Charles Owen O'Conor, the O'Conor Don

CHARLES OWEN O'CONOR, THE O'CONOR DON

Landlordism, liberal Catholicism and unionism in nineteenth-century Ireland

Aidan Enright

FOUR COURTS PRESS

Set in 11.5 pt on 13.5 pt Centaur MT for
FOUR COURTS PRESS LTD
7 Malpas Street, Dublin 8, Ireland
www.fourcourtspress.ie
and in North America for
FOUR COURTS PRESS
c/o IPG, 814 N Franklin St, Chicago, IL 60610

© Aidan Enright and Four Courts Press 2022

A catalogue record for this title is available
from the British Library.

ISBN 978-1-80151-040-0

All rights reserved. No part of this publication may be reproduced, stored in or introduced into a retrieval system, or transmitted, in any form or by any means (electronic, mechanical, photocopying, recording, or otherwise), without the prior written permission of both the copyright owner and publisher of this book.

SPECIAL ACKNOWLEDGMENT

This publication has been greatly assisted by a financial grant from the Marc Fitch Fund for Research and Publication (established by Marcus Felix Brudenell Fitch, CBE DLitt HonFBA FSA in 1956).

MARC FITCH FUND

Printed in England by
CPI Antony Rowe, Chippenham, Wilts.

Contents

Foreword   7

List of illustrations   11

List of abbreviations   12

Acknowledgments   13

Introduction   15

1. 'Amongst the great Catholic Houses of Ireland': the making of the O'Conors of Ballinagare and Clonalis, *c*.1640–1850   26

2. 'An upholder of the old liberal opinions': the O'Conor Don and his world   41

3. 'Your relations with your numerous tenantry are most creditable': the O'Conor Don and the management of his estates, 1860–1906   57

4. 'Let them get rid of the landlords altogether': the O'Conor Don and land reform, 1860–1903   85

5. 'There must be perfect equality in educational matters for all': the O'Conor Don and the Irish university question, 1860–80   108

6. 'I never will court popularity at the expense of my convictions': the O'Conor Don, liberalism and nationalism, 1860–80   135

7. 'I could not speak as an admirer or lover of the Union': the O'Conor Don, liberalism, nationalism and unionism, 1880–1900   170

Conclusion   203

Appendices

    Appendix 1: The O'Conor Don's family tree   212

    Appendix 2.1: Map of Ireland, with counties
        Roscommon and Sligo highlighted   214

    Appendix 2.2: Maps of counties Sligo and Roscommon
        with the civil parishes in which the O'Conor Don owned land   215

    Appendix 3: Landownership tables   216

Bibliography   223

Index   238

Foreword

Why does a book about a rich Catholic landlord matter? It matters mostly because of the positionality of its subject, Charles Owen O'Conor (1838–1906), in late nineteenth-century Ireland. The O'Conor Don, as he styled himself throughout his political career, was a prominent Catholic politician from the time he first won a by-election to parliament in 1860, aged 22, to 1880, when his political career declined. Best known for his contributions to the debates around education policy in Ireland, he also contributed to the debates on land reform and home rule, helped legislate for industrial schools and Sunday closing, and supported the preservation of the Irish language. Nonetheless, he was only occasionally visible at the very forefront of Victorian political life, and part of his importance was in some senses symbolic. He was, perhaps, the chief representative of the Gaelic aristocracy in Ireland. A proud descendant of the last high king of Ireland, Roderic O'Conor (d. 1198), he wore his genealogy proudly and knew it thoroughly. His own compilation of the family genealogy in 1891 drew heavily on the work of his even more illustrious relative, Charles O'Conor of Ballinagare (1701–91).

To some Irish nationalists, the O'Conor Don was a reminder of what was lost through the colonization of Ireland: his presence was that of a debased and supplicant remnant of a once-proud Gaelic aristocracy. From this perspective he was an unacceptable survivor, and his family a reminder of the cost of compromise. His prominence was only made possible by his loyalty to the forces that had debased his position. That the acceptance by Roderic of the lordship of Connaught in 1175 in return for the recognition of English suzerainty under Henry II could still dictate the family reputation is an indication of the complexity of colonial memory in Ireland. The loss of lands in the mid-seventeenth century was because of their loyalty to the Stuart monarch, and this book charts the consistent 'loyalist' theme in the O'Conor family. There was something plaintive, but also consistent, in the O'Conor Don's willingness to carry the colours of Edward VII at his coronation in 1902 at a time when the battle lines of Irish nationalism were beginning to harden. The O'Conor Don's world was coming to an end. He was, as the author puts it, a 'man out of time'. But what can we learn from this puzzling career?

It was not his status as a lost high king of Ireland that enabled the O'Conor Don's political career. Instead, it was, as Aidan Enright reveals in this book, a £50,000 legacy from his cousin Edward Moore: an enslaver and merchant who died without issue and willed most of a large legacy of £150,000 three ways between Charles, his brother Denis and their uncle Valentine O'Conor-Blake in 1851. Orphaned as a child, and with five sisters and a younger brother to support, it is clear that this inheritance is the pivotal structural change in the life of the O'Conor Don. Without it his range of professional possibilities would have been much more limited, even with an atypically large estate of somewhere in the region of 7,500 acres in Roscommon and Sligo. After he inherited, his financial affairs were never again in jeopardy and his only limitations in his lifetime were imposed by his Catholicism. This advantage, or 'privilege', as the author terms it, was derived from the profits of slave-powered plantations on the other side of the world, in Antigua and Jamaica. A high king deprived of his natural position by colonization had found his way back close to the summit of power thanks to the colonization of others. His apparent ambivalence to the issue on his tour of America in late 1865 and early 1866 reinforces the significance of this inherited wealth.

Enright is a talented contemporary of mine and the fact that this book has now emerged some ten years or so after his PhD on the same topic should provide some succour for other historians who have yet to publish their major work. PhDs very often come into conflict with, as Aidan puts it, the 'stuff of life', and few PhDs find their way onto a bookshelf immediately. His work is interested in the paradoxes apparent in the public and private lives of prominent 'loyal' Catholics. The classic narrative of Catholic elites in Ireland had often been that they did not exist at scale. The Gaelic aristocracy was broken by colonization, and the 'wild geese' had fled the island to either perish or prosper among the Catholic nobility of Europe. We now know that was not neatly the case, and while the destruction of the Gaelic nobility was considerable, it was far from total. Gaelic clans or 'septs' lived on and their directions were various and complicated. By the mid nineteenth century, a diverse layer of wealthy Catholics had emerged in Ireland, some of whom were landed and incorporating Gaelic families like the O'Conors of Clonalis, and others who could trace their roots to 'Old English' families (with Continental and often Norman origins). These older landed families sat alongside a more *nouveau riche* element of families who had made their money through merchant trade or other means, exploiting colonial and domestic markets for prominent Irish commodities as various as butter and linen, and creating plantations of their own across the Americas, enslaving Native Americans and Africans as enthusiastically as their European counterparts. These families clustered in the west of Ireland, as well as around the port cities of Cork and Dublin. Under this layer of elite Catholics could be found an expanding middle and upper middle class of Catholics, who benefited from the broad expansion of the bourgeoisie across nineteenth-century Europe, as well as the gradual opening up of the professions to Catholics in Ireland from the 1780s. Taken together these two layers coalesced to form an awkward Catholic elite in the nineteenth century, but they struggled for a coherent collective identity following the collapse of O'Connellism after Catholic emancipation. The story of the O'Conor Don gives us an insight into this complex negotiation of identity in union Ireland.

In political terms this book is interested in O'Conor's *liberalism*. His particular brand of liberalism was inflected with a conservative Catholicism. This was not at all a unique mixture in the nineteenth century, but it came to look more and more deluded as Irish politics began to divide and harden. A natural teleology takes place in Irish historiography post revolution and post partial independence, and it makes it all the more difficult to understand that one could easily be a Catholic who wished for greater domestic autonomy or home rule, while simultaneously remaining loyal to the British monarch and deeply invested in British culture. In these pages Enright gets to the heart of this complexity. What the O'Conor Don wanted was a version of the union that was more advantageous to Ireland than the one in existence in the late nineteenth century, but in most of the ways that mattered his ideology conformed with an orthodox unionist position. He wanted to maintain the union but change its terms and by doing so to strengthen its legitimacy. In his lifetime Catholics with a background similar to the O'Conor Don's saw no paradox or conflict in this position but the political axis of the world they moved in shifted perceptibly in the late nineteenth century, and they did not always shift with it. Ironically, his intensely Catholic and conservative outlook could have existed harmoniously in the 1920s and 1930s in an Ireland with limited sovereignty converted to some extent to an orthodox ultramontane state that retained a connection to the empire. But for partition, much of that might very well have appealed to the O'Conor Don as, in the words of his contemporary Edmund Dease, 'a Catholic first, [and] an Irishman Afterwards'.

The O'Conor Don's inability to clarify his somewhat muddled thinking on the subject of home rule in the late 1870s led to his election loss in 1880, from which his political career never really recovered. In this respect he is also an exemplar of the gradual takeover of popular politics by the broader middle class in Ireland, at the expense of the landed gentry. As a Catholic landlord a person such as the O'Conor Don stood to gain from his religious affiliation, but only if he could bend his principles and ideologies more to the temper of the tenantry and the popular politics of the time. He failed to do so. Once Parnell dismissed him publicly – and somewhat cruelly – as a 'symbol of West Britonism' at a pre-election meeting in Roscommon, the writing was on the wall.

The rest of his life involved a gradual retreat to his (diminishing) estate and the club circuit. He had sporadic involvement in landed and unionist politics, wrote the family history and was briefly but actively involved in the radically reformed local government at the end of the century, the significance of which is not always acknowledged in survey histories of Ireland. The fact that Enright takes the time to sketch his subject's relationships across his family networks adds much to the analysis, as does the picture that emerges of the O'Conor Don's relationship to his first and second wives and his four children. This is the sort of detail that is too often elided in political biography. Enright also forensically examines his estate management and his handling of rental negotiations with his tenantry, providing a useful and detailed window on a very complex relationship in Irish society.

Enright is correct to say that within this political career we can see tensions and contradictions that still haunt British-Irish relations down to the present. As recently as 2011 some polls showed that over half of people who identified as Catholics in Northern Ireland wanted to remain in the union. Since then, Brexit has changed all utterly, but only at a surface level. For the student of Irish history, the gift of Aidan Enright's fine study of the O'Conor Don is that it demonstrates that these paradoxes not only repeat and evolve in British-Irish relations, but that these paradoxes constitute the relationship itself.

Dr Ciaran O'Neill
Trinity College Dublin

Illustrations

Plates appear between pp 128 and 129

1. Charles O'Conor of Ballinagare.
2. Owen O'Conor of Ballinagare and Clonalis.
3. Denis O'Conor of Clonalis.
4. Charles Owen O'Conor and his brother Denis Maurice O'Conor as young boys.
5. Charles Owen O'Conor, the O'Conor Don, as a young MP.
6. Charles Owen O'Conor, the O'Conor Don, in later life.
7. Ellen O'Conor (née More O'Ferrall).
8. Old Clonalis House.
9. New Clonalis House.

Abbreviations

BL	British Library
CAC	Churchill Archives Centre
CH	Clonalis House
CMLED	Connacht & Munster Landed Estates Database
CSORP	Chief Secretary's Office Registered Papers
DAFF	Department of Agriculture, Food & Forestry
DDA	Dublin Diocesan Archives
DIB	*Dictionary of Irish biography*
DU	Drew University (New Jersey)
EDA	Elphin Diocesan Archives
HHC	Hull History Centre
HOPO	History of Parliament Online
JA	Jesuit Archives
MU	Maynooth University
NAI	National Archives of Ireland
NLI	National Library of Ireland
NUIM	National University of Ireland Maynooth
ODNB	*Oxford dictionary of national biography*
PRONI	Public Records Office of Northern Ireland
TCD	Trinity College Dublin
UC	University of Cambridge
UL	University of London
UM	University of Minnesota

Acknowledgments

I was supposed to write this book about ten years ago after I finished my PhD, but the stuff of life happened, and it never got done. I returned to the prospect of writing the book in the summer of 2020 and since then it is like the O'Conor Don never left my side.

There are many people to thank for this book's coming to fruition. Going back to where it all started in 2008, my PhD on the political life of the O'Conor Don could not have been embarked upon without the cooperation of Pyers and Marguerite O'Conor Nash, custodians of the O'Conor papers at Clonalis House, Castlerea, County Roscommon. Pyers has always been very supportive of the project to uncover the world of the O'Conor Don, even though we have not always agreed on what the uncovering means. Marguerite, for her part, deserves special praise for her patience in accommodating my research in the archive. The staff of the numerous archives and libraries I visited in Ireland and England also deserve a special word of thanks for the friendly and professional way in which they facilitated my research.

At Queen's University Belfast, where I completed my PhD in 2011, my supervisor, Professor Peter Gray, was generous with his advice and support over the course of three years. Among my contemporaries at Queen's, Jonathan Wright, Shaun McDaid, Sarah Roddy, Elaine Farrell, Pierre Ranger, Stuart Aveyard and Chris Loughlin deserve special mention for their friendship, good cheer and advice. Since embarking upon my second attempt to write the book in 2020, Ciaran O'Neill has been a great support and very kindly agreed to write the foreword.

Simon Morgan has also been very supportive, providing a platform for my research again and alerting me to the Covid recovery research fund in the School of Cultural Studies and Humanities at Leeds Beckett University, which enabled me to include the plate section in the book. A second award from the Marc Fitch Fund was crucial too. I am very grateful to the trustees of the fund for supporting my work. Nollaig Feeney, the heritage officer for Roscommon County Council, also deserves a special word of thanks for supporting the launch of this book in County Roscommon.

Others who helped with the book include Raquel Targino dos Santos, who did an excellent job of designing the maps; Liam Chambers, who provided advice and support in the initial stages of writing; and Caoimhe Nic Dháibhéid, who advised on some crucial readings in the later stages. However, this book would not be seeing the light of day without Martin Fanning at

Four Courts Press taking a risk on what probably seemed like a very uncertain prospect. For this I am very thankful.

Outside of academia, the Enright siblings and Murphy in-laws have been very supportive down through the years. I have also received much support and encouragement from friends Scott and Catherine Hardy, Alex and Sarah Ross Shaw, Caroline Firth, Lisa Davenport, Nev Owen, Matt and Sasha Stoney, Louise and Clive Nutton, Matthew and Jo Simms, and Laura Bates and Russell Bowman.

Finally, a very special word of thanks must go to my wife, Sinead, for her love, loyalty and support over the years. Our children, Maria and Connell, have shown great enthusiasm for daddy becoming an 'author', although they know that the book is going to be a 'boring' history one. I have not set myself the impossible task of converting them into enthusiasts of the O'Conor Don or nineteenth-century Irish history, but I do hope that one day they will understand that those little words of encouragement contributed handsomely to the completion of this book.

Introduction

Charles Owen O'Conor (1838–1906) was one of the most prominent Catholic landlords and politicians in Ireland during the second half of the nineteenth century. Born in 1838, he came of age in 1859, inheriting the honorary Gaelic title 'the O'Conor Don', large estates in counties Roscommon and Sligo, and a £50,000 fortune. He also inherited the mantle of local and national political leadership from his father and grandfather. The O'Conor Don was, therefore, pretty much destined for a life of prominence in high society and politics. In 1860, he was elected MP for his native County Roscommon, a seat he held until 1880. Thereafter, he maintained a certain level of public prominence until the time of his illness and death in 1906, although in popular political terms he became an increasingly marginalized figure.

As a landlord, the O'Conor Don managed his estates in an even-handed way and maintained good relations with his tenants. However, like most Irish landlords, he ended up selling off significant parts of his estates during the period of tumultuous landlord-tenant relations in the late nineteenth and early twentieth centuries. As a parliamentarian, he was hard-working, conscientious and fiercely independent-minded, but not of the first rank in terms of oratory, leadership or popularity. In politics, the O'Conor Don was a liberal who advocated a wide range of social, economic, and political reforms to advance Catholic and Irish interests within the union while resisting the advance of secularism, majoritarian democracy and home rule. The O'Conor Don was, then, in the broadest terms, a liberal Catholic and a unionist.[1]

The O'Conor Don's liberal Catholic and unionist outlook was a product of his family history and his own social and political milieu. His ancestors were significant landowners and political leaders who espoused loyalist, moderate nationalist and liberal politics at various stages between the beginnings of the campaign for the repeal of the penal laws in the 1750s through to the campaign for Catholic emancipation in the 1810s and 1820s. Post emancipation, his grandfather and father both served as Liberal MPs for County Roscommon between 1830 and 1847, with his father also serving briefly as a junior minister in the Whig-Liberal government in 1846–7. When the O'Conor Don became the MP for County Roscommon in 1860, he was one of a larger group of liberal Catholic MPs who sought to advance Catholic and Irish interests within the union through support for the British Liberal Party. Outside of parliament, the O'Conor Don and his liberal Catholic

---

1 See below for a more detailed explanation of definitions and terminologies, pp 20–3.

colleagues were part of a wider group of upper- and middle-class Irish Catholics predominantly drawn from the landed, mercantile and professional classes. Educated in English and Irish Catholic colleges, they intermarried with landed English Catholics and maintained close relations with Irish and English bishops. But they were also part of a wider Anglo-Irish and British landed and governing elite. As such, the O'Conor Don and his fellow Irish Catholics occupied a minority and somewhat awkward place in a predominantly Protestant British-Irish elite that dominated the politics, administration and governance of the United Kingdom of Great Britain and Ireland, and the wider British empire.[2]

What these transnational and cross-confessional connections instilled in the O'Conor Don was a desire to pursue a liberal middle course between the Catholic-Protestant and Irish-British divides that traditionally dominated relations between Ireland and Great Britain. Thus, although he was an Irish patriot and a staunch Catholic who often vented his frustration at Protestant bigotry towards Catholics and English indifference towards Ireland, he wished to maintain the cultural and constitutional connections between Ireland, Great Britain and the empire. He did so because of a desire for a pluralist Irish nation in which religious freedom and equality prevailed and Irish and British identities were accommodated.

HISTORIOGRAPHICAL CONTEXT

With all the above in mind, it seems more than a little obvious to say that the O'Conor Don's story does not easily fit into the dominant Catholic nationalist and Protestant unionist narratives of modern Irish history. This is not to deny that, by the end of the nineteenth century at least, culture and politics had polarized along Catholics nationalist and Protestant unionist lines, but it is to say that the dominance of these cultural-political realties can often drown out other minority forms of cultural-political expression, however unpopular they may have been at the time or however unpalatable they might remain now. The O'Conor Don undoubtedly ended up on the losing side of Irish politics in the late nineteenth century, but he was part of a minority group of Irish Catholics who were, broadly speaking, liberal and unionist in their politics and were possessed of, and torn between, Catholic, Irish and British allegiances and identities.

2 For the Irish and British landed elite, see T. Dooley, *The decline of the Big House in Ireland: a study of Irish landed families, 1860–1960* (Dublin, 2001); D. Cannadine, *The decline and fall of the British aristocracy* (London, 1996).

Given the complex nature of the O'Conor Don's cultural-political outlook, this biography seeks to engage with a relatively recent body of scholarship that has stressed the need for a more flexible understanding of the relationships between religion, politics and identity in nineteenth-century Ireland. One of the pioneers of this approach has been Jennifer Ridden, whose study of Irish liberalism in the first half of the nineteenth century demonstrates how a group of landed Protestants in County Limerick articulated a coherent liberal ideology through their support for religious and civil equality, parliamentary reform, and wider institutional and social reforms. With cultural and political ties to Ireland and Great Britain, they saw themselves as Irish and British and cleaved to the idea of a pluralist Irish nation within the union and the empire. These liberal Protestants therefore espoused a form of moderate nationalism while at the same time being firm unionists, loyalists and imperialists.[3]

To a large extent, this was the cultural-political space occupied by the O'Conor Don in the second half of the nineteenth century, although his sense of Irishness was of course distinctly Catholic and therefore often replete with a sense of grievance against Protestantism, England and British government policy in Ireland. But even so, his attachment to the union, the crown and the empire was genuine. He was pragmatic about and sometimes critical of the union, but he believed in the British connection and wanted Ireland to be part of the British imperial project. It is with this reality in mind that we can say that the O'Conor Don's sense of Irishness incorporated a sense of Britishness.

Since Ridden's pioneering work, John Bew, Gerald Hall and Jonathan Wright have produced studies that in different ways explore the British contexts and identities of Irish whigs, reformists, liberals, conservatives and unionists in nineteenth-century Ulster and Belfast. However, apart from Hall's brief exploration of middle-class Catholic opinion between 1860 and 1876, the focus of these studies is on Protestant politics and culture in the north of Ireland.[4]

Of most direct relevance to this book is Matthew Potter's biography of William Monsell (1812–94), a Catholic convert, landlord, Liberal MP for County Limerick and junior government minister. Taking account of the

3 J. Ridden, '"Making good citizens": national identity, religion and liberalism among the Irish elite c.1800–1850' (PhD, UL, 1998), pp 7–21. Gearóid Ó Tuathaigh has also encouraged this kind of flexible approach to understanding the interplay between religion, politics and identity. See G. Ó Tuathaigh, 'Ireland under the union: historiographical reflections', *Australian Journal of Irish Studies*, 2 (2002), 1–22; G. Ó Tuathaigh, 'Political history' in L.M. Geary & M. Kelleher (eds), *Nineteenth-century Irish history: a guide to recent research* (Dublin, 2005), pp 1–26.   4 G.R. Hall, *Ulster liberalism, 1778–1876: the middle path* (Dublin, 2010), pp 11–15; J.J. Wright, *The 'natural leaders' and their world: politics, culture and society in Belfast, c.1801–1832* (Liverpool, 2012), pp 7, 50–2, 239–42; J. Bew, *The glory of being Britons: civic unionism in nineteenth-century Belfast* (Dublin, 2009), pp xi–xvi, 1–21.

wider British contexts of Monsell's life during his time at the front line of Irish politics between 1847 and 1874, Potter teases out the complexities of his struggle to find a middle way between the conservatism of the Catholic Church and the increasingly secular values propounded by the Liberal Party. Overall, Potter presents Monsell as a liberal Catholic and a Catholic unionist, who, like Ridden's liberal Protestants, believed in the idea of a pluralist Irish nation within the union and the empire and was possessed of Irish and British identities.[5]

The O'Conor Don and Monsell were close friends and shared a very similar outlook on life and politics, but the content of this book is decidedly different to that of Potter's because the O'Conor Don's life and political career took a different trajectory. First, the O'Conor Don had a Catholic and liberal background, whereas Monsell's background was Protestant and tory. Second, the O'Conor Don was a much larger landowner, so his duties as a landlord dominated his life in a way that Monsell's do not seem to have done. Third, the O'Conor Don remained independent of government office and was therefore more openly critical of Liberal Party policy, particularly on education. Fourth, the O'Conor Don engaged more proactively and publicly on the issues of land reform and home rule. Overall, then, although their political outlook was more or less the same, this biography of the O'Conor Don explores in much greater detail the history of liberal Catholic politics; Catholic landownership and estate management in the wider context of Irish landlordism; and liberal Catholic opinion on land reform, education, home rule and the union in the wider contexts of Irish liberalism, nationalism and unionism.

Outside of Potter's work, Richard Keogh, James McConnel and Éamon Phoenix have also demonstrated that Catholic loyalism and unionism was a feature of the Irish political landscape in the nineteenth and early twentieth centuries. Keogh and McConnel have added an extra dimension by showing how loyalist and imperialist sentiments were part of the political outlook of leading nationalists like Sir Thomas Esmonde and John Redmond.[6] These overlaps tie in with the findings of Ciaran O'Neill's study on the education of upper- and middle-class Irish Catholics in colleges in England and Ireland between 1850

---

5 M. Potter, *William Monsell of Tervoe, 1812–1894: Catholic unionist, Anglo-Irishman* (Dublin, 2009), pp 1–5. 6 R. Keogh, '"Nothing is so bad for the Irish as Ireland alone": William Keogh and Catholic loyalty', *Irish Historical Studies*, 38:150 (2012), 230–48; R. Keogh & J. McConnel, 'The Esmonde family of County Wexford and Catholic loyalty' in O.P. Rafferty (ed.), *Irish Catholic identities* (Manchester & New York, 2013), pp 274–91; É. Phoenix, 'Catholic unionism: a case study: Sir Denis Stanislaus Henry (1864–1925)' in Rafferty (ed.), *Irish Catholic identities*, pp 292–304. J. McConnel, 'John Redmond and Irish Catholic loyalism', *English Historical Review*, 125:512 (Feb. 2010), 83–111. See also J.H. Murphy, *Abject loyalty: nationalism and monarchy in Ireland during the reign of Queen Victoria* (Cork, 2001), pp 83, 102, 187–91, 240, 245, 259, 290.

and 1900. While O'Neill demonstrates that the desire for social and political advancement was as powerful a motivator among upper- and middle-class Catholics as it was among their Protestant counterparts, he cautions against drawing a straight line between this type of education and a unionist political outlook in later life, as many of these well-heeled, well-educated Catholics and Protestants went on to become prominent nationalists and republicans.[7] This grey area in Catholic politics and identity in the nineteenth century has been further illuminated by Paul O'Brien in his study of the Glynns of Kilrush, County Clare, a wealthy business-owning family whose often limited or vague expressions of political loyalties – nationalist or unionist – reflected the low priority of politics in their everyday lives.[8] Thus, while neither O'Neill, Keogh, McConnel nor O'Brien make a particularly strong case for a dual Irish-British identity among upper- and middle-class Catholics, what these authors do make clear is the difficulties loyalist and unionist Catholics faced in articulating and displaying their sense of Irishness in the face of an increasingly anti-British Catholic nationalism, which, at its most strident, denounced them as 'West Britons'. In other words, more British than Irish.[9]

In general, what this body of work demonstrates is that the O'Conor Don's life fits into a wider and more diverse narrative of nineteenth-century Irish history that highlights the overlaps between the lives and experiences of upper- and middle-class Catholics and Protestants; between liberal, nationalist and unionist politics; and between Irish and British identities. The O'Conor Don and his fellow liberal Catholics had much in common with liberal Protestants. As such, there was, as Ridden argues, a reasonably coherent Irish liberal political tradition for much of the nineteenth century. But as Ridden, Hall and Potter demonstrate most clearly, Irish liberal politicians were notoriously bad at working together, even in the context of the loose party system that prevailed in Great Britain until the late 1860s and in Ireland until the mid-1880s. This inability to work together was partly down to a gentlemanly independent-mindedness or indifference to party action of any kind, but Irish liberals were not immune to religious divisions, with Protestants suspicious of the overmighty influence of the Catholic Church and Catholics suspicious of state bias towards Protestantism. These mutual suspicions made the alliance between Catholic and Protestant unionists an uneasy one, with the latter's rejection of home rule as 'Rome rule' not sitting easy with the former. More broadly, what these ongoing religious divisions demonstrate is that the

7 C. O'Neill, *Catholics of consequence: transnational education, social mobility, and the Irish Catholic elite, 1850–1900* (Oxford, 2014). 8 P. O'Brien, *The Glynns of Kilrush, County Clare, 1811–1940: family, business and politics* (Dublin, 2019), pp 1, 18–27, 32, 38–54, 57–62, 64–71, 90–9, 102, 113–18, 150–4. 9 O'Neill, *Catholics of consequence*, p. 17.

sense of a Catholic 'other' continued to be a rallying point for many Irish Protestants, including liberal Protestants who desired a pluralist Irish nation.[10] But it also illuminates the anti-Protestant prejudices that Irish Catholics could not shake off, including liberal Catholics who desired a pluralist Irish nation.

The O'Conor Don's story confirms the religious divisions between Catholic and Protestant liberals, but it also confirms that the liberal political outlook of Catholics like him was underpinned by an Irish national identity that incorporated or co-existed alongside some form of British identity. We must, therefore, be careful to recognize both the union and disunion among Catholic and Protestant liberals, which in turn involves a consideration for how Catholic and Protestant liberals interacted with popular nationalist and unionist politics and expressed their Irish and British identities.

Taking the general and specific contexts together, then, this biography of the O'Conor Don seeks to look beyond and between the lines of the Catholic nationalist and Protestant unionist divide that came to dominate Irish politics and culture towards the end of the century. To echo Jonathan Wright, this author does not seek to revise a nationalist narrative or revive a latent unionist narrative in Irish history.[11] But unlike Wright, this author does not seek to apply an overarching 'new' British history narrative. Rather this book presents the O'Conor Don as someone who challenges our understanding of what it meant to be a Catholic, a liberal, a conservative, a nationalist and a unionist, as well as what it meant to be Irish and British. In so doing, it strives to place the O'Conor Don's politics and identity within its Irish *and* British contexts, emphasizing the overlaps and divergences between liberal, conservative, nationalist and unionist thinking, as well as the overlaps and divergences between Irish and British identities.

DEFINITIONS AND TERMINOLOGIES

Before moving on to the structure of the book, some further explanations of the minefield of definitions and terminologies employed in this book are required. Like Hall and Jonathan Parry, this author adopts a 'broadly inclusive' definition of the term 'liberal' that accepts the existence of variation in its meaning. Broadly speaking, then, it can be said that liberals supported the principles of religious freedom and equality, freedom of the press and

---

10 L. Colley, *Britons: forging the nation, 1707–1837* (New Haven & London, 2012), p. xxii. 11 Wright, *The 'natural leaders'*, p. 7. For a more detailed case for 'new' British history see J.G.A. Pocock, 'British history: a plea for a new subject', *Journal of Modern History*, 47 (1975), 601–21; A. Grant & K.J. Stringer (eds), *Uniting the kingdom? The making of British history* (London & New York, 2014).

association, free trade, political economy, the rule of law and representative government. The practical application of these principles saw liberals support Catholic emancipation, parliamentary reform, disestablishment of the Protestant (Anglican) Church of Ireland, education and land reform, and a broad range of other social reforms.[12] The O'Conor Don supported reform in a wide range of areas, including disestablishment, university education, landownership, Irish language provision, industrial schools, factory law, Sunday closing, taxation and local government. He was, then, a fairly conventional liberal in the Irish and British sense. But as outlined at the start, there are a number of important qualifications to be considered.

First, the O'Conor Don's liberalism incorporated what could be described as a whiggish perspective on government and democracy. As such, he believed that the business of government was best carried out by a 'natural' ruling class who represented the needs and wishes of the people but remained free to make independent judgments on what they thought was in the best interests of the country, regardless of popular, majority opinion. However, while this author acknowledges that it is reasonable to preference the term whig over liberal when discussing the influence of older political traditions or describing particular points of view among Irish liberals and the wider British Liberal Party, the O'Conor Don and most of his fellow Irish liberals in the mid-Victorian period described themselves as liberals and it was not unusual for Irish or British liberals – particularly landlords with a generally paternalistic view of society – to hold such whiggish views on the 'natural' order of things.[13]

Second, the O'Conor Don's liberalism was shaped by a conservative Catholicism, which is a contemporary way of describing what was termed 'ultramontane' Catholicism in the mid- to late nineteenth century. Ultramontanism, broadly defined, was the Romanization of the Catholic Church through the papacy, hierarchy and clergy. At the highest level, this manifested itself in Pope Pius IX's syllabus of errors in 1864 and the dogma of papal infallibility in 1870, which combined were a rejection of the increasingly secular liberal values of

12 Hall, *Ulster liberalism*, pp 11–15; J.P. Parry, *The rise and fall of liberal government in Victorian Britain* (New Haven, 1993), pp 17–18. 13 Potter, *William Monsell*, pp 1–5. Potter uses the term 'whig' as an overarching term to define Monsell's combination of liberalism, Catholicism and unionism. See also D.T. Horgan, 'The Irish Catholic whigs in parliament, 1847–74' (PhD, UM, 1975). Horgan uses the term whig instead of liberal across the board, mostly on the basis of whether a Catholic MP held a government or civil service position. This author is not convinced by the historical or theoretical arguments for either Potter or Horgan's use of the term whig but accepts that terminology is not an exact science. More convincing arguments for the whig influences in liberal politics, albeit in specifically British contexts, are to be found in T.A. Jenkins, *Gladstone, whiggery and the Liberal Party 1874–1886* (New York, 1988), pp 2–11, 14–18, 46–51, 76, 111, 149, 295–304; Parry, *Liberal government in Victorian Britain*, pp 3–6, 12–13, 17–18.

the age. On a more practical level, it involved the mainstreaming of devotional religious practices and much greater clerical involvement in the everyday lives of Catholics, particularly in the provision of education and juvenile care.[14] No specific mentions of the syllabus or papal infallibility have been found in the O'Conor Don's private correspondence or public pronouncements, which suggests either a wilful silence for fear of saying something that would get him into trouble or a temperamental disinterest in theological matters or both. However, it is clear from his life in general, and his views on education more specifically, that he was a devout Catholic who revered the papacy and believed that the Catholic hierarchy and clergy ought to play a prominent role in the spiritual and temporal lives of Irish Catholics. Thus, although he was a liberal who believed in religious freedom and equality, there is little doubt that the O'Conor Don adhered to a view of the Catholic Church and its role in society that was essentially ultramontane or, to use the more contemporary term, conservative.

Third, the O'Conor Don's unionism was of the critical, constructive and national kind. In other words, although he had a strong sense of Irish national identity, supported the idea of home rule, and often criticized British government policy in Ireland (or the lack of it), he opposed home rule in practice and hoped that substantial reforms in accordance with Irish ideas would in the long run inculcate a sense of Irish nationhood that embraced the British connection and incorporated Irish and British identities. He did so because he wanted Ireland to be part of the bigger British imperial project and feared that the republican forces within nationalism saw home rule as step towards a secular Irish republic. As demonstrated by Ridden and Potter, it was not unusual for liberal Protestants and Catholics to espouse moderate nationalist sentiments while at the same time being unionists, loyalists and imperialists; that is why they articulated a pluralist Irish national identity that incorporated British identity.[15] Similarly, Colin Reid has shown how the moderate Protestant nationalist leader Isaac Butt was a unionist and imperialist who envisaged home rule as the realization of Irish nationhood within the union and the empire.[16] And as already demonstrated, one could make the same

14 E.R. Norman, *The Catholic Church in the age of rebellion, 1859–1873* (New York, 1965), pp 10, 16–19; E. Larkin, 'The devotional revolution in Ireland, 1850–75', *American Historical Review*, 77:3 (June 1972), 625–52; C. Barr, *Paul Cullen, John Henry Newman, and the Catholic university of Ireland, 1845–1865* (Herefordshire, 2003), pp 14–16, 51, 54–8, 86, 100–1, 123, 180–1; J.F. Supple, 'Ultramontanism in Yorkshire, 1850–1900', *British Catholic History*, 17:3 (1985), 274–86; V.A. McClelland, 'Church and state: the Manning-Gladstone correspondence, 1833–1891', *British Catholic History*, 32:3 (2015), 383–412. 15 Ridden, 'Making good citizens', pp 7–21; Potter, *William Monsell*, pp 1–5. 16 C. Reid, '"An experiment in constructive unionism": Isaac Butt, home rule and federalist political thought during the 1870s', *English Historical Review*, 129:537 (2014), 333–7.

argument for the Catholic nationalist leader John Redmond.[17] The O'Conor Don's opposition to home rule confirms that he was not a nationalist in any meaningful political sense of the word, but this does not distract from the fact that his unionism incorporated a moderate nationalist desire for a stronger, more unified Irish nation within the union and the empire.

SOURCES AND STRUCTURE

Finally, a brief outline of the research upon which the book is based and the structure which the book takes. The O'Conor papers, deposited at Clonalis House, Castlerea, County Roscommon, provided the bulk of the material for the book. One of the largest and most significant private archives in Ireland, the section of papers relevant to the O'Conor Don shed much light on his social circles, the running of his estates, his wide range of correspondents and his views on a broad range of social, economic and political issues.[18] It should be noted, however, that because the archive is privately held and access to it is necessarily restricted, the author had to be selective in terms of deciding which sections of the O'Conor Don's papers to consult. And even then, the sheer volume of papers is so large that the author did not get through anything near what he would have liked. To whittle things down, it was decided to focus on the themes of family, estate management, landlord-tenant relations, land reform, education reform and home rule, as these were the dominant features and issues of the O'Conor Don's life. These themes were explored through diaries, wills, rentals, draft essays and printed circulars, as well as through correspondence with land agents, bishops, priests, landlords and politicians. The O'Conor Don's trail was then followed to the landed estates court rentals, the papers of the Irish land commission (which are difficult to access) and the papers of a wide range of clergymen, landlords and politicians in Ireland and Great Britain. This manuscript material was contextualized by a range of printed primary sources, including pamphlets, journal articles, reports of select committees and royal commissions, Hansard's parliamentary debates and local and national newspapers.

In terms of style, this book is in many respects a fairly conventional political biography in that it explores the O'Conor Don's family background, social milieu, life as a landlord and some of the major political debates of his time. However, it differs in structure from most political biographies in that

17 See above, p. 18. 18 The O'Conor papers were catalogued in the 1970s by Gareth and Janet Dunleavy. See G.W. Dunleavy & J.E. Dunleavy, *The O'Conor papers: a descriptive catalog and surname register of the materials at Clonalis House* (Madison, WI, 1977).

it adopts a thematic, as opposed to chronological, approach to the analysis of its subject's life and political career. The decision to adopt this approach was part practical in that the initial identification of dominant themes in the archive naturally led in a thematic direction. But it was also partially a personal preference for a more in-depth, contextualized biography that examined the O'Conor Don's family background, experience as a landlord and views as a politician in the wider contexts of the main social, economic and political developments of his time.

With the above in mind, chapter one provides an overview of the history, economic fortunes and political traditions of the O'Conor Don's family from the 1640s to the 1850s while considering how the family's experience fits into the wider picture of an emerging Catholic landed and political elite c.1750–1850. This sets the scene for the O'Conor Don's coming of age and entry into political life in 1859–60, which, together with the education and travel that proceeded these major life events, chapter two outlines. Again, the wider context of his contemporaries' experiences is provided. Chapter three then moves on to deal with the expansion and management of the O'Conor Don's estates from 1860 to 1906. It does so by setting his experience in the wider contexts of landlord-tenant relations and the main land agitations, as well as his relationship with the bishops, clergy and prominent nationalist politicians. Intimately connected to the management of the O'Conor Don's estates was the issue of land reform. Thus, chapter four examines his views on this issue in the context of wider landed and political opinion on how landlord-tenant relations and the patterns of landownership in Ireland ought to be changed. Moving on to one of the issues that exercised him the most in politics, chapter five examines the O'Conor Don's views on the provision of university education in Ireland, assessing how they interacted with those of other Irish liberals, the bishops, the Liberal Party, the Home Rule Party, and the Conservative Party between 1860 and 1880. Chapter six then shifts the focus to look more broadly at the interplay between liberal and nationalist politics through the O'Conor Don's engagement with the Liberal Party and nationalist organizations such as the National Association and the Home Rule Party. It does so, however, while considering how his role as landlord and his views on Fenianism, government, democracy, land, education and social reform shaped his approach to national politics, the issue of home rule, and his attitude towards the union. Finally, chapter seven uses the O'Conor Don as a prism through which to examine the interplay between liberal, nationalist and unionist politics between 1880 and 1906. The focus here is his engagement with the Liberal Party, the Irish Loyal and Patriotic Union, the Liberal Union of Ireland, the Irish Landowners' Convention and

Castlerea District Council. Once again, his position as a landlord and his views on land reform are kept closely in mind, but his views on home rule and the related issue of imperial taxation provide the focus for discussion on the O'Conor Don's unionism, loyalism and imperialism.

1 / 'Amongst the great Catholic Houses of Ireland': the making of the O'Conors of Ballinagare and Clonalis, c.1640–1850

In 1889, the O'Conor Don employed the services of Sir John Bernard Burke, Ulster king of arms and chief herald of all Ireland, to verify his family's pedigree. Burke confirmed that the O'Conor Don family of Clonalis were direct descendants of the last high king of Ireland, Roderic O'Conor (d. 1198), in the twelfth century. It was this hereditary position, coupled with a 'devotion to the Catholic Church', that made the family one of 'the great Catholic Houses of Ireland'.[1] As well as confirming the O'Conor Don's royal Gaelic lineage, Burke was making an explicit reference to the fact that, due to religious wars of the seventeenth century and the penal laws of the eighteenth century, many of the old landed Catholic families converted to the established Protestant Church of Ireland in order to retain their lands.[2] That his ancestors remained Catholic at the cost of losing most of their lands in northern County Roscommon during the seventeenth century was, therefore, a badge of honour for the O'Conor Don and his family in the nineteenth century. This sense of pride was shared by other old landed Catholic families with a similar Gaelic heritage, such as the O'Donoghues of the Glens or the O'Gorman Mahons, but those from humbler backgrounds, such as the Fenians John O'Mahony and Jeremiah O'Donovan Rossa, made much of their Gaelic lineage too on occasion.[3]

On the face of it, the value placed by the O'Conor Don on the Gaelic royalty of his distant ancestors may seem somewhat irrelevant, but jealousy among the wider O'Conor clan about which branch of the family should possess the title 'Don' was not unknown.[4] More important, though, was the fact that his Gaelic pedigree was referred to again and again by political friends and opponents as evidence that he was one of Ireland's natural leaders. These

---

1 Pedigree of the O'Conor Don, 1889, O'Conor family documents, PRONI, T/ 3618/2A. For family tree, see appendix 1, pp 212–13. 2 P. Melvin, 'The landed gentry of Galway, 1820–1880' (PhD, TCD, 1991), pp 308–9. 3 S.J. Murphy, *Twilight of the chiefs: the MacCarthy Mór hoax* (Dublin, 2004), pp 30–2, 137–58, 209–16; R.V. Comerford, *The Fenians in context, Irish politics and society 1848–82* (Dublin, 1998), pp 38, 42. 4 In 1855, Roderic O'Conor of Milltown House, Castleplunkett, County Roscommon, disputed the legitimacy of the Clonalis O'Conor's claim to the title 'Don' in a series of letters to Pat O'Conor of Dundermott, County Roscommon. Pat was not interested, but Roderic also laid his claim at the door of the O'Conor Don's younger brother, Denis Maurice, in 1854, when he was just fourteen years old! See Roderic O'Conor to Denis Maurice O'Conor, 21 Dec. 1854 & Roderic O'Conor to Pat O'Conor, n.d. 1855, O'Conor papers, CAC, OCON 2/4/2.

natural leadership credentials were further bestowed upon him on account of his more recent ancestors' prominence in the campaigns for Catholic equality in the eighteenth and early nineteenth centuries. The O'Conor Don placed great store in recording and writing this family history, taking care to arrange family papers over the years and eventually publishing *The O'Conors of Connaught* in 1891.[5] Although largely a genealogical study that charts the family's royal Gaelic past, it is clear from the few political observations on the turbulent events of the seventeenth and eighteenth centuries that the O'Conor Don was keen to emphasize the traditions of loyalism and constitutional politics in the family, at the expense of any hint of disloyalty or radicalism, particularly in the rebellious 1640s and 1790s.[6]

With this in mind, understanding the O'Conor Don's family history and his perception of it is central to understanding his status as a prominent Catholic landlord and politician, as well as his views on politics, identity and British-Irish relations. This opening chapter will provide an overview of the O'Conor Don's family history, with the mid-seventeenth-century confiscations setting the scene for a more detailed account of how successive generations of the O'Conors of Ballinagare and Clonalis gradually recovered lost ground through legal battles to restore land, leasing land from sympathetic convert families, intermarrying with prosperous Catholic merchant families, merging the family estates and purchasing more land once the penal laws were relaxed. This recovery and consolidation of land and wealth went hand-in-hand with the pursuit of educational attainment, scholarly endeavour and political leadership. By the 1830s, the O'Conor Don family of Clonalis had emerged as a landed and political dynasty in Ireland. Through English education and association with high society in Dublin and London they had also become part of a transnational British-Irish landed and political class. All this paved the way for the O'Conor Don's ascendancy as a wealthy landlord and political leader in 1860, a position he sustained, albeit in gradual decline after 1880, for the rest of his life.

REBELLION, CONFISCATION AND RE-EMERGENCE

At the time of the 1641 rebellion, the O'Conors of north County Roscommon, consisting of the Ballintober, Clonalis and Ballinagare branches, were a landed dynasty whose political power was very much on the wane. Disgruntled with

5 C.O. O'Conor, *The O'Conors of Connaught: an historical memoir* (Dublin, 1891). There are several references to the O'Conor Don and his brother, Denis Maurice, arranging family papers in 1869 alone. See Diary of Denis Maurice O'Conor, 1869, NLI, p.5485.   6 See below, p. 24.

'the anti-Catholic policies of the Dublin government' and the 'puritan' English parliament, Charles O'Conor Don of Ballintober (1584–1655), the nominal 'king of Connacht', and his son Hugh, joined the rebellion of the Catholic nobility and gentry. They did so, however, while proclaiming their loyalty to the Stuart king, Charles I, which was not that unusual among landed Irish Catholics.[7] After the arrival of Cromwell in Ireland in 1652, Hugh and his cousin, Daniel O'Conor of Clonalis (1612–89), surrendered as supporters of Charles II. In 1653, Hugh and another cousin, Major Owen O'Conor of Ballinagare (1632–92), joined the king's exiled forces in France. Owen returned to Ireland in 1689 as a supporter of James II, was captured in 1692, and died in Chester Castle later that year.[8]

The family's loyalty to the Stuart cause was recounted by the O'Conor Don in his 1891 book, as were the confiscations that resulted from it, which amounted to somewhere in the region of 12,000 acres. The main beneficiaries were the Sandford family, Cromwellian settlers granted much of the Clonalis lands around the town of Castlerea. Others who gained conformed to the Protestant Church of Ireland, such as the Frenches of Frenchpark, who were granted much of the Ballinagare lands, and the Burkes of Portumna, who came to own the Ballintober lands. Despite these heavy losses, and the subsequent introduction of the penal laws that prevented Catholics from owning or leasing land, the O'Conors of Clonalis managed to hang on to some 440 acres, which they recovered through expensive litigation in the 1660s after the Stuart restoration. Although it is not clear how this came about, the Clonalis estate had more than doubled in size to 900 acres by the 1780s. Prior to this, in 1720, Denis O'Conor of Ballinagare (1674–1750) purchased the rent charge for 800 acres from the Frenches of Frenchpark, who remained on friendly terms and had been holding the Ballinagare lands in trust.[9]

The survival and re-emergence of the O'Conors was not, however, especially unusual, with the MacDermots of Coolavin, County Sligo, the Bellews

---

7 E. O'Byrne, 'O'Connor Don, An Calbhach (Charles)', *DIB*; P. Lenihan, 'O'Conor Don, Hugh', *DIB*. I have used the spelling of O'Conor with one n throughout for the sake of consistency, although *DIB* uses two 'n's in its entries for some earlier generations of the family. It would seem that the convention of spelling O'Conor with one 'n' was established in the late fourteenth century. See Matthew Potter, 'Local government in Co. Roscommon' in R. Farrell et al. (eds), *Roscommon history and society: interdisciplinary essays on the history of an Irish county* (Dublin, 2018), p. 280. For the 1641 rebellion and its aftermath, see M. Ó Siochrú, *Confederate Ireland, 1642–1649: a constitutional and political analysis* (Dublin, 1999), pp 11–54.   8 O'Conor, *O'Conors of Connaught*, pp 247–9, 264–7, 273–7, 281–3, 286–90, 382, tables iii and iv; S. Gibbon, *The recollections of S.G. from 1796 to the present year, 1829; being an epitome of the lives and characters of the nobility and gentry of Roscommon the genealogy of those who are descended from the kings of Connaught; and a memoir of Madame O'Conor Don* (Dublin, 1829), pp 83, 121–4; P. Melvin, 'Roscommon estates and landowners: diversity and durability' in Farrell et al. (eds), *Roscommon history and society*, p. 334 (footnote 36) & p. 346.   9 O'Conor, *O'Conors of Connaught*, pp 247–9, 264–7, 273–7, 281–3, 286–91, tables iii and iv; P. Lenihan, 'O'Conor Don, Hugh', *DIB*.

of Mountbellew, County Galway, the O'Donoghues of the Glens, County Kerry, the O'Reillys of Knockabbey, County Louth and the More O'Ferralls of Ballyna, County Kildare among the many old landed Catholic families who came out the other side of the confiscations and penal laws in good shape.[10] These old families were joined in the ranks of the Catholic upper and middle classes by prosperous merchants and businessmen, some of whom purchased land once the penal laws were relaxed.[11] The figure for Catholic landownership in the 1770s was estimated at five per cent, but Kevin Whelan has argued that this figure does not take account of the many friendly convert families – like the Frenches of Frenchpark – who held the title deeds of neighbouring Catholics safe or filed nominal discovery suits to distract the authorities and enable Catholics to remain on their estates. Indeed, Whelan suggests that if these nominally convert families are included, Catholic landownership was probably closer to twenty per cent towards the end of the eighteenth century.[12]

What is certain is that the gradual lifting of the penal laws from the 1770s onwards enabled Catholics to lease and own land, avail of the county franchise, obtain commissions in the British army, and establish their own schools, colleges and seminaries. Intermarriage with wealthy Catholic merchants, or becoming merchants in their own right, enhanced their financial circumstances.[13] Catholic branches of the Bellew, Blake, Browne, Kirwan, Lynch and French families of County Galway engaged in the export of wine through the ports of Bordeaux and Cadiz and on to the British West Indies. As a result, some purchased land and owned slaves in Antigua and Dominica.[14] All these developments contributed to a general rise in fortunes for old and new Catholic landowners, which in turn enabled them to carve out a place for themselves in the ranks of Ireland's mainly Protestant landed elite in the early nineteenth century.[15]

---

10 T.P. Power & K. Whelan (eds), *Endurance and emergence: Catholics in Ireland in the eighteenth century* (Dublin, 1990), p. 62; K.J. Harvey, *The Bellews of Mount Bellew: a Catholic gentry family in eighteenth-century Ireland* (Dublin, 1998), p. 41; Melvin, 'The landed gentry of Galway', p. 334; Murphy, *Twilight of the chiefs*, pp 30–2, 137–58, 209–16. 11 M. Wall, 'Catholics in economic Life' in T. Dunne & G. O'Brien (eds), *Catholic Ireland in the eighteenth century: collected essays of Maureen Wall* (Dublin, 1989), pp 73–92; P. Fagan, *Catholics in a Protestant country: the papist constituency in eighteenth-century Dublin* (Dublin, 1998), pp 45, 71–6, 97–100, 183–4; N. Yates, *The religious condition of Ireland, 1770–1850* (New York, 2006), pp 18–31; Power & Whelan (eds), *Endurance and emergence*, p. 59. 12 K. Whelan, *The tree of liberty: radicalism, Catholicism and the construction of Irish identity, 1760–1830* (Cork, 1996), pp 6–7; Wall, 'Catholics in economic life', p. 85. 13 M. Wall, 'The quest for Catholic equality, 1745–1778' in Dunne & O'Brien (eds), *Catholic Ireland*, pp 115–33; idem, 'The making of Gardiner's relief act, 1781–2', pp 135–48; idem, 'The Catholics and the establishment, 1782–93', pp 149–62; Harvey, *The Bellews*, pp 105, 111–44; Whelan, *The tree of liberty*, p. 15. 14 Harvey, *The Bellews*, pp 115–22, 122–44. 15 Whelan, *The tree of liberty*, p. 17.

THE O'CONORS IN THE EIGHTEENTH CENTURY

Although the title of the O'Conor Don had passed to the Clonalis branch of the family, it was Denis O'Conor of Ballinagare (1674–1750) who began the process of rebuilding the family's landed and political status in County Roscommon. Denis' marriage to Mary O'Rourke, daughter of Colonel Tiernan O'Rourke, a fellow scion of a Gaelic chief, was an advantageous one. By 1727 Denis had built a substantial house at Ballinagare in the early Georgian style, surrounded by smaller thatched houses, gardens and parkland. Known as Ballinagare Castle, on account of there previously having been an O'Conor castle on the site, it 'became the rendezvous for the numerous ill-fated Irish Catholic gentlemen of the province'.[16] Denis' brother-in-law, Thaddeus O'Rourke, bishop of Killala, stayed for a time, while the renowned harpist, Turlough O'Carolan, whose harp is still on display at Clonalis House today, made regular visits.[17] According to Arthur Young, the English travel writer who toured Ireland in the 1770s, Denis O'Conor of Ballinagare was considered 'a prince of the people' in north County Roscommon.[18]

The childhood of Denis' eldest son, Charles (1710–91), was thus steeped in the Gaelic tradition, the Irish language and the Catholic faith. Charles' formal education was a combination of the local hedge school, a private tutor (his uncle, Bishop O'Rourke) and Father Walter Skelton's academy in Dublin. While in Dublin, he mixed with other Gaelic scholars and antiquarian enthusiasts such as Tadhg Ó Neactain, Dr John Fergus and Geoffrey Keating.[19] The Gaelic tradition notwithstanding, Charles received something close to the classical education many young Irish and English Catholic gentleman received in France or Italy in the eighteenth century.[20] In 1731, he married Catherine O'Hagan, the daughter of a merchant from Boyle, County Roscommon. This was a profitable match that enabled him to acquire more land, although the details are not known.[21]

Charles O'Conor is, however, best known for his talents as an historian, antiquarian, pamphleteer and political activist. Although Irish was his first language, he published his first major historical work in 1753 in English, namely *Dissertations on the antient history of Ireland*. Therein he challenged David

---

16 L. Gibbons & K. O'Conor (eds), *Charles O'Conor of Ballinagare: life and works* (Dublin, 2015), pp 52–71; D. Ó Catháin, 'O'Conor, Charles (1710–1791)', *DIB*. 17 Gibbons & O'Conor, *Charles O'Conor*, p. 73; O'Conor, *O'Conors of Connaught*, p. 291. 18 Whelan, *The tree of liberty*, p. 18. 19 Gibbons & O'Conor, *Charles O'Conor*, pp 33–4, 73; O'Conor, *O'Conors of Connaught*, pp 292–3; Ó Catháin, 'O'Conor, Charles', *DIB*. 20 A. Lock, *Catholicism, identity and politics in the age of Enlightenment: the life and career of Sir Thomas Gascoigne, 1745–1810* (Woodbridge, 2016), pp 41–7; O'Neill, *Catholics of consequence*, pp 2–8. 21 Gibbons & O'Conor, *Charles O'Conor*, pp 33–5.

Hume's depiction of the Gaelic Irish as a barbarous race, extolling their virtues as a civilized and learned people, with an 'ancient constitution' complete with conceptions of freedom, liberty, nationhood and democratic forms of government.[22] O'Conor also worked on a history of the 1641 rebellion with the physician, Dr John Curry (1702?–80), which sought to review what they believed were the 'fantastically exaggerated' accounts of Catholic massacres of Protestants at the time.[23] He also penned several pamphlets on the position of Catholics under the penal laws, but anonymously as a 'moderate' or 'liberal' Protestant.[24] Influenced by the writings of George Berkeley and Charles-Louis Montesquieu, O'Conor believed that religious toleration, the rule of law and the diffusion of power between monarchy, aristocracy, church and commons were the hallmarks of a civilized polity. According to Luke Gibbons and Kieran O'Conor, his politics was a kind of nascent liberal Catholicism that ought to be viewed in the context of Catholic enlightenment thinking across Europe in the late eighteenth and early nineteenth centuries.[25] Ian McBride, on the other hand, has described O'Conor as an improbable Catholic whig who pragmatically reconciled himself to the settlement of 1688–9, adopting typically Protestant whig ideas on the balance of power between monarch and parliament, church-state relations, religious toleration, free trade and so on.[26] But the Glorious Revolution of 1688–9 had clearly not been so glorious for Catholics, so perhaps O'Conor's clandestine calls for the extension of civil and political equality to Catholics suggests a more advanced liberal-minded position than the one many Protestant whigs were prepared take at the time.

One way or another, O'Conor was determined to provide a platform for the redress of Catholic grievances. With Curry and Thomas Wyse (1701?– 70) he founded the Catholic Association in 1756, which re-formed as the Catholic Committee in 1760. Around this time, he began to advocate Catholic loyalty to the British crown to assuage Protestant fears that Catholics were still intent on reinstalling a Catholic king on the throne. In 1774, he drafted an oath of allegiance for Catholics, but its wording differed slightly from the oath passed by act of parliament that year, which he initially refused to take. In 1778, the first Catholic relief act was passed, which permitted Catholics who took the oath to own or lease land. Meanwhile, in 1777, O'Conor's younger

---

22 Ibid., pp 73–6, 89, 99, 103. **23** T. Bartlett, *The fall and rise of the Irish nation: the Catholic question 1690–1830* (Dublin, 1992), pp 51–6; C.C. Ward & R.E. Ward (eds), *Letters of Charles O'Conor*, 2 vols (Ann Arbor, MI, 1980), pp ix–xiv; J. Quinn, 'Curry, John', *DIB*; O'Cathain, 'O'Conor, Charles' *DIB*. **24** C.C. Ward & R.C. Ward, 'The Catholic pamphlets of Charles O'Conor (1710–1791)', *Studies: An Irish Quarterly Review*, 68:272 (Winter, 1979), 259–64. **25** Gibbons & O'Conor, *Charles O'Conor*, pp 9, 25–6, 35–7, 79, 99–107, 116–22. **26** I. McBride, *Eighteenth-century Ireland: the isle of slaves* (Dublin, 2009), pp 84–99.

brother, Hugh, conformed to the Church of Ireland and filed a discovery suit.[27] O'Conor was put under house arrest for a time, but his eldest son, Denis, who inherited the Ballinagare estate in 1760, took the oath in 1778 so as to avail of the terms of the relief act and secure the estate. O'Conor eventually took the oath, but the settlement of the discovery suit cost him £300.[28] However, in an amazing stroke of luck, he inherited £5,405 (some £880,000 in today's money) in 1778 from Count Charles O'Gara (1699–1777), a distant relative who had an illustrious career in the household of the Holy Roman Emperor Francis I.[29] Thereafter, O'Conor retreated from political activism to concentrate on his antiquarianism, spending the winter months trawling through manuscripts in Trinity College Dublin, and the summertime at Hermitage, a large farmhouse he had built on the outskirts of the Ballinagare estate in 1764. He became a founding member of the Royal Irish Academy in 1785 and a state pension of £100 per annum was secured for him by Charles Vallancy, a fellow antiquarian.[30]

Charles O'Conor's sons married well and thus carried on the family's seemingly inexorable rise. His eldest, Denis (1732–1804), married Catherine Browne, daughter of a merchant from Cloonfad, County Roscommon, in 1760. Charles (1736–1808) married Mary Dillon, daughter of a Dublin woollen draper, in 1765, and they settled on sizeable farm at Mount Allen, County Roscommon.[31] Denis was not as politically active as his father, but Charles was a leading member of the Catholic Committee in the 1770s and 1780s, attended the Catholic Convention in Dublin in December 1792, and was a member of the Society of United Irishmen.[32] In his history of the family in 1891, the O'Conor Don claimed that Charles withdrew from the society when it took a revolutionary turn, as he 'never intended to go outside the constitution, or ... recourse to means inconsistent with ... loyalty to the Crown'.[33] It is not clear if Charles was a loyalist, but what we do know is that his general conduct had been a cause of concern to his father before the 1790s. Moreover, he and his

27 Ward & Ward (eds), *Letters of Charles O'Conor*, i, pp 62–3, 78–80, 106, 191–5, 203, 239, 250, 276; Ward & Ward (eds), *Letters of Charles O'Conor*, ii, pp ix–xiv, 128–9, 138; Bartlett, *Irish nation*, pp 80–1, 90; Harvey, *The Bellews*, pp 147–60. 28 Denis O'Conor's oath of allegiance, 9 Nov. 1778, O'Conor papers, CH, 8.4.SH.230; Dunleavy & Dunleavy (eds), *The O'Conor papers*, pp 44, 65–7; C.J. Woods, 'O'Conor, Denis (1732–1804)', *DIB*; Melvin, 'Roscommon estates and landowners', p. 346 (footnote 37). 29 M. O'Gara-O'Riordan, 'Count Charles O'Gara 1699–1777', *Corran Herald*, 46 (2013/14), 66–9. 30 Gibbons & O'Conor, *Charles O'Conor*, pp 39, 50; McBride, *Eighteenth-century Ireland*, p. 401; Ó Catháin, 'O'Conor, Charles', *DIB*. 31 Marriage agreements of Denis and Charles O'Conor, 1760 & 1765, O'Conor papers, CH, 8.3.ES.045; C.J. Woods, 'O'Conor, Denis, and Charles O'Conor', *DIB*. 32 R.B. MacDowell et al., *The writings of Theobald Wolfe Tone, 1763–98* (Oxford, 1998), i, pp 138–9, 145, 153, 368; Woods, 'O'Conor, Denis, and Charles O'Conor', *DIB*; O'Conor, *O'Conors of Connaught*, pp 300–3. 33 O'Conor, *O'Conors of Connaught*, pp 300–18, table iv.

sons, Thomas and Denis, who were also United Irishmen, emigrated to New York after the passing of the Act of Union in 1801.[34]

THE O'CONORS IN THE EARLY NINETEENTH CENTURY

Owen O'Conor (1763–1831), Denis O'Conor's (1732–1804) eldest son, presided over the re-establishment of the family as a landed and political dynasty in the early nineteenth century. Having received his formal education at the 'academy' in Dublin, Owen returned to Ballinagare in 1778.[35] In 1791, he inherited his grandfather's house, while in 1804 he inherited the entire Ballinagare estate after the death of his father. In 1805, he bought the 900-acre Clonalis estate from his indebted cousin, Alexander (1735–1820), for £12,400. Alexander's debts were incurred through a protracted legal battle with his sister-in-law, Catherine O'Conor, who had been named as the executor of her husband Dominick's will, in which Owen was named as the chief beneficiary. Frustrated with his lot, Alexander attempted to recover the castle and lands at Ballintober by force in 1786. Although it seems to have been a totally shambolic and harmless event, government troops were dispatched and Alexander only 'narrowly escaped imprisonment'. The episode was a cause of embarrassment to the family, with Charles of Ballinagare thinking him a 'rash and silly man'.[36] Nonetheless, the family claim to the Ballintober lands remained, with the O'Conor Don purchasing part of them in 1892. Three years later, he played host to a party of the Royal Society of Antiquaries of Ireland in the ruins of the old castle.[37]

Owen's rise in fortunes was undoubtedly helped by yet another lucrative match. In 1792, he married Jane Moore, daughter of Edward Moore (d. 1787), a wealthy Dublin brewer. This marriage also forged connections with other wealthy Catholics such as Valentine O'Connor (1744–1814) and Patrick Grehan, both of whom married daughters of Edward Moore. Valentine had

34 S. Kleinman & D. Murphy, 'O'Conor, Thomas', *DIB*; G.W. & J.E. Dunleavy, 'Reconstruction, reform, and Romanism, 1865–85: America as seen by Charles O'Conor and Charles Owen O'Conor Don, MP', *Éire Ireland*, 15:3 (Fall, 1980), 15–35; Ward & Ward (eds), *Letters of Charles O'Conor*, ii, pp 124, 153. 35 C.J. Woods, 'O'Conor, Owen', *DIB*; Ward & Ward (eds), *Letters of Charles O'Conor*, ii, pp 118–19, 153, 216. 36 Woods, 'O'Conor, Owen', *DIB*; Gibbons & O'Conor, *Charles O'Conor*, pp 17, 24, 27, 54, 153; Melvin, 'Roscommon estates and landowners', pp 336–7, 346 (footnotes 34, 35 & 36); Gibbon, *The recollections*, pp 266–7; Ward & Ward (eds), *Letters of Charles O'Conor*, ii, p. 278. 37 Purchase of Pakenham-Mahon lands under the 1891 land act, July 1892, O'Conor papers, CH, 9.4.ES.294; Recollections part 2, O'Conor papers, CH, 9.4.HL.156, p. 162; Proceedings, *Journal of the Royal Society of Antiquaries of Ireland*, 5:3 (Sept. 1895), 249; C.O. O'Conor, 'Ballintubber Castle, County Roscommon', *Journal of the Royal Historical and Archaeological Association of Ireland*, 9:78 (Jan.–Mar. 1889), 24–30.

a successful mercantile business in Dublin and owned two-thirds of a sugar plantation on the island of St Vincent, in the West Indies, where he owned slaves.[38] Owen's connection to Valentine O'Connor provided him with the financial resources to purchase Clonalis in 1805, and it may have helped with the purchase of 1,051 acres in County Sligo, in 1809–10, for £14,515. Much later, in 1826–7, Owen bought 321 acres in County Roscommon for £6,043, with finance raised through a bond of £5,000 with his brother, Charles; and through William Murphy (1771–1849), a wealthy cattle dealer from Dublin, who bought 80 acres in trust.[39] Owen purchased at least another 2,549 acres, but the years and amounts paid are undetermined.[40] In 1820, he inherited the title of the O'Conor Don when its holder, Alexander of Clonalis, died without an heir. Owen then moved from Ballinagare to Clonalis to make it his principal residence.[41] Upon the death of his brother, Charles, in 1828, Owen inherited £1,250, of which £50 was to be used for the upkeep of the churches and schools in the parishes of Castlerea, Ballinagare and Ballintober. This was to be an annual donation with the stipulation that Owen and his descendants would have first preference in the nomination of clergy in these parishes.[42]

On the political front, Owen joined the Volunteers in 1781 and was a delegate for County Roscommon at the Catholic Convention in 1792. Like his uncle Charles, he was a member of the Society of United Irishmen and caught the attention of Wolfe Tone on account of his patriotic fervour. Nonetheless, although he opposed to the Act of Union, Owen's political course post-1800 followed his grandfather's example of combining patriotism, loyalism and liberal reform. As a prominent member of the Catholic Committee, he travelled to London on three occasions in the 1810s as part of a delegation petitioning for Catholic emancipation. In the 1820s, he opposed the proposed government veto on the appointment of Catholic bishops and became one of Daniel O'Connell's most trusted friends and supporters.[43] In the general election of 1830, he was returned Liberal MP for County Roscommon; and although

---

38 C.J. Woods, 'O'Connor, Valentine (1744–1814)', *DIB*; Melvin, 'Roscommon estates and landowners', pp 336–7. 39 Valentine O'Connor to Owen O'Conor, 12 May 1804, O'Conor papers, CH, 9.1.SE.073; Summary of the Ardsoreen estate, Nov. 1887, O'Conor papers, CH, 9.4.ES.291; Abstract of title to Drimina estate, July 1888, Land commission papers, DAFF, box 237/schedule C/no. 13/record no. 827; Supplemental abstract of title to Gortnagoyne, Tallaghan and part of Clooncrawfield, Apr. 1906, Land commission papers, DAFF, box 237/ schedule E/no. 6/record no. 1119; C.J. Woods, 'Murphy, William (1771–1849)', *DIB*. 40 For additional purchases in Owen's name, see O'Conor papers, CH, 9.1.EH.003. 41 Gibbons & O'Conor, *Charles O'Conor*, p. 54; Woods, 'O'Conor, Owen', *DIB*. 42 Will of Revd Charles O'Conor, 1828, O'Conor papers, CH, 9.2.HL.018; Abstract of title, 10 July 1888, Land commission papers, DAFF, box 237/schedule C/ no. 13/record no. 827. 43 Woods, 'O'Conor, Owen' *DIB*; MacDowell et al., *Theobald Wolfe Tone*, i, pp 153–4, 354, 368, 399, 407, 442; O'Conor, *O'Conors of Connaught*, pp 321–9, table iv.

subject to some local criticism over the sincerity of his support for repeal of the Act of Union, he was returned again in May 1831, having articulated a position of support for repeal without separation from the British crown.[44] Owen's sense of attachment to the crown was genuine. Indeed, in 1821, he was advised by the then Ulster king of arms, Sir William Betham, of a 'common descent' with King George IV through 'a daughter of Hugh O'Conor of Connacht, who died in 1228'. Betham recommended that Owen petition the king to have the 'former royalty' of the O'Conor family officially recognized, but nothing came of it.[45] Owen was, then, a fairly typical liberal Catholic of the early nineteenth century variety who balanced his pursuit of Catholic equality and Irish nationhood with an adherence to constitutional politics and loyalty to the crown.

Of Owen's eleven siblings, Charles (1764–1828) and Matthew (1773–1844) figured most prominently.[46] Both were sent to the Irish College in Rome to study for the priesthood, but Matthew left aged only fourteen and embarked on a tour of Europe before returning to Ireland. He went on to study law, was called to the Irish Bar, and became a successful barrister. In 1804, he married Priscilla Forbes and settled on a 2,000-acre estate at Mount Druid, near Ballinagare. An historian of some note, Matthew published a history of Irish Catholics since the Jacobite defeat in 1690, which balanced a general rebuke of English misrule in Ireland and the damaging effects of the penal laws with confident assertions of Catholic loyalty to the crown and the beginnings of an era of 'liberality, patriotism, and national glory' in Ireland.[47] Thus, Matthew, like Owen, steered the liberal course of making the patriotic case for Catholic equality and Irish nationhood while advocating loyalty to the crown.

Revd Charles O'Conor was less moderate and led a less tranquil life. In December 1790, he returned from Rome to take up the position of curate in the parish of Kilkeevan, but he done so having denounced the disciplinary and educational standards at the Irish College. His time in Kilkeevan was not a particularly happy one and he transferred to Killaracht, in County Sligo, in 1797, before leaving Ireland to take up the post of chaplain to the marquis of Buckingham, George Grenville, in 1799. In the meantime, Charles had written a memoir of his grandfather, but its publication was suppressed by the family in 1796, with his father Denis thinking its stinging criticisms of

---

44 *Freeman's Journal*, 23 July 1830; ibid., 17 Nov. 1830; ibid., 17 Jan. 1831. 45 Murphy, *Twilight of the chiefs*, pp 28–9. 46 O'Conor, *O'Conors of Connacht*, p. 320, table iv. 47 D. Murphy, 'O'Conor, Matthew', *DIB*; Matthew O'Conor, *The history of the Irish Catholics from the settlement in 1691, with a view of the state of Ireland from the invasion by Henry II to the revolution* (Dublin, 1813), pp v–vii, 262–71; Gibbons & O'Conor, *Charles O'Conor*, p. 252.

British rule in Ireland dangerous in the feverish political climate of the time, while his brother Matthew was convinced that he had fabricated some of the material attributed to their grandfather. In 1814, he published a four-volume history of Gaelic literature that was posthumously criticized by the renowned scholar John O'Donovan for the inaccuracy of its Latin and Old Irish translations. Charles' combative disposition also got him in hot water on religious matters. He dismissed the idea of papal infallibility as politically motivated and supported the British government's proposed veto on the appointment of Catholic bishops. The latter was of course opposed by his brother and led to his priestly duties being suspended by the pope.[48]

THE O'CONORS AFTER EMANCIPATION

The moulding of Denis O'Conor (1794–1847) – Owen O'Conor's eldest son – into a young Catholic gentleman reflected the change in the family's financial fortunes and broader trends in upper- and middle-class Catholic life. Between 1809 and 1813, Denis attended St Edmund's Catholic college, near the town of Ware in Hertfordshire, England.[49] As ably demonstrated by Ciaran O'Neill in his seminal study on the education of Irish Catholics in the nineteenth century, Owen's choice of education for Denis reflected a growing preference among upper- and middle-class Catholics for an English college education, which it was thought would confer social status on their sons and prepare them for university, professional jobs and political careers. Although the professions and politics were dominated by Protestants, Catholic boys who attended these colleges were now at least in a position to compete, especially after emancipation in 1829.[50]

In 1813, Denis proceeded from St Edmund's to Trinity College Dublin (TCD). Again, it was not unusual for a young Catholic gentleman to make this transition, with Denis' contemporaries Richard Lalor Sheil (1791–1851), Sir Thomas Wyse (1791–1862) and Stephen Woulfe (1787–1840) moving from Stonyhurst College, in Lancashire, to TCD.[51] Nonetheless, as we shall see in chapter five, TCD was still an overwhelmingly Protestant institution, with Catholic attendance frowned upon but not openly condemned by the Catholic hierarchy until they established a Catholic university in Dublin in

---

48 P. Boyne, *John O'Donovan (1806–1861): a biography* (Kilkenny, 1987), pp 44, 83–6; L. Lunney & A. O'Brien, 'O'Conor, Charles (1764–1828)', *DIB*; Gibbons & O'Conor, *Charles O'Conor*, pp 133–43, 154, 249–52.   49 B. Hourican, 'O'Conor, Denis', *DIB*; S. Farrell, 'O'Conor, Denis, the O'Conor Don', HOPO; Dunleavy & Dunleavy, *The O'Conor papers*, p. 98.   50 O'Neill, *Catholics of consequence*, pp 1–17, 27, 36–9, 56–9, 73–9, 112–13, 161–89.   51 Farrell, 'O'Conor, Denis', HOPO; O'Neill, *Catholics of consequence*, p. 79.

1854.[52] What Denis' attendance at TCD demonstrates is his father's aspiration and pragmatism in pursuing the best third-level education available to his son in Ireland, even though it did not meet with the approval of the bishops. In 1817, Denis was accepted at the King's Inns Dublin, but he does not seem to have ever practised law. By the early 1820s, he had, like many Catholic gentlemen of his generation, embarked on an extensive European tour.[53]

Typically, the grand tour preceded Denis' settling down to life as a country gentleman. In 1824, he married Mary Blake, daughter of Major Maurice Blake, a large landowner at Towerhill, near Carnacon, County Mayo. The Blakes and O'Conors were already connected through Maurice's marriage to Mary O'Connor, daughter of the above-mentioned Valentine O'Connor, the Dublin merchant and descendant of the Ballintober branch of the O'Conor family. Denis' younger brother, Edward (1796–1838), who was his land and political agent, married another of Maurice's daughters, Honoria, that same year.[54] Following their father's death in 1831, Denis inherited most of the Roscommon and Sligo estates, and the remainder after Edward's death in 1838. Although the specifics are not known, the estates were probably in the region of 6,000 acres at this point, but Denis continued to expand, purchasing hundreds of acres in counties Roscommon and Sligo.[55]

When Denis' father, Owen, passed away in 1831 he put himself forward to contest the vacant County Roscommon seat after Oliver John Dowell Grace (1791–1871), another prominent Catholic landlord in the county, withdrew his candidacy.[56] Like his father, he was a loyalist and a repealer, arguing at a public meeting in Roscommon in 1831 that it was 'false' to link his support for repeal with the separation of Ireland from Great Britain or the British crown. Indeed, he declared that if the campaign for repeal ever strayed in that direction, he would be 'the last to join it' and the 'readiest and … foremost to oppose it'.[57] This was not a particularly unusual position, as O'Connell himself seems to have envisaged repeal as the restoration of an Irish parliament

---

52 See chapter five, pp 110–11.   53 Farrell, 'O'Conor, Denis', HOPO; Melvin, 'The landed gentry of Galway', p. 504.   54 Indenture between Denis O'Conor and Maurice Blake, Nov. 1824, O'Conor papers, CH, 9.1.ES.457; Reference to Edward O'Conor as Denis' 'agent and manager', O'Conor papers, CH, 9.2.HS.265; For the Blake of Towehill estate, see CMLED.   55 Copy of the will of Denis O'Conor, 21 July 1847, NLI, D.17,058; Will of Denis O'Conor, n.d., O'Conor papers, CH, 9.2.ES.047; Chancery report on the will of Denis O'Conor Don, 1859?, O'Conor papers, CH, 9.3.SE.053; Chancery report on the estate of Owen O'Conor, n.d., O'Conor papers, CH, E.9.2.SE.045; Will of Owen O'Conor, 1831, O'Conor papers, CH, 9.1.EH.003; Stamp office legacy duty on residues of the personal estate of Owen O'Conor, 1831, O'Conor papers, CH, 9.2.ES.115; The estate of Edward O'Conor, 1838, O'Conor papers, CH, 9.2.EO.009; Various wills, marriage articles and land settlements, 1842, O'Conor papers, CH, 9.2.ES.358.   56 Potter, 'Local government in Co. Roscommon', p. 292; *Freeman's Journal*, 17, 30 June 1831.   57 *Freeman's Journal*, 17 Jan. 1831.

while maintaining some kind of constitutional link to the British crown and the empire.[58] Denis was, however, keen to assert the loyalty of Irish Catholics, declaring in a commons debate on the state of Ireland in 1844 'that in the wide extent of Her Majesty's dominions, there would not be found a body more devotedly attached to her than the Roman Catholic population of Ireland'. This was almost certainly wishful thinking, but Denis nonetheless went on to identify what he believed to be the main cause of Ireland's social and economic ills, namely that the country was treated by parliament as a sectarian battleground to be won or lost, rather than a country where 'Protestant, Catholic, and Dissenter – English, Irish, and Scotch – would consider themselves … fellow-citizens of the same empire – fellow-subjects of the same queen – brothers in Christian charity and civil rights'.[59] This was, essentially, a liberal plea for toleration and the politics of the common good between Great Britain and Ireland, with the latter treated as a nation in its own right under the crown and within the empire.

As we shall see, Denis' high-minded ideals on British-Irish relations were echoed by his son and the subject of this book, Charles Owen O'Conor, in the context of the debates on home rule in the 1890s. But in the context of the 1840s, this kind of liberal and nationalist-minded outlook had been in the ascendancy in Irish Catholic political representation since at least the beginning of the campaign for emancipation in the 1810s. Daniel O'Connell was the dominant figure, but Sir Thomas Wyse and Richard Lalor Sheil figured prominently too, as did Bishop James Doyle. Thus, notwithstanding O'Connell's radicalism, Denis was part of a wider group of liberal and nationalist-minded Irish Catholics, who, as demonstrated by Fergus O'Ferrall, sought the full extension of the freedoms and rights of the British constitution to Irish Catholics and supported the cause of social, economic and political reform within the union more generally. They did so, however, while emphasizing Catholic loyalty to the British crown and asserting Ireland's nationhood within a British imperial framework.[60]

Denis' desire for a liberal middle ground should not come as much of a surprise given that his family's history laid bare the results of ethnic and sectarian conflict in Ireland. He was well-schooled in the politics of moderation, with his father and great-grandfather showing him that it was possible and indeed desirable to champion Catholic equality and Irish nationhood while maintaining the constitutional link between Ireland and Great Britain. As a

---

58 A. Macintyre, *The liberator: Daniel O'Connell and the Irish Party, 1830–1847* (London, 1965), p. 128. 59 HC Deb., 20 Feb. 1844, vol. 72, cc 1209–312. 60 F. O'Ferrall, *Catholic emancipation: Daniel O'Connell and the birth of Irish democracy* (Dublin, 1985), pp 16–21, 26–7, 40–3, 52–3, 65–71, 77–80, 83–5, 96–7, 106–13, 121–3, 154, 216, 258–89.

young man his education exposed him to the institutions and customs of English Catholics and Irish Protestants, demonstrating that Irish and English, Catholic and Protestant, had shared interests and aspirations. Over the course of his time as an MP, Denis mixed freely with the political class of Ireland and Great Britain, most of whom were landed, loyalist and unionist. Indeed, even though landed Irish and English Catholics met frequently as a separate group in London, landed Catholics and Protestants from Ireland and Great Britain mixed freely at the viceregal and royal levees, in the gentleman's clubs, and in the houses of parliament.[61]

In parliament, Denis was a middle-ranking, loyal follower of O'Connell, supporting parliamentary reform, abolition of tithes, municipal reform and repeal of the corn laws, while opposing the new poor law and coercion. His political career took on a dramatically different trajectory in 1846 when he accepted the position of junior lord of the treasury in Lord John Russell's Whig-Liberal government. Although it met with O'Connell's approval, Denis' appointment was not received well by radical Irish nationalists.[62] At a meeting of the Repeal Association in Dublin in July 1846, the Young Irelander Thomas Francis Meagher lambasted him as an 'apostate' who had betrayed the cause of repeal. O'Connell quickly moved to defend him, though, arguing that he was no 'less a Repealer' for taking the position.[63] Later that month at a public meeting in Roscommon, Denis himself declared:

> that he took office under the present liberal government, not for any personal honour or aggrandizement to himself, but because he considered he could serve his country more by co-operating with the ministry in placing Ireland on an equality with England and Scotland, as to political rights and franchises.[64]

Denis' belief that Ireland could gain parity within the union was a reiteration of the views he had expressed on British-Irish relations in 1831 and 1844, but it was a very difficult position to defend as the worst effects of the Irish Famine began to take hold in 1846. In May 1847 – with a general election looming and the Famine crisis reaching its devastating height – the *Nation* declared Denis unfit to represent the people of Roscommon because, 'He will go before them

---

61 *Freeman's Journal*, 16 Oct. 1838 & 24 May 1845. 62 P. Gray, *The making of the Irish poor law, 1815–43* (Manchester, 2009), pp 185, 207, 244; D. Kerr, *'A nation of beggars'?: priests, people, and politics in Famine Ireland, 1846–1852* (Oxford, 1994), pp 24–7; O. MacDonagh, *The emancipist: Daniel O'Connell 1830–47* (London, 1989), pp 273–5, 289, 293; Macintyre, *The liberator*, pp 15–17, 44, 68, 151, 161–2, 274–5; HC Deb., 9 Mar. 1840, vol. 52, c. 1069; ibid., 15 May 1846, vol. 86, cc 722–6. 63 *Nation*, 18 July 1846. 64 *Freeman's Journal*, 25 July 1846.

again not as the O'Conor Don, but as the O'Conor Didn't ... the O'Conor who saw two millions of his nation slain by starvation, and didn't dare accuse the government of their guilt.'[65] A damning indictment to say the least, it did not take into account the considerable personal efforts Denis O'Conor made to alleviate the distress on his own estates and in the Castlerea area. In September 1846 he purchased two tons of Indian meal for his tenants, with Charles Owen later recalling how he and his younger brother Denis Maurice helped their aunts distribute these provisions at Clonalis. Moreover, after relaying 'several alarming communications' of distress to the assistant secretary of the treasury in London, Charles Trevelyan, and the chairman of the central relief commission in Dublin, Sir Randolph Routh, Denis succeeded in having a food depot opened at Castlerea.[66] Despite his personal efforts, however, Denis' ability to openly criticize the government's disastrous attempts to deal with the Famine crisis was undoubtedly compromised by his position as a junior minister. The enormity of the situation seems to have taken its toll and his health deteriorated rapidly in the summer of 1847. Although it is not clear what his ailment was, he passed away on 22 July 1847 at his London residence, 51 Pall Mall West.[67]

---

65 *Nation*, 29 May 1847. 66 Recollections part 1, O'Conor papers, CH, 9.4.HL.156, p. 6; *Correspondence from July, 1846, to January, 1847, relating to the measures adopted for the relief of the distress in Ireland. Commissariat series*, HC 1847 (761), li, 178, pp 52–3. 67 *Freeman's Journal*, 24 July 1847.

2 / 'An upholder of the old liberal opinions': the O'Conor Don and his world

Charles Owen O'Conor was born on 7 May 1838 in Lord Norbury's house, 21 Rutland Square, Dublin. He was baptized the following day in St Mary's Pro-Cathedral Church, Marlborough Street, by Archdeacon John Hamilton. His father, Denis, and mother, Mary, had already had seven daughters, five of whom survived: Jane, Kate, Josephine, Eugenia and Dionysia. In 1840, a second son, Denis Maurice, was born.[1] On 12 June 1841, Mary O'Conor died at Southampton after a short illness.[2] And as already noted, Denis died six years later in 1847, at the height of the Famine crisis. The seven O'Conor children were therefore orphaned at a young age; and as the O'Conor Don later recalled, the death of his father while he was still a minor meant the O'Conor estates 'were put under chancery' and he and his siblings 'became wards of the courts, with our aunts as guardians'. That this happened at the height of the Famine crisis seems to have led to a certain tightening of the purse strings by the aunts, Jane and Honoria, with the children spending more time at the family's Dublin residence in Kingstown (now Dún Laoghaire) over the next few years than they did at Clonalis, where 'the whole of our family establishment was reduced, most of the servants were dismissed, [and] an auction of all the stock, horses and farm requisites took place'.[3]

Whatever reduction there was in the family's circumstances during these years, Charles and his siblings were well provided for by their father. Charged to the main estate was an outlay of £10,000 for Charles and his six siblings, which was to be divided evenly in sums of £1,538 when they reached their majority. Additional sums of £2,462 were set aside for the girls if they had not joined a religious order by the age of twenty-one, or upon the event of their marriage. As well as appointing Jane and Honoria (d. 1857) as guardians to his children, Denis named them, and his brother-in-law, Valentine O'Conor-Blake (1808–79), and his cousin, Edward Moore, as executors of his will. He had his life insured for £5,000, but this money was set aside for the repayment of a £3,950 loan to Jane and Honoria, with the remainder as remuneration for their role as executors.[4] However, the determining factor in the

---

[1] Recollections part 1, O'Conor papers, CH, 9.4.HL.156, p. 2; Mary Purcell, 'Dublin Diocesan Archives: Hamilton papers (3)', *Archivium Hibernicum*, 46 (1991/1992), 22; *Freeman's Journal*, 9 May 1838. [2] Maria O'Conor to Archdeacon Hamilton, 1 June 1841, Hamilton papers, DDA, 36/4/206; *Freeman's Journal*, 16 June 1841. [3] Recollections part 1, O'Conor papers, CH, 9.4.HL.156, p. 7. [4] Copy of will of Denis O'Conor, 21 July 1847, NLI, D.17,058.

future financial stability of the O'Conor family was the fortune bequeathed to Charles and Denis by their cousin, Edward Moore, who was a partner in Valentine O'Connor's mercantile business in Dublin, owned land in South Australia, Jamaica and Antigua, and was a slave owner. Moore died in 1851 and under the terms of his will the O'Conor boys were to inherit £50,000 each (some £6.4 million each in today's money) on the event of their twenty-first birthdays.[5] It seems highly likely that the O'Conor family were aware of the provenance of Moore's wealth but, even though he visited America at the end of the Civil War in 1865 and commented on what he saw, the author has not been able to establish conclusively what O'Conor Don's views on slavery were. It also seems likely that the family's imperial connection influenced his support for the empire, but again this is not clear. One way or another, the Moore connection proved vital, as did the connection with the Blakes, with Charles' uncle, Valentine, who also inherited £50,000 from Moore, becoming a friend and confidante. Another example of a Catholic landlord on the rise in the mid-nineteenth century, Valentine bought Bunowen Castle and estate in County Galway in 1853 and was, by 1876, the owner of 11,888 acres in counties Galway and Mayo.[6]

EDUCATION AND TRAVEL

It was Denis O'Conor's wish that his children be educated in England because he felt it would enhance their 'future prospects'.[7] In 1844, the five O'Conor girls were sent to Princethorpe convent school near Coventry and all of them went on to became nuns. This may seem remarkable, but it was not that unusual for the daughters of the Catholic landed gentry to be sent down this route, most likely so their fathers could avoid having to provide multiple dowries.[8] Between 1847 and 1851 Charles and Denis were educated by a private tutor, John Leahy, both at the family's Dublin residence and at Clonalis. A former national schoolteacher who came recommended by Archdeacon Hamilton, Leahy was not entirely to the satisfaction of the boy's aunt, Honoria. Perhaps she thought he was too strict, as the O'Conor Don later recalled that although

5 Chancery report on the case of the O'Conor minors, 1858, O'Conor papers, CH, 9.2.HO.008.01; Will of Edward Moore, August 1849, O'Conor papers, CH, 9.2.ES.114. For Moore's slave owning and compensation for it, see *Centre for the Study of the Legacies of British Slavery*, https://www.ucl.ac.uk/lbs/person/view/40861. 6 Will of Edward Moore, August 1849, O'Conor papers, CH, 9.2.ES.114; For O'Conor-Blake's estates see CMLED. 7 Roderick MacDermot to the O'Conor Don, Apr. 1856, O'Conor papers, CH, 9.3.HE.055.56. 8 Recollections part 1, O'Conor papers, CH, 9.4.HL.156, p. 3; O'Neill, *Catholics of consequence*, p. 178.

Leahy was not a particularly learned man or a good teacher, 'he had a marvellous power of getting influence over his pupils and of breaking down their self[-]will'.[9]

In the autumn of 1852, Charles and Denis were sent to Downside College, Bath, where they remained until 1857 and 1858, respectively.[10] Attendance at English Catholic colleges like Downside now had the added advantage of giving upper- and middle-class Irish Catholic boys the opportunity to take a degree with the University of London, through its central examination programme for affiliated colleges, of which Downside was one.[11] This meant Irish Catholic boys did not have to attend TCD or the Queen's colleges to get a degree, although some upper- and middle-class Catholics still preferred these institutions because of their collegiate atmosphere, perceived superiority or secular ethos. This, of course, was a source of annoyance for the Catholic hierarchy, who, as well shall see, frowned upon Catholic attendance at these institutions. Although the option of sending Charles to TCD was considered, he and Denis sat the exams for the University of London.[12] This would suggest that the boys' aunts were, at the very least, keen to be seen to be following the church's direction, but one wonders if their father would have guided them in the direction of his alma matter, TCD, if he were still alive.

In any event, the O'Conor boys received a typically humanistic or 'liberal' education at Downside. Set up by Catholic religious orders in the 1790s and early 1800s, the colleges at Downside, St Edward's, Ampleforth, Stonyhurst, Oscott and elsewhere in England were attended by upper- and middle-class Catholic boys from across Europe, providing a type of education and ethos modelled on the Protestant public schools at Eton, Harrow and Winchester. Apart from religious instruction and the teaching of history, the curriculum provided was broadly similar, including Latin, Greek, French, Italian, English literature, Roman and Greek literature, music and drawing, maths, natural philosophy, history and geography. The discipline and extracurricular activities were also similar, with early morning starts, Mass, prayers and independent study all part of the daily routine, as well as an emphasis on sports,

---

9 John Leahy to Archdeacon Hamilton, 15 Nov. 1847, Hamilton papers, DDA, 37/1/202; Honoria O'Conor to Archdeacon Hamilton, 13 Sept. 1848, Hamilton papers, DDA, 37/1/359; John Leahy to Archdeacon Hamilton, 8 Nov. 1848, Hamilton papers, DDA, 37/1/382; Recollections part 1, O'Conor papers, CH, 9.4.HL.156, p. 9; Denis O'Conor to Honoria O'Conor, 27 Apr. 1851, O'Conor papers, CH, 9.3.SO.016. 10 Recollections part 1, O'Conor papers, CH, 9.4.HL.156, pp 10–16; Sale of Ardakillin to William Paine Neville, 25 June 1852, O'Conor papers, CH, 9.3.ES.048. Notably, 357 acres of O'Conor land were sold for £2,050 in June 1852, presumably by Honoria to pay for college fees and other expenses. 11 F.M.L. Thompson (ed.), *The University of London and the world of learning, 1836–1986* (London, 1990), pp xii–xvi; O'Neill, *Catholics of consequence*, p. 114. 12 For speculation about Charles Owen going to TCD, see O'Conor papers, CH, 9.2.SE.160. See chapter five, pp 110–11.

gentlemanly behaviour, correct enunciation, speechifying and debating, annual Shakespearean plays, and mock royal courts. A similar education was provided at Irish Catholic colleges such as Clongowes Wood, Tullabeg, Castleknock and Blackrock, although they did not have the same transnational element and did not have the same status as the English colleges in the minds of many landed Irish Catholics.[13]

Towards the end of the nineteenth century, the nationalist journalist D.P. Moran claimed this type of education facilitated the spread of 'West Britonism' among Catholics in Ireland, a claim based on the idea that because Catholic boys were exposed to English customs, pastimes and mannerisms, and turned out to be unionists and loyalists as adults, they were somehow not properly Irish. But the Irish boys at English colleges undoubtedly saw themselves as Irish and were perceived as being different by their English peers, with St Patrick's Day celebrations and debates on Irish politics the norm at Downside and Stonyhurst. In any event, a college education in England or Ireland just as easily had the effect of instilling nationalist or republican sympathies, as it did unionist or loyalist. For example, former students of Stonyhurst ranged from the radical nationalist Thomas Francis Meagher, to the liberal unionist, junior government minister and British diplomat Sir Thomas Wyse, while former Clongowes students included the moderate nationalist leader of the Irish Parliamentary Party, John Redmond, and the judge, chief baron of the exchequer and unionist Christopher Palles.[14] For Charles and Denis, their education at Downside seems to have reinforced an existing family tradition of loyalty to the British crown and support for the British imperial project. In 1855, at the age of seventeen, Charles was elected king at Downside's annual mock court and delivered a speech at a celebratory banquet where 'God save the queen' was sung. Denis did the same in 1857.[15] More generally, their education at Downside fostered bonds of class and kinship in the long term, with both Charles and Denis forging lifelong friendships with English Catholics, marrying English Catholics and maintaining an attachment to Downside itself.

This educational experience and its longer-term impact did not make the O'Conors feel any 'less Irish' or, if you like, 'more British', but it undoubtedly helped fostered closer connections to Great Britain and the rituals and institutions of the British state and empire. As we shall see in subsequent chapters, although the O'Conor Don was a staunch Irish Catholic who often expressed

13 O'Neill, *Catholics of consequence*, pp 21–4, 41–9, 95–8, 104–5; F.C. Burnand (ed.), *The Catholic who's who and yearbook, 1908* (London, 1908), pp 32, 105, 151, 156, 179, 220, 287–8; D.H. Norbert Birth, *Downside: the history of St Gregory's school from its commencement at Douay to the present time* (London, 1902), pp 206–12, 263–5, 270–4, 300–14, 342–8. 14 O'Neill, *Catholics of consequence*, pp 7–8, 17, 22–5, 42, 46–7, 59, 69–70, 79, 81–3, 89, 90–2. 15 Norbert Birth, *Downside*, pp 206–12, 263–5, 270–4, 300–14.

frustration at Protestant and English attitudes towards Ireland, Catholics and the Catholic Church, he was an Irishman who embraced the idea that British identity could be part of what it meant to be Irish.[16]

Questions of cultural impact aside, Charles' and Denis' everyday experiences at Downside were something of a mixed bag. They acquired a good reputation among the staff for their diligence and academic performance, but it was not all plain sailing.[17] In the summer of 1855, there appears to have been some confusion and upset regarding Charles' eligibility, on account of his age, to sit the matriculation for the University of London. Despite this, he sat and passed the exams with flying colours and subsequently decided to study for a BA degree, even though he excelled at mathematics. By September 1855, Denis was expressing his dread of getting 'in the same mess as Charlie' with the matriculation, but he also criticized Downside's course of study for a BA degree, which was 'nothing else than cramming your head for the university without teaching you anything else'.[18] This was certainly a criticism of the central examining system at the time and perhaps we should not be surprised at a bright fifteen-year-old boy having a mind of his own. But Denis was certainly in a gloomy, homesick mood, telling his cousin Roderick MacDermot (1812–99) that he felt 'more fond of Ireland' since the summer vacation and wished he 'was back again in Clonalis'. Criticizing his Italian tutor, who was trying to 'make out that' he and the Charles knew 'nothing', he signed off with: 'I am beginning to hate this place.'[19] Things were bad enough for the boys' aunt to consider moving them to another English college in the spring of 1856, but nothing came of it and Charles and Denis remained at Downside and retained an affection for the place.[20] Indeed, they both excelled in their own ways. In the summer of 1856, Charles received 'a silver gilt medal and £10', which, according to one of his teachers, was 'the greatest prize that we have ever given'. He did not, however, progress to take his degree due to a bout of ill health in 1857. Denis, on the other hand, may have been disgruntled with the system, but his time at Downside saw him gain BA and MA degrees from the University of London in 1860 and 1861, respectively. In 1866, he gained an LLD from the same institution and he was subsequently called to the Bar at the Middle Temple.[21]

16 See chapter seven, pp 182–90. 17 Letters from Downside to Honoria O'Conor, 31 July 1855 & 3 July 1856, O'Conor papers, CH, 9.3.SH.035. 18 Denis Maurice O'Conor to Roderick MacDermot, 29 Sept. 1855, O'Conor papers, CH, 9.3.SO.016. 19 The O'Conor Don to Honoria, 31 July 1855, O'Conor papers, CH, 9.3.SH.035; Denis Maurice O'Conor to Roderick MacDermot, 29 Sept. 1855, O'Conor papers, CH, 9.3.SO.016. 20 Roderick MacDermot to Charles Owen O'Conor, n.d. Apr. 1856, O'Conor papers, CH, 9.3.HE.055.56. 21 M. Stenton (ed.), *A who's who of British members of parliament: a biographical dictionary of the house of commons based on annual volumes of 'Dod's parliamentary companion' and other sources*, i: *1832–1885* (Sussex, 1976), p. 292.

After a period of convalescence at Clonalis in the spring of 1858, Charles embarked on a tour of Europe accompanied by a tutor by the name of Mr Mann, who came recommended by the English cardinal Nicholas Wiseman. He spent the next year in France, visiting Boulogne, Dieppe, Paris, Marseilles, Toulon and Hyéres before returning to Paris in May 1859 to meet up with Denis and celebrate his twenty-first birthday. He then spent the rest of the summer in Rome, where he served as chamberlain to the pope and later recalled 'the happiest days of my life were spent'. In the autumn he travelled to Germany under the supervision of William Henry Scott, a tutor who came recommended by Dr John Henry Newman, the prominent English convert who had helped found the Catholic University in Dublin in 1854 and who he had met in 1856. Scott and the O'Conor Don visited the spa town of Kreuznach in the Rhineland, where he learned some German, but in an unfortunate turn of events, Scott took ill and died in September 1859. Subsequently, the O'Conor Don returned home for a while before setting off for Rome again early in 1860.[22]

Serving in the court of Pope Pius IX was undoubtedly a seminal experience for the young O'Conor Don, instilling a reverence for the authority of the papacy and a zeal for its certainties on the necessity of denominational education and the dangers of secularism. But as we shall see in chapter five, this attachment to conservative Catholic doctrine on matters of faith and morals influenced his liberal political outlook in the sense that he thought Irish Catholics should have the freedom to practice their faith and provide the kind of education they wanted within the British state.[23] The O'Conor Don's Roman experience of 1860 was equally profound because of the anticipation of revolution, with the Italian nationalist forces of Victor Emmanuel and Giuseppe Garibaldi threatening to annex the papal territories and enter the city. On St Patrick's Day that year, the O'Conor Don and Denis attended a meeting of 300 people at the Irish College in Rome, where its rector, Tobias Kirby, spoke in defence of the pope and his territories.[24] The defence of the pope, for many Irish Catholics, was tied up with the cause of religious and political liberty at home, with anti-British sentiment and loyalty to the pope brought to the fore by dint of the British government's support for the Italian nationalist cause.[25] The Catholic hierarchy, and prominent Catholic landlords like Daniel O'Donoghue (1833–89) and Myles O'Reilly (1825–80), were prominent in popularizing the issue of the pope's plight in Ireland, helping to recruit an

---

22 Recollections part 1, O'Conor papers, CH, 9.4.HL.156, pp 10–16, 28–9; Roderick MacDermot to the O'Conor Don, 1856, O'Conor papers, CH, 9.3.HE.055. 23 See chapter five, pp 108–10. 24 D. Corcoran, *The Irish brigade in the pope's army, 1860: faith, fatherland and fighting* (Dublin, 2018), pp 51–3 25 Ibid., pp 157–61

Irish brigade for the pan-European papal army got up to defend the pope and his territories.[26] Indeed, O'Reilly, a captain in the County Louth militia who trained at the Curragh and Aldershot, went on to lead the Irish brigade in the summer and autumn of 1860. Although he seems to have acquitted himself well, the papal army was poorly organized and easily defeated. Nonetheless, O'Reilly and the brigade returned home to a hero's welcome in November 1860, as defeat was 'turned into triumph' in Ireland.[27] As we shall see, O'Reilly and the O'Donoghue were parliamentary colleagues of the O'Conor Don, but although their concern for the pope's plight was the cause of anti-English sentiment and frustration with the Liberal Party, it also instilled in them a deep suspicion of the republican, anti-clerical impulses of Fenianism.

FAMILY STATUS AND ELECTION

Immediately after the gathering at the Irish College on 17 March 1860, the O'Conor Don left Rome to contest a by-election in County Roscommon. He had been urged to stand in the general election of the previous year by his cousin and land agent, Thomas MacDermot (1810–79), but had declined to do so. Writing from Hyéres in April 1859, he told 'Big Tom' that:

> I cannot possibly think of putting myself forward as a candidate for the representation of my native county. My youth, inexperience, and delicate health forbid my doing so, but nevertheless it is ... of great satisfaction to me to find that the memory and service of my father have not been forgotten, and there exists, on account of this, such a friendly feeling in favour of me his son.[28]

Here we get the first real sense of the O'Conor Don's awareness of what his family's reputation meant in the county, but he was clearly reluctant to take on the mantle of political leadership just yet. Since emancipation, County Roscommon had always returned two Liberal MPs (one Catholic and one Protestant), but the 1859 general election upset this electoral equilibrium.[29] The Protestant landlord, Fitzstephen French (1801–73), stood again, but the sitting Catholic MP, Oliver Grace, decided to stand down, which is why MacDermot asked the O'Conor Don to stand.[30] Although it was rumoured that the Catholic landlord and former MP for County Mayo George Henry

26 Ibid., pp 45–9. 27 Ibid., pp 66, 148, 154, 157 28 The O'Conor Don to Thomas MacDermot, 24 Apr. 1859, O'Conor papers, CH, 9.3.HS.080. 29 Potter, 'Local government in Co. Roscommon', p. 292. 30 The O'Conor Don to Thomas French, 24 Mar. 1859, O'Conor papers, CH, 9.3.HE.055.

Moore was being lined up to replace Grace, this did not materialize.³¹ The liberal candidate who stood in Grace's place, Edward King-Tenison, was a Protestant landlord with large estates in counties Roscommon and Leitrim, but he was defeated by the conservative, Captain Thomas Goff, another Protestant landowner in the county.³² This upset was not that unusual, however, as the Liberal government's support for Italian nationalism saw the Catholic hierarchy and clergy generally withhold their support for liberal candidates.³³ As the O'Conor Don later recalled, much 'to the just indignation of the catholic laity of the upper classes who were all strong liberals', the bishop of Elphin, Lawrence Gillooly, and the local clergy supported Goff. However, a petition to unseat Goff, citing the use of 'bribery and undue influences', was immediately submitted. On 12 January 1860, the O'Conor Don was proposed to contest the expected by-election at a meeting of Roscommon's liberal gentry at Kilronan Castle, the home of Edward King-Tenison.³⁴ The following day, Thomas MacDermot, who was instrumental in rallying the local liberals, wrote to the O'Conor Don telling him that he had the support of the bishop and clergy. Goff was eventually unseated on or before 9 March and, after 'much doubt and hesitation', the O'Conor Don decided to return and contest the seat.³⁵ In his election address, published on 10 March, he vowed to uphold the 'old liberal opinions' of his father and grandfather, whom the county had 'not yet forgotten', but in terms of specific policies he pledged his support for disestablishment, denominational education, tenant right and the secret ballot.³⁶ On 17 March, his candidature was publicly endorsed by Bishop Gillooly, who instructed his clergy to canvass on the O'Conor Don's behalf.³⁷

The O'Conor Don arrived back in Roscommon on 22 March, staying the night at Mountplunkett, the home of Catholic landlord and family friend Patrick Grehan, near Athlone. The following day, he gave his first public speech in Athlone from atop Grehan's coach. Although 'intensely shy and timid' and possessed of 'the greatest dread of public speaking', the O'Conor Don recalled how he 'rattled away the first thoughts that came into my head', finding that he could 'speak with satisfactory fluency' and 'that it was not after all a difficult

---

31 Roderick MacDermot to unknown, 22 Mar. 1858, O'Conor papers, CH, 9.3.HS.283. 32 A. Coleman, *Riotous Roscommon: social unrest in the 1840s* (Dublin, 1999), pp 8–12; P. Connolly, *The landed estates of County Roscommon* (Galway, 2018), pp 170–1. 33 A. Shields, *The Irish Conservative Party: land, politics and religion, 1852–1868* (Dublin, 2007), pp 86–7; K.T. Hoppen, 'Tories, Catholics, and the general election of 1859', *Historical Journal*, 13:1 (1970), 48–67. 34 Recollections part 1, O'Conor papers, CH, 9.4.HL.156, pp 29–33; Thomas MacDermot to Denis O'Conor, n.d., O'Conor papers, CH, 9.3.HS.080; P. Slattery, 'Tenison, Edward King', *DIB*; Connolly, *Landed estates*, p. 243. 35 Thomas McDermot to the O'Conor Don, 13 Jan. 1860, O'Conor papers, CH, 9.3.HS.080; Recollections part 1, O'Conor papers, CH, 9.4.HL.156, p. 33; *Roscommon Messenger*, 10 Mar. 1860. 36 *Roscommon Journal*, 10 Mar. 1860. 37 Ibid., 10 Mar. 1860.

task'.³⁸ On 24 March, Goff resigned from the contest and the O'Conor Don travelled to Roscommon town to deliver his victory speech. He thanked his liberal colleagues and the local clergy for organizing and running the campaign in his absence, with Bishop Gillooly getting a special mention. Moreover, as well as reaffirming the liberal principles set out in his election address, he declared 'that the Holy Father should be left in possession of all his dominions'. This show of loyalty to the pope was not unusual, but in an utterly bizarre turn of phrase, he went on to assert that the pope 'should be left perfectly at liberty to "wallop his own n____s"', suggesting that 'a little walloping would do the said n____s no great harm'.³⁹ According to someone present at the hustings, this comment was meant as a 'hustings joke', made in reference to 'a well-known witticism of a certain facetious gentleman in the county, who is a prominent member of the Conservative party'.⁴⁰ The O'Conor Don did attribute the comments to those 'of certain gentleman in this county', but even so, this was an extraordinary choice of words for a prospective MP to use in public, even by the mid-nineteenth century's low standards of casual racism.

POLITICAL AND SOCIAL MILIEU

And so the political career of the O'Conor Don had commenced. Introduced to the house of commons by Fitzstephen French, the O'Conor Don took his place on the liberal and government side of the House. Tellingly, he feared that he might be considered just another 'regular Whig or English party hack ... waiting to receive office' and was 'determined if possible to prove that this suspicion had no foundation'.⁴¹ The O'Conor Don would undoubtedly have been conscious of the controversy that surrounded his father's position in Lord John Russell's Whig-Liberal government during the height of the Famine, but the taking of government jobs by Irish Catholic MPs had been a cause of controversy since O'Connell's alliance with the Whigs in the 1830s. It continued to be so after the Famine, with the defection of the nominally independent MPs John Sadlier and William Keogh to Lord Aberdeen's Liberal-Peelite ministry in 1853 the most recent example.⁴² But it was not just those who took government jobs that were denounced by Irish nationalists as

---

38 Recollections part 1, O'Conor papers, CH, 9.4.HL.156, pp 34–5. For Patrick Grehan's estate, see CMLED. 39 *Freeman's Journal*, 27 Mar. 1860. 40 *Dublin Evening Post*, 29 Mar. 1860. 41 Recollections part 1, O'Conor papers, CH, 9.4.HL.156, pp 36–8. 42 R.V. Comerford, 'Churchmen, tenants, and independent opposition' in W.E. Vaughan (ed.), *A new history of Ireland, v: Ireland under the union, I, 1801–70* (Oxford, 1989), pp 399–406; K.T. Hoppen, *Elections, politics and society in Ireland, 1832–1885* (Oxford, 1984), pp 17–33.

whigs. For a Catholic to be labelled a whig in post-Famine Ireland variously and negatively meant being part of the landed elite, a government minister or administrator, an opponent of home rule or a loyalist. It was, in other words, to be a 'West Briton' or a 'Castle Catholic' by another name. As we shall see, the O'Conor Don was from time to time labelled a whig, a West Briton and a Castle Catholic, but he did not accept any of these labels, even though he eventually fulfilled all the typical criteria assigned by his opponents, excepting that of a government minister. He did hold what could be described as whiggish views on representative government and democracy, but he saw himself as a liberal and many liberals, especially those drawn from the landlord class, held similar views on these issues.[43]

One thing is for certain, though, the O'Conor Don was starting out in life from a position of power and privilege. Upon his coming of age in 1859, he inherited somewhere in the region of 7,650 acres in counties Roscommon and Sligo. And as we shall discover in the next chapter, the £100,000 windfall from his cousin Edward Moore enabled the O'Conor Don and his brother Denis to add considerably to their estates.[44] On a local political level, the O'Conor Don was appointed justice of the peace for counties Roscommon and Sligo in 1860 and 1877, respectively; magistrate and deputy lord lieutenant of County Roscommon in 1888; lord lieutenant of County Roscommon in 1896; chairman of the Castlerea board of guardians in 1887; and chairman of the Castlerea District Council in 1899.[45] On a national level, he was MP for County Roscommon from 1860 to 1880, appointed to the privy council in 1881 and became an executive committee member of the Landowners' Convention in 1887. Moreover, both during and after his time as an MP, he served on numerous select committees and royal commissions on a wide variety of social issues. His very keen interest in educational matters saw him appointed a lay trustee on the governing board of Maynooth College in 1868; vice-president of the Society for the Preservation of the Irish Language in 1877; a commissioner on the Intermediate Education Board in 1878; and a senator of the Royal University of Ireland in 1891, from which he received an honorary LLD in 1892. He was also a council member of the Royal Irish Academy and the Royal Dublin Society and was elected President of the Royal Society of Antiquaries of Ireland in 1897. Finally, his interest in financial matters saw him made a director of the National Bank in 1892.[46]

---

43 See introduction, pp 20–3. See chapter four, p. 94; Chapter six, pp 150, 152–3, 165–6. 44 See chapter three, pp 60–1. 45 Commission of the peace for County Roscommon, 1860, O'Conor papers, CH, 9.3.SH.190; Commission of the peace for County Sligo, 1877, O'Conor papers, CH, 9.4.SO.290; Recollections part 1, O'Conor papers, CH, 9.4.HL.156, p. 125. 46 Charles Russell to the O'Conor Don, 9 June 1868, O'Conor papers, CH, 9.3.SE.285; Notice from the Society for the Preservation of the Irish

This world of power and privilege was underpinned by a wide and varied network of friendships and connections. His primary social circle was that of the Catholic gentry, aristocracy and hierarchy in Ireland and Great Britain. This was a relatively small circle of Irish and English Catholics who sometimes rather awkwardly moved within a wider and predominantly Protestant British-Irish elite. Although accepted as part of this elite on the basis of class and education, there was a mutual religious suspicion that saw these Catholics band together as an elite within an elite, particularly on issues such as disestablishment of the Church of Ireland, the temporal power of the pope and Catholic education. Disagreement notwithstanding, the O'Conor Don's main parliamentary allies on these issues included the likes of Myles O'Reilly, Edmund Dease, Daniel O'Donoghue ('the O'Donoghue') and William Monsell. This group of liberal Catholic MPs were in the ascendancy between 1860 and 1874 but, although they met regularly to discuss their approach to commons legislation, they did not operate as a disciplined group or party in the commons. Indeed, even by the loose party standards of the mid-Victorian period, they were decidedly bad at acting together in a coherent fashion. Some like Edmund Dease were inconspicuous and ineffective, while others like the O'Donoghue were conspicuously opportunist and ill-disciplined. But most, like the O'Conor Don, were active and serious about their work, with Monsell and O'Reilly two of his closest friends and colleagues in the House. The O'Conor Don and his fellow liberal Catholic MPs had a wider network of connections and friends among landed Catholic peers and middle-class Catholics who were similarly well-educated and worked in Dublin Castle, the colonial service, the civil service and the legal system.[47]

The Catholic hierarchy and clergy were of course highly influential in Irish politics and particularly active on the education question. On that score, the O'Conor Don was closest to Bishop Lawrence Gillooly, Father William Delany, Monsignor Bartholomew Woodlock, Cardinal Paul Cullen and Archbishop Edward McCabe. These could be strained and politically

---

Language to the O'Conor Don, 9 Mar. 1878, O'Conor papers, CH, 9.4.LH.081; Notice from the Royal Dublin Society to the O'Conor Don, O'Conor papers, CH, 9.4.LH.082; Recollections, parts 1 and 2, O'Conor papers, CH, 9.4.HL.156, pp 50, 87, 142, 147–8, 172; *Royal Irish Academy list of members 2001, giving the names of the council and officers, members, honorary members and Cunningham medallists, with an appendix listing the officers of the Academy since its foundation* (Dublin, 2001), p. 31; Proceedings, *Journal of the Royal Society of Antiquaries of Ireland*, 5:3 (Sept. 1895), 249. **47** Other liberal Catholic MPs included Richard More O'Ferrall, Thomas O'Hagan (Lord O'Hagan), Sir Rowland Blennerhassett, Sir George Errington, William Henry Cogan, Myles O'Reilly, Sir Colman O'Loghlen and Sir Dominic Corrigan. Catholic peers included the earls of Kenmare, Fingall, and Granard, and Viscount Gormanston. Similarly well-educated middle-class Catholics included Sir Patrick Keenan, James Kavanagh, William Keogh, Thomas Henry Burke, Sir Anthony MacDonnell, Sir Nicholas O'Conor and Hugh Hyacinth MacDermot.

awkward relationships, with the O'Conor Don often walking the tightrope of taking the views of the hierarchy and clergy on board while trying to prevent them becoming too meddlesome in Westminster politics and damaging the prospect of meaningful political action or progress. His relationship with Gillooly was the most important one given that he was the bishop of his diocese, Elphin, but they certainly had their disagreements and clashes. The English hierarchy also sought to influence Irish educational policy, with the hope of gaining similar concession for English Catholics. The O'Conor Don's closest English confidantes were Cardinal Herbert Vaughan and Archbishop George Errington, with cardinals Newman and Manning encountered on the odd occasion.[48]

Outside the world of high politics in Dublin and London, among the gentry of County Roscommon, the O'Conor Don was closest to other branches of the O'Conor family, his cousins the MacDermots and the numerous other landed Catholics in the county. Regionally, in the west of Ireland, he mixed regularly with his cousins the Blakes of Towerhill, County Mayo, and other landed Catholics in counties Galway and Mayo. This local and regional world of landed Catholic friendship and association revolved around intermarriage, Mass, country house visits, dinner parties, horse racing, agricultural shows, cattle fairs, hunting and shooting game.[49]

The O'Conor Don and many of his Irish Catholic peers forged close ties and friendships with landed English Catholics.[50] The result of this was intermarriage and the formation of a transnational Catholic elite in the second half of the nineteenth century. In 1868, the O'Conor Don married Georgina Perry (1847–72), daughter of Thomas Perry of Bitham Hall, Warwickshire, a wealthy landowner and businessman. This was undoubtedly a match made for reasons of class and religion, but it is also clear from their diaries that Charles and Georgina were very much in love. Their marriage was, however, cut tragically short. Although Georgina gave birth to four sons in four years (Denis, Owen and twins Charles and Roderick), she was plagued by consumption throughout

---

48 Diaries of the O'Conor Don, 1861–4 & 1872–4 O'Conor papers, CH, 9.3.SH.306; Diaries of the O'Conor Don, 1880 & 1886–7, O'Conor papers, CH, 9.4.HS.270. Other landed Catholics in County Roscommon included the Balfe, De Freyne, Murphy, Grace, Strickland, Woulfe Flanagan, Irwin, Taafe, Mapother and Raleigh Chichester families. Other landed Catholics in the Galway and Mayo included the Lynch, Joyce, Blake, Moore and Redington families. **49** Diaries of the O'Conor Don, 1860, 64, 76, 77, 80 & 84, O'Conor papers, CH, 9.3.SH.306; Diary of Georgina O'Conor, 1868, O'Conor papers, CH, 9.3.SE.307; Diary of Denis Maurice O'Conor, 1869, NLI, p. 5485. **50** Diaries of the O'Conor Don, 1864, O'Conor papers, CH, 9.3.SH.306; Diary of Georgina O'Conor, 1868, ibid., 9.3.SE.307; Diary of Denis Maurice O'Conor, 1869, NLI, p.5485; M. Bence Jones, *The Catholic families* (London, 1992). Other landed English Catholic families included the Howard, Robinson, Fielding, Trafford, Blundell, Gerard, Jerningham, Petre, Blount and Clifford families.

and died at Clonalis on 18 August 1872, aged only twenty-five. Georgina's death left the O'Conor Don feeling 'all alone in the world', and after her funeral and burial on 24 August he left Clonalis for Dublin 'with a broken heart'. Indeed, he got as far away from Clonalis as he possibly could, travelling with Denis to America in October 1872.[51] Six years later, in October 1878, his twin son Roderick died prematurely from a brain tumour. In 1879, the O'Conor Don married a second time, to Ellen More O'Ferrall (1857–1932), daughter of John Lewis More O'Ferrall of Granite Hall, Kingstown, County Dublin, who was commissioner of the Dublin Metropolitan Police. This seems to have been more of a settled match, and they had no children together.[52] His brother, Denis, married Ellen Kevill Davies, daughter of Revd William Trevelyan Kevill Davies of Croft Castle, Herefordshire, in 1873. They had one son, Charles.[53]

The O'Conor Don and his brother therefore moved in an exclusive, transnational world of Catholic landowners and prelates, a fact that challenges Mark Bence Jones' claim that there was a 'growing estrangement between the Catholic worlds of England and Ireland' in the post-emancipation period.[54] There were different attitudes and approaches to politics and religion, but the bonds of religion and class often gave these Irish and English Catholics a sense of common purpose and identity in the face of a still potent anti-Catholic mindset among their Protestant counterparts. The O'Conor Don met regularly with landed Irish and English Catholics at Clonalis, the St Stephen's Green Club in Dublin, the Perry home at Bitham Hall and the Stafford Club in London. This was especially the case while he was married to Georgina, but the Perrys remained family friends long after her passing, and socializing with English Catholics continued in London.[55]

The O'Conor Don did not, however, exist in a Catholic bubble. His status as a large landowner and role as a justice of the peace in County Roscommon necessitated engagement with the local Protestant gentry on the grand jury and assizes, but he was anyway on close personal terms with the Wills-Sandford, Crofton, King-Harman and King-Tenison families.[56] Indeed, he had been

---

51 Diaries of the O'Conor Don, 17–24 Aug. 1872, O'Conor papers, CH, 9.3.SH.306; Recollections part 1, O'Conor papers, CH, pp 60–2. 52 Recollections parts 1 & 2, O'Conor papers, CH, 9.4.HL.156, pp 49, 55, 57, 62, 86, 91; Marriage agreement of the O'Conor Don and Georgina Perry, Apr. 1868, O'Conor papers, CH, 9.3.ES.280. Marriage agreement of the O'Conor Don and Ellen More O'Ferrall, Sept. 1879, O'Conor papers, CH, 9.4.SE.067. 53 Marriage agreement of Denis O'Conor and Ellen Kevill Davies, Aug. 1873, O'Conor papers, CH, 9.3.ES.328; Burnand (ed.), *The Catholic who's who*, p. 306. 54 Bence Jones, *Catholic families*, p. 137. 55 Diary of Denis Maurice O'Conor, 1869, NLI, p.5485; Diary of the O'Conor Don, 19 Jan. 1877, O'Conor papers, CH, 9.4.SH.247. B. Share & C.F. Smith (eds), *Whigs on the green: the Stephen's Green Club, 1840–1900* (Dublin, 1990), pp 68, 160. 56 Diaries of the O'Conor Don, 1861–4 & 1872–4, O'Conor papers, CH, 9.3.SH.306; Recollections part 1, O'Conor papers, CH, 9.4.HL.156, p. 43; Diary of Denis Maurice O'Conor, 1869, NLI, p. 5485.

engaged to a daughter of Edward King-Tenison in February 1864, with their impending marriage widely reported in the papers in June of that year, before marrying Georgina Perry.[57] As already noted, the O'Conor and King-Tenison families were political allies and the O'Conor Don's diaries in the early 1860s make frequent references to meetings with the family in Roscommon, Dublin, London and Rome.[58] Such a marriage would have caused quite a stir, and it perhaps demonstrates the young O'Conor Don's willingness to challenge authority, as the Catholic hierarchy would have taken a very dim view of it. But whether he was driven by the prospect of acquiring part of the King-Tenison's large estates, or he simply fell in love with Miss Tenison, or a bit of both, the engagement was broken off in June of that year. It is not clear why, but the most likely scenarios are disagreement over the marriage settlement, the O'Conor Don baulking at the prospect of marrying a Protestant or Miss Tenison refusing to convert. Whatever the reason, Edward King-Tenison never forgave him for it. Indeed, King-Tenison's 'hatred' of the O'Conor Don blocked the latter's path to the lord lieutenancy of County Roscommon in 1872 because the former refused to swap the position for the lord lieutenancy of County Leitrim, which would have been convenient for him.[59] And as an aside, the prospect of this match was raised years afterwards as a slight on the O'Conor Don's character by Kate O'Conor, his cousin Arthur's wife, in letters to the rector of the Irish College in Rome, Tobias Kirby.[60]

Among the wider group of Irish landlords, the O'Conor Don was on good personal terms with the Protestants Arthur Kavanagh and lords Dufferin, Clonbrock and Castletown. Like the O'Conor Don, they were all large landowners with forthright views on the land reform. In the 1880s, the O'Conor Don was member of the Kildare Street Club, the privy council and the executive committee of the Irish Landowners' Convention, all of which were predominantly Protestant and unionist organizations. Through these associations and friendships, he was able to influence debate and policy on land reform, but there was a shared opposition to Gladstonian home rule too.

---

57 *Catholic Telegraph*, 18 June 1864; Connolly, *Landed estates*, p. 250. Edward King-Tenison had two daughters, Louisa and Florence, but it is not clear which one the O'Conor Don was due to marry. 58 Diaries of the O'Conor Don, 1861–4, O'Conor papers, CH, 9.3.SH.306. 59 Connolly, *Landed estates*, p. 250; Recollections part 1, O'Conor papers, CH, 9.4.HL.156, p. 43; For King-Tenison's dislike of the O'Conor Don, see Earl Spencer to Lord O'Hagan, 11 Aug. 1872, O'Hagan papers, PRONI, D2777/8/204. 60 Kate O'Conor (*née* Blake) to Tobias Kirby, 10 Jan. 1879 & 30 July 1890, Kirby papers, Irish College, Rome. See http://san.beniculturali.it/web/san/dettaglio-oggetto-digitale?pid=san.dl.SAN:IMG-01000634 & http://san.beniculturali.it/web/san/dettaglio-oggetto-digitale?pid=san.dl.SAN:IMG-01202443, accessed 2 Nov. 2021. The O'Conor Don was an executor of Arthur's will and Kate was convinced that he was trying to rob her and her sons of their inheritance. The details of the will and its execution are not known to the author.

The O'Conor Don also maintained close relations with the Dublin Castle administration throughout his life, meeting with lord lieutenants and chief secretaries on a regular basis, whether liberal or conservative. Once again, influencing policy on land reform was always a primary concern, but law and order and investment in land reclamation schemes and railways figured prominently too. The O'Conor Don also had a wider, more diverse set of connections and acquaintances with Irish Protestants, which reflected his support for the temperance movement, radical land reform, agricultural improvement and the Irish language. In London, the Reform Club and the lobbies of Westminster were places for the O'Conor Don, on the odd occasion, to meet or even dine with prime ministers.[61] He had huge admiration for W.E. Gladstone and met and corresponded with him on quite a few occasions, but they ended up disagreeing on land reform and home rule. Finally, the O'Conor Don, as a firm loyalist, attended the queen's levees throughout his life. In 1902, he was the standard bearer for Ireland at the coronation of King Edward VII, which he remarked at the time was a 'most Catholic' ceremony.[62]

This myriad of friendships and connections reflect the fact that the O'Conor Don was very much part of the landed and political establishment of Ireland and Great Britain. They also reveal a liberal Catholic politician who was open-minded and politically moderate enough to move relatively freely in Protestant circles, often working across the religious and political divides to achieve significant reforms. But as we shall see, he was possessed of a fierce independent streak, which sometimes served him well, but on the whole worked to his disadvantage and helped ensured that he became an increasingly marginal figure in Irish politics.

Political considerations aside, though, such varied social circles reveal a genial and sociable man who was well-liked and regarded as a man of sincere convictions, even by those who did not agree with him. He placed a high value on family and friends, and was fiercely loyal to both. And although he moved in the highest circles in Dublin and London, he did not live a particularly lavish or extravagant lifestyle, relative to many of his fellow landlords. A frugal, devout and hardworking man, the O'Conor Don regularly attended

---

61 Diaries of the O'Conor Don, 1861–4 & 1872–4, O'Conor papers, CH, 9.3.SH.306; Diaries of the O'Conor Don, 1880, 1886–7 & 1893, O'Conor papers, CH, 9.4.HS.247; Diaries of the O'Conor Don, 1901–2, O'Conor papers, CH, 0.1.SH.041. Over the year, the O'Conor Don met frequently with Chichester Fortescue (Lord Carlingford), W.E. Forster, Earl Spencer, the earl of Aberdeen, the Balfours, Lord Cadogan, George Wyndham and Lord Dudley. His Protestant connections included Jonathan Pim, Thomas Wallace Russell, Horace Plunkett, Lord Monteagle and Douglas Hyde. 62 Newspaper report of King Edward VII's coronation ceremony, 1902, O'Conor papers, CH, 0.1.SH.046; Diaries of the O'Conor Don, 1903, O'Conor papers, CH, 0.1.SH.041.

Mass and Confession; was constantly moving between Clonalis, Dublin and London meeting with friends, politicians and other landlords; spent a lot of time inspecting his estates and meeting with tenants; and always made time for shooting game. Thus, we have a man who, in August 1902, attended the royal coronation in London on the 9th; went to Mass in Kingstown on 12th; got the train down to Castlerea with Hyde on the 13th; supervised sheep dipping and getting the hay in with his steward, Fitzsimmons, on the 21st; and met with the executive committee of the Landowners' Convention in Dublin on the 29th to discuss Wyndham's land bill.[63] This schedule neatly encapsulates how the O'Conor Don was a man of power and influence who nonetheless kept himself grounded with faith, friendship and the affairs of his estate.

---

63 Diary of the O'Conor Don, Aug. 1902, O'Conor papers, CH, 0.1.SH.041.

3 / 'Your relations with your numerous tenantry are most creditable': the O'Conor Don and the management of his estates, 1860–1906

Upon the event of his marriage to Georgina Perry in April 1868, the O'Conor Don received a memorial from 'the inhabitants of Castlerea and ... the Parish of Kilkeevin', who wished to express their delight at his recent union and their gratitude for his conduct as a landlord. In rather glowing terms, they declared that:

> [O]ur hearts are with you and we hold [you] in the same regard and respect as if your brow were encircled with the Diadem of the Ancient Monarch of Ireland ... your relations with your numerous tenantry are most creditable ... they are happy and contented ... your exemplary dignified yet humble demeanour must have the salutary effect of suggesting to others 'Go and do likewise'.[1]

Compare this, however, with a police report from 1879 that claimed the O'Conor Don 'was loathed by the majority of his constituents' and there emerges a conflicting picture regarding his popularity as a landlord and politician.[2] This is symptomatic of the general picture regarding the likely popularity or unpopularity of Irish landlords. As a Catholic who could trace his ancestry to the last high king of Ireland, the O'Conor Don was less likely to be exposed to what Terence Dooley identifies as the 'sense of resentment' directed towards the many Protestant landlords who acquired their estates via the confiscations of the seventeenth century. But Dooley and other historians of Irish landlordism have also argued that deference towards landlords, Catholic or Protestant, was a significant factor in landlord-tenant relations. In many cases, the good character of the landlord meant deference towards him as the natural leader of the local community prevailed. On the other hand, the same historians emphasize the difficulty in discerning how genuine this deference might have been, with tenants at the very least making exaggerated displays of deference because it was in their interest to do so, given their dependency on their landlords for land, rent levels and work.[3]

---

1 Memorial to the O'Conor Don, Apr. 1868, O'Conor papers, CH, 9.3.SO.018.   2 G. Moran, 'James Daly and the rise and fall of the Land League in the West of Ireland, 1879–82', *Irish Historical Studies*, 29:114 (Nov. 1994), 197.   3 Dooley, *The decline of the Big House*, p. 9; Melvin, 'The landed gentry of Galway', p. 166; J. Clarke, *Christopher Dillon Bellew and his Galway estates, 1763–1862* (Dublin, 2003), pp 6–7; W.E. Vaughan,

Deference towards the O'Conor Don as a 'natural' leader in the community was a significant factor in his relationship with his tenants, which in turn gave him a paternalistic sense of his duty towards them and the local community. Nonetheless, although his Gaelic ancestry did play its part in bolstering his status, the language of the above memorial was exaggerated, and it seems far more likely that the O'Conor Don was well-liked and respected because of the way he interacted with his tenants and the paternalistic way in which he managed his estates. A secure financial position undoubtedly helped, but his pro-active and even-handed approach to estate management played a significant part in his leading something of a charmed existence amid the widespread agitation on surrounding estates in north County Roscommon in the 1880s, 1890s and early 1900s. This does not mean that he was totally immune to the effects of the land agitations, but if the O'Conor Don had the poor financial circumstances and confrontational temperament of his neighbour and fellow Catholic landlord Lord De Freyne, then his Gaelic ancestry would have counted for very little indeed.[4] And there are many other examples of overbearing Catholic landlords. William Scully carried out numerous evictions on his estates in County Tipperary in the 1860s and was shot at while trying to carry out one.[5] Walter Bourke, who had a reputation for harshness, was assassinated in June 1882 after serving ejectment notices on some of his tenants in County Mayo.[6] Thus, the claim of Protestant landlord Lord Dufferin that Catholic landlords were treated differently by their tenants simply because they were Catholics does not stand up to scrutiny.[7] Indeed, the one thing that can reasonably be said to have set the O'Conor Don and his fellow Catholic landlords apart from their Protestant counterparts was their anger and frustration over clerical support for the land agitations and their attempts to use their influence at Westminster and Rome to have it condemned.

CATHOLIC LANDOWNERSHIP

As already noted, the O'Conor experience of survival and re-emergence in the eighteenth century was indicative of the rise of a relatively small but

Landlords and tenants in mid-Victorian Ireland (New York, 1994), pp 2, 33. For other very useful studies on the subject of paternalism, see K. McKenna, 'Power, resistance, and ritual: paternalism on the Clonbrock estates, 1826–1908' (PhD, NUIM, 2011); B.J. Casey, 'Land, politics and religion on the Clancarty estate, east Galway, 1851–1914' (PhD, NUIM, 2011).   4 D. Dyer Wolf, 'Two windows: the tenants of the De Freyne rent strike, 1901–1903' (PhD, DU, 2019), pp 64, 71, 74, 79–82, 145.   5 H.E. Socolofsky, 'William Scully: Ireland and America, 1840–1900', *Agricultural History*, 48:1 (Jan. 1974), 163–5.   6 J. Murphy, *The Redingtons of Clarinbridge: leading Catholic landlords in the nineteenth century* (Dublin, 1999), pp 240–2.   7 E.D. Steele, *Irish land and British politics: tenant-right and nationality, 1865–1870* (London, 1974), p. 78.

prosperous Catholic landowning class in Ireland.⁸ This pattern of growing Catholic landownership continued apace in the early nineteenth century, with the O'Conor's building of a large landed estate emulated by others like the Blakes of Towerhill, the Bellews of Mountbellew and the Redingtons of Clarinbridge.⁹ During and after the Famine, the sale of indebted land through the encumbered and landed estates courts enabled minor, medium and large Catholic landowners to purchase more land.¹⁰ The O'Conor Don is a prime example of this trend from the older, larger landowning families, as were his cousins Denis O'Conor of Mount Druid and Arthur O'Conor of Elphin. Those new aspiring Catholics landowners who expanded in the aftermath of the Famine included the likes of Patrick Grehan of Mountplunkett and Daniel Henry Ferrall of Beechwood, County Roscommon; Hugh and Connell O'Beirne of Drumsna, County Leitrim; and Walter Bourke of Rahasane Park, County Mayo.¹¹ Finally, converts increased the number of Catholic landowners in the pre and post-Famine periods too, with Arthur French (Lord De Freyne) of Frenchpark, County Roscommon; George Forbes (earl of Granard) of Newtownforbes, County Longford; and William Monsell (Lord Emly) of Tervoe, County Limerick among the most high-profile examples.¹² Catholic landlords were most numerous in the province of Connaught, particularly in counties Galway, Mayo and Roscommon, but the provinces of Munster and Leinster contained significant numbers too. Ulster had relatively few.¹³

Putting a figure on Catholic landlords as a proportion of the larger group of Irish landlords is not an exact science, but it is possible to make some estimations. The first house of commons record of landownership in nineteenth-century Ireland in 1876 revealed that just 6,461 landlords owned roughly ninety per cent of the land mass in a country of 5.5 million people.¹⁴ The majority of these landlords – especially those owning between 10,000 and 30,000 acres – were still Protestant. And this Protestant dominance was overwhelmingly the case with magnates who owned 50,000 acres or more.¹⁵

8 See chapter one, pp 30–7. 9 Clarke, *Christopher Dillon Bellew*, p. 6; Murphy, *The Redingtons*, pp 72–3. 10 P.G. Lane, 'The encumbered estates court, Ireland, 1848–1849', *Economic and Social Review*, 19 (1972), 413–53. 11 Melvin, 'Roscommon estates and landowners', p. 339. For O'Conor-Blake, see above, pp 41–2. For Bourke see Murphy, *The Redingtons*, pp 240–2. For Grehan, Farrell & O'Beirne, see CMLED. 12 Dyer Wolf, 'Two windows', pp 190–4; Potter, *William Monsell*, pp 1–5; T. Dooley, 'Landlords and mortgagees in late nineteenth century Ireland: the case of Lord Granard and the trustees of Maynooth College, 1871–89', *Journal of the County Kildare Archaeological Society*, 18 (1998), 612–25. 13 Melvin, 'The landed gentry of Galway', pp 334, 441–92; O. Purdue, *The Big House in the north of Ireland: land, power and social elites, 1878–1960* (Dublin, 2009), pp 2, 24–5. 14 *Return of names of proprietors and area and valuation of properties in counties in Ireland, held in fee or perpetuity, or long leases at chief rents*, HC 1876 (412), lxxx, 395, pp 176–8. Hereafter referred to as *Return of names of proprietors … in Ireland*. 15 W.E. Vaughan, 'Ireland, c.1870' in idem (ed.), *A new history of Ireland* (1989), v, p. 740; Dooley, *The decline of the Big House*, pp 10–12.

Nonetheless, the census of 1861 estimated that Catholics owned forty per cent of Irish land.¹⁶ This figure includes those who owned between 100 and 500 acres, the largest category of landowners who were not, strictly speaking, *landlords*, in the sense that they rented much, or any, land to others. Indeed, this group of landowners are more accurately described as large famers. Thus, the figure for Catholic landlords was probably somewhere between thirty and forty per cent by the 1860s. There is much work to be done in cross-referencing the many sources now available for Irish landownership, but a more accurate figure for Catholic landlords and a more complete account of the extent of Catholic landownership before the break-up of Irish landed estates is a research project in itself, for another day.¹⁷ What we can say, however, is that the O'Conor Don was part of a large minority of Catholic landlords within the larger group of mainly Protestant Irish landlords who owned the overwhelming majority of land in Ireland. In that sense, he was by no stretch of the imagination a rarity as a wealthy landed Catholic.

THE O'CONOR DON'S ESTATES

Although life as a landlord officially began on the occasion of the O'Conor Don's coming of age on 7 May 1859, it was not until March 1860, when he returned from Rome, that he took up the reins of power in a practical sense. Up to that point, the young O'Conor Don's affairs were managed by his aunt Honoria, with Charles Strickland of Loughglynn and his cousins, Thomas and Roderick MacDermot, acting as agents. After Honoria's death in January 1857, Valentine O'Conor-Blake stepped in to oversee the execution of the O'Conor Don's father's will, and Thomas MacDermot was charged with the practical day-to-day management of the O'Conor Don's estates and business affairs.¹⁸

With the £100,000 Moore inheritance, MacDermot proceeded to buy up as much land as he could through the landed estates court. In 1858, he purchased

---

16 Potter, *William Monsell*, p. 195. 17 Theo Hoppen's mid-nineteenth century estimate of twenty per cent is low given Whelan's estimate of twenty per cent by the late eighteenth century. See Hoppen, *Elections, politics, and society*, p. 122. It also seems low based on this author's admittedly limited exploration of the sources available. A cross reference of the following sources is the best way to ascertain who the Catholic landlords were and to get a more accurate figure for how many of them there were: *Declaration of Irish Catholic laity in favor of religious equality* (Dublin, 1860), pp 1–27; *Copy of declaration of the Catholic laity of Ireland, on the subject of university education in that country, lately laid before the prime minister*, HC 1870 (140), liv, 645; U.H. Hussey De Burgh, *The landowners of Ireland: an alphabetical list of the owners of estates of 500 acres or £500 valuation and upwards in Ireland, with the acreage and valuation in each county* (Dublin, 1878); *Return of names of proprietors ... in Ireland*, pp 176–8; Burnand, *The Catholic who's who*; CMLED & *DIB*. 18 The O'Conor Don's rentals, 1850–7, O'Conor papers, CH, 9.3.ES.305; Chancery report on the estate of the O'Conor minors, 1859, O'Conor papers, CH, E.9.2.HO.008.01.

just over 1,613 acres for £12,285 from the estate of Col. Fulkes Greville in the parish of Kiltullagh, near the village of Ballinlough and about eight miles from Clonalis.[19] In 1859, he purchased just over 115 acres for £3,000 from the estate of Marcus McCausland in the parish of Kilnamanagh, which bordered the O'Conor Don's existing lands in the parish of Killaraght in neighbouring County Sligo. He also bought a further eight acres from McCausland for £1,500 in 'the best part of Roscommon town', for which the O'Conor Don had to spend £500 on additional 'permanent buildings'.[20] Once again in 1859, MacDermot bought just over 260 acres from the estate of Viscount Lorton in the parish of Killaraght, County Sligo, which again was close to existing land.[21] In 1860, the O'Conor Don bought just over 637 acres for £14,580 on the estate of William Lloyd in the parish of Kilkeevin, close to Clonalis.[22] That same year, a further 928 acres was purchased for £10,000 on the estate of Patrick Balfe in the parish of Tibohine, near Ballaghaderreen.[23] In 1861, the O'Conor Don is thought to have purchased land worth £24,000 in counties Roscommon and Sligo on the estates of 'Mr O'Beirne' (almost certainly Hugh and/or Connell above), but the details are not known. Of this purchase, the *Roscommon Messenger* claimed it 'would be rather difficult to describe the joy of the tenantry ... as they apprehended a different fate' with the O'Conor Don as their landlord, although it was felt that his popularity was as much down to the 'excellent' Thomas MacDermot, whose 'high character' was 'well known'.[24] This was exuberant language, but the reputation of the family was such that the O'Conor Don received a number of memorials from tenants requesting

19 Sale of part of the estate of Colonel Fulke Southwell Greville, landed estates court rentals, NLI, 26 Nov. 1858; Copy of landed estates court rental, 18 July 1859, O'Conor papers, CH, 9.3.ES.047. See also www.findmypast.co.uk/search-ireland-records-in-census-land-and-surveys/and_land-and-estates, accessed 12 Jan. 2022. See also Abstract of title, Apr. 1884, Land commission papers, DAFF, box 237/schedule B/no. 1/record no. 827; Abstract of title, May 1882, Land commission papers, DAFF, box 237/schedule A/no. 3/ record no. 837. 20 Copy of landed estates court rental, Feb. 1859, McCausland papers, PRONI, D1550/43; Sale of part of the estate of Marcus McCausland, landed estates court rentals, NLI, 17 Feb. 1859; Thomas MacDermot to Bishop Gillooly, 18 Mar. 1859, Gillooly papers, EDA, BI/5/2 (2). 21 The O'Conor Don to Denis Maurice O'Conor, n.d. but likely 1858/9, O'Conor papers, CH, 9.3.SO.068. MacDermot purchased a further 694 acres for Denis Maurice on the Taafe estate for £15,000, located in the parish of Baslick, near Castlerea. See Marriage agreement of Denis Maurice O'Conor and Ellen Kevill Davies, Aug. 1873, O'Conor papers, CH, 9.3.ES.328. 22 Sale of part of the estates of William and Richard Nathaniel Lloyd, landed estates court rental, NLI, 29 Nov. 1860. See also www.findmypast.co.uk/search-ireland-records-in-census-land-and-surveys/and_land-and-estates, accessed 12 Jan. 2022. 23 Sale of part of the estates of Patrick Balfe, landed estates court rental, NLI, 20 Nov. 1860; *Royal commission of inquiry into the procedure and practice and the methods of valuation followed by the land commission, the land judge's court, and the civil bill courts in Ireland under the land acts and the land purchase acts*, vol. II, minutes of evidence, HC 1898 (41), xxxv, p. 770. Hereafter referred to as *Royal commission into ... methods of valuation*. 24 *Roscommon Messenger*, 3 Aug. 1861. Hugh O'Beirne did sell land in Roscommon and Sligo in June 1861, but it not known which parts of it the O'Conor Don bought. See landed estate court rentals, 1850–85, www.findmypast.co.uk/search-ireland-records-in-census-land-and-surveys/and_land-and-estates, accessed 12 Jan. 2022.

that he buy the estates they resided on.²⁵ Much later, in 1876, the O'Conor Don bought 1,023 acres for £7,850 on the estate of Dominick Trant, in the parishes of Baslick and Kilcorkey, near Castlerea.²⁶ In 1878, a further 150 acres were purchased on the estate of John McCreery, in the parish of Kilkeevin, near Castlerea, for £503, while another £1,380 was expended on some 95 acres on the estate of Michael Fox, in the parish of Tibohine, near Frenchpark.²⁷

The O'Conor Don therefore went from inheriting somewhere in the region of 7,650 acres in counties Roscommon and Sligo in 1859 to owning 12,650 acres in 1878. From the above, we can see that he purchased some 4,569 acres at a price tag of £51,098, another 260 acres that we cannot monetarily account for, and a further £24,000 was expended on an amount of land unknown. Further purchases were made in County Roscommon in the early years, but again the details are not known. It has not, therefore, been possible to fully account for the exact acreage and money spent between 1859 and 1878, but by De Burgh's reckoning in 1878, the O'Conor Don owned 11,466 acres in County Roscommon, with a rental value of £4,948, and 1,184 acres in County Sligo, valued at £487. His brother Denis owned 2,016 acres in County Roscommon, valued of £1,583, and 760 acres in County Sligo, valued at £447.²⁸ That put them in the second tier of large landlords in County Roscommon and the middle rank nationally.²⁹

Most of the O'Conor Don's Roscommon estates were concentrated in the north-western part of the county, in the parishes of Kilkeevin and Kilcorkey, clustered around Clonalis House, just outside the town of Castlerea, and around the village of Ballinagare, some seven and a half miles to the north-east of Castlerea. The smaller parts of his estates were close to the nearby village of Ballinlough, and the towns of Frenchpark, Ballaghaderreen, Tulsk and Strokestown, all of which are between five and twenty miles from Clonalis. The land around Clonalis and Ballinagare was mostly good quality, with grazing farms of between fifty and 400 acres, but the overwhelming majority of holdings on his Roscommon estates were under twenty acres, with many of

---

25 Memorials from tenants on the Lloyd and Pakenham-Mahon estates, 1 Oct. 1860, O'Conor papers, CH, 9.3.SH.316. 26 Landed estates court rental, 17 Nov. 1876, O'Conor papers, CH, 9.3.ES.047. 27 Landed estates court rental, 7 June 1878, O'Conor papers, CH, 9.3.ES.047; Abstract of title, 1897, Land commission papers, DAFF, box 237/schedule BB/no. 5/record no. 827. 28 De Burgh, *The landowners of Ireland*, p. 347. For the fullest account of what the author knows regarding land inherited, purchased, and sold by the O'Conor Don, see tables 1 and 2 in appendix 3, pp 216–22. The O'Conor estates were estimated to be 10,467 acres in 1853. See P.J. Carty, 'Roscommon: landownership, land occupation and settlement' in Farrell et al. (eds), *Roscommon history and society*, p. 413. However, a search of Griffith's valuation for 1857/8 puts the estates of the O'Conor Don and his brother Denis at around 9,500 acres. Griffith's valuation can be searched by name, county, parish, barony, and townland at www.askaboutireland.ie/griffith-valuation/, accessed 2 Nov. 2021. 29 Carty, 'Roscommon: landownership', p. 413; Cannadine, *British aristocracy*, pp 9–11.

these under ten. There were also some tracts of bog, varying from thirty to 140 acres, the majority of which the O'Conor Don held directly. The main parts of his Sligo estates were close to the town of Tobercurry, in the west of the county, and to the southern border with County Roscommon, on the shores of Lough Gara. The smaller part was close to Kilmactranny, on the eastern border with County Roscommon. His land in Sligo was generally of poorer quality, with the large majority of holdings under ten acres.[30]

The purchases in 1876 and 1878 seem odd at first glance, given that the O'Conor Don was by that time advocating state-sponsored compulsory purchase for the transfer of land from landlords to tenants.[31] But this land was adjoining his existing properties and three of the four townlands were single-hold grazing farms. Given his keen interest in livestock farming, the O'Conor Don may have been hoping to transition to a type of landownership concentrated on a small number of large, more profitable grazing farms, as opposed to renting out hundreds of small, subsistence-style properties.[32] One final purchase was made in July 1892 when the O'Conor Don bought just over 207 acres in the parish of Ballintober, County Roscommon, for £5,100. He already rented this land from the Pakenham-Mahon family in Strokestown, but it was of particular significance to him as it contained the family's former royal seat of Ballintober Castle.[33] The O'Conor Don therefore acquired this land because of his family's long-standing connection to the place. Overall, then, he probably had both the future of landholding and personal attachment as motivations when buying land at a time when landlords in general were not. But much of the land he purchased, including the sentimental Ballintober purchase, ended up being sold again in his own lifetime, or shortly thereafter.[34]

The Moore inheritance also enabled the O'Conor Don's brother, Denis, to purchase two properties in London: one at Ashley Moon and the other at Queen's Gate. The O'Conor brothers also supplemented their finances through investment in Irish, English, American, Australian and Indian stocks, shares and rail bonds, which in the 1860s provided them with yearly returns of between £1,500 and £2,000.[35] Finally, the O'Conor Don struck lucky once again in 1884 when he inherited £2,000 from Helen Blake of Kensington. It is

30 The O'Conor Don's rentals, 1850–76, O'Conor papers, CH, 9.3.ES.304 & 9.3.ES.305. See also Griffith's valuation. Finlay Dun gives the impression that most of his Roscommon estates was made up of large grazing farms, which was not the case. F. Dun, *Landlords and tenants in Ireland* (London, 1881), pp 208–11. For a visual impression of where the O'Conor Don's lands were located in counties Roscommon and Sligo, see appendix 2.1 & 2.2, pp 214–15. 31 See chapter four, pp 85–6. 32 Landed estates court rental, 17 Nov. 1876, O'Conor papers, CH, 9.3.ES.047. 33 Purchase of Pakenham-Mahon lands, July 1892, O'Conor papers, CH, 9.4.ES.294; O'Conor, *O'Conors of Connaught*, pp 250–1 34 See land sales below, pp 81–4. 35 The O'Conor Don's investments, 1864–8, O'Conor papers, CH 9.3.EO.030; Settlement of Denis O'Conor's estate, 1883, O'Conor papers, CH, 9.4.SE.173; Diary of the O'Conor Don, Jan. 1893, O'Conor papers, CH, 9.4.SH.247.

not clear what the connection was here, but Blake was a native of Claremorris, County Mayo, who died intestate in 1876 with a fortune of £140,000.[36]

Thus, the O'Conor Don combined the very lucky circumstances of his inheritances with sound investments in land and financial markets. He was not, however, averse to spending money. In the late 1860s, new farmyard buildings were constructed to the rear of what became old Clonalis House, which included a barn, turf house, stables, coach house, steward's room, servant's room and rent offices.[37] These buildings are still extant, operating as holiday cottages and apartments.[38] However, by far the biggest outlay in the O'Conor Don's lifetime was the construction of the new Clonalis House between 1878 and 1880.[39] This was a somewhat unusual undertaking given that relatively few landlords were building new houses by the 1870s, but, again, there was a personal motivation.[40] As already noted, the O'Conor Don's first wife, Georgina, died prematurely at Clonalis in August 1872. This painful association with the old house, combined with a recurring issue of flooding and dampness in the basement, drove him to build the new house, which he dedicated to Georgina's memory.[41] In 1877, he sought the services of the renowned English architect, Fredrick Pepys Cockerell, who, throughout the 1860s and 1870s, designed several country houses in England and, to a lesser extent, Ireland. The 'plain Italianate style' of Georgina's home in England, Bitham Hall, was the guiding architectural principle for the new Clonalis House, which was one of the first concrete-built houses in Ireland at the time, comprising forty-five rooms. Although Cockerell thought that English contractors would be better equipped to take on the work, the O'Conor Don feared that this would not be well received in the locality. Expressing a 'natural wish to employ a countryman', he fixed on the Irish contractor John Townsend Trench (1834–1909) to carry out the building work, which cost £10,582.[42] It was and still is a grand house, but

---

36 A.K. Stephenson to the O'Conor Don, 28 Apr. 1884, O'Conor papers, CH, 9.4.SE.202. It is not clear if there was a family connection or if the O'Conor Don knew Helen Blake (née Sheridan). She married Captain Robert Dudley Blake, a wealthy British army officer from Northumberland. For the extraordinary story of the 'Blake Millions', see http://www.thehelenblake.com/benefactor/, accessed 2 Nov. 2021. 37 Building works at the old Clonalis House, 1866–9, Clonalis House, O'Conor papers, 9.3.ES.024. 38 See https://clonalishouse.com/country-house-hotel-ireland/#cottages, accessed 2 Nov. 2021. 39 Letters, drawings, plans and costs relating to the building of the new Clonalis House, 1878–80, O'Conor papers, CH 9.4.EA.232. 40 Dooley, *The decline of the Big House*, pp 28–9. 41 See chapter two, pp 52–3. I was not able to locate any reference in the papers to flooding and dampness in the old house, but it is remarked upon by Pyers O'Conor Nash here https://clonalishouse.com/historic-house/?sfw=pass1630333627, accessed 2 Nov. 2021. 42 Letters, drawings, plans and costs relating to the building of the new Clonalis House, 1878–80, O'Conor papers, CH 9.4.EA.232; The O'Conor Don to Pepys Cockerell, 18 & 22 Aug. 1877, O'Conor papers, CH, 9.4.EA.232. For Cockerell see D. Watkin, 'Cockerell, Frederick Pepys (1833–78)', *ODNB*. For Townsend see G.J. Lyne, 'Trench, Richard Steuart ('William Steuart

it was relatively small in comparison to other Big Houses in the county, such as Loughglynn (Dillon), Frenchpark (De Freyne), Castlerea (Wills-Sandford), Rockingham (King-Harman), Strokestown (Pakenham-Mahon) and Kilronan (King-Tenison). The O'Conor Don could probably have afforded the risk of building a much larger Big House, but he was by instinct a thrifty man who was keen for his architect to avoid over-elaborate and costly designs, as well as a cautious man keen to avoid the negative attention from the locality that ostentation would undoubtedly have attracted.[43]

In 1893, renovation works were carried out on Hermitage, the farmhouse built by Charles O'Conor of Ballinagare in the 1760s. The purpose here was for his eldest son, Denis Charles (1869–1917), to use this large two-storey farmhouse as his country residence after he completed his studies for an LLB degree at the University of London.[44] Finally, the O'Conor Don's Dublin residence at Granite Hall, Kingstown, also required maintenance. Under the combined ownership of lords Longford and De Vesci, the O'Conor Don took over the lease on this property in July 1883 from his then deceased father-in-law, John Lewis More O'Ferrall, who had been chief commissioner of the Dublin Metropolitan Police. With sites for four more houses on the property, pressure was being brought to bear on the O'Conor Don towards the end of 1890 to construct 'at least 4 houses … on the sites … approved by their Lordships', or face losing the lease altogether.[45] He subsequently sold the lease in May 1892 for £1,200 but bought it back a year later for £1,100. Things came to head again in January 1898 and the O'Conor Don sold the lease again, only to buy it back shortly afterwards because his wife, Ellen, 'regretted having lost it'.[46] The lease was renewed with the stipulation that some building work be carried out on the property by 1903. By December 1899, the O'Conor Don had received five estimations, ranging from £2,294 to £3,927, 'for the making of a new road at Granite Hall'. It is not clear if this or any building work was carried out at Granite Hall, but it seems likely given that he managed to maintain the lease beyond 1903.[47]

Trench') (1808–72)', *DIB* & idem, 'John Townsend Trench's reports on the Lansdowne estates in Kerry', *Journal of the Kerry Archaeological and Historical Society*, 19 (1986), 5–64. **43** Connolly, *Landed estates*, pp 35, 103, 145, 163, 179, 195; The O'Conor Don to Pepys Cockerell, 18 & 22 Aug. 1877, O'Conor papers, CH, 9.4.EA.232. **44** Letters from J.J. Kelly to the O'Conor Don re building works at Hermitage, 1893, O'Conor papers, CH, 9.4.ES.281; Gibbons & O'Conor, *Charles O'Conor*, pp 68–9; Burnand, *Catholic who's who*, p. 306. **45** Papers relating to the lease of Granite Hall, 1887–99, O'Conor papers, CH, 9.4.ES.259; Recollections part 2, O'Conor papers, CH, 9.4.HL.156, p. 107; D. Murphy, 'O'Ferrall, John Lewis More', *DIB*. **46** The O'Conor Don to Lord De Vesci, 16 Jan. 1898, O'Conor papers, CH, 9.4.ES.259; Recollections part 2, O'Conor papers, CH, 9.4.HL.156, pp 145, 162. **47** Stewart & sons' solicitors to the O'Conor Don, 27 Jan. 1898, O'Conor papers, CH, 9.4.ES.259; Papers relating to lease of Granite Hall, 1887–99, O'Conor papers, CH, 9.4.ES.259.

ESTATE MANAGEMENT

Having a reputation for being a 'good' or 'excellent' landlord mattered and the O'Conor Don had such a reputation. The expectation that he would be a good landlord was partly based on the track record of his father, who was known for being pro-active and generous-minded, both before and during the Famine.[48] In that way, the O'Conor Don was similar to Charles Strickland in County Roscommon or Lord Clonbrock in County Galway, both of whom maintained good reputations before, during and after the Famine. Other local landlords like the De Freynes of Frenchpark and Pakenham-Mahons of Strokestown did not. The latter was one of the most troubled estates in the country before and during the Famine, with hundreds of evictions and the assassination of the landlord, Denis Mahon, in 1847.[49]

Expectations of benevolence were also reinforced by the fact that his cousin and agent, Thomas MacDermot, had a good reputation. A shrewd man who had the complete confidence of the O'Conor Don, MacDermot had the support of his younger brother, Roderick, who acted as a kind of deputy, while also being the main agent for the O'Conor Don's younger brother, Denis. The MacDermots were themselves minor landowners in County Sligo, with their eldest brother, Charles (1794–1873), the holder of the honorary Gaelic title, the 'Prince of Coolavin'. Charles was forced to sell 800 of his 1,600-acre estate to the encumbered estates court in 1852, but Thomas and Roderick bought this land back at a cost of £5,410, with the help of Edward O'Conor's widow, Honoria (*née* Blake of Towerhill), who lent them £2,125. Thomas never married and lived with Roderick and their sister, Fanny, at Hermitage near Ballinagare. Both he and Roderick were keen farmers and rented large farms of 366 and 166 acres on the O'Conor Don's Ballinagare estates.[50]

The employment of cousins or sons as agents was not unusual among Irish landlords, and while it did not guarantee the smooth running of an estate, it just so happened that it did with MacDermot.[51] Like Charles Strickland of Loughglynn he had a good reputation among the tenants as a pro-active and fair-minded man.[52] Such good and long-established relations were harder to engender for agents who came from outside the counties they worked in,

---

[48] *Royal commission of inquiry into state of law and practice in respect to occupation of land in Ireland, minutes of evidence, part II*, 1845 (616), xx.1, pp 225–9; Dunleavy & Dunleavy, *The O'Conor papers*, p xvii. [49] Connolly, *Landed estates*, pp 154–5, 168–9, 206–9; McKenna, 'Clonbrock estates', p. 87. [50] Recollections part 2, O'Conor papers, CH, 9.4.HL.156, p. 91; D. MacDermot, *MacDermot of Moylurg: the story of a Connacht family* (Nure, Co. Leitrim, 1996), pp 245–95; The O'Conor Don's rentals, 1874, O'Conor papers, CH, 9.3.ES.304. For the MacDermot's estates, see CMLED. [51] Melvin, 'The landed gentry of Galway', p. 159. [52] Connolly, *Landed estates*, pp 153–7.

but conscientious paternalists like Thomas Bermingham on the Clonbrock estate in County Galway, or Tristram Kennedy on the Bath estate in County Monaghan, proved that it could be done.⁵³ Conversely, on the De Freyne estate in County Roscommon, a series of exacting agents – some of whom were local – exacerbated the ongoing disputes between the quarrelsome landlord and his tenants.⁵⁴

The O'Conor Don struggled to find someone to replace Thomas MacDermot when he died in 1879, but this did not lead to any drastic change in his relationship with his tenants, despite the general upsurge in land agitation from 1879 onwards. Although Roderick took over as agent for the Ballinagare lands, it would seem that he was not trusted enough to take over the entire agency. Indeed, Roderick fell out with the O'Conor Don in 1889 over a relationship with a member of his house staff, Mary Cullinan, who was forty-eight years his junior. It would seem the O'Conor Don considered terminating his post, but Roderick saved him the trouble when he and Mary left Roscommon for Clontarf in 1890.⁵⁵ Another cousin of the O'Conor Don's, Valentine Blake (b. 1843), son of Valentine O'Conor-Blake of Towerhill, took on part of the agency for a brief period in 1880.⁵⁶ Elliott Graham Armstrong of Emalroy, County Roscommon, replaced Blake as agent for some of his Roscommon estates between February 1881 and January 1882, while Edward Whitby Lynch of Boyle, County Roscommon, managed some of his Roscommon and all of Sligo estates for much of the 1880s. Once described by John Dillon as 'one of the worst agents in Connaught', Lynch also worked on the Taafe estate in County Mayo and the De Freyne (briefly), Woufle Flanagan and Murphy estates in County Roscommon.⁵⁷ In January 1890, J.J. Kelly, a minor landowner from Essex Lawn, near Roscommon town, took over as full-time agent, but he died in October 1893.⁵⁸ Subsequently, the

---

53 McKenna, 'Clonbrock estates', pp 17–51; Casey, 'Clancarty estate', p. 257; C. Kenny, 'Paradox or pragmatist? "Honest" Tristram Kennedy (1805–85): lawyer, educationalist, land agent and member of parliament', *Proceedings of the Royal Irish Academy*, 92:1 (1992), pp 1–35. 54 Dyer Wolf, 'Two windows', pp 71, 82, 145. 55 Letters from Roderick MacDermot to the O'Conor Don re estate management, 1883–5, O'Conor papers, CH, 9.4.ES.213; MacDermot, *MacDermot of Moylurg*, pp 245–95. 56 Diaries of the O'Conor Don, Mar., Apr. & Oct. 1880, O'Conor papers, CH, 9.4.SH.247. Burnand, *Catholic who's who*, p. 33. 57 Elliott Graham Armstrong's appointment as 'rent collector', 22 Feb. 1881, O'Conor papers, CH, 9.4.SE.075; Recollections part 2, O'Conor papers, CH, 9.4.HL.156, p. 99. Armstrong was a minor landowner on the Caulfield estate in County Roscommon, a justice of the peace and a member of the Roscommon Board of Guardians. See *Irish Times*, 7 Feb. 1862 and *Roscommon Journal*, 17 Sept. 1864. For Whitby Lynch see the O'Conor Don's Sligo rentals 1881, O'Conor papers, CH, 9.4.ES.246. Lynch was also a justice of the peace for County Roscommon and a Boyle town commissioner. See *Irish Times*, 4 Dec. 1880; *Sligo Independent*, 19 Nov. 1881; *Freeman's Journal*, 7 June 1884 & 16 Oct. 1885. 58 Letters from J.J. Kelly to the O'Conor Don regarding estate management, 1890–3, O'Conor papers, CH, 9.4.ES.281; Recollections part 2, ibid., 9.4.HL.156, pp 138, 165; For Kelly's estate see CMLED.

O'Conor Don's eldest son, Denis Charles O'Conor, took charge of the agency and resided at Hermitage. He duly inherited the family title and lands after the O'Conor Don's death on 30 June 1906.[59]

The continuation of relatively cordial relations with his tenants after Thomas MacDermot's death was largely due to the O'Conor Don's hands-on and fair-minded approach to estate management. He was a creature of habit who took his duties as a landlord seriously and remained in touch with the day-to-day running of his estates by maintaining a hectic schedule of travel between Clonalis, Dublin and London. He was often in direct contact with his tenants to discuss the marking out of roads and drains, disputes over fences and bog, rent reductions and land purchase terms.[60] He was also a keen farmer, keeping 370 acres of grazing and 30 acres of tillage on the Clonalis demesne and adjacent townlands, where he reared cattle and sheep, kept horses and grew potatoes and other vegetables. To manage all this, he employed a steward, a herdsman and thirty labouring men all year round.[61] He sometimes attended fairs and bought his own cattle, although this job was normally left to his agents or herdsmen.[62] As already noted, he built new stables and farm buildings in the late 1860s, but he also had sheds for housing cattle in the winter and keeping hay, turf and potatoes dry. Indeed, it is clear from his diaries that he was regularly present at the getting in of these supplies. In the 1880s, he moved with the times and constructed silage pits at Clonalis and Ballinagare.[63] He was also a keen hunter, never missing an opportunity to shoot game when he visited the Blakes at Towerhill, while at home at Clonalis, or when he visited Downside. At Clonalis, his regular companions were his long-serving gamekeeper James Gaffrey, the MacDermots, his sons and other family members, and local and visiting gentry. In later years, Lord De Freyne and Douglas Hyde were regular companions.[64]

---

59 Irish land commission certificates for judicial rents, 1890s, O'Conor papers, CH, 9.4.ES.255; Accounts of Denis Charles O'Conor, 1890–9, O'Conor papers, CH, 9.4.ES.257; Rentals of Denis Charles O'Conor, 1900–1, O'Conor papers, CH, 0.1.ES.111; Will of Charles Owen O'Conor, 1891, O'Conor papers, CH, 0.1.ES.151;   60 Diaries of the O'Conor Don, 1861–5 and 1867–74, Clonalis House, O'Conor papers, 9.3.SH.306; Diaries of the O'Conor Don, 1875–99, ibid., 9.4.SH.247.   61 Dun, *Landlords and tenants*, pp 208–11; *Royal commission on labour: the agricultural labourer, vol. iv, Ireland, part iv, reports by Mr Arthur Wilson Fox (assistant commissioner), upon certain selected districts in the counties of Cork, Mayo, Roscommon and Westmeath; with summary report prefixed*, HC 1893–4 (341), xxxvii, pp 20, 28, 90–7. Hereafter referred to as *Royal commission on labour*.   62 Diary of the O'Conor Don, Jan. 1861, O'Conor papers, CH, 9.3.SH.306.   63 Diaries of the O'Conor Don, Sept. 1873, O'Conor papers, CH. 9.3.SH.306 & Aug. 1902, O'Conor papers, CH, 0.1.SH,041; *The agricultural districts of Ireland, for the year 1887*, HC 1888 (106), cvi, p. 132.   64 Diaries of the O'Conor Don, Jan., Apr. & May 1861 & Mar. 1864, O'Conor papers, CH, 9.3.SH.306; Diaries of the O'Conor Don, Jan. 1880, O'Conor papers, CH, 9.4.SH.247; Diaries of the O'Conor Don, Jan. 1900, O'Conor papers, CH, 0.1.SH.041; Diary of Denis Maurice O'Conor, 1869, NLI, P.5485.

The O'Conor Don was also an improving landlord, spending thousands of pounds on drainage, land reclamation and road making in the 1860s and 1870s. This was a source of employment for his tenants, but payment was often partially in wages, partially in rent-arrears write-offs.[65] In 1879–80, as the economic depression took hold, the O'Conor Don took out public works and land-improvement loans worth thousands of pounds, which was spent on drainage, gravelling and liming, the reclamation of bogland, the making of roads, fences, bridges and gullets, and the improvement of tenants' houses. Although many landlords took out similar loans at the time, the O'Conor Don was carrying on a tradition of doing such work.[66] As chairman of the River Suck Drainage Board, he helped provide employment for up to 1,000 skilled and unskilled labouring men on a temporary basis in the late 1880s and 1890s.[67] Given that the river flowed through several landed estates in counties Roscommon and Galway, the scheme had the support of other landlords including Patrick Balfe, Henry Sandford Pakenham-Mahon, Thomas George Willis-Sandford, the earl of Clancarty and Lord Clonbrock. However, the scheme was an incredibly drawn-out and unsuccessful affair with numerous disputes with contractors over delays in work. The O'Conor Don himself admitted that 'fatal' mistakes were made by the board regarding initial estimations of costs and the timescale for completion of the work.[68] In 1903, Anthony MacDonnell, under-secretary to the Irish chief secretary, who the O'Conor Don thought 'a most intelligent' man, described the project as an 'expensive failure'. He did so because it cost double what it was supposed to and still failed to prevent flooding or improve the land to any significant degree. For this mismanagement, MacDonnell blamed the project's promoters, the landlords.[69]

Despite this failure, the O'Conor Don maintained his reputation as a benevolent landlord and employer. Indeed, he was thought to be 'exceptional' among landlords in the area in that he paid his full-time labourers when they were off sick. He also paid pension contributions for his gamekeeper, James Gaffrey, so it seems likely that he would have done the same for other long-serving staff.[70] Conversely, he did not hesitate to sack a workman called

---

65 Receipts of rents paid and works done, 26 Feb. 1872, O'Conor papers, CH, 9.3.ES.142; List of bills, rent arrears and works done, 1874, O'Conor papers, CH, 9.4.ES.246. 66 Public works and land improvement loans, 1879–80, O'Conor papers, CH, 9.4.ES.241; *Relief of Distress (Ireland) Acts (loans)*, HC 1881 (99), p. 42. 67 *First report of the royal commission on Irish public works*, HC 1887 (471) (509), xxv, pp 211–13. 68 Documents and letter relating to the River Suck Drainage Scheme, 1879–84, O'Conor papers, CH, 9.4.ES.233; *Roscommon Journal*, 27 Oct. 1888; Casey, 'Clancarty estate', pp 27–8, 46. 69 Documents and letters relating to the River Suck Drainage Scheme, 1888–9, 1903, CSORP, NAI, 1907/4265; Diary of the O'Conor Don, 12 Dec. 1902, O'Conor papers, CH, o.1.SH.041. 70 List of bills, rent arrears, and works done, 1874 (Clonalis House, O'Conor papers, 9.4.ES.246); Connolly, *Landed estates*, p. 231; *Royal commission on labour*, pp 90–1.

Hynes on the spot when he failed turn up for work on a Monday morning due to drunkenness.[71] He also established a national school on his estate at Cloonboniffe, near Clonalis, and made regular donations to other schools, local churches and priests. In addition, he received many requests to use his influence to help constituents get jobs in local government administration, the police and the civil service.[72]

Considering the extent of his influence over the lives of the people in the local community, it seems more than reasonable to suggest that there was a considerable degree of deference towards the O'Conor Don among his tenants and the among the local population more generally. This deference reinforced the paternalistic sense of duty that he undoubtedly felt as a landlord and politician. But as we shall see, this did not mean he was totally immune to trouble on his estates. In any event, such influence was not that unusual among landlords, with the earl of Clancarty and Lord Clonbrock in County Galway both examples of paternalistic landlords who carried out extensive land improvements, employed many people, contributed to local charities, and supported local schools, while also experiencing relatively low levels of agitation on their estates from time to time.[73]

TENANT RIGHT, RENT AND ARREARS

Like many Irish landlords, the O'Conor Don permitted the practice of tenant right on his estates. Loosely defined, tenant right was the right of a tenant to sell the 'interest' in their holding, which was taken to be the value of the improvements they had made. The landlord either compensated the departing tenant for the value of these improvements if there was no incoming tenant or permitted them to sell the value of the improvements to an incoming tenant. For many tenant farmers, the right to sell their interest ought to be secured with fixity of tenure and fair rents. This in turn manifested itself in the popular demand for the 3fs: free sale, fixity of tenure and fair rent.[74]

As per the general pattern of rental agreements between landlord and tenant, the year-to-year tenancy prevailed on the O'Conor Don's estates. After Gladstone's 1870 land act, the O'Conor Don, like many landlords, was more

71 Diary of the O'Conor Don, 7 Feb. 1870, O'Conor papers, CH, 9.3.SH.306. 72 M. Moran, 'Father Michael O'Flanagan' in Farrell et al. (eds), *Roscommon history and society*, p. 561; Local school teacher to the O'Conor Don, 13 May 1860, O'Conor papers, CH, 9.4.SE.260; Bishop Gillooly to the O'Conor Don, 11 Nov. 1867, O'Conor papers, CH, 9.3.ES.179; Letters regarding local donations, 1859, O'Conor papers, CH, 9.3.HS.212; Letters to the O'Conor Don seeking favours, 1860–3, 1878 & 1882, O'Conor papers, CH, 9.3.HS.076, 9.4.SO.078 & 9.4.HS.230. 73 Casey, 'Clancarty estate', pp 22–93; McKenna, 'Clonbrock estates', pp 17–76. 74 Vaughan, *Landlords and tenants*, pp 67–76; Steele, *Irish land and British politics*, pp 5–15.

inclined to use the formal lease. Although he and the majority of landlords supported Gladstone's act, its attempt to make compensations for improvements legally binding proved complicated and expensive to enforce. The drawing up of new leases that would not be subject to the terms of the new legislation was therefore seen by landlords as a way to avoid the complication and expense.[75] The O'Conor Don's leases, generally issued for a period of thirty-two years, stipulated his right to enter a property to make drains and roads; to access all mines, minerals and other natural resources; and to shoot and kill game. If rent was not paid on the first of May or November in a given year, or was behind by more than twenty-one days, he reserved the right to enter a property and recoup the value of the rent in livestock or other available assets. The lessee was obliged to look after their holding 'in a good and husband-like manner', with under-letting and house building forbidden. In some cases, tenants were not permitted to plough or till the land.[76]

The officialism of the lease was not, however, reflected in the O'Conor Don's actual attitude to estate management. He certainly allowed tenants to build new houses and make improvements to old ones, providing an allowance for the undertaking.[77] But it was in the collection of rent where leniency manifested itself most clearly, with the landlord and judge William O'Connor Morris claiming the O'Conor Don was 'too good-natured' and consequently 'allowed his arrears to accrue' beyond what was reasonable or normal to expect.[78] Although there is a large degree of truth in this, losses accrued during the Famine, and in the bad years in the early 1860s, had a knock-on effect on the accumulation of arrears over the longer-term.[79] Thus while the yearly rental on the O'Conor Don's Roscommon estates between 1864 and 1873 was around £5,000, actual receipts averaged £4,300, while accumulated arrears averaged £3,900. This was despite an abatement of twenty per cent in 1864 and the fact that the O'Conor Don did not raise his rents throughout the period in question, which, as it happens, was not particularly exceptional behaviour on his part.[80] The general pattern on his estates was that rents were reduced

---

75 The O'Conor Don's rentals, 1861–5 and 1867–73, O'Conor papers, CH, 9.3.ES.304; The O'Conor Don rentals, 1848–53, 1856–8 & 1860–1, O'Conor papers, CH, 9.3.ES.305; J.S. Donnelly Jnr, *The land and people of nineteenth-century Cork: the rural economy and the land question* (London, 1975), pp 204–10; Vaughan, *Landlords and tenants*, pp 5–7. See chapter four, pp 86–90. 76 Papers relating to Thomas MacDermot's management of the O'Conor Don's estates, 1860–70, O'Conor papers, CH, 9.3.ES.142; Copies of leases drawn up by the O'Conor Don, 1881 & 1885, O'Conor papers, CH, 9.4.ES.288. 77 Thomas MacDermot to the O'Conor Don, 12 Dec. 1870, O'Conor papers, CH, 9.3.HE.055. 78 P. Geoghegan, 'Morris, William O'Connor', *DIB*; *Royal commission of inquiry into … methods of valuation*, p. 347. 79 The O'Conor Don's rentals 1848–53, 1856–8 & 1860–1, O'Conor papers, CH, 9.3.ES.305. 80 The O'Conor Don's rentals, 1861–5 & 1867–73, O'Conor papers, CH, 9.3.ES.304; W.E. Vaughan, 'Landlord and tenant relations in Ireland between the Famine and the Land War, 1850–1878' in L.M. Cullen & T.C. Smout (eds), *Comparative aspects of Scottish and Irish economic history, 1600–1900* (Edinburgh, 1977), pp 216–18; Donnelly, *The land and people*, pp 187–94.

by thirty per cent in 1847 and stayed at that level until 1876, when they were restored to pre-Famine levels.[81]

The issue with accumulated arrears persisted to the extent that, in 1882, 362 of the O'Conor Don's roughly 500 holdings, mostly under twenty acres, and with a rental value of £2,733, had accumulated arrears of £6,781. Under the Arrears Act of 1882, these arrears were struck off as landlords were compensated for complying with the legislation.[82] The O'Conor Don welcomed the act, thinking it would go some way to keeping the peace in Ireland; and although he was keen to comply, he was not averse to arguing the toss with the leader of the Home Rule Party, Charles Stuart Parnell, who made several 'rather troublesome' representations on behalf of tenants between November 1882 and February 1883.[83] This must have been somewhat irritating for the O'Conor Don given that Parnell had played a significant part in his electoral defeat two years earlier, but they seemed to have remained on fairly civil terms. In any event, the O'Conor Don received £1,949 in compensation under the act, which meant a loss of £784 or twenty-nine per cent of the rental income on those properties for that year.[84] However, if one considers that this was in large part the writing-off of accumulated Famine arrears after a period when he almost doubled the size of his holdings and restored pre-Famine rent levels, it can be said that the O'Conor Don had done good business as a landlord while remaining lenient in the collection of rent.

By way of comparison, much larger landlords in County Roscommon such as the King-Harmans, King-Tenisons and Pakenham-Mahons, who submitted a similar number of properties with a similar acreage and rental value under the arrears act, had not accumulated arrears to the same extent.[85] Indeed, the only one to surpass him in the county was his fellow Catholic landlord Lord De Freyne. He submitted 1,126 holdings with a rental value of £7,156 and arrears of £16,499, for which his was compensated £5,945.[86] Relatively speaking then, he fared slightly better than the O'Conor Don, losing £1,211 or seventeen per cent of rental income on those properties. The crucial difference between the O'Conor Don and De Freyne, though, is that the latter's problem with arrears was more because his tenants simply refused to pay, rather than having let arrears slide from year to year without pursuing them.

81 The O'Conor Don's Ardsoreen rentals, 1829, 1842, 1847 & 1876, O'Conor papers, CH, 9.4.ES.291. 82 *Return of payments made to landlords by the Irish land commission, pursuant to the 1st and 16th sections of the act; and also a return of rent-charges cancelled pursuant to the 15th section of the Arrears of Rent (Ireland) Act 1882*, HC 1884 (97), lxiv, pp 150, 239. Hereafter referred to as *Return of payments made to landlords … Arrears of Rent*. 83 The O'Conor Don to Earl Spencer, 11 Aug. 1882, Althorp papers, BL, 1869–81, add. 76997, art. 1; C.S. Parnell to the O'Conor Don, 17, 27 Nov. & 20 Dec. 1882 & 3 Feb. 1883, O'Conor papers, CH, 9.4.HE.223. 84 *Return of payments made to landlords … Arrears of Rent*, pp 150, 239. 85 Ibid. 86 Dyer Wolf, 'Two windows', p. 74.

De Freyne inherited huge debts when he took over the estate in 1876 and compounded them in 1877 by taking on a mortgage loan of £44,000 from Maynooth College, approved by Archbishop Paul Cullen. There had been a no-rent campaign on his estates since 1880, to which his response was to refuse rent abatements and issue hundreds of eviction notices.[87] Although he had just built a new house, the O'Conor Don was financially secure and adopted a more generous-minded and pragmatic approach, letting arrears accrue, granting further abatements, applying for government loans, making improvements, creating employment, evicting very few tenants, and selling outlying parts of his estates in County Sligo.[88] A similar approach was adopted by Lord Clonbrock in County Galway, who had seen his arrears rise from £990 in 1879 to £3,649 in 1889.[89]

Under Gladstone's land act of 1881, tenants were granted fixity of tenure and could apply to have their rents judicially fixed to levels that were deemed fairer by the newly established land commission.[90] As we shall see in chapter four, the O'Conor Don was opposed to the act, preferring instead the radical policy of compulsory state-aided land purchase to convert tenant farmers into owner-occupiers, rather than instituting what he saw as a system of dual ownership of land where neither party would be satisfied.[91] Nonetheless, between 1884 and 1898, seventy-seven holdings on his estates were judicially fixed, of which the overwhelming majority were small holdings of less than twenty acres. Collectively they amounted to some 1,160 acres, with a rental value of just over £681. Fixed at £400, the O'Conor Don lost £281, which amounted to an overall drop of forty-two per cent in income on these holdings. Underneath these headline figures, however, a small number of rents stayed the same, while the majority of rent reductions ranged from fifteen to twenty per cent, which was roughly the same or just above the national average of judicial reductions of ten to fourteen per cent.[92] This suggests two things:

87 Ibid., pp 167–70. 88 For improvements, see above p. 69. For sale, see below pp 81–4. 89 McKenna, 'Clonbrock estates', pp 178–208 90 Purdue, *The Big House*, p. 49. 91 See chapter four, pp 85–6. 92 *Return according to provinces and counties of judicial rents fixed by sub-commissions and civil bill courts, as notified to the Irish land commission during the month of December 1882*, HC 1883 (121), lvi, pp 78–9. For succeeding years, the references are shortened to *Return ... of judicial rents fixed ... during the month of etc. Return ... of judicial rents fixed ... January 1883*, HC 1883 (237), lvi, pp 84–5; *Return ... of judicial rents fixed ... October 1883*, HC 1884 (233), lxv, pp 164–5, 236–7; *Return ... of judicial rents fixed ... April 1884*, HC 1884 (413), lxvi, pp 84–7; *Return ... of judicial rents fixed ... November 1884*, HC 1884–5 (193), lxv, pp 44–5; *Return ... of judicial rents fixed ... January and February 1888*, HC 1888 (229), lxxxiv, pp 120–1; *Return ... of judicial rents fixed ... May and June 1888*, HC 1888 (621), lxxxiv, pp 50–2; *Return ... of judicial rents fixed ... January and February 1889*, HC 1889, lxiii, pp 16–17; *Return ... of judicial rents fixed ... May, 1890*, HC 1890 (477), lxi, pp 62–3; *Return ... of judicial rents fixed ... June, 1890*, HC 1890 (653) (811), lxi, pp 140–1; *Return ... of judicial rents fixed ... August 1890*, HC 1890–1 (219), lxv, pp 76–7, 166–7; *Return ... of judicial rents fixed ... September, October, and November 1891*, HC 1892 (177), lxvi, pp 28–9, 56–7; *Return ... of judicial rents fixed ... March and April, 1893*,

that a significant minority of his tenants were not happy with their rent levels, and that his rents were, in some cases, relatively high. Indeed, he compares unfavourably with the likes of Lord Clonbrock, who, between 1888 and 1893, had thirty-five holdings judicially fixed at or just below the national average of reductions.[93] Looking at the general picture again, the O'Conor Don's restoration of pre-Famine rent levels meant his rents were in some cases high when compared to the judicial rents. Indeed, many of his judicial rents were set close to the reduced rents granted by his father in 1847.[94] However, the fact that he complied with requests for reductions to such a significant extent, as well as continuing to let arrears slide and being a hands-on landlord, seems to have contributed to the relatively tranquil state of affairs on his estates.

EVICTIONS AND LAND LEAGUE AGITATION

Although the O'Conor Don was thought to be 'an excellent landlord', evictions, or more commonly the threat of them, were not unknown on his estates.[95] Like on many Irish estates, notices to quit were served by the O'Conor Don's agents as a reminder for those in arrears. But even when tenants were served with these notices, they were almost always never actually evicted, with some arrangements made for 'working off' the rent and arrears owed, or the further postponement of collection if there were extenuating circumstances.[96]

For example, in May 1874, Thomas MacDermot reported how eviction notices were served on Luke Conway and Pat and Luke Brennan on the O'Conor Don's Sligo estates, but in all cases MacDermot had no intention of actually evicting the tenants; he thought the Brennans would 'pay more punctually' after receiving their notice, and he was prepared for money to be 'allowed in work' in the case of Conway. On the Roscommon estates, Loughlin Broderick had possession taken of his holding for long-standing arrears and non-payment of rent, but he was soon reinstated, with some of the property to be let out to another tenant for grazing. MacDermot also complained of John Flanagan, who had to 'be served with ejectment' for the same reasons, but with the same outcome.[97] The O'Conor Don also showed compassion towards tenants with difficult personal circumstances. In one case

HC 1893–4 (553), lxxv, pp 60–1; *Return ... of judicial rents fixed ... September and October 1893*, HC 1893–4 (871), lxxv, pp 30–3; *Return ... of judicial rents fixed ... May and June 1895*, HC 1895 (583), lxxxii, pp 18–19; *Return ... of judicial rents fixed ... September, October, November, and December 1895*, HC 1896 (85), lxx, pp 42–3; *Return ... of judicial rents fixed ... November 1897*, HC 1898 (375), lxxv, pp 32–3.   93 McKenna, 'Clonbrock estates', p. 197.   94 The O'Conor Don's Ardsoreen rentals 1829, 1842, 1847 & 1876, O'Conor papers, CH, 9.4.ES.291.   95 *Roscommon Journal*, 9 Feb. 1878.   96 Vaughan, 'Landlord and tenant relations', pp 219–24.   97 The O'Conor Don's rentals, 1861–5 & 1867–74, O'Conor papers, CH, 9.3.ES.304.

MacDermot attributed the tenant's difficulty in meeting the rent to the death of two children from smallpox, noting that arrears would be paid in instalments, with the option of the tenant working off some of the rent owed. There were similar circumstances for a tenant who was to be given extra time to pay due to the death of his wife. Here MacDermot commented on how the O'Conor Don had 'allowed him five pounds for his house' and an 'additional grant', which assisted the tenant in the part-payment of his rent.[98]

Conversely, in July 1880, the Frenchpark branch of the Land League reported a dispute over the value of land on one of the O'Conor Don's holdings, where the tenant in question sought a reduction in his rent but none was forthcoming and the threat of an eviction was thought to be imminent.[99] In February 1882, the Castlerea branch of the Ladies' Land League reported the eviction of John Byrne from one of the O'Conor Don's estates, and how he had not been '[re-] admitted as caretaker'.[100] Land League branches were hardly impartial observers, but there are records of the O'Conor Don paying bailiffs' expenses, so it seems likely that these or other evictions did in fact take place.[101] Despite these cases, the *Roscommon Journal* still considered the O'Conor Don 'to rank amongst the best landlords in Ireland', making much of the fact that tenants who had been served with possession orders owed 'from seven to ten years rent'.[102] Nonetheless, the threats of eviction due to accumulated arrears continued into the 1890s.[103] In August 1891, the O'Conor Don's then agent, J.J. Kelly, complained of an evicted tenant who had re-entered the property and 'stocked and tilled' it. According to Kelly, the solicitor's advice was 'to summon him [the tenant] for trespass or eject him again', urging swift action 'before the crop [was] removed'.[104]

As we shall discover in chapters four and six, the O'Conor Don's popularity as a politician was in sharp decline by the time the Land War commenced in 1879, with his opposition to home rule and fixity of tenure doing little to endear him to his constituents. But there is clearly a distinction to be drawn between constituents in the county and tenants on his estates, as he did not experience any notable agitation between 1879 and 1882. Thus, although MacDermot received many reports of distress and requests for rent reductions in 1878 and 1879, the usual policies of letting arrears accumulate, making arrangements for working off some of the arrears or waiting for men and their wages to return from England, ensured that there was no trouble

98 Ibid. 99 Correspondence regarding the O'Conor Don's estates, Land League papers, NLI, MS 17,706 (3). 100 *Freeman's Journal*, 5 Feb. 1882. 101 List of bills, rent arrears and works done, 1874, O'Conor papers, CH, 9.4.ES.246. 102 *Roscommon Journal*, 7 Jan. 1882. 103 List of decrees of possession, 1892, O'Conor papers, CH, 9.4.ES.267. 104 J.J. Kelly to O'Conor Don, 22 Aug. 1891, O'Conor papers, CH, 9.4.ES.281.

on the O'Conor Don's estates during the first phase of intense land agitation.[105] It would therefore seem reasonable to argue that his unpopular political views did not overly distract from the on-the-ground practical reality of him being, and being perceived to be, a good landlord. Obviously feeling secure in his position, the O'Conor Don did not feel the need to join the Irish Land Committee in 1879 or the Property Defence Association (PDA) in 1881, both of which were formed to provide financial assistance to landlords impacted by the no-rent campaigns of the Land League.[106] The similarly benevolent and generally popular lords Clonbrock and Clancarty in County Galway both got through the Land War unscathed, with Clancarty also feeling there was no need to join the PDA.[107]

THE PLAN OF CAMPAIGN AND THE CHURCH

Having escaped the worst effects of the Land League agitations, the O'Conor Don was, by September 1883, warning the lord lieutenant, Earl Spencer, that National League meetings in County Roscommon were leading to tenants refusing to pay rent and that this would inevitably lead to 'outrages' being committed. Indeed, he thought he could find himself in 'hot water' if the government did not do something 'to prevent such meetings', emphasizing that 'the priests find it very difficult to control the people' afterwards.[108] But apart from an arson attack on the coach house to the rear of old Clonalis in June 1884, there does not appear to have been any serious outbreak of violence on the O'Conor Don's estates throughout the 1880s.[109] That said, after the commencement of the Plan of Campaign in October 1886, the orchestration of a no-rent campaign on his estates was attempted by John Dillon, who, along with other leading members of the National League, helped devise the no-rent manifesto of the Plan.[110] At a National League meeting in Dublin on 9 November 1886, Dillon alleged that 'rack renting' on the O'Conor Don's Cartronmore and Carrowgarve lands, near Ballaghaderreen, was nothing short of a 'public scandal', with his agent Whitby Lynch being singled out for special criticism for the harsh treatment of the tenants. The O'Conor Don was incensed by the accusation, immediately writing a letter to the editor of the

105 Letters from tenants to Thomas MacDermot, Nov. 1878–Oct. 1879, O'Conor papers, CH, 9.4.SH.009.   106 A. Pole, 'Landlord responses to the Irish Land War, 1879–82' (PhD, TCD, 2006), pp 39–40, 218–19, 229–31, 344–55.   107 McKenna, 'Clonbrock estates', pp 177–8; Casey, 'Clancarty estate', pp 12, 140, 205.   108 The O'Conor Don to Earl Spencer, 19 Sept. 1883, Althorp papers, BL, add. 76997, art. 1.   109 Owen Wynne to the O'Conor Don, 1 July 1884, O'Conor papers, CH, 9.4.SH.199; Diaries of the O'Conor Don, June 1884, O'Conor papers, CH, 9.4.SH.247.   110 L.M. Geary, *The Plan of Campaign, 1886–1891* (Cork, 1986), pp 21–4; F.S.L. Lyons, *John Dillon: a biography* (London, 1968), pp 75–86.

Freeman's Journal strenuously refuting it, explaining how he had bought the properties at the specific request of the tenants, and had only realized afterwards that rents were high and arrears were owed. Having been thus enlightened, the O'Conor Don rather sarcastically remarked that his 'first act of tyranny and oppression … was to have a new valuation made on the land … which resulted in a reduction of the net rental' by twenty per cent. His 'next act of systematic oppression' was to 'spend large sums in drainage, road making, and other improvements for which I never charged the tenants 1s'. The O'Conor Don further stated that 'indulgence was given' to the extent that, in some cases, rents had not been paid for eight years; and this was despite abatements of twenty-five and fifteen per cent in 1879 and 1881, respectively. Dillon had also alleged that 'judicial rents' were forced on the tenants after the 1881 land act, but the O'Conor Don insisted that all rents were fixed by mutual agreement, and that the tenants had their arrears quashed under the arrears act of 1882. He also disputed Dillon's figure of twelve eviction notices, claiming that only eight had been taken out in October 1885, and that these were not enforced until May 1886, so as to allow the tenants to return as caretakers while some form of settlement was reached.[111] Determined to protect his reputation as a good landlord, the O'Conor Don went on to declare that:

> During the time that I have had anything to say to them [the tenants] my relations with them have been of the most friendly and cordial character. There is scarcely one of them that I do not personally know … During the twenty odd years I have had connection with the property several sales of tenants [interest] … have taken place, and large sums, varying from ten to fifteen years purchase of the rents have been obtained.[112]

Although naturally a biased view, this was, based on the evidence, a largely accurate depiction of his relationship with his tenants. But still, Dillon's failure to instigate a no-rent campaign on the O'Conor Don's estates is notable given that their very public spat occurred at a time when the Plan of Campaign had taken hold on the surrounding De Freyne, Dillon, Wills-Sandford, Pakenham-Mahon, Murphy, O'Grady and Worthington estates in north County Roscommon, where the National League had a very able and committed local leader in John Fitzgibbon. Indeed, Fitzgibbon, a draper in Castlerea, was no fan of the O'Conor Don.[113] The O'Conor Don's Catholicism could not have been much of a factor given that De Freyne and Murphy

---

111 *Roscommon Journal*, 13 Nov. 1886.   112 *Roscommon Journal*, 13 Nov. 1886.   113 Geary, *The Plan of Campaign*, pp 21–4, 77–8, 154–78; J. Bligh, 'John Fitzgibbon of Castlerea: "A most mischievous and dangerous agitator"' in Brian Casey (ed.), *Defying the law of the land: agrarian radicals in Irish history* (Dublin, 2013), pp 201–19.

were both Catholics and the Catholic earl of Granard's estate in neighbouring County Longford was another high-profile case.¹¹⁴ And while Dillon and William O'Brien complained of a lack of 'unity' among the tenants on the generally popular Catholic earl of Kenmare's huge estates in County Kerry, they still managed to organize a no-rent campaign on part of his estates in 1888.¹¹⁵

Catholic landlords were therefore not immune to agitation and received no special treatment from their tenants or the National League. The absence of the Plan of Campaign on the O'Conor Don's estates was therefore almost certainly down to his conduct as a landlord who was lenient in the collection of rent, carried out few evictions, and generally treated his tenants well. The Protestant lords Clonbrock and Clancarty in County Galway, both of whom behaved in a similar way, did not entirely escape the Plan, but they did make terms with their tenants relatively quickly and remained generally popular landlords in their respective localities.¹¹⁶ The O'Conor Don was, therefore, something of an anomaly, but it was clearly not for the want of trying on the part of Dillon and one can only assume that the tenants themselves were not interested in provoking a fight. In any event, the National League's focus was on estates in precarious financial circumstances, in the hope that they could break them with a no-rent combination. The De Freyne, Granard and Kenmare estates were all severely indebted, with the first two receiving loans from Maynooth College to try and manage their financial woes, while the latter embarked on the construction of a massive new mansion in the 1870s that proved to be a financial disaster.¹¹⁷ As already noted, the O'Conor Don had no such worries, managing to balance the building of a relatively modest new house with the sale of his Sligo estates. Hence, much like the land committee and the PDA during the Land War, the O'Conor Don felt no compulsion to join the Anti-Plan of Campaign Association when requested to do so by the County Carlow landlord, Arthur Kavanagh, in June 1887.¹¹⁸ And this was despite the fact that 1887 was, by his own admission, the worst year he had experienced as a landlord, with many groups of tenants refusing to pay their rents unless reductions were granted.¹¹⁹

Similar demands for reductions were made by tenants on the aforementioned Cartronmore and Carrowgarve lands, near Ballaghaderreen, in

114 Geary, *The Plan of Campaign*, pp 45–6, 165. 115 J.S. Donnelly Jnr, 'The Kenmare estates during the nineteenth century', *Journal of the Kerry Archaeological and Historical Society*, 3:23 (1990), 20–33; Geary, *The Plan of Campaign*, p. 167. 116 McKenna, 'Clonbrock estates', pp 177–8; Casey, 'Clancarty estate', p. 237; Geary, *The Plan of Campaign*, p. 159. 117 Dyer Wolf, 'Two windows', pp 167–70; Geary, *The Plan of Campaign*, pp 45–6; J.S. Donnelly Jnr, 'The Kenmare estates during the nineteenth century', *Journal of the Kerry Archaeological and Historical Society*, 1:21 (1988), 29–41. 118 Arthur Kavanagh to the O'Conor Don, 18 June 1887, O'Conor papers, CH, 9.4.HS.216. 119 Recollections part 1, O'Conor papers, CH, 9.4.HL.156, pp 128–9.

November 1890.¹²⁰ One year later, his agent J.J. Kelly reported difficulties in collecting rents at Ballinagare. He also complained of 'interference' from the local clergy in relation to the payment of rent in the townland of Clonalis.¹²¹ By November 1892 Kelly had reason to believe that there was 'no combination on the Clonalis estate but almost a general request for time until the next fair at Castlerea'. From the Strokestown tenants, he reported a refusal 'to pay without a reduction but ... no specific percentage was demanded'. The situation in Ballinlough seemed to pose the greatest problem, with Kelly certain that the tenants were displaying an 'undoubted show of determining combination'. Once again, a local priest met with Kelly and, on behalf of the tenants, requested an abatement of twenty-five per cent in light of the previous 'bad season for both crops and cattle'. Kelly informed the O'Conor Don that he had not committed to the request because he thought it too high, but nonetheless felt the necessity of reaching some form of compromise.¹²²

Despite Kelly's frustrations, the involvement of the clergy seems to have been welcomed by the O'Conor Don when it was a case of mediating negotiations for rent reductions or purchase terms. Their tacit support of the Plan was, however, a source of anger and frustration for him.¹²³ As early as 1885, George Errington – fellow Catholic landlord, MP for County Longford and friend – had brought the issue of clerical involvement in land agitation to the attention of Gladstone and Pope Leo XIII. However, Errington's unofficial role as a diplomatic link between London and Rome, as a means to supressing clerical support for the Plan, was a conspicuous failure.¹²⁴ In October 1886, the O'Conor Don joined his fellow landed Catholics Captain John Ross, Sir Rowland Blennerhassett, the duke of Norfolk, the earl of Denbigh and lords Emly and Clifford on a delegation to meet with the conservative prime minister, Lord Salisbury, to try and persuade him of the need for cooperation between London and Rome in combating the clergy's involvement in the Plan. Once again, however, nothing came of the initiative.¹²⁵ The pope had been receiving reports of clerical involvement in the Plan from the coadjutor bishop of Clonfert, John Healy, and his initial response was to dispatch a papal legate to Ireland in the summer of 1887 to investigate the matter. Although Monsignor Ignazio Persico did visit landlords to get their views on the agitation, turning up at the earl of Granard's estates while evictions were

120 J.J. Kelly to the O'Conor Don, 13 Nov. 1890, O'Conor papers, CH, 9.4.ES.281. 121 J.J. Kelly to the O'Conor Don, 21 & 27 Nov. 1891, O'Conor papers, CH, 9.4.ES.281. 122 J.J. Kelly to the O'Conor Don, 19 Nov. 1892, O'Conor papers, CH, 9.4.ES.281. 123 Recollections part 1, O'Conor papers, CH, 9.4.HL.156, p. 99. 124 Geary, *The Plan of Campaign*, p. 83; E. Larkin, *The Roman Catholic Church and the Plan of Campaign in Ireland, 1886–88* (Cork, 1978), pp 248, 294. 125 A. Macaulay, *The Holy See, British policy and the Plan of Campaign in Ireland, 1885–93* (Dublin, 2002), pp 5–40.

taking place would not have generated much sympathy for the landlord side of the argument.[126] The O'Conor Don was apparently put out by Persico's failure to call at Clonalis, but he got to meet him at Archbishop William Walsh's residence in Dublin in July 1887, and at the residence of the Catholic lord chief justice, Michael Morris, where they had 'a long chat'. The general reaction of landed Catholics to the mission was to welcome it as a positive sign of papal support for their position. After Persico's departure at end of 1887, an address was drawn up conveying their appreciation for the pope's action and their continued loyalty to his temporal power.[127] But in a way that neatly highlighted the dual loyalties of landed Catholics, a pledge of allegiance was also addressed to the queen in June of that year.[128]

In April 1888, a papal decree was issued condemning the boycotting and no-rent combinations of the Plan, but this was not the end of the matter for the O'Conor Don and his landed Catholic colleagues. In August of that year, he joined Edmund Dease and William Monsell in condemning the conduct of the clergy in letters to Captain John Ross, who subsequently forwarded their letters to Cardinal Rampolla, the secretary of state to the Vatican.[129] The O'Conor Don claimed that 'boycotting' was 'rife' in the Castlerea area, with the curates and parish priest in the town 'eloquently silent as to the decree'. He blamed the clergy's waywardness on the lack of 'direction' from Bishop Gillooly, whom he claimed had 'made no ... outward public' condemnation of such activities in the diocese. He also criticized Archbishop Walsh, who 'never said one word in support of the decree', further suggesting that Ireland needed 'some ecclesiastical head, who would enforce the pope's decree and make the Bishops obey'. Although the O'Conor Don believed the Plan was 'nearly extinct', he did not think it was 'on account of the Papal condemnation'.[130] By December 1889 he was writing directly to Archbishop Walsh remonstrating about the clergy's conduct and insisting that tenants should 'formally' renounce the Plan by holding official meetings and 'passing ... resolution[s]' to that effect.[131] But Walsh was having none of it, arguing that the Plan was 'up to a certain date ... a thoroughly justifiable proceeding', and rejecting the O'Conor Don's demands as wholly unrealistic, which indeed they were.[132]

By January 1902, the O'Conor Don's son Denis was in possession of the troubled Cartronmore and Carrowgarve lands, which at that point were being

126 Lyons, *Dillon*, p. 91; Macaulay, *The Holy See*, pp 112–13. 127 Macaulay, *The Holy See*, pp 112–14, 260. 128 Recollections part 2, O'Conor papers, CH, 9.4.HL.156, pp 125, 128; *Times*, 30 June 1887. 129 John Ross to Cardinal Rampolla, 24 Aug. 1888, Bladensburg papers, PRONI, D2004/4/50. 130 The O'Conor Don to John Ross, 14 Aug. 1888, Bladensburg papers, PRONI, D2004/4/45. 131 Archbishop Walsh to the O'Conor Don, 28 Dec. 1889, O'Conor papers, CH, 9.4.HE.079; The O'Conor Don to Archbishop Walsh, 29 Dec. 1889, O'Conor papers, CH, 9.4.HE.079. 132 Archbishop Walsh to the O'Conor Don, 28 Dec. 1889, O'Conor papers, CH, 9.4.HE.079.

monitored by the then Irish chief secretary, George Wyndham, for signs of a no-rent combination and any 'undue or unfair pressure upon either the landlord or the tenants' by outside forces.[133] That County Roscommon was on Dublin Castle's radar was no surprise, as it was once again the scene of numerous no-rent campaigns, this time organized by the United Irish League, under the direction of William O'Brien and John Dillon. Campaigns were active on the De Freyne, Wills-Sandford, Murphy and O'Grady estates, which collectively became known as the 'Associated Estates'. Once again, however, the O'Conor Don and Denis escaped the worst of it and felt no compunction to join the latest organization of landlord defence, the Irish Land Trust, in 1902.[134] At some point in 1902, Denis agreed terms with the Cartronmore and Carrowgarve tenants to sell to the Congested Districts Board (CDB), but, as we shall see below, this did not actually happen until 1909. Whether he agreed to sell to the CDB under threat of a no-rent combination is not clear, but the sale of Lord Dillon's neighbouring estates to the CDB in 1899 almost certainly put pressure on him to at least indicate that he was willing to follow suit.[135] Indeed, the O'Conor Don told his cousin, Sir Nicholas O'Conor (1843–1903), a British diplomat, that Dillon's sale to the CDB, at the 'very bad price' of fifteen and a half years purchase, would bring down the selling price of other estates in the county. On the upside, however, he encouraged Nicholas to buy Loughglynn House, which he thought would be 'sold very cheap' by the CDB, who had restored it after a fire. The O'Conor Don recommended the shooting on the demesne, but worried that all this would be 'destroyed' if the house was not 'bought by some gentleman'.[136]

SALE AND DECLINE

Under pressure from all sides, Irish landlords were now faced with the prospect of having to sell their estates. The next chapter will reveal how the O'Conor Don had been an advocate of compulsory state-aided land purchase since at least 1877; and how, from that point on, he tried to persuade successive British governments to pass legislation along those lines. It will come as no great surprise, then, that he tried to avail of the voluntary land-purchase schemes of the 1880s, 1890s and early 1900s.

133 Inspector general's reports on Roscommon, 21 Jan. 1902, CSORP, NAI, 1883.   134 Dyer Wolf, 'Two windows', pp 107–40, 149–59. See also land trust documents, 1902, De Freyne papers, NLI, MS 50,329/7/1–30. It should be noted that Daphne Dyer Wolf very kindly shared these documents and their reference with me. I did not consult the documents directly.   135 Dyer Wolf, 'Two windows', p. 135.   136 The O'Conor Don to Sir Nicholas O'Conor, 21 Sept. 1899, O'Conor papers, CAC, OCON2/4/32; Connolly, *Landed estates*, p. 147.

It was in February 1879, however, through the landed estates court, that the O'Conor Don first sold 653 acres from his Sligo estates for £3,500, although the completion of sale for some holdings dragged on until the late 1880s.[137] In January 1882 he attempted to negotiate the sale of part of his Clonalis estate, but, despite the mediation of the parish priest, Father Neary, nothing came of it. Efforts to sell to tenants on his Ballinlough estates in January 1884 also came to nothing.[138] After the passing of the Ashbourne act in 1885, tenants were more inclined to buy as they could now borrow the full purchase price of their holdings, repayable at four per cent over forty-nine years. Initially, £5 million of treasury money was made available for the scheme, and due to the demand for purchases the government provided an additional £5 million in 1888.[139] In 1889, under the terms of the 1885 act, the O'Conor Don sold 55 acres in County Roscommon and 359 acres in County Sligo for £1,200 and £3,561, respectively.[140] The early sale of much of his Sligo estates supports Dooley's assertion that landlords were more inclined to sell smaller or outlying parts of their estates to clear debts.[141] The building of the new Clonalis House would have put a strain on the O'Conor Don's finances and it is likely these sales went a long way towards footing the bill.

In April 1890, the agent J.J. Kelly made further attempts to persuade more of the O'Conor Don's tenants to buy their holdings, but once again nothing came of it.[142] The land acts of 1891 and 1896 made a combined total of £69 million available for land purchase, but the terms were not as favourable as the Ashbourne act, and the transfer of land therefore remained slow as 'landlords were unwilling to sell and the tenants reluctant to buy'.[143] For tenants, annuities were high in comparison to the relatively low rents fixed under the 1881 land act, which meant repayments could be stretched out over a period of anything up to seventy years. Landlords, on the other hand, were to be paid in government land stock rather than cash payments, which meant the returns on sales were at the mercy of fluctuating prices for land stock on the open market.[144] In February 1893, the O'Conor Don met with the unhappy tenants on the Cartronmore and Carrowgarve lands to discuss purchase terms, presumably under the 1891 act. Although they agreed to give seventeen years purchase for their holdings, nothing came of it, but it is not clear if this was due to a change of heart on their or

---

137 Sale of Drimina estate, County Sligo, 14 Feb. 1879, landed estates court rental, NAI, MRGS 39/60 vol. 135; *Freeman's Journal*, 15 Feb. 1879. 138 Recollections part 2, O'Conor papers, CH, 9.4. HL.156, pp 110–11. 139 Purdue, *The Big House*, pp 70–1. 140 *Return giving the names of the landowners the purchase of whose properties under 'the Land Purchase (Ireland) Act, 1885', has been sanctioned by the Irish land commission since 1st January 1889*, HC 1890 (115), lx, 171, p. 12. 141 Dooley, *The decline of the Big House*, p. 106. 142 J.J. Kelly to O'Conor Don, 16 Apr. 1890, O'Conor papers, CH, 9.4.ES.281. 143 Dooley, *The decline of the Big House*, pp 103–6; Purdue, *The Big House*, pp 70–1; Macaulay, *The Holy See*, p. 333. 144 J.E. Pomfret, *The struggle for land in Ireland, 1800–1923* (Princeton, NJ, 1930), pp 271–5.

the O'Conor Don's part.¹⁴⁵ Nonetheless, between 1896 and 1902, the O'Conor Don sold approximately 1,223 acres for £11,200 under the 1891 act.¹⁴⁶ That he did not sell much of his lands in the 1890s would suggest that he, like many landlords, was not enamoured with the prospect of being paid in land stock, as opposed to cash. That said, he clearly tried to sell more land than he did even though indebtedness was not a major issue for him. In contrast, Lord Crofton, a landlord of comparable size in County Roscommon who was experiencing financial difficulties, sold almost five times as much land in the 1890s.¹⁴⁷

Like on many Irish estates, sales increased under the more favourable terms of Wyndham's land act of 1903, which provided a further £70 million for land purchase. Tenants' annuities were now calculated in such a way that they would not exceed existing rents levels, while landlords received the purchase money in advance as a cash payment, with the added incentive of a twelve per cent bonus upon the successful completion of the sale.¹⁴⁸ When the O'Conor Don passed away at Clonalis House on 30 June 1906, the majority of his Roscommon estates were still intact and bequeathed to his eldest son and heir, Denis Charles O'Conor. In addition to the landed estates, the O'Conor Don left £33,272 4s. 4d. in his will. Of that, £20,000 was left to Denis Charles, with Charles and Owen getting £4,000 each if they entered a religious order. £300 was left to the bishop of Elphin and £200 to charities of Ellen O'Conor's choice. Ellen was left the Granite Hall real estate at Kingstown.¹⁴⁹ However, in December of that year, Denis sold 5,471 acres under the 1903 land act for £57,160. What this suggests is that although there was some reluctance on the O'Conor Don's part to sell, it seems very likely that the purchase terms for the Wyndham sale were agreed before he passed away.

In February 1909, a further 572 acres was sold by Denis Charles for £10,496 to the Congested Districts Board – the Cartronmore and Carrowgarve lands.¹⁵⁰ No land was sold under the less favourable terms of Birrell's 1909 land act, which offered no bonus and reverted back to payment in land stock. This was not unusual, however, as it was not uncommon for landlords who were initially reluctant to avail of Wyndham's 1903 act to rush to sell under its terms before

---

145 Diary of the O'Conor Don, Feb. 1893, O'Conor papers, CH, 9.4.SH.247. 146 *Return of advances under the Purchase of Land (Ireland) Act, 1891, 1899–1900*, HC 1900 (302), lxix, 757, pp 144–7; *Return of advances … 1900–1901*, HC 1901 (308), lxi, 563, p. 228; *Return of advances … 1901–1902*, HC 1902 (334), lxxxiv, 929, pp 244, 265; *Return of advances … 1902–1903*, HC 1903 (335), lvii, 31, pp 229, 258. 147 Dooley, *The decline of the Big House*, p. 114. 148 F. Campbell, *Land and revolution: nationalist politics in the west of Ireland, 1891–1921* (New York, 2005), p. 79; Purdue, *The Big House*, pp 82–3; Dooley, *The decline of the Big House*, p. 113. 149 G.L.G. Norgate & A. O'Day, 'O'Conor, Charles Owen', *ODNB*; *Irish News*, 21 Sept. 1906. 150 Abstract of the sale of the estate of Denis Charles O'Conor, Apr. 1906, Land commission papers, DAFF, box 237/schedule K/no. 3/record no. E.C. 1119A; Abstract of title for the sale of lands to the Congested Districts Board, May 1908, Land commission papers, DAFF, box 237/schedule A/no.5/record no. CDB6452.

the terms of Birrell's act of 1909 came into force.[151] In total, then, between 1879 and 1909, some 8,333 out of 12,650 acres of untenanted O'Conor lands were sold for £87,117. However, 1,143 acres in demesne and other lands around Clonalis and Ballinagare were re-purchased under Wyndham's act for £18,875. The incentive here for Denis Charles O'Conor was to sell and re-purchase lands held directly by him for the same price, while at the same time benefitting from the twelve percent bonus on the overall sale under the Wyndham act. Therefore, in 1909, Denis Charles was still the owner of some 5,452 acres, 1,143 of which was untenanted.[152] Another 2,768 acres was sold to the CDB in 1916, while a further 2,260 acres was sold in 1934 under the Irish Free State land acts. Although the latter included almost all the untenanted land around Clonalis and Ballingare, marking the end of an era of O'Conor Don dominance in landownership, the lateness of the sale demonstrates the strength of the family's attachment to the land.[153]

In the end, while the O'Conor Don embarked on the sale and attempted sale of his lands from 1879 onwards, he was, like Lord Clonbrock, 'too sentimentally attached' to let go completely.[154] Indeed, in a speech to the Irish Landowners' Convention on the 1903 land act, he remarked how he was, like many Irish landlords, reluctant to sell the 'old lands' and break the 'old relationship' with his tenants.[155] This was evidently the case with the lands of Clonalis and Ballinagare, some of which he farmed himself and on which were two of the three old seats of O'Conor power in County Roscommon. By comparison in the county, the absentee Lord Dillon sold all of his Roscommon estate to the CDB in 1899; most of the Crofton estate was sold in the 1890s; most of the King-Harman estate was sold under Wyndham's act after 1903; and the combative Lord De Freyne sold almost all of his estates to the CDB in 1906. The latter two were much larger estates than the O'Conor Don's, but both families had their financial troubles and did not have the same consistently cordial relations with their tenants. The King-Harmans, King-Tenisons, De Freynes, Croftons, Pakenham-Mahons and Talbots all maintained a reduced presence in Roscommon until well after the creation of the Irish Free State in 1922,[156] but the O'Conors were different and have remained in place until the present day.

151 Dooley, *The decline of the Big House*, pp 114–16. 152 Abstract of the sale of the estate of Denis Charles O'Conor, Apr. 1906, Land commission papers, DAFF, record no. E.C. 1119A); Abstract of title for the sale of lands to the Congested Districts Board, May 1908, Land commission papers, DAFF, box 237/schedule A/no. 5/record no. CDB6452; *Return of untenanted lands in rural districts, distinguishing demesnes on which there is a mansion, showing: rural district and electoral division; townland; area in statute acres; valuation (poor law); names of occupiers as in valuation lists (land-landlord and tenant (Ireland): untenanted lands)*, HC 1906 (250), c. 177, pp 380–2. 153 Court of the Irish land commission (Land Acts 1923–33), Land commission papers, DAFF, box 8169/schedule B/no. 6/record no. S.5103; For O'Conor Don sales in 1916, see CMLED. 154 Dooley, *The decline of the Big House*, p. 116. 155 C.O. O'Conor, *The Irish land bill, 1903: speech of the right hon. the O'Conor Don at the Irish Landowners' Convention, Dublin, 24 April, 1903* (Dublin, 1903), pp 11–12. 156 Connolly, *Landed estates*, pp 118, 157, 177; Dyer Wolf, 'Two windows', p. 140

4 / 'Let them get rid of the landlords altogether': the O'Conor Don and land reform, 1860–1903

In 1878, during a house of commons debate on land reform, the O'Conor Don stated his support for a policy of compulsory state-aided land purchase, so as to enable the wholesale transfer of land from landlords to tenant farmers.[1] As an alternative to the popular call for free sale, fixity of tenure and fair rents (the 3fs), it was seen as too radical and/or self-interested by most nationalists, liberals and conservatives in parliament. The practice of tenant right – compensation for tenants' improvements and the right to sell the value of these improvements – was conceded in Gladstone's 1870 land act, and this was followed by the fixing of tenure and rents in Gladstone's second land act in 1881. Broadly speaking, these land acts instituted a type of dual ownership, overseen by the government through the land commission, that satisfied neither landlord nor tenant. Therefore, the idea of a scheme of state-aided land purchase – where the state would purchase land from the landlords and lend the purchase price of the land to the tenant farmer, who would then pay it back over a long number of years – became more popular in parliament once the issue of home rule became a live one in 1885–6. Indeed, it was supported by liberals, conservatives and unionists who opposed home rule, as well as liberals and nationalists who supported it. But a policy of voluntary land purchase prevailed in the various land acts between 1885 and 1903, with compulsory purchase not implemented until the 1909 land act.

The O'Conor Don's support for compulsory land purchase was therefore ahead of its time. But the idea of a landlord proposing a radical policy to address the highly contentious issue of land ownership in Ireland is not one that sits well in a history of the land question that has, understandably, focused on landlord-tenant relations before and during the Famine, as well as the long years of land agitations between 1879 and 1909.[2] Irish landlords were of course a self-interested group, but they did have views on the subject of land reform that were not entirely based on the opportunism of availing of favourable land purchase schemes when Conservative governments were seeking to 'pacify' Ireland and 'kill' home rule with 'kindness' towards the end

---

1 HC Deb., 6 Feb. 1878, vol. 237, cc 1193–4. 2 Pomfret, *The struggle for land*; Donnelly, *The land and people*; Vaughan, *Landlords and tenants*; Steele, *Irish land and British politics*; Dooley, *The decline of the Big House*; Purdue, *The Big House*; Campbell, *Land and revolution*; P. Bew, *Land and the national question in Ireland, 1858–82* (Dublin, 1978); idem, *Conflict and conciliation in Ireland, 1890–1910 – Parnellites and radical agrarians* (New York, 1987); B.L. Solow, *The land question and the Irish economy* (Cambridge, 1971).

of the nineteenth century.³ The O'Conor Don's support for land purchase was shaped by self-interest and other political motivations, but it was not entirely shaped by these factors. A paternalistic landlord who adopted an even-handed approach to estate management, he knew his tenants well and this informed his views on land reform. He was also a firm believer in the benefits of private ownership while at the same time believing in a form of political economy that advocated, where necessary, greater state intervention in the economy for the public good. He therefore moved from a moderate position of endorsing tenant right in the mid-1860s to the advanced position of supporting state-aided land purchase in the mid-1870s. From that point on, through to the first large-scale land purchase act of 1903, the O'Conor Don played a significant, although often isolated role in pushing the idea of land purchase forward. He did so by arguing that only compulsory purchase would facilitate a transfer of land on the extensive scale required to create a numerous class of owner-occupiers with an interest in protecting property rights, upholding the rule of law and maintaining political stability in Ireland.

TENANT RIGHT AND THE 1870 LAND ACT

When the young O'Conor Don declared his support for tenant right in his 1860 election address, it seems likely that he did so without much knowledge or conviction. He had, after all, no experience of estate management or political affairs at that point. The MacDermots did, however, keep him abreast of both when he was at Downside, so he probably had at least a vague idea of what tenant right meant and of the recent history of political agitation on the issue through the tenant-right movement and the Independent Irish Party in the 1850s.[4]

He certainly had a distinct boyhood memory of the Famine, handing out provisions to tenants at Clonalis with his brother and aunt.[5] It was during the Famine that the poverty and insecurity of Ireland's small tenant farmers and landless labourers became such an acute problem, with an estimated million people dying and millions more emigrating due to the repeated failure of the potato crop and the mostly inept response of the British state to the crisis. However, the inequality of the majority of land being in the hands of a

---

3 P. Bull, *Land, politics and nationalism: a study of the Irish land question* (Dublin, 1996); A. Gailey, *Ireland and the death of kindness: the experience of constructive unionism, 1890–1905* (Cork, 1987).   4 Letters from Thomas & Roderick MacDermot to the O'Conor Don re estate matters and politics, n.d. & 4 May 1856, O'Conor papers, CH, 9.3.HE.055.   5 See chapter two, p. 40.

small minority of landlords was seen as a major contributing factor.[6] In 1846, the Catholic nationalist leader Daniel O'Connell, himself a large landlord in County Kerry, called for the legalization of some form of tenant right. That same year, the Protestant radical William Sharman Crawford, a landlord in County Down, formed the Ulster Tenant Right Association.[7] In 1850, the Tenant Right League formed under the leadership of the former Young Irelander Charles Gavan Duffy, and the English Catholic convert Frederick Lucas, demanding the 3fs.[8] The Independent Irish Party was also formed in 1850 as the parliamentary wing of the tenant-right movement, with Duffy, Lucas and George Henry Moore at its head. It had the support of radicals, nationalists and liberals, with forty-two candidates pledging to form an independent party in the commons after 1852 general election.[9] When William Keogh and John Sadlier accepted junior government positions in Lord Aberdeen's Liberal-Peelite ministry in 1853, the credibility of the party was shattered.[10] Thereafter, opposition to any kind of tenant-right legislation in a landlord-dominated house of commons contributed to the party's demise. Lord Palmerston, the owner of large estates in England and Ireland, epitomized this opposition, having once labelled tenant right as landlord wrong. When Palmerston became prime minister in February 1855, any remaining hopes of progress on the issue were well and truly quashed.[11] In the meantime, the liberal policy of encouraging a free market in land, as a way to create a more numerous, supposedly thriftier class of landowners, was implemented through the encumbered and landed estates courts. As already demonstrated, the O'Conor Don and other large and medium-sized Catholic landowners availed of this policy by purchasing tens of thousands of acres through the landed estates court.[12]

In his early years as landlord, then, the O'Conor Don was probably supportive of the idea of tenant right as a way to compensate tenants for their improvements, while at the same time taking advantage of the opportunity provided by his inheritance and buying up more land. Reality soon kicked in, however, with successive bad harvests, the partial failure of the potato crop

---

6 C. Kinealy, *This great calamity: the Irish Famine, 1845–52* (Dublin, 2006); P. Gray, *Famine, land and politics: British government and Irish society, 1843–50* (Dublin, 1999).   7 Gray, *Famine, land and politics*, pp 151–3; S. Lee & A. O'Day, 'Crawford, William Sharman', *ODNB*.   8 P. Bew & F. Wright, 'The agrarian opposition in Ulster politics, 1848–87' in S. Clark & J.S. Donnelly Jnr, *Irish peasants: violence and political unrest, 1780–1914* (Madison, WI, 1983), p. 194; Bull, *Land, politics and nationalism*, pp 37–8.   9 J.H. Whyte, *The Independent Irish Party, 1850–9* (London, 1958); S. Knowlton, 'The voting behaviour of the Independent Irish Party, 1850–59', *Éire-Ireland* (Spring, 1991), 57–62; Comerford, 'Churchmen, tenants, and independent opposition', pp 399–406.   10 Whyte, *Independent Irish Party*, p. 89; Knowlton, 'Independent Irish Party', pp 62–6.   11 Shields, *The Irish Conservative Party*, pp 35–7, 55–75.   12 Gray, *Famine, land and politics*, pp 151–3, 217–26. Chapter three, pp 58–62.

and the inability of many tenants to pay their rents focusing his attention in 1861–2.[13] Bishop Gillooly impressed the urgency of the situation upon him towards the end of 1861, requesting that he and other prominent landlords in the county make an appeal to the lord lieutenant on the need for relief of the poverty-stricken tenant farmers.[14] The O'Conor Don obliged, leading a deputation on 14 January 1862 to Lord Carlisle, which called for the provision of outdoor relief for tenant farmers owning more than a quarter acre, as well as land-improvement loans for landlords to help create employment.[15] He did not, however, make any public calls for land reform in these early years. Indeed, as we shall see in the next chapter, the issue that he took up in parliament with the most fervour at this time was Catholic education.

It is not until 1866 that we get any real sense of the O'Conor Don's early views on land reform. In an essay on tenant right that year, he expressed the belief that 'many landlords in Ireland … would not be adverse to a measure which would secure to the tenant' some form of compensation for improvements, but he qualified this with the observation that compensation for improvements was 'a very difficult thing to define', and that the 'difficulty of legislating … on the question' lay in the 'assumption that the interests of landlord and tenant are antagonistic'. Of the rather optimistic view that 'the interests' of his tenants were not 'opposed to my own', the O'Conor Don believed this to be a false assumption, arguing that anything that benefitted the tenant, benefitted the landlord. He praised the good intentions of Gladstone, whose land bill of that year sought to provide compensation for improvements for tenants not under the obligation of a lease. But Gladstone's bill failed, and the O'Conor Don's optimism is perhaps indicative of the somewhat naïve views of a young landlord and politician. Nonetheless, he expressed some early frustration with 'English' misgovernment in Ireland, lamenting the fact that, although the 'English nation' boasted 'of its love of fair play', the natural resources of the 'sister' island were not being developed in the same way as they were in England, with the Irish people emigrating in their droves as a result.[16] This sense of Irish injustice at the hands of England was not unusual among Irish politicians of all political hues, but liberals like the O'Conor Don put great faith in Gladstone's commitment to Ireland and Irish reforms.[17]

In December 1868, Gladstone formed his first Liberal government and declared his intention to tackle the issue of land reform, as well as

---

13 *Roscommon Journal*, 17 Mar. 1860. 14 Bishop Gillooly to the O'Conor Don, 13, 18 & 29 Dec. 1861 & 8 Jan. 1862, O'Conor papers, CH, 9.3.HS.309. 15 *Freeman's Journal*, 15 Jan. 1862. 16 Essay on tenant right, 1866, Clonalis House, O'Conor papers, 9.3.HL.308; B. Kinzer, *England's disgrace?: J.S. Mill and the Irish question* (Toronto, 2001), pp 171–3. 17 See chapter five, p. 116.

disestablishing the Church of Ireland and reforming Ireland's university system. The O'Conor Don was preoccupied with the issue of a Fenian amnesty at this time, but tenant-right associations were cropping up around the country and County Roscommon was no different.[18] At a meeting in Roscommon town on 29 November 1869, it was resolved that relations between landlord and tenant were 'unsatisfactory' and required not only legislating for tenant right, but for fixity of tenure and fair rents. The O'Conor Don was in attendance and agreed to convey these views to Gladstone, but the bill introduced by the latter on 15 February 1870 did not propose legislating for the 3fs. Rather it sought to legalize the practice of tenant right where it existed, granting compensation for improvements upon the quitting of a lease or for disturbance upon eviction. After pressure from the radical MP and cabinet member John Bright, Gladstone included a clause that gave tenants the option of purchasing their holdings by borrowing two-thirds of the price from the government, but only if the landlord was willing to sell.[19] Conceding the principle of an extremely limited form of land purchase in Ireland was, at this stage, preferable to conceding the principle of the state fixing land tenure and rent. This was all to change eleven years later.

The majority of Irish landlords in the commons, including the O'Conor Don, supported Gladstone's land bill and it passed through both houses without much trouble, becoming law in August 1870.[20] Such landlord acceptance was not particularly surprising given that many already allowed some form of tenant right to operate on their estates, which meant the bill did not significantly alter their existing position.[21] This was the case with the O'Conor Don, but he would have preferred it if Gladstone had incorporated a scheme for the purchase of tenant right, at a rate of ten years the annual rental, as suggested by the former judge of the landed estates court, Mountifort Longfield.[22] His support for such a scheme at this stage would suggest that he was at least considering the idea of some form of state-funded solution to make tenant farmers owners in their own right.

The failure of the 1870 land act to accomplish what it set out to achieve has been well documented by historians. In the first instance, it became clear

18 V. Crossman, *Politics, law and order in nineteenth-century Ireland* (Dublin, 1996), pp 114–15. See chapter five, p. 116; see chapter six, pp 143–8. 19 Circular of Roscommon tenant-right meeting, 29 Nov. 1869 (Clonalis House, O'Conor papers, 9.3.HE.173); Vaughan, *Landlords and tenants*, pp 93–102; Bull, *Land, politics and nationalism*, pp 52–3; Steele, *Irish land and British politics*, pp 298–315. 20 HC Deb., 7 Mar. 1870, vol. 199, cc 1406–7; ibid., 8 Mar. 1870, vol. 199, c. 1583; ibid., 28 Mar. 1870, vol. 200, cc 764–5; ibid., 14 June 1870, vol. 202, cc 60–2; ibid., 10 Aug. 1870, vol. 202, c. 1792; Steele, *Irish land and British politics*, pp 298–315; Potter, *William Monsell*, p. xii; A. Jackson, *Colonel Edward Saunderson: land and loyalty in Victorian Ireland* (New York, 1995), p. 34. 21 Purdue, *The Big House*, pp 34–6; F. Thompson, *The end of liberal Ulster: land agitation and land reform, 1868–1886* (Belfast, 2001), p. 61. 22 HC Deb., 29 June 1876, vol. 230, cc 674–86; S.P. Donlan, 'Longfield, Mountifort', *DIB*.

that the absence of a precise definition of tenant right allowed for evasive action on the part of landlords in dealing with their tenants' claims. Even when claims were admitted, the legal process was so cumbersome and expensive that it largely favoured the landlord. Moreover, because rents were not regulated by the act, landlords could easily raise them and subsequently evict their tenants if they could not afford the increase. In general, rents were not raised and landlords preferred to draw up new leases that would not fall under the remit of the act, but Gladstone's aim of curbing landlord power did not succeed and landlord-tenant relations carried on much the same as before.[23]

ISAAC BUTT'S LAND BILL

When the leader of the Home Rule Party, Isaac Butt, introduced his land bill in March 1876, he identified the threat of eviction and the consequent lack of secure tenure as the outstanding issues consequent from Gladstone's land act. Butt therefore sought to place the principle of tenant right on a firmer footing by making provision for fixity of tenure at a fair rent, along with free sale of the interest on the holding. Once again, this was a call for the full implementation of the 3fs.[24]

Landlord opinion on the measure was divided: the O'Conor Don, Myles O'Reilly and Arthur Kavanagh opposed the bill while the O'Donoghue and Rowland Ponsonby Blennerhassett supported it.[25] In his speech on the bill in June 1876, the O'Conor Don argued that fixity of tenure across the board would be unworkable because of the diversity of existing lease arrangements, which, if interfered with, would undermine freedom of contract and what he believed were the cordial arrangements that existed between many landlords and tenants. But the major concern for him was combining fixity of tenure with fixed rents, which he felt would wholly undermine the principle of private ownership, making the landlord a 'mere rent charger', disinterested in making improvements or compensating his tenants for their improvements. He argued that dual ownership of this kind could not be fairly imposed by the state without some form of compensation for landlords, given than many had recently purchased land through the landed estates court, which the state had encouraged. If the aim was to make tenant famers the owners of the land on which they worked, then 'this great and radical change' could only be achieved by making them absolute owners.[26] Although he did not elaborate on how this

23 Purdue, *The Big House*, pp 34–6; Thompson, *The end of liberal Ulster*, pp 88–103; Vaughan, *Landlords and tenants*, pp 93–102; Steele, *Irish land and British politics*, pp 312–15. 24 HC Deb., 29 Mar. 1876, vol. 237, cc 771–90. 25 Ibid., 29 Mar. 1876, vol. 228, cc 805–13. 26 HC Deb., 29 June 1876, vol. 230, cc 624–714.

might be achieved, the O'Conor Don was clearly concerned with preserving freedom of contract and protecting ownership rights from government regulation. Since at least 1866 he had been happy to admit the justice of tenant right, but he had also considered Longfield's proposals for state-aided purchase of tenant right in 1870. Moreover, having paid out 'large sums' in tenant right, he had perhaps concluded that fixity of tenure would more or less extinguish his interest in his own land, much of which he had paid for in hard cash through the landed estates court.[27]

The view that fixity of tenure would undermine existing property rights was certainly shared by Colonel Charles Raleigh Chichester, a relatively small and largely unknown English Catholic landlord, who had married into the Balfe family of Southpark, Castlerea, and resided at Runnamoat, near Roscommon town, when in Ireland.[28] In a letter to the O'Conor Don in August 1876, Chichester delivered a damning critique of Gladstone's land act, which he felt had instituted a system of 'joint proprietorship' that was 'immoral and vicious politically and ignoring human nature'. It was so because, as Chichester went on to argue, 'where there is a joint proprietorship Human nature prompts either or both of the co-proprietors to get rid of each other'. As for Butt's bill, he congratulated the O'Conor Don on his speech, describing it 'as a very valuable attempt to put public opinions in this much-be-bothered-by-agitators country … in a wholesome state'. Because Chichester was certain that fixity of tenure would 'practically' get 'rid of the landlord' and transfer 'the land encumbered with a rent charge to the tenant', he felt the only alternative was to make it so 'that the land should belong absolutely to either' the landlord or the tenant.[29]

Chichester and the O'Conor Don were well known to each other, moving in the same gentry circles in County Roscommon; and although the extent to which the O'Conor Don's views were influenced by Chichester's is not entirely clear, it seems likely that they at least exchanged views on land reform. In a further commons debate on Butt's bill in March 1877, the O'Conor Don, in a way that reflected Chichester's views, declared that the British state now had to 'face the matter boldly – let them get rid of the landlords altogether, pay them the money value of their rights, and secure the occupiers as owners both really and nominally, and leave them free'. A pretty astonishing turn of phrase for any landlord, he nonetheless went on to state that this was the only 'statesman-like course' of action to take because introducing fixity of tenure and creating a set of new government regulations to determine the relationship between

27 See chapter three, pp 60–2. 28 Diary of Charles Raleigh Chichester, 1866, Chichester papers, HHC, DDCH/102. There are frequent mentions of country house visits in County Roscommon. 29 Raleigh Chichester to the O'Conor Don, 6 Aug. 1876, Clonalis House, O'Conor papers, 9.4.HS.133.

landlord and tenant was bound to fail.³⁰ One year later, in another debate on the bill, he declared that the only way to bring about this radical transfer of land in Ireland was through compulsory purchase by the state. Although willing to admit that his ideas were in stark contrast to the principle involved in Butt's bill, the O'Conor Don believed such a policy would deal head-on with 'the evil which was sought to be removed'. Moreover, he ambitiously envisaged that such a radical transfer of land would:

> tend to establish an independent class of yeomen in Ireland, everyone one of them interested in preserving freedom of contract for the future, everyone of them interested in maintaining law, and order, and the institutions of the country. He thought that for the establishment of such a class in Ireland no sacrifices would be too great; and, as a landlord himself, he would only say that he would be willing to give up any of the rights to which he had been alluding, if that result could only be brought about.³¹

Not too discretely hidden between the lines here is, one suspects, an argument against home rule: assist the tenant farmer in becoming a landowner and disgruntlement with the political status quo might be appeased. As chapter six will demonstrate, the O'Conor Don opposed Butt's federal home rule scheme in 1873, so it would seem reasonable to suggest that his thinking on land reform was influenced by his opposition to home rule. Indeed, the O'Conor Don had already joined the two issues together, arguing in a debate on Butt's land bill in 1876 that it would have little prospect of gaining the assent of a prospective Irish house of lords, which would be entirely comprised of landlords.³²

Other political motivations aside, it was not that unusual for landlords to propose radical policies. Henry Villers Stuart, a Liberal MP for Waterford in 1873 and 1880–5, supported state-aided land purchase and state provision of houses and allotments for agricultural labourers.³³ However, although the O'Conor Don's proposal for compulsory purchase was a radical one in the house of commons at the time, he was not the first to advocate state intervention for the creation of a class of owner-occupiers in Ireland. The English political economists William Thornton Thompson and John Stuart Mill both advocated this policy in the 1840s and 1850s, although the former favoured the even more radical policy of land nationalization.³⁴ Whether the O'Conor Don was influenced

---

30 HC Deb., 21 Mar. 1877, vol. 233, c. 296.   31 Ibid., 6 Feb. 1878, vol. 237, cc 1193–4.   32 HC Deb., 29 June 1876, vol. 230, cc 674–86.   33 Ian d'Alton, 'A "first voice": Henry Villers Stuart (1827–95) and the cause of the Irish agricultural labourers' in Casey (ed.), *Defying the law of the land*, pp 164–70.   34 W.T. Thompson, *A plea for peasant proprietors; with the outlines of a plan for their establishment in Ireland* (London, 1848); Kinzer, *England's disgrace?*, pp 4–5, 53–6, 108–17; Steele, *Irish land and British politics*, pp 48–55.

by Thompson or Mill is not known for certain, but it seems likely that Mill's work crossed his path. He was influenced by the work of Mill's friend, the Irish economist and academic John Elliott Cairnes; and both Mill and Cairnes were advocates of a new type of political economy, which, through a combination of 'English theory and Irish facts', sought to modify the worst effects of *laissez-faire* capitalism by advocating unprecedent levels of state intervention in the market to secure tenure and rent and facilitate ownership for tenant farmers.[35] The O'Conor Don did not wholly subscribe to Mill's thinking on Irish land reform, given that he rejected fixity of tenure as the wrong kind of state intervention, even as an interim measure. Nonetheless, he clearly embraced the idea that the state should intervene to enable tenant farmers to own land and to compensate landlords for their loss. This aligned him closely with the views of fellow landlord Lord Dufferin, who was also influenced by Mill's thinking on Irish land reform. The O'Conor Don stayed with Dufferin at Clandeboy, County Down, in 1867, and was influenced by his views on land reform.[36]

THE BACKLASH

At a public meeting in Roscommon town in March 1876, the O'Conor Don was roundly criticized for his opposition to Butt's bill and the principle of fixity of tenure. His response to this criticism did nothing to help his case. In a decidedly Burkean interpretation of what he thought the role of an MP ought to be, the O'Conor Don claimed to have 'never solicited the honor of representing' the county 'on any condition except that he should be at perfect liberty to act as his conscience dictated to him, and he never would accept the position on any other terms'.[37] Echoing these sentiments in a commons debate on the bill the following June, he argued that while he owed his present position to the electors of Roscommon, he was convinced that MPs were required 'to do something more than record our votes in favour of proposals that might be approved by our constituents'.[38]

Although declaring such views made a bad situation worse, the O'Conor Don's land purchase proposals were also the target of criticism. In February

35 C. Ó Gráda, 'Cairnes, John Elliot', *DIB*; T. Duddy, *A history of Irish thought* (London & New York, 2002), pp 243–50. 36 F. Clarke, 'Blackwood, Frederick Temple Hamilton-Temple', *DIB*. See below for the O'Conor Don's endorsement of Dufferin's views, p. 82. See also F. Temple Blackwood, *Irish emigration and the tenure of land in Ireland* (London, 1867); J.E. Cairnes, *The character and logical method of political economy* (London, 1857); idem, *Political essays* (London, 1873); idem, *Some leading principles of political economy newly expounded* (London, 1874). The O'Conor Don possessed copies of all three, which are still on display in the library at Clonalis House. 37 *Roscommon Journal*, 11 Mar. 1876. 38 HC Deb., 29 June 1876, vol. 230, cc 674–86.

1878, the *Boyle Herald* dismissed them as the impractical musings of a self-interested landlord.[39] But despite his growing unpopularity, an olive branch of sorts was extended at a Land League meeting in Castlerea in December 1879 when Martin McDonnell, a local organizer, remarked that if the O'Conor Don 'could be got to put his views into the groove adopted by Mr. Parnell he would be as good a representative as they could have'.[40] Parnell was, of course, a landlord himself, but he had been one of the leading 'obstructionist' nationalist MPs in parliament since his election in 1875, seeking to disrupt the ordinary business of the House by making long-winded speeches. In 1877, he stated his support for Butt's bill while at the same time endorsing land purchase as the best long-term solution to the land question. By 1879, Parnell had formed an informal alliance with the leader of the Land League, Michael Davitt, and the leader of Clan na Gael in America, John Devoy. This alliance became known as the 'New Departure', bringing together the forces of moderate nationalism, republicanism and agrarianism to further the causes of land reform and home rule.[41]

It would seem that Parnell was keen to get the O'Conor Don on board with this new style of politics in the run-up to the general election of April 1880, but this was never going to work on a man with such liberal sensibilities. As a result, at a public meeting in Roscommon on the eve of polling day, Parnell scolded the assembled crowd for their 'reluctance ... to part ... with a gentleman like The O'Conor Don', who he declared was nothing more than 'a symbol of West Britonism in Ireland ... [and] of the rights of England and Englishmen to rule Ireland'.[42] This was a classic piece of electioneering that sought to portray the O'Conor Don as someone who was more British than Irish and therefore did not have the best interests of Ireland at heart. Notwithstanding the irony of an Anglo-Irish landlord labelling anyone a 'West Briton', Parnell's depiction of the O'Conor Don as a patsy for English rule in Ireland was of course unfair. The O'Conor Don moved in Anglo-Irish circles, and he was opposed to federal home rule, but this did not make him any less Irish, any more than Parnell's Anglo-Irish background made him any less Irish. Often critical of what he saw as English misgovernment in Ireland, the O'Conor Don was a liberal and a patriotic Irishman. Nonetheless, his views on land reform and home rule were unpopular. Parnell knew this and, neatly combining the two issues, he told the assembled crowd in Roscommon that:

> The dismissal of The O'Conor Don from your representation will be a warning sent out from Roscommon that Ireland is still determined to

39 *Roscommon Journal*, 9 Feb. 1878.   40 Ibid., 13 Dec. 1879.   41 HC Deb., 1 May 1877, vol. 234, cc 177–80; *Nation*, 23 Nov. 1878; F.S.L. Lyons, *Charles Stewart Parnell* (Dublin, 2005), pp 60–108.   42 *Roscommon Journal*, 3 Apr. 1880.

recover her own Parliament. It will be a declaration that Ireland believes in the right of the tillers of the soil to live in their soil free from the arbitratory [sic] caprice of rack-renting landlords.[43]

This portrayal of the O'Conor Don as the enemy of home rule and the tenant farmer was a deciding factor in his election defeat on 6 April 1880, although, as we shall see later, hubris about his invincibility played a significant part too. A letter from a disgruntled supporter informed him that 'it is your own fault that you are not returned wit[h] a large majority' because the 'tenant farmers ... were led to believe you did not take sufficient interest in the "Land Question"'.[44] The O'Conor Don did, of course, take a keen interest in the land question; the problem was his interest in it appeared to be opposed to that of the tenant farmer. When the policy of land purchase was endorsed at a Land League conference on 29 and 30 April 1880, the O'Conor Don must have been left wondering where he went wrong. But support for the 3fs was still preferred by many within the League on the grounds that it was realistically achievable, while Michael Davitt was against a proposed scheme of twenty years purchase, arguing that it was too generous an offer to landlords. Parnell, on the other hand, preferred to emphasize the need for more immediate measures like the writing-off of arrears to prevent the eviction of the more vulnerable small tenant farmers. Such ambiguity suited Parnell given his reluctance to attach himself to a position that the new Liberal government might be unlikely to accept. In an effort to tone down the League's land purchase scheme amid accusations from the moderate nationalist *Freeman's Journal* that he supported 'complete confiscation', he subsequently recommended the appointment of a government commission for the orderly transfer of land.[45] Although this was a less radical policy than the O'Conor Don's, it was more politically astute.

THE 1881 LAND ACT

Regardless of his election defeat the O'Conor Don still maintained a high public profile as a member of the land law commission in 1880. More commonly known as the 'Bessborough commission' – named so after its chair, the sixth earl of Bessborough – it was set up to investigate the effects of Gladstone's 1870 land act and make suggestions for remedial legislation. When

---

43 *Roscommon Journal*, 3 Apr. 1880.   44 Anon. to the O'Conor Don, Apr. 1880, O'Conor papers, CH, 9.4.HS.083.   45 Lyons, *Parnell*, pp 123–4; Bew, *Land and the national question*, pp 99–106.

the commission published its report in January 1881, the full implementation of the 3fs was the recommended course of action. Although he consented to put his signature to the commission's final report, the O'Conor Don submitted a separate report that, despite Bessborough's opposition, outlined his support for state-aided compulsory land purchase as the best solution.[46] He argued that simply reviewing and attempting to reform the current land laws would not suffice because:

> any Act based merely or mainly on proposals [to modify] the conditions under which the occupier is brought into relation with the owner, will be only like the Act of 1870, a mere temporary expedient, fit for a transition period, but containing within itself the seeds of failure as a permanent settlement.[47]

Although the O'Conor Don admitted to the Irish chief secretary, W.E. Forster, that 'security of tenure' was the popular demand, and that it might lead to 'the greatest inducement to the carrying out of improvements', he insisted that 'the most perfect form of security would be ownership'. Furthermore, he rejected Forster's suggestion that compulsory purchase was an unrealistic proposal. Citing Lord Dufferin, the O'Conor Don argued that a scheme could be financed by the issuance of government-backed bonds to the banks, with tenants in turn borrowing the purchase money from the banks at twenty-two and a half times the annual rent, repayable at four per cent interest over fifty-two years. Landlords, for their part, could sell on the basis of receiving payment in the guaranteed bonds.[48] While the O'Conor Don admitted that many of the landlords questioned before the commission were opposed the idea of compulsory purchase, he believed 'the disadvantages of having the ownership of land held by a mere handful of the population' ought to be the overriding concern for the government.[49]

The O'Conor Don's reference to Lord Dufferin was timely. In January 1881, Dufferin once again declared his support for the creation of peasant proprietorships in a pamphlet for the Irish Land Committee.[50] Much like the O'Conor Don, he thought the 1870 land act had sown the seeds of discontent by putting the tenant 'into the same bed with his landlord', which in turn

---

46 *Report of Her Majesty's commissioners of inquiry into the working of the Landlord and Tenant (Ireland) Act, 1870, and the acts amending the same*, HC 1881 (73) xviii & (825) xxix, pp 38–46. Hereafter referred to as *Bessborough commission*; Earl of Bessborough to the O'Conor Don, 25 Dec. 1880, O'Conor papers, CH, 9.4.HS.219; R.A. Jones, 'Ponsonby, Frederick George Brabazon, sixth earl of Bessborough', *ODNB*. 47 *Bessborough commission*, pp 38–46. 48 The O'Conor Don to W.E. Forster, n.d. but most likely Dec. 1880 or Jan. 1881, Gladstone papers, BL, add. 44158, f. 97. 49 *Bessborough commission*, pp 38, 45–6. 50 F. Temple Blackwood, *The land question, Ireland*, vi: *Lord Dufferin on the three f's* (Dublin, 1881), pp 1–22.

resulted in the tenant attempting 'to kick his landlord out of the bed'. The implementation of the 3fs, he argued, would indicate the government's willingness to appease the agitations of the Land League 'by giving the tenant a little more of the bed', the effect of which he claimed would be to encourage the tenant to 'say to himself, "One kick more, and the villain is on the floor"'. Again, much like the O'Conor Don, Dufferin concluded that the aim of such a radical transfer of land was to 'render Ireland conservative' by making tenant famers owners 'upon a very extensive scale', thereby making it in their 'interest ... to support law and order, recognise the sanctity of property, and the reasonableness and necessity of rent'.[51]

Having gotten into considerable debt and consequently sold most of his County Down estates by the mid-1870s, Dufferin was hardly an impartial advocate of land purchase.[52] But he did not see land purchase as the only solution. For the numerous tenant farmers on poor quality land in the west of Ireland, Dufferin argued that it would be impossible to try and 'convert these poor people into peasant proprietors', even if the land was given to them 'for nothing'. He therefore reasoned that emigration was 'the only remedy' to the problems facing this part of the country, it being 'simply inhuman to perpetuate from generation to generation a state of things which has been deplored by every traveller who has visited those parts during the last eighty years'.[53] The O'Conor Don and the County Carlow landlord Arthur Kavanagh both agreed, supporting a policy of state-assisted emigration from parts of counties Kerry, Clare, Galway and Mayo. Although Kavanagh opposed land purchase, he argued that assisted emigration was the only way to alleviate distress in these areas because the tenant farmers were 'simply labourers with farms' who could get no employment other than in the harvest time of the year. The O'Conor Don concurred, arguing that the evidence put before the commission demonstrated that over-population on unworkable land was the genesis of the problem in distressed areas, with rent levels having little or no effect on the overall situation.[54]

In the end, the O'Conor Don's and Dufferin's pleas for land purchase made no impression on Gladstone and his government. Quite the contrary. In a letter to Forster on 7 December 1880, Gladstone expressed his 'alarm' at the suggestion 'that the State i.e. the people of the country are to compensate the Irish landowners ... for a portion of their property, now to be taken away from them'. He described the O'Conor Don's proposals as 'utterly wild', worrying what effect they might have 'on the public mind'. Under increasing pressure

---

51 Blackwood, *The land question*, pp 14–16. 52 L.P. Curtis, 'Incumbered wealth: landed indebtedness in post-Famine Ireland', *American Historical Review*, 85:2 (Apr. 1980), p. 359. 53 Blackwood, *The land question*, p. 22. 54 *Bessborough commission*, pp 51, 60.

from the agitations of the Land League, and a strengthened Home Rule Party under Parnell's leadership, Gladstone ruefully observed that the proper course of action for the Bessborough commissioners would have been to 'simply ... record their differences in a few general terms ... rather than produce Essays some of which might act as firebrands'.[55] Not surprisingly then, the implementation of the 3fs was the course adopted by Gladstone in his 1881 land act. Parnell and the Home Rule Party tentatively supported the measure with a view to 'testing' it to see how it might work. There were, however, radical nationalists such as Jasper Tully and Matt Harris who condemned it as a feeble attempt to shore up the institution of landlordism.[56] Ironically, Harris, a relentless and severe critic of Irish landlords, congratulated the O'Conor Don on his views on land purchase in July 1881, remarking how 'he was much struck by the similarity of our views on some important points'.[57]

As it turned out, the 1881 land act introduced a form of dual ownership between landlord and tenant that ultimately satisfied neither party. The fixing of rents by the newly established land commission proved to be a cumbersome and expensive process for tenant farmers, while the general result for landlords was a reduction in their incomes and in their ability to set rent levels. The arrears act of 1882 was another blow to landlords' revenues, but some fared better than others, with the O'Conor Don's losses in rental income amounting to a minor setback when viewed in the context of twenty years of expansion as a landlord.[58]

LANDLORDS AND LAND PURCHASE, 1885–96

As the effects of Gladstone's second land act became more and more apparent, increasing numbers of landlords began to advocate land purchase.[59] William Monsell (now Lord Emly) had been inclined to favour fixity of tenure, but was now willing to support land purchase so that 'a greater proportion of the population' could have a 'stake in the status quo'.[60] Christopher Redington, the duke of Abercorn, the earls of Antrim and Belmore, and Lord De Vesci were all, by the mid-1880s, advocates of some form of land purchase.[61] In 1884, Sir Rowland Blennerhassett published a pamphlet, which, similar to Parnell,

---

55 H.C.G. Matthew (ed.), *The Gladstone diaries with cabinet minutes and prime-ministerial correspondence*, ix: *January 1875–December 1880* (Oxford, 1986), pp 630–1. 56 Bew, *Land and the national question*, pp 99–132; Vaughan, *Landlords and tenants*, p. 226. 57 Matt Harris to the O'Conor Don, 5 July 1881, O'Conor papers, CH, 9.4.HE.206. 58 Purdue, *The Big House*, pp 48–63. See chapter three, pp 70–4. 59 Purdue, *The Big House*, pp 49–50. 60 Potter, *William Monsell*, p. 71. 61 Murphy, *The Redingtons*, p. 246; Purdue, *The Big House*, pp 64–72; Lord De Vesci to O'Conor Don, 17 June 1885, O'Conor papers, CH, 9.4.HS.215.

endorsed the setting up of a government commission 'for the purpose of converting large tracts of Irish land into peasant properties'. Like the O'Conor Don and Monsell, one of Blennerhassett's chief motivations for supporting the policy of land purchase was the desire to see 'the pacification of Ireland' and the protection of those with a legitimate 'interest' in 'property of any kind'.[62]

In January 1885, Edward William O'Brien, son of the Young Irelander William Smith O'Brien, joined the chorus, informing the O'Conor Don that he was convinced 'there [were] many farmers who would be glad to purchase their holdings if they got a chance'.[63] More important was a letter the O'Conor Don received from Edward King-Harman in July 1885, explaining how he had 'been meeting [with] our people about a Purchase Bill', and that he was hopeful that 'something may be brought in'. Our people, as it turned out, was Edward Gibson, Irish lord chancellor in Lord Salisbury's first Conservative government. King-Harman, a Protestant landlord in County Roscommon and MP for County Dublin, warned the O'Conor Don that Gibson would be 'hard to convince' on the merits of land purchase and thought that if he wrote 'to him at once ... it would be very useful'.[64] Later that month, Gibson drew up the provisions of what became known as the Ashbourne act, named so on account of him being subsequently made Baron Ashbourne. As noted in the previous chapter, this was the first voluntary scheme of land purchase that tenant farmers could realistically avail of.[65] It is not clear how influential the O'Conor Don was in the run-up to the passing of the act, but Gibson and other leading conservatives such as W.H. Smith had been considering the idea of land purchase since 1882.[66] Whatever the case, it seems unlikely that the act went far enough for him.

What the Ashbourne act did, however, was force Gladstone and the liberals to rethink their opposition to land purchase. This rethinking was also influenced by the issue of home rule, with the likelihood of the Home Rule Party holding the balance of power in the commons after the next election a distinct possibility, and negotiations on home rule between Parnell and the conservative Irish viceroy, Lord Carnarvon, coming to light.[67] When Gladstone returned to power in February 1886 on a home rule platform, he did so with a view to incorporating a scheme of land purchase. On 16 April, eight days after

---

62 Rowland Blennerhassett, *Peasant proprietors in Ireland* (London, 1884), pp 9–12, 24–8; J. Quinn, 'Blennerhassett, Sir Rowland', *DIB*. 63 Edward O'Brien to the O'Conor Don, 25 Jan. 1885, O'Conor papers, CH, 9.4.HS.219. 64 Edward King-Harman to the O'Conor Don, 10 July 1885, O'Conor papers, CH, 9.4.HS.219. 65 See chapter three, p. 82. 66 Pomfret, *The struggle for land*, pp 222–3; P. Maume, 'Gibson, Edward (1837–1913), 1st Baron Ashbourne', *DIB*. 67 R.F. Foster, *Modern Ireland, 1600–1972* (London, 1988), p. 422; A. O'Day, *Irish home rule, 1867–1921* (Manchester, 1998), pp 97–108.

the introduction of his home rule bill, Gladstone brought forward another bill proposing the outlay of £113 million for land purchase. However, this amount was reduced to £50 million when it became clear that many within the Liberal Party were opposed to such a large sum of money being expended on what was perceived to be nothing more than a payoff for Irish landlords. Indeed, the cabinet ministers Joseph Chamberlain and G.O. Trevelyan were opposed to the bill altogether.[68]

Part of Gladstone's thinking at the time was that a favourable settlement of the land question might bring Irish landlords over to the cause of home rule, and he met privately with Parnell before the bill's introduction to discuss this very prospect.[69] However, the problem with this line of thinking was that most landlords hoped that land purchase would eventually neutralize agitation for home rule, rather than make them more amenable to it. Such reasoning was once again evident in February 1886 when Lord Monteagle speculated with the O'Conor Don on whether 'buying out the landlords compulsorily and making the tenants the owners' would put a stop to calls 'for an Irish Parliament'. The O'Conor Don hoped that land purchase would give tenant farmers an interest in protecting 'the institutions of this country', but he told Monteagle that he was not convinced that any attempt to legislatively combine the two issues would work.[70] He confirmed this position with the liberal Irish viceroy, Earl Spencer, in May 1886, arguing that it would be disingenuous of the government to 'drop the land purchase bill and ... proceed' with the home rule bill simply because 'Irish landlords did not show their willingness to accept and support the entire policy of the government in regard to Ireland'. Indeed, it caused him the greatest 'alarm' and 'the deepest disappointment' that Spencer and his 'great chief have most emphatically stated that you considered the land purchase bill simply an Act of justice' only if home rule was passed.[71] From a purely practical point of view, the O'Conor Don's assessment was correct. Gladstone's land bill stood little chance of success as long as it was wedded to the issue of home rule, but the principle of land purchase had already been conceded by the House and the bill may have passed on its own. As it turned out, both measures were defeated in the commons, which brought down Gladstone's second Liberal government.[72]

Although the liberals returned to power in 1892, Gladstone's second home rule bill was defeated in 1893 and the conservatives were the party of

---

68 G.D. Goodlad, 'The Liberal Party and Gladstone's land purchase bill of 1886', *Historical Journal*, 32:3 (Sept. 1989), 627–41; Pomfret, *The struggle for land*, pp 233–43. 69 P. Bew, *Charles Stewart Parnell* (Dublin, 1980), pp 78–85. 70 Lord Monteagle to the O'Conor Don, 4 Feb. 1886, O'Conor papers, CH, 9.4.HS.219. 71 The O'Conor Don to Earl Spencer, 5 May 1886, Althorp papers, BL, add. 76997, art. 1. 72 Goodlad, 'Gladstone's land purchase bill', pp 627–41; Pomfret, *The struggle for land*, pp 233–43.

'Let them get rid of the landlords altogether'

government between 1895 and 1905. Undoubtedly biased towards the cause of Irish landlords, they took up where they left off in 1885 and introduced land purchase acts in 1888, 1891 and 1896.[73] During this time, the O'Conor Don had the ear of the Irish chief secretary, Arthur Balfour, who he met on several occasions to discuss the land purchase bills of 1888 and 1891. He also had the ear of many landlords in the house of lords through his connections on the Irish Landowners' Convention, of which he became an executive committee member in 1887.[74] But this does not disguise the fact that the O'Conor Don's demand for compulsory land purchase was not being heeded, something which he complained of to Lord Morris in relation to the 1891 act.[75] He was also deeply unimpressed with the Balfour's establishment of the Congested Districts Board (CDB) that same year. Balfour hoped that the board would help improve and consolidate agricultural holdings in the west of Ireland through the purchase of untenanted grazing land in the better parts of the region, the promotion of modern farming practices and assisted migration from the poorer parts of the region.[76] For the O'Conor Don the CDB was yet another cumbersome government agency that would impair the rate of land purchase rather than improve it. When Balfour offered him a position on the board, he turned it down.[77] His poor opinion of the board was, however, as much influenced by his views of the customs and practices of Irish tenant farmers, as it was by his concerns around land purchase. Indeed, the O'Conor Don was convinced that it would be:

> absolutely impossible, unless the people's own ideas are changed, to prevent subdivision of ... enlarged holdings. There is a firm conviction in the minds of the people that an addition to a holding is a new holding. If you give a man that has ten acres a holding that lies beside him, and which has been vacated by a neighbour, and which consists also of ten acres, he will consider that he now has two holdings, and he will certainly divide them amongst his children. Landlords with all their power

73 H.W.C. Davis & H.C.G. Matthew, 'Cadogan, George Henry, fifth earl Cadogan', *ODNB*; Pomfret, *The struggle for land*, pp 260–2; Bull, *Land, politics and nationalism*, p. 197. See chapter three, p. 86.   74 Recollections part 2, O'Conor papers, CH, 9.4.HL.156, pp 122–40; Duke of Abercorn to the O'Conor Don, 15 June 1887, O'Conor papers, CH, 9.4.HS.219; Lord Carlingford to the O'Conor Don, 22 Sept. 1890, O'Conor papers, CH, 9.4.HS.192; Walter Hussey Walsh to the O'Conor Don, 4 & 25 July 1891, O'Conor papers, CH, 9.4.HS.192; Gailey, *Ireland and the death of kindness*, pp 35–40.   75 The O'Conor Don to Lord Morris, 28 May 1891, O'Conor papers, CH, 9.4.HS.219; P.M. Geoghegan, 'Morris, Sir Michael', *DIB*.   76 C. Breathnach, *The Congested Districts Board, 1891–1923: poverty and development in the west of Ireland* (Dublin, 2005), pp 33–4; Pomfret, *The struggle for land*, pp 263–8. Bull, *Land, politics and nationalism*, p. 197.   77 The O'Conor Don to Lord Clonbrock, 4 Dec. 1901, Clonbrock papers, NLI, MS 35, 774 (5); The O'Conor Don to Lord Clonbrock, 6 Sept. 1902, Clonbrock papers, NLI MS 35, 774 (6); A.J. Balfour to the O'Conor Don, 22 May 1891, O'Conor papers, CH, 9.4.HS.189.

could not prevent it. No public Board can prevent it. A division will secretly take place. Marriages will be made. Two families will grow up on the land, and public opinion, where this has taken place, never tolerates the eviction of men who have paid and are willing to continue to pay their annuity or rent.[78]

The O'Conor Don's thoughts here represent an assessment that was fairly typical of a landed class who placed much of the blame for the status quo regarding fractious landlord-tenant relations and rural poverty firmly at the doorstep of tenant farmers and their representatives in Parnell's Home Rule Party, who supported agrarian agitation. Nonetheless, it is one of the clearest expositions of the thinking behind his insistence that compulsory land purchase was the only way to force landlords to sell and tenants to buy. As for the CDB, although inadequate funds for the purchase of untenanted land meant the relocation of tenant farmers did not take place in any significant numbers, the board's work did significantly reduce the likelihood of famine-like distress in the west of Ireland by the turn of the century.[79] However, the fact that many landlords in the west resorted to letting their untenanted land as large grass farms for periods of eleven months, rather than twelve, so as to avoid the rent-fixing legislation of the 1881 land act, did little to help the CDB's cause or improve progress on land purchase more generally.[80]

LANDLORDS AND THE WYNDHAM LAND ACT OF 1903

The rates of land purchase did not significantly increase under the legislation of the 1890s, as neither landlord nor tenant was entirely satisfied with the terms on offer.[81] One of the catalysts for further and more extensive reform was the establishment of the United Irish League (UIL) in 1898 under the leadership of William O'Brien. With the encouragement of T.W. Russell, a radical Ulster unionist and junior minister in Salisbury's third administration, O'Brien adopted compulsory land purchase as UIL policy.[82] The O'Conor Don had known Russell since 1878 through his position on the Intermediate Education Board and one must wonder if he influenced the Ulsterman on compulsory purchase, or if it was the other way round.[83]

78 Memorandum on small tenancies in the west of Ireland by the O'Conor Don, 1902, Clonbrock papers, NLI, MS 35, 775 (4). 79 Campbell, *Land and revolution*, pp 26–8; Breathnach, *Congested Districts Board*, p. 174. 80 Bew, *Conflict and conciliation*, pp 10–11. 81 See chapter three, p. 82. 82 Campbell, *Land and revolution*, pp 1–7, 24–41, 47–9, 70, 81–4. 83 Diary of the O'Conor Don, Apr. 1880, O'Conor papers, CH, 9.4.SH.247; J. Loughlin, 'Russell, Sir Thomas Wallace', *DIB*.

One way or another, Irish landlords did not have it entirely their own way in terms of influencing government policy. The O'Conor Don was no doubt acutely aware of the UIL's power given its particularly high levels of organization in County Roscommon.[84] Indeed, he was, by May 1900, convinced that 'the beginning of a new land agitation of a most serious character' was in the offing.[85]

The response of the Conservative government to the mounting agitation was more land purchase. However, the bill introduced by the Irish chief secretary, George Wyndham, in March 1902, made land purchase 'less attractive' for tenants, as their annuities were not reduced and the rate of purchase was more likely to be set at twenty-five years, rather than twenty-two as under the previous land acts. Even worse, landlords could set the purchase prices on their holdings where requests for rent revisions had been lodged; and if tenants declined to purchase at the set price, they could not make any further requests for rent revisions for another fifteen years. Being so heavily weighted in the favour of landlords, Wyndham's bill was rejected by John Redmond, a Catholic landlord who was now the leader of a re-united Home Rule Party, commonly known as the Irish Parliamentary Party (IPP).[86]

At this stage of the debate on land purchase, the O'Conor Don's views were well known and generally well-respected within Irish and British political circles. Wyndham – who first began work on his bill while staying at Clonalis in the autumn of 1901 – thought him to be 'particularly well acquainted' with the issue.[87] And following the proposal for a land conference in June 1902 after the failure of Wydham's bill, Redmond described the O'Conor Don as the potential 'man in the gap' between the landlord and tenant positions.[88] The proposers of the land conference, in a series of letters to the *Times*, and quite independent of the executive committee of the Landowners' Convention, were the relatively unknown landlords Captain John Shawe Taylor and Lindsay Talbot Crosbie.[89] On 8 September, Shawe Taylor wrote to the O'Conor Don requesting that he attend, as he was convinced the government would 'do a big thing in the way of land purchase' if a scheme was agreed at the conference.[90] The O'Conor Don's reply was to provide the rather tame excuse that he was not entitled to participate in the conference because he was no longer

---

84 Campbell, *Land and revolution*, pp 1–7, 24–41, 47–9, 70, 81–4. 85 Diary of the O'Conor Don, 7 May 1900, O'Conor papers, CH, 0.1.SH.041. 86 Campbell, *Land and revolution*, p. 73. 87 George Wyndham to the O'Conor Don, 19 Nov. 1902, O'Conor papers, CH, 0.1.HE.011. 88 J.W. Mackail & G. Wyndham, *Life and letters of George Wyndham* (London, 1925), ii, p. 427; George Wyndham to the O'Conor Don, 19 Nov. 1902, O'Conor papers, CH, 0.1.HE.011; Lindsay Talbot Crosbie to the O'Conor Don, 23 Sept. 1902, O'Conor papers, CH, 0.1.HE.011. 89 Gailey, *Ireland and the death of kindness*, p. 221; Bull, *Land, politics and nationalism*, pp 144–5; A. Jackson, *Home rule: an Irish history* (London, 2003), p. 89. 90 John Shawe Taylor to the O'Conor Don, 8 Sept. 1902, O'Conor papers, CH, 0.1.HE.011.

an elected representative.[91] However, in a draft letter that was never sent, he revealed his distaste for the conference initiative, suggesting that 'What we have to do in this country is to disregard the white flags which a section of the landlords are raising', adding that it was 'quite useless to enter into a conference' with the likes of William O'Brien given that he was the sworn enemy of Irish landlords. As for Shawe Taylor, he hoped 'the Irish people would turn a deaf ear for the moment to the suggestions coming from the few … who speak without authority'.[92]

Oblivious to the O'Conor Don's hostility, Shawe Taylor wrote again on 17 and 23 September, pleading with him to attend. To further convince him of the necessity for action, Shawe Taylor claimed that Lord Clonbrock was favourably 'disposed' towards a land purchase scheme he had devised, but Clonbrock – obviously having been informed of the fact by the O'Conor Don – rejected the claim of the 'young man' from Galway who he felt, 'having only just left the Army', was 'neither a landlord [n]or a tenant' and had 'as little knowledge or experience of the matter as any man in Ireland'.[93] Thinking Shawe Taylor not 'right in the head', Clonbrock was 'very sorry' that the O'Conor Don was too 'considerate' in toning down his reply to him, as he felt 'no snub could have been too direct'. Clonbrock feared that if Shawe Taylor 'had the audacity' to write the O'Conor Don inviting him to the conference, 'he may have done so to others'. Indeed, Clonbrock warned the duke of Abercorn that Shawe Taylor was 'always jumping at conclusions, and making out that what he wishes to happen, or thinks ought to happen, has actually happened'. Of even graver consequence for Clonbrock was the possibility that Wyndham's judgment, something he did not think much of in any case, had been unduly influenced by Shawe Taylor's scheming.[94]

Lindsay Talbot Crosbie also had a go at persuading the O'Conor Don to attend, staying at Clonalis on 12 September and following this up with a letter that lavished praise on him as 'the one man in Ireland' who could 'come forward now and take the same bold independent stand that you did at the convention'.[95] The allusion here was to the O'Conor Don's opposition to a resolution of the executive committee of the Landowners' Convention at a

---

91 The O'Conor Don to John Shawe Taylor, 9 Sept. 1902, O'Conor papers, CH, o.1.ES.013. 92 The O'Conor Don to Anon., 20 Sept. 1902, O'Conor papers, CH, o.1.ES.013. 93 John Shawe Taylor to the O'Conor Don, 17 Sept. 1902, O'Conor papers, CH, o.1.HE.011; John Shawe Taylor to O'Conor Don, 23 Sept. 1902, O'Conor papers, CH, o.1.HE.011; Lord Clonbrock to the O'Conor Don, 10 Sept. 1902, O'Conor papers, CH, o.1.HE.011. 94 Lord Clonbrock to the O'Conor Don, 10 Sept. 1902, O'Conor papers, CH, o.1.HE.011. 95 Lindsay Talbot Crosbie to the O'Conor Don, 17 Sept. 1902, O'Conor papers, CH, o.1.HE.011.

meeting on 29 August 1902, which offered conditional support to Wyndham's land bill 'as an honest and ingenious attempt to promote the working of the Purchase Acts upon voluntary lines'. The O'Conor Don opposed the resolution on the grounds that he could not support the bill without the inclusion of compulsory purchase.[96] Clearly hoping that flattery would change his mind, Talbot Crosbie informed the O'Conor Don that his actions at the convention had gained him 'the respect of the whole country', and that he would 'not suffer' if he stood 'alone now' and supported the conference.[97] The O'Conor Don remained resolute, however, even though he met Talbot Crosbie again on 25 November in Roscommon town where they 'had a long chat on the land question' with T.W. Russell.[98] He declined a further invitation from the earl of Mayo, again arguing that the 'transfer of ownership ... must be accompanied with compulsion'.[99] Towards the end of November, the earl of Dunraven tried his luck too but the O'Conor Don would not be moved.[100]

The majority of landlords on the executive committee of the Landowners' Convention were opposed to the idea of a conference with tenant representatives, mostly on the grounds that they could not countenance sitting down with the leader of the UIL, William O'Brien.[101] The O'Conor Don was clearly of a similar mind, but fairly typically he clashed with those on the anti-conference side too. On 28 November 1902, the executive committee accused Dunraven and the pro-conference provisional committee of creating divisions among landlords by passing a resolution in favour of the land conference at a recent meeting of the Landowners' Convention, stating that it was 'unfortunate that a body so generally and deservedly discredited as the Irish Parliamentary Party, representing the United Irish League', should be entered into discussions with by a 'body of Irish noblemen and gentlemen'.[102] The following day, the O'Conor Don wrote to the County Fermanagh landlord Hugh de Fellenberg Montgomery, expressing his extreme 'disappointment' with the statement, which to 'all intents and purposes [was] a declaration of war with the tenants parliamentary representatives'. Threatening to resign from the executive committee, he wondered how Montgomery thought 'their accusations' would bring about a 'return to United action on the landlords' side'. Moreover, he felt that 'no matter what we may think of them', the reality was the IPP would have 'far more power than we can ever hope for in manipulating

---

96 *Irish Times*, 25, 30 Aug. 1902; The O'Conor Don to George Wyndham, 17 Nov. 1902, O'Conor papers, CH, 0.1.ES.013. 97 Lindsay Talbot Crosbie to O'Conor Don, 17 Sept. 1902, O'Conor papers, CH, 0.1.HE.011. 98 Diary of the O'Conor Don, 25 Nov. 1902, O'Conor papers, CH, 0.1.SH.041. 99 The O'Conor Don to the earl of Mayo, 20 Oct. 1902, O'Conor papers, CH, 0.1.ES.013. 100 The O'Conor Don to the earl of Dunraven, 30 Nov. 1902, O'Conor papers, CH, 0.1.HE.011. 101 Anon. to the O'Conor Don, 20 Sept. 1902, O'Conor papers, CH, 0.1.ES.013. 102 *Irish Times*, 29 Nov. 1902.

the details of the land bill when before parliament'. In other words, it made absolutely no sense to weaken the landlords' already comparatively weak position by attacking other landlords.[103]

Montgomery's response was unrepentant. He felt the O'Conor Don was overreacting, claiming that 'Dunraven and Mayo are much more thick-skinned and our letter is much less offensive than you think'; and while expressing regret over the possibility of his resignation from the executive committee, Montgomery hoped his 'disclaimer' would 'not put into Dunraven and Co's heads to consider themselves insulted!' Determined to fight the 'Dunraven faction' by convincing 'neutral landlords' in the Landowners' Convention that they had been misled about the popularity of the idea of a conference, Montgomery claimed the majority of 'landlords, press, and public ... wanted nothing to do with the United Irish League'. He also rejected the O'Conor Don's charge that calling 'the Irish Parliamentary Party a discredited body' would 'increase their power'. On the contrary, he argued that 'To acquiesce in the treatment of them by Dunraven and Co as if they were not a discredited body would certainly tend to fortify their power.' Unsurprisingly, then, Montgomery finished by impressing upon the O'Conor Don that he, the duke of Abercorn and Lord Clonbrock were determined 'to take this opportunity of making it clear, by the use of sufficiently emphatic language, that we were not going to be bullied or manoeuvred or coerced into any sort of acquiescence in their conference schemes'.[104]

On the 5 December 1902, the O'Conor Don received another letter from Talbot Crosbie, who on this occasion tried to shame him into attending the conference by suggesting that he could be held personally 'responsible for that very unwise letter written by your Ex[ecutive] Com[mittee]'.[105] Although the O'Conor Don was obviously fretting over the possibility of being associated with the views expressed by the committee, he was not driven to attend the conference by way of disassociating himself from Montgomery and Co. In light of this, his so-called role as the 'man in the gap' proved to be wishful thinking.

The land conference went ahead in December 1902 and Wyndham's land act became law in August 1903. A measure that attempted to strike a balance between enticing landlords to sell and tenants to buy, the average purchase price worked out at twenty-two and a half years, and over time the act enabled some 200,000 tenant farmers to become owner-occupiers.[106] Although the

103 The O'Conor Don to Hugh Montgomery, 29 Nov. 1902, O'Conor papers, CH, o.1.ES.013. 104 Hugh Montgomery to O'Conor Don, 2 Dec. 1902, O'Conor papers, CH, o.1.HE.011. 105 Lindsay Talbot Crosbie to O'Conor Don, 5 Dec. 1902, O'Conor papers, CH, o.1.HE.011. 106 Campbell, *Land and revolution*, pp 79–80, 88.

O'Conor Don reluctantly supported the measure, he believed the absence of compulsion meant it would not 'lead to that immediate and universal transfer of ownership which is looked forward to by its authors'.[107] As it happened, he was proved right, as landlords were still reluctant to sell and, as a result, widespread agitation was resumed in 1904 by the UIL. It was only when compulsion was introduced in the Birrell land act of 1909 that sales really began to increase in anything like significant numbers under the Wyndham act.[108] Nonetheless, in an echoing of the misguided optimism of many Irish landlords, the O'Conor Don had hoped that the Wyndham act would 'slowly and gradually, [bring] about the pacification of Ireland and the re-establishment of good feeling between the different classes in the country'.[109]

---

107 O'Conor, *Irish land bill, 1903*, p. 10. 108 Campbell, *Land and revolution*, pp 85–123. 109 O'Conor, *Irish land bill, 1903*, p. 10.

5 / 'There must be perfect equality in educational matters for all': the O'Conor Don and the Irish university question, 1860–80

In 1872, the O'Conor Don penned a pamphlet on education that posed the question: what is meant by freedom of education? His answer was that Irish Catholics should have the freedom to obtain a Catholic education, supported by the state, if they so wished, just as Irish Protestants had the freedom to obtain a Protestant education. According to him, the overwhelming majority of Irish Catholics, lay and clerical, wanted a Catholic education, rather than the system of secular education promoted by the state.[1] The truth of this contention was the cause of much controversy in the debate on the provision of university education in Ireland during the second half of the nineteenth century, which centred on three things: whether it ought to be secular or denominational in character; what influence, if any, the Catholic hierarchy and clergy ought to have over its governance and provision; and to what extent the state should provide financial support for it. For the O'Conor Don, it was clear that the majority of Catholics were in favour of denominational education and demanded a state-chartered and endowed Catholic university. However, successive British governments, both liberal and conservative, refused to concede this demand. Indeed, most liberal and conservative Protestants in Great Britain and Ireland tended to interpret this demand as the opinion of the Catholic hierarchy voiced through Catholic MPs, who in turn exaggerated the degree of public support for it. Moreover, there were many liberal Protestants and Catholics who were in any event in favour of secular education.

Any consideration of the views of the Catholic hierarchy on university education ought to recognize the degree to which lay Catholics both challenged and reinforced those views.[2] That said, it cannot be denied that the

---

1 C.O. O'Conor, *What is meant by freedom of education, or, the Catholic objections to pure secularism considered* (Dublin, 1872), p. 24. 2 S. Pašeta, 'The Catholic hierarchy and the Irish university question, 1880–1908', *History*, 85 (2000), 268–84; A. Enright, 'Catholic elites and the Irish university question: European solutions for an Irish dilemma, 1860–1880' in B. Heffernan (ed.), *Life on the fringe? Ireland and Europe, 1800–1922* (Dublin & Portland, OR, 2012), pp 177–95. Other notable exceptions to the clerical focus include D. McCartney, 'Lecky and the Irish university question', *Irish Ecclesiastical Record*, 5 (1967), 102–12 & B. Kinzer, 'John Stuart Mill and the Irish university question', *Victorian Studies*, 31 (Autumn, 1987), 59–77. For the influence of the hierarchy and clergy see T.W. Moody, 'The Irish university question of the nineteenth century', *History*, 43 (1958), 90–109; Norman, *Catholic Church* (1965); T.J. Morrissey SJ, *Towards a national university: William Delany SJ (1835–1924): an era of initiative in Irish education* (Dublin, 1983); E. Larkin, *The Roman Catholic Church and the emergence of the modern political system, 1874–1878* (Dublin, 1996); J. Phillips, 'The Irish university question, 1873–1908' (PhD, UC, 1978).

Catholic Church was a dominant force in nineteenth-century Irish politics, particularly in the debates on education. A by-product of the church's influence was a power struggle between it and the state, which, as part of a broader European phenomena of 'secular-Catholic' conflicts, centred around the issues of papal authority, the role of the hierarchy and clergy in civic society, and the provision of education.[3] It is clear, however, from examining the O'Conor Don's views on education that this church-state struggle was cut across by a secular-denominational debate among lay Catholics and Protestants. The O'Conor Don believed religious instruction by the clergy should be part of the education of Irish Catholics, but the fact that he shared this view with the hierarchy does not imply that he was simply reflecting their views. First, he was a devout man with genuine religious convictions who had received a denominational education and supported the principle of it. Second, he was a liberal who believed in freedom of religion within what we would today call a pluralist state. For him, this meant the state should support denominational education for all denominations or none at all. Third, he was a pragmatic politician who differed with the bishops on what was an acceptable compromise to a Catholic university, on the extent of their involvement in the provision of education, and on the extent of their involvement in politics. As we shall see, he was not alone in holding these views and adopting this approach, but other liberal Catholics supported a secular system of education in one form or another and were more wary of what they saw as the over-mighty influence of the Catholic hierarchy in Irish society.

What all liberal Catholics sought to do, however, was influence opinion within the predominantly Protestant British Liberal Party, which, notwithstanding serious reservations, they supported as the best prospect for meaningful reform in Ireland. Indeed, as a liberal, the O'Conor Don's instinct was to try and make the union work. One way to achieve this was to provide university education for a greater number of Irish Catholics, who in turn might become morally upright, economically secure and politically mature citizens who could see and reap the benefits of Ireland's place within the union and the wider British empire. In other words, liberal Catholics like the O'Conor Don saw the concession of the seemingly popular demand for a Catholic university as something that might lead to a rapprochement between Catholic Ireland and the British state. But liberal Protestant opinion was mostly opposed to the idea of a Catholic university. And even though liberal Catholics and Protestants could agree on some practical compromise solutions, the secular vs denominational debate on university education, fuelled

---

[3] C. Barr, *The European culture wars in Ireland: the Callan schools affair, 1868–1881* (Dublin, 2010), pp 1–16.

by suspicions of the ultramontane designs of the bishops and Catholic MPs, proved detrimental to the already weak cause of liberalism in Ireland.

IRISH UNIVERSITY EDUCATION

By 1860, the provision of university and university-type education in Ireland was vested in five institutions. The oldest of these, Dublin University, and its constituent college, Trinity College Dublin (TCD), was established in 1592 by Queen Elizabeth I as an exclusively Protestant institution. Maintained by the rentals of substantial landed estates and an annual state grant, the university lifted its ban on nonconformist attendance in 1793 at a time when Pitt the younger was trying to appease Catholic and Presbyterian discontent with the political status quo in Ireland, heightened by the revolution in France.[4] In a similar vein, the revolutionary atmosphere on the Continent was the motivation for Pitt's establishment of St Patrick's College in Maynooth in 1795, a seminary under the control of the bishops and in receipt of a state grant.[5] Presbyterians were left to fend for themselves until 1814 when the Synod of Ulster established the Belfast Academical Institution, which sought to provide a university education for laymen and clergy. It received an annual state endowment, but this was temporarily withdrawn by the government in 1817 over the perceived radicalism of some of the institution's managers and supporters.[6] In 1845, Sir Robert Peel's Tory government established the secular Queen's colleges in Belfast, Cork and Galway, while at the same time increasing the state grant for the Catholic seminary at Maynooth. In receipt of an annual state grant and eventually affiliated to the Queen's University in 1850, Peel's hope was that the Queen's colleges would assuage lay Catholic and Presbyterian concerns with TCD.[7]

Although a lack of means would have been the main obstacle in the way of most young Catholic and Protestant men attending the Queen's colleges and TCD, middle- and upper-class Catholics were left in no doubt by Pope Pius IX's rescripts of 1847–9, and the subsequent ruling of the Irish bishops in 1850, that attendance at these institutions was very much frowned upon. Under the direction of the newly appointed archbishop of Dublin, Paul Cullen, the bishops set about implementing Pius IX's recommendation that a Catholic university be established in Ireland. The Catholic University of Ireland, at St Stephen's Green, Dublin, was duly established in 1854, with Cullen appointing the prominent English convert, John Henry Newman, as rector. Both men

---

4 Moody, 'The Irish university question', pp 90–109; *Return showing the gross and net revenues of Trinity College, Dublin for the year 1888 ...*, HC 1889 (334), lix, 389, pp 1–6. 5 Moody, 'Irish university question', pp 95–9. 6 Wright, *The 'natural leaders'*, pp 85–8, 160–70. 7 Moody, 'Irish university question', pp 95–9.

had high hopes of emulating the University of Louvain in Belgium, but they struggled to see eye to eye on educational ethos, student discipline and overall management. However, the refusal of successive liberal governments to grant a charter for its degrees was the greatest barrier to success, with the university facing an ongoing struggle to attract students in significant numbers. Newman resigned in 1858, but even his more compliant and activist successor, Monsignor Bartholomew Woodlock, struggled to improve student numbers.[8]

Given the complexity and controversy surrounding the provision of university education in Ireland, the preferred option for the majority of upper- and middle-class Irish Catholics continued to be to send their sons to Catholic colleges in England and Ireland, from which they could proceed to take their degrees by central examination through the University of London, or instead proceed to TCD or the Queen's colleges.[9] As we have seen, the O'Conor Don attended Downside College, Bath, and would have taken a degree from the University of London but for bad health. For him and many of his contemporaries, it was possible to receive a Catholic education and obtain a legitimate university degree, which in turn paved the way for social and political advancement. But despite being able to work their way through and take advantage of the system, liberal Catholics like the O'Conor Don – when they entered the world of politics – expressed their dissatisfaction with it because the 'freedom' to obtain a Catholic university education in Ireland was, in their view, being denied by the state. Many Catholics were clearly happy to send their sons to TCD and the Queen's colleges, either on pragmatic grounds or because they actually endorsed the idea of secular education, but the majority of Catholic bishops and liberal and nationalist Catholic MPs were not satisfied with what they saw as the unfairness of denying the majority Catholic population the Catholic university education they seemingly wanted. It was liberal MPs like the O'Conor Don, who dominated Irish Catholic representation between 1860 and 1874, who pursed reform of Ireland's university system most forcefully.

THE UNIVERSITY QUESTION, 1860–73

When the O'Conor Don entered the house of commons in 1860, any hope of having the university question addressed by the Liberal Party was

8 Barr, *Catholic University of Ireland*, pp 133–76; F. McGrath, *Newman's university: idea and reality* (London, 1951), pp 43–6; S. Pašeta, 'Trinity College, Dublin, and the education of Irish Catholics, 1873–1908', *Studia Hibernica*, 30 (1998/9), pp 10–12; Moody, 'Irish university question', pp 93–4; Norman, *Catholic Church*, pp 5, 18–19. 9 O'Neill, *Catholics of consequence*, pp 1–13, 30–41, 54–9, 66–88, 100–9, 111–14, 206–8; Thompson, *The University of London*, pp xii–xvi.

significantly reduced by the hostile attitude of its leader, Lord Palmerston, towards Catholicism – and towards Irish reforms more generally. His support for Italian unification in 1859, at the potential expense of the pope's territories, together with his appointment of the hapless Sir Robert Peel as Irish chief secretary in 1861, were the most obvious manifestations of this attitude.[10] All this was a source of great annoyance for the O'Conor Don and his fellow liberal Catholic MPs William Monsell and Richard More O'Ferrall, who were highly critical of the government's Italian policy and were resigned to the fact that the prospect of Irish reforms, let alone university reform, were slim as long as Palmerston and Peel remained in place.[11]

The unlikelihood of university reform did not, however, prevent the O'Conor Don from criticizing various other aspects of the education system. In his maiden commons speech on 17 May 1861, he raised the issue of the provision of religious instruction in Ireland's national schools, which, although secular in principle, were denominational in character, with the majority of schools under the control of the Catholic Church, the Church of Ireland or the nonconformist churches, depending on their location in the country.[12] However, the O'Conor Don claimed there were several parishes of mixed denomination, particularly in the north of Ireland, where Protestant clergymen controlled the schools and prevented Catholic priests from carrying out their pastoral duties, while the national board prevented Catholics from establishing their own schools in these parishes.[13] In June 1864, he complained of the absence of endowments for convent schools, comparing them unfavourably to the state-funded model and teacher-training schools, most of which were run by Protestants. In July 1866, he tabled a resolution recommending that the prison ministers act of 1863 better provide for the religious instruction of Catholic inmates in British prisons.[14] And when he first brought the Irish industrial schools bill before the House in March 1867, the O'Conor Don sought to ensure that adequate religious instruction would be provided for children of all denominations.[15]

---

10 Hoppen, *Elections, politics, and society*, pp 260–1, 273; J.P. Parry, *Democracy and religion: Gladstone and the Liberal Party* (Cambridge, 1989), pp 25, 130, 136.   11 The O'Conor Don to Archbishop Cullen, 26 Feb. 1862, Cullen papers, DDA, 340/5; The O'Conor Don to Monsignor Woodlock, 25 Apr. 1865, Woodlock papers, DDA, 106/49; Richard More O'Ferrall to William Monsell, 30 June 1865, Monsell papers, NLI, MS 1075/20/3.   12 D.H. Akenson, *The Irish education experiment: the national system of education in the nineteenth century* (London & Toronto, 1970), pp 4–5, 102–22, 157–224; P.J. Dowling, *A history of Irish education: a study in conflicting loyalties* (Cork, 1971), pp 159–83; C. Barr, *The European culture wars*, pp 84–7.   13 HC Deb., 17 May 1861, vol. 162, cc 2225–32. See also *Copy of a letter on the subject of national education in Ireland, addressed to the chief secretary in the month of July last by certain members of parliament*, HC 1861 (212), xlviii, 683, pp 1–4.   14 HC Deb., clxxvi, 176–83 (23 June 1864); ibid., clxxxiii, 990–1032 (15 May 1866); ibid., clxxxiv, 1417–41 (24 July 1866).   15 HC Deb., 13 Mar. 1867, vol. 185, cc 1741–5.

The O'Conor Don also took an interest in the promotion of scientific education. In 1864, he and his fellow liberal Catholics Myles O'Reilly, William Cogan and Sir Colman O'Loghlen sat on a select committee investigating the state of Ireland's scientific institutions. The committee's report called for additional government funding for institutions such as the Museum of Irish Industry, the Royal Zoological Society, the Royal Dublin Society and the Royal Irish Academy, arguing that it would help maintain 'persons of high intelligence and attainments', thereby elevating the overall standard of scientific knowledge in Irish society.[16] He subsequently became a council member of the Royal Dublin Society and the Royal Irish Academy, as well as attending the conference of the National Association for the Promotion of Social Science in Belfast in September 1867.[17] All this was of a piece with the liberal outlook of the O'Conor Don and his colleagues, who believed that social and scientific inquiry could and indeed should lead to practical reforms to improve social, economic and political conditions in Ireland, and to assimilate the country's laws with those of the rest of the United Kingdom where it was sensible to do so.[18]

Meanwhile, in May 1862, the O'Conor Don delivered his second commons speech, which condemned the state's promotion of secular education at university level and called for reform. Later that year and in 1863, his colleagues Monsell and O'Reilly published pamphlets that called for reform of Ireland's system of university education.[19] However, it was not until June 1865 that the first tangible parliamentary action was taken when the O'Donoghue put down a motion for a charter for the Catholic University.[20] Something of a maverick who was almost certainly trying to curry favour with the clergy in the run-up to an election, the O'Donoghue acted without the prior agreement of many of his liberal Catholic colleagues, which was symptomatic of their inability to work together in parliament. It would seem that the rector of the Catholic University, Monsignor Woodlock, had previously asked the O'Conor Don to do it, but he was of the view that any motion should be for a charter for a new 'central examining university'.[21] This is the first indication of the O'Conor Don's acceptance that a Catholic university was not a realistic

---

16 *Report from the select committee on scientific institutions (Dublin); together with the proceedings of the committee, minutes of evidence, appendix and index*, HC 1864 (495), xiii; Notice from the Royal Dublin Society to the O'Conor Don, n.d., O'Conor papers, CH, 9.4.LH.082; *Royal Irish Academy list of members 2001*, p. 31. 17 Lord Dufferin to the O'Conor Don, 12 Sept. 1867, O'Conor papers, CH, 9.3.HS.275. 18 Potter, *William Monsell*, p. 56. 19 HC Deb., 22 May 1862, vol. 162, cc 2031–82; W. Monsell, 'University education in Ireland', *Home and Foreign Review*, 2 (Jan. 1863), 32–58; M. O'Reilly, 'The connection of the state with education in England and Ireland', *Dublin Review*, 52 (Nov. 1862), 106–54; idem, 'University education', *Dublin Review*, 52 (Apr. 1863), 423–67. 20 Norman, *Catholic Church*, pp 194–5. 21 The O'Conor Don to Monsignor Woodlock, 25 Apr. 1865, Woodlock papers, DDA, 106/49.

legislative goal, and that compromise was therefore needed. The response of a now Lord Russell-led, and Gladstone-influenced, Liberal government was to propose a 'supplemental charter' for the Queen's University, which would allow Catholic students to sit the exams for its degrees without having to attend the Queen's colleges.[22] It is not clear if the O'Conor Don supported this proposal, but it seems likely given that it was supported by Monsell, O'Reilly and other liberal Catholics like John Brady, Charles Moore, Dominic Corrigan and Thomas O'Hagan.[23] But Monsell and O'Hagan, both of whom were close to Gladstone, sought to go one step further and draw up a proposal for the affiliation of a Catholic college (the Catholic University reformed) to the Queen's University. This plan was shared with ministers and bishops in the spring of 1866, but much to Monsell's frustration, Cullen rejected it because he did not think there was enough clerical influence on the university senate or the governing body of the Catholic college. Moreover, when these behind-the-scenes negotiations were made public, the conservative Protestant press and the Queen's Graduates' Association expressed their stern opposition to any clerical influence over the Queen's University. In any event, on 18 June 1866, Lord Russell's government was defeated on an amendment to Gladstone's franchise reform bill, which occasioned a speedy request for a royal patent for the supplemental charter.[24]

With the future of the supplemental charter in limbo due to a legal challenge from the convocation of the Queen's University, Lord Derby's minority Conservative government, led by Disraeli in the commons, hinted at providing its own solution to the university question. By October 1867, the Irish chief secretary, the earl of Mayo, was corresponding with Cardinal Cullen's intermediaries, Archbishop Patrick Leahy and Bishop John Derry, on the possibility of a charter for the Catholic University. Mayo's efforts foundered on Cullen's demand for control of the senate and the episode was a considerable cause of embarrassment for all concerned when the correspondence was made public in May 1868.[25] In a letter to Woodlock after the fact, the O'Conor Don 'candidly' expressed the view that there would not have been 'the slightest chance of getting a declaration' of laymen to support the bishops' proposal for absolute control of the governance of the Catholic University.[26] This was

22 Norman, *Catholic Church*, pp 196–9.   23 HC Deb., 20 June 1865, vol. 200, cc 541–90; Potter, *William Monsell*, pp 112–19; E. O'Brien, *Conscience and conflict: a biography of Sir Dominic Corrigan, 1802–1880* (Dublin, 1983), pp 281–313.   24 Norman, *Catholic Church*, pp 198–239; Parry, *Liberal government in Victorian Britain*, pp 197–8; P. MacSuibhne, *Paul Cullen and his contemporaries: with their letters from 1820–1902* (Naas, 1961), iii, p. 253.   25 *Copy of further correspondence relative to the proposed charter to a Roman Catholic University in Ireland*, HC 1867–8 (288) (380), liii, 779, 791, pp 1–15; Norman, *Catholic Church*, pp 240–81; Potter, *William Monsell*, pp 115–16.   26 The O'Conor Don to Monsignor Woodlock, 30 May 1868, Woodlock papers, DDA, 106/68.

not surprising given that he supported 'the legitimate influence of the laity' in the governance of any state-supported educational institution, but it is noteworthy as a clear sign of his wariness of Cullen's unrealistic aims, and of clerical interference in the politics of the education question more generally.[27]

With the return of the liberals under Gladstone's leadership in December 1868, the O'Conor Don and many of his liberal Catholic colleagues had great hopes for Irish reforms and strengthening the cause of liberalism in Ireland. Indeed, they had held been telling him of this hope since 1865.[28] Their excitement in 1868 was further heightened by Gladstone's pledge to govern Ireland with 'Irish ideas', which in policy terms meant disestablishing the Church of Ireland and tackling the issues of land and university education. As a pious high church Anglican, Gladstone was not hostile to Catholicism in the same way that many low church and nonconformist liberals in Great Britain and Ireland were, but he was determined to counter the influence of ultramontane Catholicism in Ireland by placing the 'control of education, especially higher education' in the hands of lay liberal Catholics who were willing to challenge it. He was undoubtedly influenced by the views of Monsell and O'Hagan on Ireland and Catholicism, with both now part of his administration, as under-secretary for the colonies and lord chancellor, respectively.[29] What they and the O'Conor Don had in common was a desire to reach an accommodation between Protestants and Catholics on the education question, by bridging the divide between the conservative religious values of the church and the increasingly secular values of the Liberal Party.[30] Indeed, the O'Conor Don wished for there to be a pragmatic admittance of the differences between secularists and denominationalists on the education question, so that an accommodation could be reached. This was evident in April 1870 when Henry Fawcett, the radical MP for Brighton, proposed the abolition of the remaining religious tests at TCD. Although this meant Catholics would be able to compete for TCD's fellowships and prizes, the O'Conor Don argued that the proposal failed to address Catholics' objection to secular education; and that it was, in any event, a cynical move to pre-empt the possibility of TCD losing some or all of its state grant in Gladstone's expected university bill.[31]

This was not the first time the O'Conor Don questioned the logic of TCD's endowment when the policy of the government was to promote secular education.

---

27 O'Conor, *freedom of education*, p. 51. 28 Thomas O'Hagan to W.E. Gladstone, 27 Apr. 1865, Gladstone papers, BL, 44406, f. 93 & 5 Dec. 1867, Gladstone papers, BL, 44413, f. 255; Colman O'Loghlen to W.E. Gladstone, 28 Apr. 1865, Gladstone papers, BL, 44406, f. 96; Sir Rowland Blennerhassett to W.E. Gladstone, 5 Dec. 1868, Gladstone papers, BL, 44416, f. 299. 29 Parry, *Democracy and religion*, pp 156, 193, 314–15. Potter, *William Monsell*, pp 1–3, 127, 139–41, 159–66. 30 Potter, *William Monsell*, pp 2–3. 31 HC Deb., 1 Apr. 1870, vol. 200, cc 1090–146; HC Deb., 20 Mar. 1872, vol. 210, cc 327–77.

During the committee stages of the disestablishment bill in May 1869, he argued that cutting the Maynooth College grant – one of the provisions of the bill – was not justified given that 'similar endowments' for the education of Protestant clergymen at TCD 'were left untouched'. His comparison of Maynooth and TCD invoked the ire of Protestants who insisted the former was a religious endowment and the latter educational. As a trustee on the governing board of Maynooth College, the O'Conor Don obviously had an interest in defending the college's position, but his raising of the issue was not a statement of his opposition to the endowment of Protestant religious instruction; rather it was to highlight the inconsistency of government policy on educational endowments. Nonetheless, he thought disestablishment was 'a great measure of justice' and was satisfied that the termination of the Maynooth grant had been augmented by a lump-sum compensation payment from the disestablished church fund.[32]

The tensions between Protestant and Catholic MPs on the education question were further exacerbated by the declaration of papal infallibility in July 1870.[33] While it is not clear what the O'Conor Don thought of making papal infallibility part of church teaching, he did not openly question it. This was the position of Monsell, Blennerhassett and the English Catholic Lord John Acton, all of whom accepted the concept of papal infallibility but opposed its enshrinement in church teaching as unnecessary, politically inopportune and a blow to the cause of liberalism within the church and among lay Catholics more generally.[34] It seems likely that the O'Conor Don's pragmatic political instincts would have led him to the same conclusions, but this did not stop him from chairing a meeting in Castlerea in support of the pope and his territories, which had fallen into the hands of Italian nationalist forces in September 1870.[35] This did not make him unusual among Catholic politicians, as many attended similar meetings throughout the country in November and December of that year. But while it was one thing to sympathize with the pope's plight in the face of Italian nationalist annexation of his territories, it was quite another to openly declare one's support for a dogma that was anathema to liberal Protestants and made Irish reforms, favourable to Catholics, considerably more difficult. Indeed, the O'Conor Don's public silence on the issue was most likely for the same reasons as Monsell's: that it would jeopardize progress on the university question, which could in turn lend greater force to the argument for home rule.[36]

32 HC Deb., 4 May 1869, vol. 196, cc 107–49; Recollections part 1, O'Conor papers, CH, 9.4.HL.156, p. 50; Norman, *Catholic Church*, pp 368–76.   33 Norman, *Catholic Church*, pp 412–15   34 Potter, *William Monsell*, p. 145.   35 Recollections part 1, O'Conor papers, CH, 9.4.HL.156, pp 56–7; Norman, *Catholic Church*, pp 412–15.   36 *Freeman's Journal*, 3, 4, 16, 18, 21, 22, 29 Nov. 1870 & 1, 5, 7, 8, 12, 16, 23, 27 Dec. 1870; Parry, *Democracy and religion*, p. 315.

Meanwhile, the English and Welsh campaigns for educational reform played into the Irish debate, exacerbating frictions within the Liberal Party. Fawcett and his secularist allies pushed for the abolition of all religious tests and the establishment of a secular national education system in England and Wales, but the education act of 1870 was not to their satisfaction, with denominational schools able to receive state funding if they operated a conscience clause restricting instruction to certain times of the day. Moreover, when the Oxford and Cambridge religious tests were repealed in February 1871, Gladstone resisted Fawcett's attempt to have the abolition of clerical fellowships included in the legislation. In light of these developments, radicals and nonconformists in the Liberal Party were determined not to concede any ground when the Irish university question came up for debate.[37] When Fawcett brought forward his TCD tests bill again in March 1872, the O'Conor Don once again spoke strongly against it. Gladstone did so too, but this put him in the rather embarrassing position of opposing a reform he in fact supported and would introduce in his own bill. Fawcett withdrew his bill when Gladstone threatened to resign over the matter.[38]

THE IRISH DEBATE ON UNIVERSITY REFORM

At the same time English liberals were quarrelling over educational reform, the divisions between Irish liberals on the subject were becoming more pronounced. As already noted, the O'Conor Don published a pamphlet on education in 1872, in which he declared 'that there must be perfect equality in educational matters for all'.[39] When he said equality, he meant religious equality, with his central argument being that the function of a truly liberal state was to enable all denominations to provide religious instruction as part of their education, rather than impose a system of secular education on a people that was largely opposed to it. In the case of national schools, the O'Conor Don argued that the will of the Irish people had made a mockery of the state's secularist policy by making the system denominational in practice. At intermediate level, he pointed to the unfairness of model and teacher-training schools run by Protestants receiving state funding while Catholic colleges and convent schools received nothing.[40] But it was in the sphere of university education that the O'Conor Don thought the state most blatantly contravened its own secular policy, with the 'avowedly Protestant' TCD in receipt

---

37 Parry, *Democracy and religion*, pp 289–348. 38 HC Deb., 20 Mar. 1872, vol. 210, cc 327–77; Parry, *Democracy and religion*, pp 298, 308, 345–8. 39 O'Conor, *Freedom of education*, p. 24. 40 O'Conor, *Freedom of education*, pp 24–36.

of substantial state funds while the Catholic University received none.⁴¹ In order for Gladstone's government to resolve the situation, the O'Conor Don suggested that two 'truths' had to be admitted: that Catholics were overwhelmingly opposed to the present system of university education; and that the system was not in fact secular, but openly biased towards the teaching of Protestantism in its various forms.⁴² Quite apart from that, he questioned the very idea that secular education was practically achievable, reasoning that the state unduly interfered with what constituted religious instruction by determining the criteria for endowment based on whether institutions provided it or not.⁴³ More importantly, he argued that it was impossible to exclude religious bias – Catholic or Protestant – from the teaching of subjects such as history and philosophy, even if the 'idea of God [were] … regard[ed] … in the light of unbelief'.⁴⁴ This argument is particularly significant because it reflected the general thinking of Cullen and Newman, both of whom held that the teaching of history, philosophy, literature and the natural sciences could not be properly understood without taking account of Catholic religious doctrine. It was also the position of more nationalist-minded Catholics such as John O'Hagan and Frank Hugh O'Donnell.⁴⁵

In making suggestions for reform, the O'Conor Don posited a number of solutions: a chartered and endowed Catholic university with affiliated colleges; the affiliation of a Catholic college to Dublin University, alongside TCD, with endowment; the amalgamation of all existing universities into one national university, with affiliated and endowed colleges of all denominations and none; and, finally, the establishment of an examining university along the lines of the University of London, with students from affiliated and unaffiliated colleges obtaining their degrees by sitting standard examinations.⁴⁶ Although he favoured the idea of one national university, it was a central examining university that the O'Conor Don believed most English MPs were likely to concede because all the others invoked their misguided suspicions of 'clerical domination'. But even so, he conceded that an examining university was not in-keeping with the traditional, collegiate ethos of university education. Indeed, he thought such a university could end up being 'a mere examining body', a judgment he perhaps came to as a result of his own

---

41 Ibid., pp 36–41. 42 Ibid., p. 47. 43 Ibid., pp 11–12. 44 Ibid., pp 12–13. 45 Barr, *Catholic University of Ireland*, pp 74–91; I. Ker, *John Henry Newman: a biography* (Oxford, 1988), pp 388–93; J. O'Hagan, 'The constitutional history of the University of Dublin, with some account of its present condition and suggestions for improvement', *Dublin Review*, 22 (Sept. 1847), pp 245–50; S. Sturgeon & J. Quinn, 'O'Hagan, John', *DIB*; F.H. O'Donnell, *Public education: its necessity, and the ideas involved in it: an essay on the principles of national instruction: with some of their applications to Irish university systems* (Dublin, 1867), pp 18–20, 30–1; A. O'Day, 'O'Donnell, Frank Hugh', *DIB*. 46 O'Conor, *Freedom of education*, pp 48–9.

experience of studying for his degree with the University of London.⁴⁷ These views were to large extent shared by William Monsell and Myles O'Reilly, who had both called for 'freedom' of education in the same sense, favoured the option of one national university, but similarly concluded that a central examining university was the solution most likely to meet with approval in an English-dominated parliament.⁴⁸

There were, however, voices of dissent in liberal Catholic circles. Thomas Maguire, Robert Kane and James Lowry Whittle were all opposed to denominational education and the creation of an 'ultramontane' university under the influence of the bishops. As graduates of TCD, they obviously harboured no fears of the supposed dangers secular education presented to the faith and morals of Catholics. Indeed, both Maguire and Kane fully embraced the idea of secular education, with the former professor of Latin at Queen's College Galway and the latter president of Queen's College Cork. Whittle is a somewhat more obscure figure, but he was known to and well regarded by J.J. Ignaz Von Döllinger, the German academic who opposed the doctrine of papal infallibility. He was also known to Lord Acton, a pupil of Döllinger's and a fierce critic of ultramontanism; and to Gladstone, who of course knew both Acton and Döllinger.⁴⁹ The O'Conor Don did not normally keep such elevated company, but he was close to Monsell and they both, along with Acton, believed in the importance of religious instruction in the education of Catholics. Where they sometimes differed was how this might be practically achieved in the world of politics, and to what extent the hierarchy ought to influence that process.⁵⁰

Whittle, on the other hand, was convinced that the bishops dictated the position of Catholic MPs on the university question because of their influence in Irish elections. As a result, he felt 'gentry and moneyed' Catholics could not be taken seriously as true representatives of lay liberal Catholics, who he thought found the bishops' 'extreme Ultramontane opinions … a source of permanent political embarrassment'.⁵¹ Maguire expressed a similar view when he questioned the sentiment behind a Catholic petition to parliament in 1870, which called on Gladstone to recognize their conscientious objections to secular education.⁵² As the principal organizer of the petition, the O'Conor Don

---

47 Ibid., pp 50–1.   48 Monsell, 'University education', pp 32, 54–5; O'Reilly, 'The connection of the state with education', pp 137–8; O'Reilly, 'University education', pp 441–4.   49 Barr, *The European culture wars*, pp 101–2; Parry, *Democracy and religion*, p. 163; J. Adelman, *Communities of science in nineteenth-century Ireland* (London, 2009), pp 62–7, 150, 167; P. Long, 'Maguire, Thomas', *DIB*.   50 Quinn, 'Blennerhassett, Sir Rowland', *DIB*; Potter, *William Monsell*, p. 145; J.L. Altholz, *The liberal Catholic movement in England: the rambler and its contributors, 1848–1864* (London, 1962), pp 60, 203, 211–13.   51 J.L. Whittle, *Freedom of education: what it means* (Dublin, 1866); idem, 'How to save Ireland from an ultramontane university', *Fraser's Magazine for Town and Country*, 77 (Apr. 1868), pp 436, 441.   52 T. Maguire, *Letter to Henry Fawcett on the Irish university question* (Galway, 1872), pp 1–4.

responded angrily by stating that it was 'idle' and 'insulting' to try and 'represent the expressed opinions' of independent-minded Catholics 'as merely clerical'.⁵³ William Sullivan, professor of chemistry at the Catholic University, also sought to defend the integrity of lay Catholic opinion in the face of Whittle's and Maguire's criticisms. Claiming that the real 'liberal Catholic party' supported the role of the bishops and the clergy in education, he felt Whittle had failed to understand that the opponents of ultramontanism in the Catholic Church – Acton, Newman and Döllinger – still supported the idea of a Catholic university.⁵⁴

Nonetheless, the problem for the O'Conor Don and Sullivan was that Maguire's and Whittle's suspicions of clerical influence were shared by leading liberal Protestants in Ireland. John Elliott Cairns, a Protestant graduate of TCD, argued that the call for 'freedom of education' was in reality a call for clerical supremacy. He opposed a charter for the Catholic University on the basis that it would impose a system of 'medieval' education on a Catholic population who did not desire such a thing, but he also opposed a supplemental charter for the Queen's University and the abolition of TCD's religious tests because he believed it would facilitate an ultramontane takeover of the governance of these institutions. Furthermore, he rejected proposals for an examining university on the grounds that one already existed in London, where Catholics were taking degrees in significant numbers. In other words, Cairnes believed the system as it stood was quite adequate and in keeping with the liberal values of the time. This was essentially Maguire's position too.⁵⁵

The Presbyterian minister Thomas Croskery took a more nuanced position. On the one hand, he argued that disestablishment of the Church of Ireland could not be logically followed with the endowment of a Catholic university given that the state had now disassociated itself 'from every sectarian institution in the country'.⁵⁶ But unlike Cairnes and Maguire, he thought the abolition of TCD's religious tests would help complete this 'liberal policy' and destroy the pretext of the hierarchy's argument for an endowed Catholic university. To further his argument, Croskery referenced the views of Albert William Quill, another Catholic graduate of TCD, who had argued that the abolition of religious tests at Oxford and Cambridge confirmed that the

53 *Copy of declaration of the Catholic laity of Ireland, on the subject of university education in that country, lately laid before the prime minister*, HC 1870 (140), liv, 645, pp 1–7; O'Conor, *freedom of education*, pp 51–2.   54 W.K. Sullivan, *University education in Ireland; letter to Sir John Dalberg Acton* (Dublin, 1866), pp iii–iv, 1–5, 12–13, 28, 48–50; D. Murphy & L. Lunney, 'Sullivan, William Kirby', *DIB*.   55 J.E. Cairnes, 'University education in Ireland', *Theological Review*, 3 (Jan. 1866), pp 116–18, 122–7, 129, 140, 142–9; C. Ó Gráda, 'Cairnes, John Elliot', *DIB*; Maguire, *Letter to Henry Fawcett*, pp 1–4.   56 T. Croskery, 'Irish university education', *Edinburgh Review*, 125 (Jan.–Apr. 1872), pp 168, 172–3, 180–2; T. Hamilton & D. Huddleston, 'Croskery, Thomas', *ODNB*.   57 Croskery, 'University education', p. 185; *Freeman's Journal*, 9 Nov. 1871.

British state had now fully turned away from the endowment of denominational education.[57] Such enlightened views were praised by Croskery and he described Quill, Whittle, Maguire and O'Hagan as members of the 'small but intelligent minority' of liberal Catholics who resisted the 'spiritual terrorism' of 'clerical dictation'.[58] But Croskery did not think that simply abolishing TCD's religious tests would solve the problem. Instead, he endorsed the 'only two practical plans' available: the establishment of one national university via a re-constituted Dublin University, with TCD, the Queen's colleges, a Catholic college and the Presbyterian Magee College, in Londonderry, affiliated; or a re-constituted Queen's University, with the Queen's colleges, a Catholic college and Magee College affiliated. Significantly, Croskery argued that under either arrangement the 'denominational' Catholic college and Magee College could not receive the same endowments as the 'unsectarian' TCD and the Queen's colleges.[59]

GLADSTONE'S UNIVERSITY BILL

The university bill brought before parliament on 13 February 1873 by Gladstone was essentially Croskery's plan for a national university.[60] There were, however, some crucial additional features. First, although TCD maintained its state grant, half of its private monies from landed estates were to be allocated for the running of the university. Second, its theological department was made separate and put under the auspices of the Representative Body of the Church of Ireland; like Maynooth College, it would receive a one-off compensation payment from the disestablishment fund. Third, the Queen's college in Galway was to be wound-up, as it was deemed to be unviable from an academic and financial point of view. Fourth, although the new university was to have both examining and teaching functions, it was decided, for the purposes of 'securities of conscience', that there would be no chairs in modern history and moral philosophy.[61]

It was, however, the absence of direct state endowment for the Catholic college, while TCD and the remaining two Queen's colleges maintained their existing endowments, that drove the O'Conor Don and the majority of liberal and nationalist Catholic MPs to vote against the second reading of the bill, a significant factor in its defeat by the narrow margin of three votes. Indeed, only four liberal Catholic MPs voted for the bill: William Monsell (postmaster general at this stage), Sir Dominic Corrigan, Sir Rowland Blennerhassett

58 Croskery, 'University education', pp 170, 173–5, 181–2. 59 Ibid., pp 184–7. 60 HC Deb., 13 Feb. 1873, vol. 214, cc 377–429. 61 Ibid.

and George Gavin.⁶² E.R. Norman's conclusion that 'the influence of the bishops ... secured the defeat of the Government' would suggest that Whittle's claim that most Catholic MPs were under the electoral thumb of the hierarchy was well-founded.⁶³ However, Woodlock's reports back to Cullen from Westminster, in the lead-up to the second reading of the bill on 3 March, were of a body of Catholic MPs in several minds as to what to do. Myles O'Reilly and Edmund Dease were his chief points of contact in his undoubted efforts to convey Cullen's opposition, but the O'Conor Don kept a wide berth, telling Woodlock on 18 February that it was his hope that 'the bishops will consider very well before they condemn this scheme as I fear no better is possible'. Indeed, he felt such a condemnation would be 'most detrimental' given that Gladstone and 'this House of Commons' were already against the policy of a 'direct grant for a Catholic College'.⁶⁴ This would suggest two things: that the O'Conor Don was fearful of the bishops putting him and his colleagues in an awkward position by making their views on the bill officially known; and that he was hopeful that changes in the funding model would enable him to support the bill.

As it turned out, the bishops heavily criticized the bill at a meeting in Dublin on 27 February, and Cullen made public his opposition on 9 March.⁶⁵ On the fourth and final night of debate on 11 March, the O'Conor Don wearily announced that it 'was with considerable pain' that he found himself in opposition to the bill. While he thought that Gladstone had 'comprehended the grievance', he felt that parliament had not been able to admit the sincerity of it. This he claimed was evidenced by the repeated attempts to discredit Catholic opposition to secular education as nothing more than a priestly conspiracy. On a personal level, he admitted the hierarchy's opposition to the measure was influential, but typically added that 'he would not hold his seat for an hour on condition of yielding his convictions in such a case'. In this regard, his initial conviction was to support the bill if the government indicated its willingness to concede changes on the exclusion of the chairs of modern history and moral philosophy, and on the endowment of the Catholic college. The O'Conor Don argued that the former would render the college completely secular in character, something he could not accept as a firm believer in the 'principle of denominationalism'. Indeed, he would have preferred it if Gladstone had proposed a 'mere Examining Board', which

---

62 HC Deb., 6 Mar. 1873, vol. 214, cc 1450–60 & 11 Mar. 1873, vol. 214, cc 1741–868; Potter, *Monsell*, pp 160–3. 63 Norman, *Catholic Church*, p. 451. 64 Monsignor Woodlock to Cardinal Cullen, 4, 5 & 7 Mar. 1873, Woodlock papers, DDA, XIV 45/5; The O'Conor Don to Monsignor Woodlock, 18 Feb. 1873, Woodlock papers, DDA, 106/68; Norman, *Catholic Church*, pp 451–2. 65 Norman, *Catholic Church*, pp 451–2; Parry, *Democracy and religion*, p. 363.

would have left the Catholic college to teach these subjects as it saw fit. In relation to the absence of endowment, the O'Conor Don wondered:

> could there be a stronger argument in favour of Home Rule than the action taken on this occasion by the right hon. Gentleman? The Irish Roman Catholics had in every constitutional manner expressed their opinion in favour of denominational education, and yet, whilst the other educational religious bodies in that country were endowed, the Prime Minister dared not pronounce that word in connection with Roman Catholics. The result of this continued refusal to attend to the wants of the Roman Catholics of Ireland ... must lead to very strong agitation on the subject of Home Rule.[66]

It was a statement born out of frustration. The O'Conor Don was not speaking in favour of home rule, but rather reminding the House that its failure to adequately legislate for Catholic Ireland might create problems on that score further down the road. This is not to suggest that the O'Conor Don had a unique insight into Irish politics. It would have been obvious to any political observer that the home rule movement was gathering some momentum, but the failure of Gladstone's bill was a boost for it and what the O'Conor Don's comments do reveal is his sense of foreboding on the matter. Indeed, the following chapter will demonstrate that his attitude to home rule at the national conference in November 1873 was one of extreme scepticism.

The more immediate consequences of the bill's failure were the resignation of Gladstone and his cabinet, their reinstatement as a result of Disraeli's refusal to form an interim minority government, and, to add insult to injury for the O'Conor Don, the passing of Fawcett's TCD tests bill.[67] The difficult political situation for Catholic MPs was further exacerbated by the growing controversy surrounding the dismissal of Revd Robert O'Keefe from his post as manager of five national schools in the parish of Callan, County Kilkenny. The controversy surfaced in April 1871 when O'Keefe, parish priest of Callan, took a libel action against two curates who had publicly accused him of lying about the bishop of Ossory's stance on pupil recruitment to a recently established Christian Brothers school in the area – O'Keefe implied that Bishop Walsh favoured his schools. Cullen suspended O'Keefe in November 1871 and the education commissioners subsequently dismissed him on the grounds that

---

66 HC Deb., 11 Mar. 1873, vol. 214, cc 1781–5.   67 K.T. Hoppen, *The mid-Victorian generation, 1846–1886* (Oxford, 1998), p. 609; HC Deb., 21 Apr. 1873, vol. 215, cc 727–77 & 5 May 1873, vol. 215, cc 1520–35.

a suspended cleric could not, under the rules of the board, hold the position of school manager. O'Keefe contested his dismissal and early in 1872 lobbied both Lord Russell and Gladstone to take up the matter in parliament. When it eventually came before the House in May it was grist for the mill of the critics of ultramontanism in Ireland who saw O'Keefe's dismissal as further evidence of Cullen's pernicious influence. After sustained parliamentary pressure, Gladstone appointed a select committee to investigate the circumstances of the case in May 1873.[68]

The O'Conor Don was selected as a committee member, most likely on the basis that he was a safe pair of hands to represent the Catholic interest. This was certainly how Cullen saw it; he had already written directly to the O'Conor Don in May 1872 outlining the seriousness of the matter and the need for him to be vigilant on the question in parliament. When the committee was in session, Cullen encouraged Bishop Gillooly to impress upon the O'Conor Don the need to defend both the position of the church and the board. As Colin Barr has shown, the O'Conor Don proved to be a useful committee member on both fronts. He established the precedent for the board's actions by asking Sir Patrick Keenan, the board's resident commissioner, 'a series of leading questions', the answers to which described how similar actions had been taken in the past regarding suspended priests. Moreover, through his and the other committee members' 'aggressive' line of questioning, O'Keefe was very much portrayed as an incompetent eccentric.[69] The O'Conor Don later remarked how Keenan, a friend, had said that 'only for my exertions and the assistance I gave him … the case would have gone against the commissioners'. A somewhat boastful claim, it almost certainly confirms Barr's claim that he and Keenan had rehearsed a set of questions beforehand.[70] Although the committee provided no report, its evidence, presented to the House on 18 June 1873, essentially vindicated the actions of the commissioners and cleared Cullen of wielding any direct influence over their decision to dismiss O'Keefe.[71] In the space of a few months, then, the O'Conor Don the liberal had helped bring down a Liberal government; the O'Conor Don the denominationalist had helped save the blushes of the, in theory, non-denominational national board of education; and the O'Conor Don the conservative Catholic had helped an essentially anti-conservative Catholic government clear an embattled conservative cardinal from any wrongdoing – a bizarre sequence of seemingly irreconcilable actions.

68 Barr, *The European culture wars*, pp 79–80, 94–5, 190–240. 69 Ibid., pp 95, 225. 70 Recollections part 1, O'Conor papers, CH, 9.4.HL.156, p. 67. 71 Barr, *The European culture wars*, pp 190–240; *Report from the select committee on Callan schools; together with the proceedings of the committee, minutes of evidence, and appendix*, HC 1873 (255), ix, 1, pp 1–161; Norman, *Catholic Church*, pp 431–40, 459.

BUTT'S UNIVERSITY BILL

Gladstone eventually called a general election in February 1874, the result of which was the defeat of his party and the formation of a majority Conservative government under Disraeli's leadership. Most significantly in Ireland, the election result saw the return of fifty-nine home rule MPs under the leadership of Isaac Butt.[72] Butt set about providing his own solution to the university question, producing a pamphlet on the subject in 1875, which endorsed the affiliation of an endowed Catholic college to Dublin University, alongside TCD.[73]

As early as May 1874, Woodlock had been busying himself with drafting a bill along these lines and approached the O'Conor Don about bringing it before the House.[74] The O'Conor Don declined to do so on the grounds that he and his fellow Catholic MPs could not 'see any way to our interfering at all in the arrangements of Trinity College ... under Fawcett's Act', adding with a hint of bitterness that 'what they [Trinity] ... do amongst themselves is no business of ours as anything they would do would be unacceptable to us'.[75] This would appear to have been the end of the matter until October 1875 when Woodlock informed the O'Conor Don of his desire to have Butt take charge of the bill. The O'Conor Don's response was to state that while he thought Butt was probably the best man for the job, he feared his position as the leader of the Home Rule Party would lessen the bill's chances of success.[76]

Butt pressed ahead and introduced his university bill to the commons on 16 May 1876.[77] The bill envisaged the affiliation of a Catholic college to Dublin University on an equal footing with TCD in terms of endowment. It also proposed the establishment of a committee of founders for the Catholic college, under the control of the bishops, which would decide upon issues of faith and morals, and have the power to appoint the rector, vice-rector and professors of religious studies.[78] Despite having put his name to the bill, the O'Conor Don privately did not think much of it. In a letter to the marquess of Ripon – a recent English convert to Catholicism who took an interest in the Irish education question – he condemned the bill as 'an extremely weak half [-] hearted measure' that 'would work out most unjustly ... as regards Catholic interests', and 'if passed in its present state ... would be most disastrous to religious

---

72 Hoppen, *The mid-Victorian generation*, p. 609.   73 I. Butt, *The problem of Irish education: an attempt at its solution* (London, 1875), pp 30–4.   74 Larkin, *Catholic Church ... 1874–1878*, pp 159–71, 209–10.   75 The O'Conor Don to Monsignor Woodlock, 13 May 1874, Woodlock papers, DDA, 106/109.   76 Larkin, *Catholic Church ... 1874–1878*, p. 201.   77 HC Deb., 16 May 1876, vol. 229, cc 805–29.   78 D. Thornley, *Isaac Butt and home rule* (London, 1964), pp 277–8; Larkin, *Catholic Church ... 1874–1878*, pp 158–256.

education generally'.⁷⁹ This was a severe and unfair assessment of the bill given that it offered Catholics considerably more than Gladstone's bill. It may have been that the O'Conor Don was somewhat annoyed by the fact that Butt, not him, was leading the charge on university reform, but this is pure speculation. What we do know is that the O'Conor Don had strenuously opposed Butt's land bill as recently as March 1876, and they differed on the issue of home rule, so they were hardly political allies.

In any event, Butt failed to get a second reading for the bill during the remainder of the parliamentary session.⁸⁰ In the meantime, Woodlock sought to foster public support for the bill by organizing a series of provincial meetings.⁸¹ Significantly, in December 1876, he tried to persuade the O'Conor Don to meet privately with him and a delegation of clergymen to discuss the bill's provisions, but he refused to partake on the grounds that if the meeting was made public it would only serve to undermine the bill's chances of success.⁸² Not surprisingly he also declined William Dillon's invitation to attend a conference on the bill in the library of the Catholic University on 28 and 29 January 1877.⁸³ Dillon – brother to John and a former student of the Catholic University – told the O'Conor Don that Butt was 'anxious to know' if he had his support, arguing that 'if the Bill is to be brought in again next session it would be highly desirable that ... it should be clearly ascertained that the main body of Irish MPs' supported it.⁸⁴ As it turned out, the O'Conor Don once again put his name to the bill and Butt finally managed to get a second reading in July 1877.⁸⁵ To privately condemn the bill and refuse to hold public discussions on its provisions while at the same time supporting it in the House was a highly ambiguous position for the O'Conor Don to take. Having said that, his refusal to publicly engage with Butt outside Westminster is consistent with his insistence on remaining independent of the Home Rule Party – something the next chapter will discuss in detail. His support for the bill in the commons therefore reflects the pragmatism of a man willing to make the best of what he personally thought was a bad job. After all, having been a long-time advocate of university reform favourable to Catholics, it would have been very odd indeed for the O'Conor Don to oppose the bill.

79 The O'Conor Don to marquess of Ripon, 15 June 1876, Ripon papers, BL, add. 43626, f. 1; A.F. Denholm, 'Robinson, George Frederick Samuel, first marquess of Ripon', in *ODNB*. 80 HC Deb., 19 June 1876, vol. 230, cc 8–9 & 7 Aug. 1876, vol. 231, cc 704–12. 81 Larkin, *Catholic Church ... 1874–1878*, pp 228–9. 82 The O'Conor Don to Monsignor Woodlock, 16 Dec. 1876, Woodlock papers, DDA, 106/68. 83 Larkin, *Catholic Church ... 1874–1878*, pp 235–6. 84 B. O'Cathaoir, *John Blake Dillon: Young Irelander* (Dublin, 1990), pp 122, 151; Lyons, *Parnell*, pp 36–9; William Dillon to the O'Conor Don, 18 & 23 Jan. 1877, O'Conor papers, CH, 9.4.HS.178. 85 Larkin, *Catholic Church ... 1874–1878*, pp 248–52; Thornley, *Isaac Butt*, p. 316.

INTERMEDIATE EDUCATION

Although the obstructionist tactics of Parnell and his supporters in Butt's Home Rule Party had been slowing down the normal business of parliament, Disraeli's Conservative government had been reluctant to introduce any Irish legislation. Nonetheless, in January 1878, it was announced that an Irish intermediate education bill would be introduced in the coming session, which eventually happened through the back door of the house of lords on 21 June 1878.[86] The liberals Sir Patrick Keenan and William Monsell (now Lord Emly) both had hands in preparing the bill, styling it on a scheme of 'payment by results' they had devised for Trinidad in 1870, when the former was chief inspector of Irish national schools and the latter was in the colonial office.[87] The O'Conor Don was supportive of the bill, with Butt telling the chancellor of the exchequer, Sir Stafford Northcote, that they had 'a long conversation' about it and agreed that it should be proceeded with before the estimates of the costs of the Queen's colleges were published, as they would spring the obstructionists into action again.[88] Significantly, during the bill's second reading, the O'Conor Don proposed that the Irish language be placed on the curriculum of the new board. This initiative was a product of his interest in the Irish language, which manifested itself in his appointment as vice-president of the Society for the Preservation of the Irish Language (SPIL) in 1877. Although this was an honorary position, and he did not attend the society's meetings, the O'Conor Don's association with SPIL and the Gaelic Union was based on a genuine interest in the language and Celtic culture more broadly. SPIL had already successfully petitioned the commissioners of national education to have Irish included on its curriculum and, in light of this, the O'Conor Don's proposal that it be part of the intermediate curriculum was taken on board by the Conservative government.[89]

The significance of the O'Conor Don's support for the preservation of the Irish language will be considered again in chapter seven but suffice to say at this point that it was reflective of a cultural nationalism which did not make him a nationalist in any meaningful political sense. In any event, the cause of preserving the Irish language was not the preserve of Catholics or nationalists,

---

86 HC Deb., 17 Jan. 1878, vol. 237, cc 59–153; HL Deb., 21 June 1878, vol. 241, cc 7–19; K.T. Hoppen, *Governing Hibernia: British politicians and Ireland, 1800–1921* (Oxford, 2016), pp 251–2; Phillips, 'Irish university question', pp 62–8.   87 Potter, *William Monsell*, pp 142–3.   88 Isaac Butt to Stafford Northcote, 12 June 1878, Iddesleigh papers, BL, add. 50040, f. 109.   89 HC Deb., 15 July 1878, vol. 242, cc 1482–536 & 12 Aug. 1878, vol. 242, cc 1776–828; Dunleavy & Dunleavy, *The O'Conor papers*, pp 273, 288. For SPIL and Gaelic Union meetings, see *Freeman's Journal*, 20 Mar. 1883, 31 Dec. 1883, 24 & 29 Mar. 1886, 31 Mar. 1893.

with many Protestants and unionists being members of SPIL and the Gaelic Union in the 1870s and 1880s.[90]

Returning to the matter in hand, however, the intermediate education bill was generally well received by MPs and passed through the House on 12 August 1878. The act provided for the establishment of the Intermediate Education Board, through which the state would provide funds for Catholic colleges based on their students' examination results. One million pounds from the disestablished church fund was made available for the provisions of the act, out of which £32,000 per annum was put at the disposal of the board for distribution among the colleges. The Irish viceroy, the duke of Marlborough, was granted the power to nominate the board members and he did so along suitably denominational lines. John Thomas Ball, the earl of Belmore, Revd George Salmon and James Corry MP represented the Protestant interest, while Lord O'Hagan, the O'Conor Don and Christopher Palles represented the Catholic interest.[91]

The passing of the Intermediate Education Act seemed to spur the government into action on university reform. In November 1878, the secretary of state for colonies and former Irish chief secretary Michael Hicks Beach met privately with Woodlock to discuss the possibility of a central examining university on the model of the University of London. Marlborough had been considering the same option since 1877 and, working on his own initiative, met Woodlock and a number of bishops on 9 January 1879 to try and gauge their willingness to accept such a plan. The response was positive enough for him to submit a memorandum to the cabinet, which advocated the establishment of a central examining 'Royal University of Ireland', to which would be affiliated the Queen's colleges and a Catholic college. Marlborough also envisaged a scheme of indirect endowment for the affiliated colleges based on the example of the intermediate system.[92] With the Irish chief secretary, James Lowther, harbouring decidedly misplaced enthusiasm for the prospects of a Catholic-Tory alliance at the next election, a bill was drawn up and presented to the cabinet in early February 1879.[93]

As already demonstrated, the O'Conor Don and many of his liberal Catholic colleagues had been favourable to the idea of an examining university

---

90 B. Ó Conchubhair, 'The culture war: the Gaelic League and Irish Ireland' in T. Bartlett (ed.), *The Cambridge History of Ireland* (Cambridge, 2018), iv, pp 196–219; R.F. Foster, 'The Irish literary revival' in Bartlett (ed.), *Cambridge history of Ireland* (2018), iv, pp 169–82; T. Garvin, *Nationalist revolutionaries in Ireland, 1858–1928* (Oxford, 2005), pp 78–99. 91 S.V. Ó Súilleabháin, 'Secondary education' in P.J. Corish (ed.), *A history of Irish Catholicism* (Dublin, 1971), vi, p. 70; F. McGrath, 'The Irish university question' in Corish (ed.), *A history of Irish Catholicism*, pp 106–8; *Report of the Intermediate Education Board for Ireland for the year 1879*, HC (1880), xxiii, 31. 92 Memorandum on the university question, n.d. but most likely Jan. 1878, Iddesleigh papers, BL, add. 50040, ff 137–41; Phillips, 'Irish university question', pp 70–5. 93 Phillips, 'Irish university question', pp 77–82.

1 Charles O'Conor of Ballinagare. (Pyers O'Conor Nash, Clonalis House)

2 Owen O'Conor of Ballinagare and Clonalis. (Pyers O'Conor Nash, Clonalis House)

3 Denis O'Conor of Clonalis. (Pyers O'Conor Nash, Clonalis House)

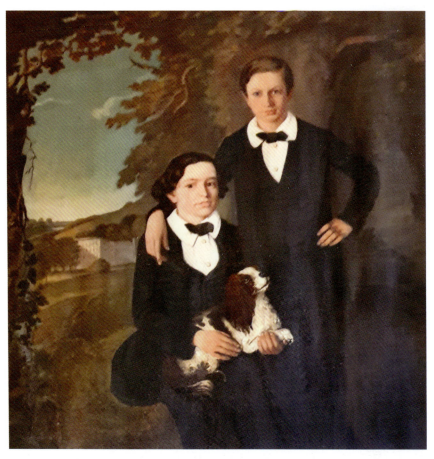

4 Charles Owen O'Conor and his brother Denis Maurice O'Conor as young boys. (Pyers O'Conor Nash, Clonalis House)

5 Charles Owen O'Conor, the O'Conor Don, as a young MP. (© National Portrait Gallery, London)

6 Charles Owen O'Conor, the O'Conor Don, in later life. (Pyers O'Conor Nash, Clonalis House)

7 Ellen O'Conor (née More O'Ferrall). (Pyers O'Conor Nash, Clonalis House)

8 Old Clonalis House. (Pyers O'Conor Nash, Clonalis House)

9 New Clonalis House. (Pyers O'Conor Nash, Clonalis House)

since the mid-1860s; and, in a 'seminal' letter to Lord Castletown on the university question early in 1879, Edmund Dease confirmed that this was still the case.[94] But despite Marlborough's and Lowther's enthusiasm for the plan, Disraeli and the cabinet thought it inadvisable to attempt a resolution of the Irish university question before an election, and the bill failed to make it into the government's programme of legislation for the coming session.[95] This was a cause of much disappointment for Butt, who thought the absence of a university bill was a missed opportunity for the government to build on the success of the intermediate act and win the support of the Catholic 'clergy and upper classes'. Indeed, he told Northcote that Catholic support for the Conservatives could become 'a great element in Irish politics' if encouraged, which was either hopelessly naïve or a desperate attempt to appeal to any delusions the Conservatives may have held about winning over Irish Catholics in significant numbers.[96]

THE O'CONOR DON'S BILL

Electoral delusions aside, the Conservatives' omission of a university bill spurred the O'Conor Don, Woodlock and Father William Delany into action. On 21 March 1879, the O'Conor Don told Delany, a teacher at Tullabeg College, County Offaly, that he was 'doing all he [could] to get the government to reconsider their decision', suggesting that if they could not be persuaded to do so 'action must be taken by the Catholic members' in the form of drafting a bill of their own.[97] The following week Woodlock conveyed Delany's report of Marlborough's recent meeting with the cabinet, from which it materialized that the government was sticking to its decision 'but would give support to a private bill, so as to secure (at least) its second reading'.[98] On this assurance Woodlock and the O'Conor Don set about drafting a bill in early April.[99]

On 15 May 1879, the O'Conor Don introduced a bill to parliament proposing the establishment of a new central examining university for Catholic colleges, to be symbolically named the University of St Patrick. Although he did not think it contained everything that Catholics 'believed that they were justly entitled to', and 'the establishment of one great

94 Edmund Dease to Lord Castletown, 1879, Castletown papers, NLI, MS 35, 313 (9). 95 Phillips, 'Irish university question', pp 82–4. 96 Isaac Butt to Stafford Northcote, 4 Feb. 1879, Iddelseigh papers, BL, add. 50040, f. 136. 97 The O'Conor Don to Father Delany, 21 Mar. 1879, Delany papers, JA J456/225; Morrissey, *Toward a national university*, pp 19–20, 50–1. 98 Monsignor Woodlock to the O'Conor Don, 28 Mar. 1879, O'Conor papers, CH, 9.4.HS.178. 99 Recollections part 1, O'Conor papers, CH, 9.4.HL.156, pp 88–9.

National University for Ireland ... would most please him', he felt that any attempt to reconstitute Dublin University and TCD, or the Queen's University, would be 'impracticable'. Like the intermediate act, the bill outlined a scheme of payments by results to be paid in instalments as students completed each year of their course. And although not envisaged as a teaching university, it was proposed that the senate would pay the salaries of professors teaching secular subjects in the affiliated colleges, and that it would provide monies to assist in the establishment of libraries, laboratories and museums. Once again, the source of funding was the disestablished church fund, with a proposed yearly endowment of £30,000.[100] The bill was very similar to proposals submitted by Butt to cabinet in February 1879, and even though he died on 5 May it would seem likely that the O'Conor Don was at least made aware of the proposals by Butt before his death, or by Woodlock or Marlborough.[101]

One way or another, the O'Conor Don was clear in his mind that the bill was not a definitive solution to the university question, but he felt that something ought to be done to try and force the government's hand.[102] As for the bishops, he was eager to gain their approval but remained apprehensive about their tendency to make unhelpful public pronouncements.[103] With this in mind he turned to Bishop Gillooly, suggesting a private meeting to go over the provisions of the bill, but he also pressed Gillooly to canvas nationalist MPs for their support.[104] Gillooly subsequently requested the support of all the bishops and wrote to Parnell and other home rule MPs with the same purpose in mind. It became clear, however, that Archbishop Thomas Croke of Cashel was not going to be easily won over.[105] Indeed, Croke was no admirer of the O'Conor Don, describing him in a letter to Archbishop Edward McCabe of Dublin 'as a Whig in disguise and in some sense a political renegade'.[106] Apparently oblivious to Croke's dim view of him, the O'Conor Don directly requested his support, but the archbishop's reply was to declare that the bill would 'get no substantial support' in parliament, where it would 'be either quietly shelved or shamefully defeated'.[107] The clerical difficulties worsened when, on 5 May, Delany told the O'Conor Don that many of the bishops were annoyed with Gillooly's 'taking ... it [up] on himself to be their spokesman'.[108]

100 HC Deb., 15 May 1879, vol. 246, cc 475–93; Morrissey, *Toward a national university*, pp 50–1; Phillips, 'Irish university question', pp 89–91.   101 Memo on the Irish university question by Mr Butt, 7 Feb. 1879, Iddesleigh papers, BL, add. 50040, ff 142–3.   102 The O'Conor Don to Anon., 30 Apr. 1879, O'Conor papers, CH, 9.4.HS.178.   103 Father Delany to the O'Conor Don, 27 May 1879, O'Conor papers, CH, 9.4.HS.178.   104 Phillips, 'Irish university question', pp 88, 93.   105 Bishop Gillooly to the O'Conor Don, 27 Apr. 1879, O'Conor papers, CH, 9.4.HS.178.   106 Quoted in Phillips, 'Irish university question', p. 93.   107 Archbishop Croke to the O'Conor Don, 2 May 1879, O'Conor papers, CH, 9.4.HS.178.   108 Father Delany to the O'Conor Don, 5 May 1879, O'Conor papers, CH, 9.4.HS.178.

In light of these internal tensions, the O'Conor Don's decision to limit his dealings with the bishops was a wise one.[109]

Reaction to the bill in parliament was something of a mixed bag. The O'Conor Don's claim that consensus had been reached 'on both sides of the House' among those who held the 'most opposite political views' was somewhat verified by the fact that the conservatives Arthur Kavanagh and Lord Beresford, as well as the moderate home rulers William Shaw and Mitchell Henry, had put their names to the bill. Parnell was initially reluctant to support the measure, but the O'Conor Don called on Archbishop McCabe to persuade him otherwise.[110] Even then, although he assured the O'Conor Don that his 'usual judgement and determination' would ensure the bill's safe passage through the House, Parnell displayed little interest in the measure.[111] Outside of this, however, English and Scottish liberal opposition to the bill was considerable, with Leonard Courtney, MP for Liskeard, arguing that the proposed university would be a direct threat to the existence of the Queen's University, while the MP for Edinburgh City, Duncan McLaren, raised his opposition to what he viewed as a Catholic university funded by the state. This prompted a fiery response from the O'Conor Don, who wondered how McLaren could object to the proposed university given that Scotland's four universities, in receipt of state funding, were 'far more for ... one particular creed' than the university proposed in his bill. To make matters worse, Northcote spoke neither for nor against the measure, and would not guarantee a day for a second reading.[112]

Despondent, the O'Conor Don told Delany the bill was 'killed as dead as Julius Caesar' because the government had 'been frightened by the Protestant bigots'.[113] Delany remained upbeat, however, insisting to Arthur Kavanagh that the government could not avoid dealing with the question in light of the O'Conor Don's action. Indeed, in a similar vein of optimism to Butt and Lowther, he felt that if the conservatives did not settle it on this occasion, their chance of winning 'a very large section' of Irish Catholic support would 'not be easily had again', hastening to add that this support would not come from 'the Fenian element of course – but the higher clergy and the better classes'.[114] Meanwhile, out-of-doors opposition to the bill was gathering momentum, with the *Irish Times* criticizing the lack of clerical influence on the proposed senate; the graduates' association of the Queen's University claiming that all

---

109 Bishop Gillooly to the O'Conor Don, 3 May 1879, O'Conor papers, CH, 9.4.HS.178. 110 Phillips, 'Irish university question', p. 97. 111 C.S. Parnell to the O'Conor Don, 8 Apr. 1879, O'Conor papers, CH, 9.4.HS.268; HC Deb., 21 May 1879, vol. 246, c. 1002. 112 HC Deb., 15 May 1879, vol. 246, cc 495–6; ibid., 21 May 1879, vol. 246, cc 930–1003. 113 The O'Conor Don to Father Delany, 21 May 1879, Delany papers, JA, J456/225. 114 Father Delany to Arthur Kavanagh, 26 May 1879, Delany papers, JA, J456/231.

'the friends of liberal education' in Ireland were opposed to the endowment of denominational education; and the Presbyterian General Assembly condemning it for the 'demand ... made in the interests ... of Ultramontanism'.[115]

In the face of growing opposition, the O'Conor Don pressed Northcote to allocate time for a second reading and he was assured something would be done.[116] However, when the debate resumed again on 25 June, the home secretary, Richard Assheton Cross, made clear the government's position: they strongly opposed the O'Conor Don's proposed university, which he described as 'theological endowment with State money'. However, he felt 'it would be right' for the government to provide an alternative, which the lord chancellor, Hugh Cairns, would do in 'another place'. Cairns duly presented the government's university bill to the house of lords on 30 June.[117] As Croke had predicted, the O'Conor Don's bill had been 'quietly shelved', but it had at least forced the government to think again and act.

THE ROYAL UNIVERSITY OF IRELAND

The government's bill provided for the establishment of a new central examining university with the secular Queen's colleges and other unspecified denominational colleges to be affiliated. This necessitated the dissolution of the Queen's University, but Dublin University and TCD remained untouched. In terms of the financial arrangements, the Queen's colleges were to maintain their existing endowments, but there was no pronouncement on funding for the other colleges. Like the University of London, the new university would have the power to confer degrees in subjects other than theology on all students who passed its examinations.[118]

The O'Conor Don's initial reaction was to proceed with caution, and he advised Archbishop McCabe and the bishops to adopt a similar approach. Convinced that 'the government want us to throw out the bill ... [so] that they could work on the no popery feeling in some of the [English] constituencies', he thought it wise to embrace the idea of having 'a new University ... and to have the Queen's University dissolved'.[119] The bishops met the following day and, although they deemed the bill unacceptable in its present form, they

---

115 *Irish Times*, 19 May 1879; Association of Graduates, *The Queen's University and the O'Conor Don's university bill: report of proceedings at a meeting held in Belfast, 2 June 1879* (Belfast, 1879), pp 1–16; *Belfast Newsletter*, 13 June 1879. 116 The O'Conor Don to Stafford Northcote, 6 & 11 June 1879, Iddesleigh papers, BL, add. 50040, ff 159 & 164. 117 HC Deb., 25 June 1879, vol. 247, cc 596–670; HL Deb., 30 June 1879, vol. 247, cc 931–45. 118 *A bill intituled an act to promote the advancement of learning, and to extend the benefits connected with university education in Ireland*, HL 1878–9 (250), vii, 591. 119 The O'Conor Don to Archbishop McCabe, 1 July 1879, McCabe papers, DDA, 337/6/II.

expressed the hope that amendments in the interests of Catholics might be made.[120] On 23 July the O'Conor Don called for the discharging of his bill, and a discussion on the government's bill took place in the commons the following day.[121] During this debate, he pressed the government on whether the bill would be altered to provide indirect funding for prospective Catholic colleges through fellowships and prizes for their students; and, if so, whether the Queen's colleges would be eligible to compete for them. If the latter turned out to be the case, the O'Conor Don thought the bill would be 'utterly valueless'. Northcote subsequently indicated that it was the government's intention to introduce a clause during the committee stages of the bill that would provide a 'liberal grant' of money.[122] Introduced on 1 August 1879, the clause proposed a scheme whereby all students taking their degrees with the university would be eligible for its fellowships and prizes, except those already in receipt of state funds through their colleges.[123] This went some way towards easing the O'Conor Don's concerns about an unfair advantage for the Queen's colleges, and he subsequently expressed his satisfaction with the amendment and gave his support to the bill. He did so, however, with the view that it was not a definitive settlement of the university question. Indeed, the O'Conor Don expressed the hope that a more comprehensive measure would be forthcoming in the future, which fully reflected the wishes of Irish Catholics.[124]

The Conservative government's university bill became law on 15 August 1879, but it was left to Gladstone's second Liberal government to put the legislative seal on the Royal University of Ireland, which received its charter on 20 April 1880.[125] The duke of Abercorn and Lord O'Hagan were made chancellor and vice-chancellor, respectively, while the thirty-six-member senate consisted of a suitable mix of academics, laymen and clerics from Protestant and Catholic backgrounds. Some of the O'Conor Don's closest Catholic associates were appointed to the senate, including Lord Emly (Monsell), the earls of Granard and Kenmare, Edmund Dease, Archbishop McCabe and Woodlock, by then a bishop. He himself was made a senator in June 1891.[126] When a formula for the university's scheme of fellowships and prizes was finally agreed upon in April 1882, somewhere in the region of £20,000 per annum was made available for distribution among the affiliated colleges,

---

120 Phillips, 'Irish university question', p. 111.   121 HC Deb., 23 July 1879, vol. 248, c. 1099.   122 HC Deb., 24 July 1879, vol. 248, cc 1182–273.   123 Ibid., 29 July 1879, vol. 248, c. 1631; ibid., 1 Aug. 1879, vol. 248, cc 1940–1; *A bill [as amended in committee] intituled an act to promote the advancement of learning, and to extend the benefits connected with university education in Ireland*, HL 1878–9 (283), vii, 599.   124 HC Deb., 5 Aug. 1879, vol. 249, cc 187–232; ibid., 6 Aug. 1879, vol. 248, cc 290–362; ibid., 11 Aug. 1879, vol. 248, cc 720–43.   125 *Copy of the charter of the Royal University of Ireland*, HC 1881 (203), lxxiii, 283; Phillips, 'Irish university question', p. 120.   126 *Copy of list of the names of the members of the senate of the Royal University of Ireland*, HC 1881 (204), lxxiii, 291; Recollections part 2, O'Conor papers, CH, 9.4.HL.156, p. 142.

which included the secular Queen's colleges, the Presbyterian Magee College, the Catholic University College (formerly the Catholic University) and, over time, a number of mostly Catholic intermediate colleges.[127]

What the O'Conor Don and other liberal Catholic MPs thought would be the most likely solution to the university question had therefore become a reality. In practical terms, the establishment of the Royal University of Ireland arrived at an opportune time in terms of the Intermediate Education Act of the previous year, which enabled intermediate Catholic colleges to produce greatly increased numbers of students for a university degree over the next thirty years. Like the University of London, the university maintained high standards in its examinations and its degrees, prizes and scholarships were open to both men and women. However, the Royal University satisfied none of the parties interested in the Irish university question, and the debate rumbled on.[128] Indeed, the O'Conor Don gave evidence to a royal commission on university education in 1903 where he reiterated his preference for denominational education and the view that this preference was shared by the majority of Irish Catholics. Notably, though, he expressed his regret at having opposed Gladstone's bill because he believed one national university, with affiliated colleges of all denominations and none, in receipt of equal funding from the state, was still the best possible solution.[129] The final settlement of 1908, enacted by a Liberal government, failed to realize this solution. Instead, it abolished the Royal University of Ireland and created the two new universities: the National University of Ireland and Queen's University Belfast. Affiliated to the former were the predominantly Catholic university colleges in Dublin, Cork and Galway, while the latter was a mainly Presbyterian institution. The mainly Church of Ireland TCD remained untouched. Given that all were in receipt of some form of state funding, the government's policy of no state endowment for denominational education proved to be a mere pretence.[130] Indeed, the university education system in Ireland had been not too discreetly divvied up along sectarian lines.

---

127 J.J. Auchmuty, *Irish education: a historical survey* (London, 1937), p. 141. Phillips, 'Irish university question', p. 116. 128 F. Campbell, *The Irish establishment, 1879–1914* (New York, 2009), pp 76–9; J.C. Beckett & T.W. Moody, *Queen's Belfast, 1845–1949: the history of a university* (London, 1959), i, pp 288–9, 296–7; S. Parkes, 'Higher education in Ireland, 1793–1908' in W.E. Vaughan (ed.), *A new history of Ireland, vi: Ireland under the union, II, 1870–1921* (Oxford, 1996), p. 561. 129 Draft of speech on the university question by the O'Conor Don, 1903, O'Conor papers, CH, 9.4.HS.095. 130 Pašeta, 'Irish university question', pp 282–4.

6 / 'I never will court popularity at the expense of my convictions': the O'Conor Don, liberalism and nationalism, 1860–80

Given that it has already been well-established that the O'Conor Don was an independent-minded man, it should come as no surprise that he would state so bluntly, at a national conference on home rule in 1873, his unwillingness to follow the current of popular opinion if it diverged from what he thought was best for the country. Up to that point, his support for disestablishment, tenant right and denominational education had generally been in line with popular Catholic opinion, but the O'Conor Don's refusal to 'court popularity' or fully engage with party politics, liberal or nationalist, saw him chart a somewhat tortuous and often isolated course in Irish politics between 1860 and 1880.

In one sense, this independent-mindedness was a matter of temperament; he was clearly temperamentally unsuited to toeing the party line, so to speak, whether that be liberal or nationalist. Thus, even though adherence to strict party lines was still in its infancy in the 1860s and 1870s, especially by landlords of independent means, the O'Conor Don demonstrated a particular zeal for independent thought and a particular squeamishness for committing to a fixed position on home rule. In another sense, however, this independent-mindedness was bound up with the whiggish and conservative elements of his liberal political outlook. Although the O'Conor Don was a critic of the union, he still preferred the constitutional status quo to a union with a home rule parliament dominated by nationalists and republicans and subject to the whim of popular opinion. Like many liberals in mid-nineteenth-century Ireland and Great Britain, he believed that a 'natural' ruling class, presumably comprised of landed and well-educated gentlemen, were best placed to represent the wishes of the people in a limited form of representative government. If their views aligned with popular opinion, all good and well, but if they did not, they reserved the right to independent judgment and action in the best interests of the country – what might be described today as the 'national interest'. These views of government and democracy could be, and indeed were, described as whiggish, but the O'Conor Don saw himself as a liberal and many Irish and British liberals held similar views on these issues. To simply dismiss them as anachronistic whigs would be to misunderstand the varied nature of liberal thought in the mid- to late nineteenth century, not least because liberal Catholics like the O'Conor Don also held conservative Catholic views on the moral necessity of religious and church influence in society that made them instinctively suspicious of the secular influences within Irish nationalism, particularly the Fenian threat of a secular Irish republic.[1]

The O'Conor Don sought to represent the interests of the people as he interpreted them. In the case of land reform, his advanced position on compulsory state-aided land purchase did not entirely represent the people's wishes, or at least that is how it seemed; in the case of university education, his support for a Catholic university appeared to be in line with that of the majority of Catholics, but this was hotly debated by other liberals and of course excluded Protestant opinion. The O'Conor Don's views on political representation, representative government, democracy and home rule reflected a liberal preference for maintaining the constitutional status quo while at the same time pursuing an agenda of sometimes advanced social and economic reforms. But he struggled and ultimately failed to maintain this position because he stood aloof from the Liberal Party on the education question and the Home Rule Party on home rule. This was broadly reflective of the fate of Irish liberals, who, even though they agreed on a wide range of social, economic and political issues, did not organize along anything remotely resembling party lines; succumbed to old religious divisions on the education question; and opposed home rule and the rise of popular politics. Thus, liberal Catholics like the O'Conor Don were not, as Hoppen would have it, political opportunists who latched on to the coattails of the Liberal Party, the National Association or the Home Rule Party in order to survive.[2] Rather he was an independent-minded liberal who was unsuited to party politics and refused to play, or was not very good at playing, the political game to save his electoral bacon. Nonetheless, despite his support for a wide range of social and economic reforms to improve Ireland's lot within the union, his independent-mindedness, unpopular views on home rule and land reform, the influence of Parnell and his own hubris all played their part in his election defeat in 1880.

LIBERALISM, NATIONALISM AND FENIANISM, 1860–74

As noted already, the relationship between Irish Catholic MPs and British whigs and liberal governments were at times close and controversial, with liberal Catholics taking junior positions in Lord Melbourne's administration in 1835–41, Lord Russell's in 1846–52 and Lord Aberdeen's, 1852–5. Clearly, many

---

1 See introduction, pp 20–3.   2 Hoppen, *Elections, politics and society*, pp 258–78. A similar argument is made in G.L. Bernstein, 'British liberal politics and Irish liberalism after O'Connell' in S.J. Brown & D.W. Miller (eds), *Piety and power in Ireland 1760–1960: essays in honour of Emmet Larkin* (Belfast, 2000), pp 43–65.

Catholic MPs were driven, to some degree, by self-interest, with some more self-interested than others, but what is less well considered is that many liberal Catholics were also convinced that any opportunity to influence whig or liberal government policy in Ireland was both the pragmatic and patriotic course of action to take. As Potter has shown, the O'Conor Don's friend, William Monsell, is a good example of this mentality, but there were many, many more liberal Catholics like him who served as ministers, judges and civil servants.³ Although the O'Conor Don did not serve as a minister or civil servant, he did not remain independent of office to challenge the constitutional status quo. Rather, he did not want to be perceived as an 'English party hack', and he may have wanted to give himself the space to openly criticize British government policy in Ireland.

In any event, cooperation of any kind with the Liberal Party in the early 1860s would have been controversial in Ireland, with Palmerston's support for Italian nationalist annexation of the papal territories in 1859–60 not endearing the party to the O'Conor Don, his liberal Catholic colleagues or Irish Catholics more generally. However, it was as much Palmerston's unwillingness to address some of the main Irish issues, such as land and education reform, that rendered cooperation impossible, which in turn highlighted the ineffectiveness of Irish liberals in parliament. In July 1864 the nationalist *Nation* newspaper surmised that public anger with the inability of Irish liberal MPs to have any effect on Liberal Party policy in Ireland was reaching a tipping point, with the people no longer prepared to return 'whig' place-seeking landlords who dominated 'many a hustings and call the farce an election'. The O'Conor Don was named in a list of mostly liberal Catholic MPs who were advised to pay heed to the warning that any 'Irish representative who is found on the side' of Palmerston's Liberal Party in the expected general election 'deserves execration and expulsion'.⁴

All the while, the O'Conor Don and his liberal Catholic colleagues repeatedly called for religious and educational equality in Ireland and worked towards moderate social reforms through parliamentary committees, commissions and legislation. The use of select committees and royal commissions became more and more pronounced from the 1830s onwards, becoming one of the defining characteristics of the British parliamentary system. In the case of Ireland, this

---

3 Potter, *Willam Monsell*, p. 4. Other examples throughout post-emancipation nineteenth-century Ireland include Sir Thomas Wyse, Denis O'Conor, Richard Lalor Sheil, Sir Thomas Redington, Richard More O'Ferrall, Lord Thomas O'Hagan, Sir Patrick Keenan, Thomas Henry Burke, Lord Michael Morris, Sir Nicholas O'Conor, Sir Anthony MacDonnell and many, many more. 4 *Nation*, 2 July 1864. Others mentioned were William Monsell, Richard More O'Ferrall, Myles O'Reilly, the O'Donoghue, William Cogan and Sir Colman O'Loghlen.

meant that almost every feature of society was scrutinized, but the rate of committee/commission to any kind of meaningful reform was a very poor one.⁵ Nonetheless, for liberal Catholics like the O'Conor Don, these official organs provided the space and time for MPs – away from the heat of commons disagreement and popular calls for radical change – to consider a broad range of Irish issues and how they could be addressed by reviewing the effects of previous legislation, taking evidence from experts in the field and making recommendations for further administrative changes and legislative reforms. Indeed, it was this moderate, gradualist approach to politics and reform that, as much as anything else, defined the O'Conor Don's political life, given that he was a regular select committee and royal commission member both during and after his time as an MP.

His first foray into royal commissions came in 1863, when he sat on the commission on penal servitude, which examined ways to strengthen legislation on sentencing, punishment and rehabilitation, and the transportation of convicts.⁶ This led to the Penal Servitude Act of 1864, which increased the length of minimum sentences and gave the central government in London, and the Irish administration in Dublin, greater powers to ensure the rules on punishment and prisoner release licensing were enforced by local authorities.⁷ In 1864, the O'Conor Don was a member of the select committee set up to investigate Ireland's tax contribution to the imperial exchequer. The aim here was to consider whether Ireland's tax contribution was disproportionately higher than Great Britain's in light of Gladstone's introduction of the income tax and increase of spirit duties in his landmark 1853 budget. The committee concluded that it was not, mostly on the basis that Ireland could not be taxed differently on account of its relative poverty because to do so would be to admit the same to other parts of the United Kingdom.⁸ The O'Conor Don typically dissented and published his own pamphlet on the subject, which concluded that Ireland was taxed disproportionately higher than Great Britain on the basis that Ireland's social and economic conditions were demonstrably different (worse) to those of Great Britain's. Indeed, he felt that it was patently obvious that:

> there is something more than a mere geographical distinction between Great Britain and Ireland. The habits of the people, their mode of living,

---

5 D.G. Boyce & A. O'Day (eds), *Defenders of the union: a survey of British and Irish unionism since 1801* (London & New York, 2001), p. 8; Parry, *Liberal government in Victorian Britain*, pp 115–16, 180. 6 *Royal commission to inquire into operation of acts relating to transportation and penal servitude: report, appendix, minutes of evidence*, HC 1863 (3190) (3190-I), xxi.1, 283. 7 *Royal commission to inquire into working of penal servitude acts: report, minutes of evidence, appendix, index*, HC 1878–9 (C.2368) (C.2368-I) (C.2368-II), xxxvii.1, 67, xxxviii.1. 8 Hoppen, *Governing Hibernia*, pp 159–62.

the productions of the two countries, and their sources of wealth, are not at all similar; and though separated only by a narrow expanse of water, there is perhaps as great a difference between them as between nations at different extremities of the globe.[9]

This was a blunt articulation of the social, economic and cultural differences that did indeed exist between Ireland and Great Britain. Nonetheless, although highlighting these differences raised difficult questions around Ireland's place in the union, it did not lead the O'Conor Don to think that Ireland's grievances should be agitated upon strictly national lines. Indeed, when Bishop Gillooly urged him to join the National Association and attend its inaugural meeting in December 1864, he declined to do so.[10] Formed under the direction of Archbishop Cullen, who was concerned about the rise in Fenian activity in the country, the association had the support of nationalist and liberal MPs and settled on an ambitious programme of reform, which included tenant right, the disestablishment of the Church of Ireland and denominational education.[11] Although the O'Conor Don told Gillooly that the association's objectives represented some of the most important issues of the day, he felt that such a meeting would lead to 'scenes so often displayed in this country of magnificent … promises being made [only] to be broken shortly after'. He wished the association well but predicted that it would serve no great purpose.[12] Some of the O'Conor Don's other, more revealing reservations were made clear to his friend Myles O'Reilly, who also tried to persuade him to attend. While he agreed there was a 'desirability of a thorough union between the ecclesiastical and lay portion of the Catholic community', and a 'profound need for political action viz fair settlement of the Tenant, Church, and Education questions', the O'Conor Don thought such a comprehensive programme of reform was unrealistic and feared that the 'moderate' men in the organization would be 'disregarded' after a short time once it became clear that such 'great expectations' were not immediately achievable. Indeed, he disagreed with O'Reilly's assertion that 'the whole liberal party' and 'all the influential and moderate lay Catholics of the Kingdom' would join the association, arguing that, while some liberals would inevitably join, they would not be able to 'control and direct' it for very long because 'men of a different stamp having other objects in view'

---

9 C.O. O'Conor, *A few remarks on the evidence received by the Irish taxation committee: together with a brief review of the subject* (Dublin, 1865), p. 84. 10 The O'Conor Don to Bishop Gillooly, 7 Dec. 1864, Gillooly papers, EDA, B1/5/1/2. 11 Norman, *Catholic Church*, pp 135–82. The National Association had the support of John Blake Dillon, George Henry Moore, John Francis Maguire, John Aloysius Dease, the O'Donoghue and Myles O'Reilly. 12 The O'Conor Don to Bishop Gillooly, 7 Dec. 1864, Gillooly papers, EDA, B1/5/1/2; Norman, *Catholic Church*, p. 141.

would take over.¹³ Clearly, then, the O'Conor Don and O'Reilly had some conception of there being a liberal party in Ireland, but the former's caution or disinterest in being associated with a nationalist-type organization perhaps goes some way to explaining why liberal politics in Ireland failed.

With the benefit of hindsight, the O'Conor Don's gloomy predictions were validated, as the National Association foundered on whether the questions of land, education or disestablishment should receive primacy, and on the question of parliamentary independence. Cullen and the majority of the bishops plumped for disestablishment and education in that order, while more nationalist-minded MPs tended to emphasize the importance of the land question. As for parliamentary conduct, Cullen endorsed a policy of members maintaining individual independence, rather than independent opposition *en masse*. Indeed, he was happy for the O'Donoghue and O'Reilly to work with non-association members like Monsell and the O'Conor Don in lobbying the government for a charter for the Catholic University. Monsell was also working towards reform of the separate parliamentary oath for Catholics, which essentially prevented them from openly campaigning for disestablishment and holding certain high offices. Indeed, this was another example of moderate, gradual reform, with Monsell working behind the scenes with liberals and conservatives *c*.1865–7 to eventually get a new, single parliamentary oath on the statue book in 1868. This new act permitted Catholic MPs to campaign for disestablishment and led to the appointment of Thomas O'Hagan as the first Catholic lord chancellor since the reign of James II.¹⁴

While the old parliamentary oath prevented Monsell and O'Hagan from joining the National Association in 1865, the O'Conor Don did not mention it as a factor in his decision and it did not stop Myles O'Reilly and John A. Dease from joining. It seems more plausible, therefore, that his decision was based on a determination to remain an independent liberal in parliament. When attempts were made to impose a strict rule of independent opposition on National Association members in parliament, O'Reilly and Dease seem to have come to same conclusion and left the association.¹⁵

The O'Conor Don's refusal to join the association also demonstrates the first real sign of his political independence from the Catholic hierarchy. Indeed, in advance of his unopposed return in the 1865 general election, he rather nonchalantly pointed out to Bishop Gillooly that while he would be grateful for his public blessing, he did not need it.¹⁶ This independence

---

13 The O'Conor Don to Myles O'Reilly, 11 Dec. 1864, O'Conor papers, CH, 9.3.HS.181.   14 Potter, *William Monsell*, pp 124–7; Norman, *Catholic Church*, pp 182–9.   15 Norman, *Catholic Church*, pp 182–9; Potter, *William Monsell*, p. 124.   16 The O'Conor Don to Bishop Gillooly, June 1865, Gillooly papers, EDA, B1/5/1/2.

from clerical influence was further illustrated in October 1865 when Gillooly tried to persuade the O'Conor Don to work more closely with his Catholic colleagues in parliament. His response was to inform Gillooly of 'some conversations' he'd had 'last August with … Sir R[owland] Blennerhassett and other Irish members' regarding the possibility of a meeting at Westminster. Although he expressed a willingness to attend 'if it were thought expedient by those more experienced than myself to join in getting it up', he had planned a trip to America to visit his cousin, Charles O'Conor of New York (1804–84), in November 1865. In light of this, the O'Conor Don told Gillooly that he would have 'of course disregard[ed] my private inconvenience' if he thought it a public duty to attend the meeting, but he did not think his 'actual presence' could 'be of much importance', and therefore saw little point in signing a petition in support of the proposed meeting. Despite this blasé attitude, he assured Gillooly that, upon his return, he 'would be ready to support in parliament any fair and practical measure proposed at the intended meeting'.[17]

A meeting of twenty-two liberal and nationalist MPs did take place in Dublin in December 1865, which rather ambitiously called for disestablishment, land and university reform; reform of the railways, grand jury laws and the parliamentary oath; investment in Irish industry and agriculture; and measures to prevent the spread of the cattle plague (rinderpest) from England to Ireland. However, even though the drafting of land and grand jury bills was proposed, nothing concrete materialized in parliament. On the other hand, it was clearly hoped that government measures would materialize given that the meeting also endorsed cooperation between Irish MPs and the '"advanced section" of the English Liberal Party', which it thought 'largely share[d] our political views'.[18] This was not an unrealistic aim given the recent passing of Palmerston and his replacement by Russell and Gladstone, but as we know from previous chapters the Liberal government's attempts at land and university reform in 1866 failed.

Upon his return from America in February 1866, the O'Conor Don sat on select committees investigating funding for art unions, animal welfare in transit and the provision of tramways in Ireland.[19] This approach again reflected his prioritizing of parliamentary process over any kind of party politics; and

17 The O'Conor Don to Bishop Gillooly, 15 Oct. 1865, Gillooly papers, EDA, B1/5/1/2; Diaries of the O'Conor Don, Nov. & Dec. 1865, O'Conor papers, CH, 9.3.SH.306. 18 *Freeman's Journal*, 8 Dec. 1865. Those in attendance included Myles O'Reilly, the O'Donoghue, John Francis Maguire, John Blake Dillon, Sir Patrick O'Brien and Sir John Gray. 19 *Select committee on art union laws: report, proceedings, minutes of evidence, appendix, index*, HC 1866 (332) (332-I) vii.1, 97; *Select committee on home and foreign trade in animals by sea and railroad: report, proceedings, minutes of evidence, appendix, index*, HC 1866 (427) (427-I) xvi.423, 831; *Report from the select committee on tramways (Ireland) acts amendment bill; together with the proceedings of the committee, minutes of evidence, and appendix*, HC 1866 (418) xi.643.

although not frontline issues, preventing the spread of disease in livestock and extending Ireland's rail network were issues of personal interest to him and had been proposed at the meeting of Irish MPs in December.

The O'Conor Don's determination to plough his own furrow was further illustrated in May 1866 when he turned down Lord Russell's offer of a junior lordship in the treasury, despite Gladstone urging him to reconsider.[20] Both men clearly felt the O'Conor Don was someone who could see the benefits of being part of the government and be trusted to toe the party line, but the O'Conor Don informed Gillooly that he turned down the post because of differences of opinion on the education question, which, although he believed Russell's government had 'a sincere desire' to address, would have put him 'in a false position'.[21] Given the O'Conor Don's public support for denominational education, he would have been exposed to accusations of hypocrisy, but he accepted that compromise was necessary and would likely be forthcoming from the Liberal government side. Maybe his refusal was as much about being perceived as a placeman or the fact that he was a man of independent means who did not need the salary, but maybe he genuinely felt it would compromise his position as an independent-minded liberal Catholic. One way or the other, he was still happy to support Russell's government when he could. In June 1866, he opposed Lord Dunkillen's motion to amend Gladstone's franchise reform bill, which passed and precipitated the fall of Russell's government.[22] And when the debate on electoral reform resumed under Lord Derby's minority Conservative government in March 1867, the O'Conor Don and the majority of his liberal Catholic colleagues opposed Disraeli's bill. However, with many British liberals either voting with the Conservative government or abstaining altogether, the reform bill passed in April 1867 and was followed by the passing of an Irish reform bill in June 1868.[23]

Irish liberal opposition to a slightly more advanced reform of the franchise was, on this occasion, more about supporting Gladstone, who they held in high esteem, but it was also reflective of their reluctance to embrace the idea of an expanded electorate. This reluctance was fuelled by the rise of Fenian activity in Ireland and Great Britain. In December 1866, the O'Conor Don's neighbour, Oliver Grace, a Catholic landlord and former Liberal MP for County Roscommon, expressed his concern about the rise of Fenian activity in the county and wondered whether a statement of loyalty should be issued by 'persons of influence and lovers of Law and Order'. Grace thought

20 Lord Russell to the O'Conor Don, 5 May 1866, O'Conor papers, CH, 9.3.HS.323. 21 The O'Conor Don to Bishop Gillooly, May 1866, Gillooly papers, EDA, B1/5/1/2. 22 Hoppen, *The mid-Victorian generation*, p. 248; *Freeman's Journal*, 19 June 1866. 23 Hoppen, *Elections, politics and society*, pp 31–2; idem, *The mid-Victorian generation*, pp 246–53.

such action would have the threefold effect of maintaining the county 'in its present undisturbed state'; providing a 'sense of security to those engaged in the peaceful pursuits of farming and commerce'; and preventing 'the seeds of Fenianism' from growing to 'dangerous' levels.[24] Although Fenian activity had been reported in the county in February 1866, the O'Conor Don urged caution, arguing that such a declaration was unnecessary given the county's comparably peaceable state and because no one, in any case, doubted the loyalty of the gentry.[25] An assessment that probably factored in the likely adverse reaction among Fenians in the county, and maybe even on his estates, the O'Conor Don was nonetheless very much aware of the increased support for Fenianism, not only in Ireland and Great Britain, but in North America also. During his travels there between November 1865 and February 1866, he noted the anti-English feeling among Irish Americans, many of whom had fought in the civil war and were now bent on returning to Ireland and instituting an American form of democracy by force of arms.[26] Large numbers of suspected Fenians had already been arrested in the provinces of Munster and Leinster in September 1865, and more were rounded up after the failed rebellion of March 1867. Subsequent attempts to rescue some of those imprisoned resulted in the shooting dead of a police officer in Manchester in September, and the death of several innocent bystanders after an explosion at Clerkenwell prison in London in December. The shooting in Manchester led to the execution of three Fenians and a furore of anti-Irish feeling in the English press. Conversely, the execution of the 'Manchester Martyrs' received widespread condemnation in Ireland.[27]

The O'Conor Don witnessed such condemnation at a public meeting in Roscommon in December 1867, where the 'most determined Fenian spirit', some of which found its voice in the speeches of the local clergy, 'inculcated hatred against England'. Indeed, he thought the clergy's remarks were 'thoroughly disloyal' and wondered whether they considered that such disloyalty would not influence 'the people to follow their teachings'.[28] Here we see early signs of the O'Conor Don's resistance to the sometimes-anti-English rhetoric of Irish nationalist sentiment, as well as his concern about the impact of the clergy's promulgation of such rhetoric. Thus, although he was not averse to the odd private and public outburst of ant-English sentiment, he clearly felt

---

24 Oliver Grace to the O'Conor Don, Dec. 1866, O'Conor papers, CH, 9.3.HS.181. 25 The O'Conor Don to Oliver Grace, 12 Dec. 1866, O'Conor papers, CH, 9.3.HS.181; Clipping from the *Roscommon Journal*, 10 Feb. 1866, O'Conor papers, CH, 9.3.HE.167. 26 Notes on the O'Conor Don's tour in America, Dec. 1865, O'Conor papers, CH, 9.3.HS.249; Dunleavy & Dunleavy, 'Reconstruction, reform, and Romanism', pp 30–5. 27 Comerford, *The Fenians in context*, pp 117–18, 131–50. 28 Recollections part 1, O'Conor papers, CH, 9.4.HS.156, p. 48.

it had no place in national political discourse. Moreover, although he clearly felt the clergy had a legitimate role influencing the minds of the people, this should be done within the parameters of keeping them on the loyal, law-abiding straight and narrow. Indeed, this was what he expected of them during the land agitations of later years.

Meanwhile, in 1867–8, the O'Conor Don continued along the path of parliamentary scrutiny and moderate social reform, chairing a select committee investigating grand jury revenue and introducing an industrial schools bill for Ireland.[29] Although the former reflected his interest in local government reform and recommended the replacement of the landlord-dominated grand juries with more representative baronial and county boards elected along the lines of the poor law boards, it did not lead to anything.[30] His industrial schools bill, on the other hand, led to the passing of the Irish industrial schools act in 1868. Having sat on a commission that investigated the provision of education for destitute children in England and Wales in 1861, the O'Conor Don was already familiar with the British state's attempts at providing care for orphaned, neglected and 'criminal' children through a system of ragged, industrial and reformatory schools.[31] With this knowledge and Monsell's support, he ushered the industrial schools bill through the House and the subsequent act led to the establishment of reformatory and industrial schools across Ireland, largely run by religious orders.[32] The O'Conor Don continued to take an interest in juvenile care, lobbying for the opening of a new industrial school in Athlone, making regular visits to industrial schools in Dublin throughout his life, and sitting on a royal commission on reformatory and industrial schools in 1884.[33] Nonetheless, although the intention behind these schools was a good one and of a piece with the O'Conor Don's liberal outlook on the proactive role the state should take in improving the social, economic and moral fabric of society by equipping uncared-for children with the skills for gainful employment in adulthood, it should be noted that the legacy of these institutions in post-independence Ireland has

29 *A bill to extend the Industrial Schools Act to Ireland*, HC 1867–8 (6), ii, 523; *Select committee on laws under which monies are raised by grand jury presentments in Ireland: report, proceedings, index*, HC 1867–8 (392) (392-I) x.47, 477. 30 *Select committee on ... grand jury presentments*, pp iii–vii; W. Feingold, 'The tenants' movement to capture the Irish Poor Law Boards, 1877–1886' in A. O'Day (ed.), *Reactions to Irish nationalism, 1865–1914* (London, 1987), p. 79. 31 *Select committee to inquire how education of destitute and neglected children may be assisted by public funds: report, proceedings, minutes of evidence, appendix, index 1861*, HC 1861 (460) (460-I), vii, 395, 647; J. Barnes, *Irish industrial schools, 1868–1906: origins and development* (Dublin, 1989), pp 40–3, 57, 67–8, 71–5, 88–104, 113–17, 141–52. 32 Barnes, *Irish industrial schools*, pp 38–43, 57, 67–75, 88–104, 113–17, 141–52. 33 Diaries of the O'Conor Don, 12 Feb. 1877, O'Conor papers, CH, 9.4.SH.247 & 21 Apr. 1901, O'Conor papers, CH, 0.1.SH.041; *Freeman's Journal*, 18 Aug. 1880, 15 & 17 July 1893; *Royal commission on reformatories and industrial schools: report, minutes of evidence, appendices, index*, HC 1884 [C.3876] [C.3876-I], xlv.1, 89.

been a largely harmful one, with widespread abuse of vulnerable children over many years, leading right up to recent times.³⁴

Returning to the issue of Fenianism, the rise in activity and the threat of revolt was partly viewed by liberal Catholics as an indictment of British misrule in Ireland.³⁵ Gladstone was now of a similar mind and fought the 1868 general election campaign on a policy of governing Ireland with 'Irish ideas', promising disestablishment and land and education reform. In so doing, Gladstone managed at once to outmanoeuvre the minority Conservative government and draw Irish liberals, particularly liberal Catholics, closer to the Liberal Party.³⁶ With the support of the Catholic clergy and the mainstream press, sixty-five Irish Liberal MPs were returned in November/December 1868 – most on a platform that supported disestablishment and land and educational reform.³⁷ The O'Conor Don was returned unopposed again, while his brother, Denis, was returned for the neighbouring county of Sligo, where he defeated one of the sitting Tory candidates, Colonel Edward Cooper. At a hustings during the contest, the O'Conor Don assured the assembled crowd that Gladstone, 'One of England's greatest men', was sure to do right by Ireland.³⁸

The overall election result in 1868 brought about a liberal majority of 106 in the commons and the formation of Gladstone's first Liberal government. Nonetheless, although the disestablishment act passed through both houses with relative ease in March 1869, the tenuous alliance between Irish and British liberals was to be severely tested on the issues of an amnesty for Fenian prisoners, land reform, law and order, and education.³⁹ As early as October 1868, the O'Conor Don had received a letter from Charles French, a local Catholic landlord, who feared the possibility of public discontent over a Fenian amnesty and wondered whether petitioning the queen for clemency would not be a sensible course of action.⁴⁰ In a commons debate on the subject the following February, the O'Conor Don asked the Irish chief secretary, Chichester Fortescue, whether the government would consider advising the queen to 'extend' a 'Royal clemency … to persons suffering imprisonment or penal servitude for offences of a political character in connection with Ireland?'⁴¹ Sensitive to the potential for Irish agitation on the amnesty question, the cabinet had already made the decision to release forty-nine Fenian prisoners, which it seems likely the O'Conor Don was already aware of. But

34 See the 2009 report (the Ryan report) of the commission to inquire into child abuse in the Republic of Ireland here: www.childabusecommission.ie/rpt/pdfs/, accessed 2 Nov. 2021. 35 Potter, *William Monsell*, p. 130. 36 A. Hawkins, *British party politics, 1852–1886* (Basingstoke, 1998), pp 142–8. 37 O'Day, *Irish home rule*, p. 25; Thornley, *Isaac Butt*, pp 25–7; Hawkins, *British party politics*, pp 142–8; Crossman, *Politics, law and order*, pp 114–15. 38 *Sligo Champion*, 10, 17, 24 Oct. & 5 Dec. 1868. 39 Thornley, *Isaac Butt*, pp 22, 62–82. 40 Charles French to the O'Conor Don, Oct. 1868, O'Conor papers, CH, 9.3.HS.187. 41 HC Deb., 22 Feb. 1869, vol. 194, c. 159.

despite this concession, the issue continued to gather momentum and an Amnesty Association was formed in June 1869 under the leadership of Isaac Butt, a nationalist-minded Protestant unionist who, as a lawyer, had made representations on behalf of the Young Irelanders after the 1848 rebellion and the Fenians after the 1867 rebellion.[42] The association had the support of a large section of the clergy and, together with the renewal of tenant-right clubs, reinvigorated nationalist politics and raised Butt's profile as a national leader in 1869.[43]

The O'Conor Don typically kept his distance from the Amnesty Association, but, when Gladstone introduced a coercion bill alongside his land bill in February 1870, his anxiety about the influence of the amnesty question over the popular mind came to the fore. On 15 March 1870, he urged Thomas O'Hagan (now Lord O'Hagan) to impress upon the government that such a policy left him and his colleagues in a precarious position. Indeed, in a letter to the viceroy, Earl Spencer, O'Hagan colourfully described how:

> The O'Conor Don was with me here this morning, almost in agony of mind, to tell me of the straits, in which he and many of the best Irish Members find themselves. They ... will be howled at, with double virulence, if they support a measure of coercion. They feel the need of such a thing; but he thinks they will be driven to oppose it, or be swept from the face of the political earth, unless it be accompanied by some such concession as the liberation of the Fenians, on the terms of their leaving the country.[44]

While the O'Conor Don admitted to O'Hagan that it would be hard to convince 'English opinion' of the merits of such a proposal, he emphasized the difficulty for Irish MPs in supporting any measure of coercion. Taking this into consideration, O'Hagan conveyed the O'Conor Don's thoughts on the matter to Lord Granville, who in turn promised to 'communicate with Gladstone on the subject'.[45] One week later, however, the O'Conor Don and William Cogan were again pleading with O'Hagan to lobby the government on the issue. According to the latter, both men 'said that their foolish and deluded constituents were angry' about the land bill-coercion bill scenario and felt 'the moment was opportune for letting out the Fenian prisoners'. Although O'Hagan was sure the government would not go in for such an arrangement, he was nonetheless 'seriously afraid' that Irish MPs would vote against the

---

42 Reid, 'Isaac Butt, home rule and federalist political thought', pp 333–7; Comerford, *The Fenians in context*, pp 170–4; O'Day, *Irish home rule*, pp 22–38. 43 Thornley, *Isaac Butt*, pp 13–24, 65–8. 44 Lord O'Hagan to Earl Spencer, 15 Mar. 1870, O'Hagan papers, PRONI, D2777/8/102. 45 Ibid.

land bill if the government did not do something to assuage their fears. With this in mind, he thought the promise of 'an amnesty on the earliest ... occasion which might arise on the restoration of tranquillity' in Ireland would allow the O'Conor Don and his colleagues to support coercion without any fear of political retribution.[46] As it turned out, O'Hagan was essentially correct in his assessment. The peace preservation act passed through the House in 1870 and the government released another thirty-three Fenian prisoners in February 1871. In May 1872, the government introduced a further coercion bill with two clauses: one for the continuation of the peace preservation act and the other for the suspension of habeas corpus. The O'Conor Don was happy to support the latter but put forward a motion to amend the bill so the former would not be continued. Apart from his brother Denis, he received little support from Irish MPs, who either opposed or supported the bill outright.[47] Overall, however, what this episode demonstrates is that the O'Conor Don was extremely fearful about the influence of Fenianism in Ireland and about the ability of his electorate to accept what he thought were sensible political decisions around the necessity to maintain law and order.

LIBERALISM, DEMOCRACY AND THE HOME RULE MOVEMENT

Gladstone's land act passed through the House in the summer of 1870, but as outlined in the previous chapter the weakness of the British-Irish liberal alliance was brutally exposed with the defeat of his Irish university bill in the spring of 1873. In the meantime, however, the Home Government Association (HGA) was established on 19 May 1870 under Butt's leadership, forming a committee of sixty-one members that initially brought together a peculiar mix of conservatives, liberals, constitutional nationalists and Fenians. When the committee met and finalized its programme in September of 1870, it advocated the establishment of a parliament in Dublin within a federal United Kingdom.[48]

The idea of an Irish parliament within a federal union was first proposed in the early 1840s by the radical Protestant MP William Sharman Crawford, largely as a reaction to Daniel O'Connell's campaign for repeal of the Act Union, which vaguely envisioned the restoration of 'Grattan's Parliament' of 1782–1800. But O'Connell's repeal campaign petered out and the federal ideal did not receive much attention until Butt published a pamphlet on the subject

46 Lord O'Hagan to Earl Spencer, 22 Mar. 1870, O'Hagan papers, PRONI, D2777/8/104. 47 O'Day, *Irish home rule*, p. 26; *Freeman's Journal*, 20 May 1871; HC Deb., 19 May 1871, vol. 206, cc 1039–73. 48 Thornley, *Isaac Butt*, pp 92–103.

in 1870. Concerned about the influence of Fenianism in the Irish body politic and influenced by the federal settlement in Canada in 1867, Butt envisaged the establishment of domestic parliaments in England, Scotland and Ireland under one imperial parliament in London (Wales did not figure). The Irish parliament would have a house of lords and commons, while 105 Irish MPs would continue attending the imperial parliament. Butt's explanation of how and when all three sets of domestic MPs would converge in Westminster for imperial purposes, and whether the English and Scottish parliaments would work separately or together, was confused and ill-defined. However, despite the lack of clarity, the debate over whether Ireland should have some form of self-government had been recommenced.[49]

As the O'Conor Don feared, the fall of Gladstone's government in March 1873 over the defeat of his Irish university bill gave renewed emphasis to debate on home rule, even though conservative support for it, based on the perceived injustice of disestablishment, had largely fizzled out and membership of the HGA became more Catholic and nationalist.[50] The O'Conor Don did not attend the HGA's inaugural meeting in 1870, declining to give his support to the federal plan. And when the Roscommon branch of the HGA requested his 'cooperation in carrying ... into effect' the principles of federalism in April 1872, his response was to state his belief 'in the principle of self-government' while making vague assurances that he would 'not be wanting in supporting these principles to the best of my ability'.[51] His reply to a direct request to join the association from its secretary, L.P. Hayden, on 30 September 1873, was less evasive. While he thought a federal arrangement might have 'great advantages', he hesitated 'to join the committee' because he thought it would be 'unwise' to agitate 'on this subject without very good prospects of success'.[52]

The O'Conor Don's initial evasiveness seems to have been a combination of the political and the personal. On the former, he told Monsell that he was considering not standing at the next election in light of the failure of Gladstone's university bill and because he could not support Butt's federal plan.[53] On the latter, his wife, Georgina, had died prematurely on 17 August

---

49 J. Kendle, *Ireland and the federal solution: the debate over the United Kingdom constitution, 1870–1921* (Kingston, Ontario, 1989), pp 8–15; Reid, 'Isaac Butt, home rule and federalist political thought', pp 349–59; O'Day, *Irish home rule*, p. 7. 50 Thornley, *Isaac Butt*, pp 83–137; L.J. McCaffrey, 'Isaac Butt and the home rule movement: a study in conservative nationalism', *Review of Politics*, 22:1 (Jan. 1960), 77–82. 51 Circulars from the Home Government Association, 1870–2, O'Conor papers, CH, 9.3.HS.220; Letter to the O'Conor Don from Anon., 7 July 1870, O'Conor papers, CH, 9.3.HS.226; L.P. Hayden to the O'Conor Don, 4 Apr. 1872, O'Conor papers, CH, 9.3.HS.266; The O'Conor Don to L.P. Hayden, 10 Apr. 1872, O'Conor papers, CH, 9.3.HS.266; Thornley, *Isaac Butt*, p. 96. 52 L.P. Hayden to the O'Conor Don, 30 Sept. 1873 & the O'Conor Don to L.P. Hayden, Oct. 1873, O'Conor papers, CH, 9.3.HS.266. 53 William Monsell to the O'Conor Don, 17 Sept. 1873, O'Conor papers, CH, 9.4.HS.230.

1872, aged only twenty-five, from consumption.⁵⁴ This undoubtedly left the O'Conor Don 'with a broken heart' and he effectively dropped out of public life for the following five months, going on visits to Blackpool and Llandudno 'for the waters', and embarking on his second trip to America with his brother, Denis.⁵⁵ Moreover, in the weeks leading up to Georgina's death, he had lobbied Lord O'Hagan and Earl Spencer for the positions of deputy lord and lord lieutenant of Roscommon. Although not one of those liberals who was 'rabid for jobs', he was an obvious contender for any honorary local position and was not shy of reminding Spencer of this fact. Thus, the O'Conor Don does seem to have been looking for a way out of frontline politics during the time of his wife's illness and death in the autumn of 1872, but any hope of getting either of these positions was blocked by his sworn enemy in the county, Edward King-Tenison.⁵⁶

In any event, Monsell seems to have persuaded the O'Conor Don to rethink the matter, telling him that 'Hardly any Catholic of weight' would be in the next parliament if he stood down, with the few remaining probably having their places taken by 'low demagogues or insincere professors of Home Rule'.⁵⁷ Monsell also felt 'sure' that he would 'carefully weigh and consider … any scheme … giving Ireland more control over her own concerns you are thinking of putting forward'. Nothing was forthcoming, however; and as we shall see in the next chapter, the extent to which it can be said that the O'Conor Don had a credible, alternative scheme of home rule in mind is highly debateable. Monsell's own view of home rule was that 'nothing like a representative assembly' could be allowed because:

> What would property be worth if an assembly chosen by the present Irish constituencies were to have the sole and uncontrolled power of dealing with it? How certain too any such assembly would be … anti[-] English and Fenian in its spirit, and to use Federalism as a means to … separation, or at all means complete independence – again what possible chance, against Ulster and the property of the other 3 provinces, is there of forcing G[reat]t Britain to consent to such a scheme?⁵⁸

What is evident from this disclosure is that Monsell's extremely wary attitude towards the idea of home rule was based on his distrust of the electorate

---

54 Diary of the O'Conor Don, Aug. 1872, O'Conor papers, CH, 9.3.SH.306.   55 Diaries of the O'Conor Don, Aug.–Dec. 1872, O'Conor papers, CH, 9.3.SH.306.   56 Hoppen, *Elections, politics and society*, p. 262; The O'Conor Don to Earl Spencer, 10 Aug. 1872, Althorp papers, add. 76997, art. 1; Earl Spencer to Lord O'Hagan, 11 Aug. 1872, O'Hagan papers, PRONI, D2777/8/204.   57 William Monsell to the O'Conor Don, 17 Sept. 1873, O'Conor papers, CH, 9.4.HS.230.   58 Ibid.

and of the motives of those MPs who professed to support federalism. However, it also pointed to the rather obvious but largely unrecognized issue of Protestant opposition, particularly in Ulster. As we shall see, the O'Conor Don's views on home rule largely reflected those of Monsell, but he had already reached his own conclusions on government and democracy, which almost certainly influenced his views on home rule. In a draft essay penned in 1865–6, he surmised that the seventeenth-century French mathematician and Catholic philosopher Blaise Pascal provided the 'most beautiful expression and most precise definition' of representative government, i.e. 'That Multitude which is not reduced to Unity is confusion and that Unity which does not comprise Multitude is Tyranny.' For the O'Conor Don, this meant the majority needed to possess a general unity of mind on the basic principles that should govern society, but these principles – 'divine law', 'duty', 'justice' and 'reason' – were possessed by 'the man who feels himself truly free, and in ... that freedom always acknowledges some natural law by wh[ich] he is guided ... wh[ich] ought to regulate his will'. He therefore rejected Rousseau's 'primitive' social contract, which claimed equality among all men and advocated a form of direct democracy. He did so because he believed that there was a 'natural inequality' among men, which meant 'the tendency of all society is to be governed by the best ... by those who have greatest knowledge of and the greatest desire for truth and justice'. In other words, the O'Conor Don thought that government was best conducted by some kind of quasi meritocratic, representative ruling class who understood that their duty was to protect society from the 'tyranny' of absolutism and majoritarian democracy. Indeed, he felt both aristocratic and democratic government tended towards despotism. A limited form of representative government, as existed under the British constitution, recognized the reality of a natural inequality in society, where people's abilities and stations in life differed, and where those 'less able' and of 'inferior intellect' recognized 'those superior' to them and let them get on with the business of good government.[59] He therefore held the fairly typical mid-Victorian liberal view that government by an intelligent and benevolent ruling class, representing the interests of the majority, was the best way to maintain stability in society.[60]

Inegalitarian high-mindedness aside, the O'Conor Don's thinking on government and democracy was also influenced by his tour of North America

---

59 Essay on representative government, 1865–6, O'Conor papers, CH, 9.3.HL.308; H. Bouchilloux, 'Pascal and the social world' in N. Hammond (ed.), *The Cambridge companion to Pascal* (Cambridge, 2003), pp 206–13. 60 Essay on representative government, 1865–6, O'Conor papers, CH, 9.3.HL.308; B. Russell, *History of Western philosophy* (London, 2000), pp 669–74; Parry, *Liberal government in Victorian Britain*, pp 4–6, 12–13, 18; J. Gray (ed.), *John Stuart Mill: 'On liberty' and other essays* (New York, 1998), pp 302–25.

between November 1865 and February 1866. Indeed, his essay on representative government may have been written while on his travels. Arriving in New York, his hosts were his cousin Charles O'Conor, William Sloane (presumably the luxury furniture and carpet business owner) and Ernest McCracken. While there he met the archbishop of the city, John McCloskey; visited Tammany Hall, where he met General Ulysses S. Grant; and spent a day at West Point, where he met Lieutenant William Thomas Clarke and Colonel Daniel McCallum. From New York, he travelled across the border into Canada, visiting Montreal and Quebec, where he met Father Patrick Dowd at the Séminaire de Saint-Sulpice and Bishop Charles-François Baillargeon. From Montreal, he travelled to Buffalo, visiting Niagara Falls; and from there on to Chicago, where he met Bishop James Duggan. The O'Conor Don then headed south via St Louis, taking in New Orleans, Mobile, Montgomery, Atlanta, Augusta, Charleston and Richmond. In the latter, he met the leader of the Confederate army, General Robert E. Lee, who he thought 'a most ... handsome man', much loved by the people of Richmond, many of whom regretted 'that he had not been made dictator'.[61] His travel party between Charleston and Richmond included a southern planter, Mr Nicholls, who used to own seventy-three slaves, as well as a 'negro boy' named Cupid who helped with the baggage wagon. Unsurprisingly, Nicholls was not convinced that emancipation would be beneficial to slaves, claiming that they did not want to work for themselves or under any kind of contract, and in general did not know what to do with their freedom. Indeed, Nicholls left the O'Conor Don with the distinct impression that speaking up for black people in the south would be met with open hostility. In Atlanta, he met a Catholic chaplain, Father Whelan, who relayed the 'hell on earth' which 35,000 Confederate prisoners were subjected to in a camp at Andersonville. In Charleston, he met the Irish immigrant and Confederate-supporting bishop of the diocese, Patrick Lynch, who relayed similar accounts of the poor treatment of Confederate prisoners of war by Union forces. Lynch also told the story of a black man who was shot in the street by an 'officer' because he had the temerity to speak to a white woman. Apparently, 'nothing was thought of it no more than if a dog had been shot'. And in a similar vein to Nicholls, Lynch gave an account of a 'n___r' who turned up at the federal offices in Columbia to 'seek his freedom', as he did not 'rightly understand what freedom meant'. Apparently, the federal officer informed him he was already free and needed to go and find work to support himself and his family.[62]

61 Notes on the O'Conor Don's tour in America, Nov. 1865–Feb. 1866, O'Conor papers, CH, 9.3.HS.249. 62 Notes on the O'Conor Don's tour in America, Nov. 1865–Feb. 1866, O'Conor papers, CH, 9.3.HS.249.

From Richmond, the O'Conor Don travelled north to Washington D.C., where he attended two receptions at the White House. There he saw President Andrew Johnson, who he thought looked young for his age and possessed a 'rather good natural countenance', but whose daughters were 'very plain' and 'unassuming' on account of their not being of 'high birth'. Indeed, the O'Conor Don was not terribly impressed by the general class of people in attendance, observing that such receptions were not attended by the upper classes of the city. It would seem the latter did not think much of Congress either, which they felt was packed with 'adventurers to whom the salary is of importance'. Nonetheless, the O'Conor Don thought the Capitol a fine building 'in many respects … superior' to the 'British Houses' of parliament, although he felt the towers and the library of 'our building' superior to anything in America.[63]

Overall, the O'Conor Don was struck by 'the deadly hatred [that] existed between North and South', but his views on slavery were not made explicit one way or the other. His cousin, Charles O'Conor, was a Democrat and a lawyer who supported slavery and represented the Confederate leader, Jefferson Davis, after the war, but this does not imply that the O'Conor Don agreed with his pro-slavery views. He did seem wary of expressing a view on the subject while in the company of the former owner of enslaved people Mr Nicholls, which would suggest that he was opposed to slavery. On the other hand, his causally racist comments in his 1860 election victory speech suggest at the very least a disregard for black people. On American politics more generally, he was clearly not enamoured with the calibre of politician on show in Washington, expressing some rather elitist views about fashionable society in the capital. Moreover, he took a dim view of what he saw as the corrupt and populist nature of majoritarian democracy in America, which, in his opinion, led to politicians being too easily swayed by powerful private interest groups on the one hand, and public opinion on the other.[64] Like many nineteenth-century British and Irish liberals, then, the O'Conor Don thought the idea of democracy was all good and well, but the idea of the 'sovereignty of the majority' was a dangerous one based on the erroneous 'supposition that each man possesses by right of birth not only an equal right to be well governed but also an equal right to govern others'. The restricted franchise of the United Kingdom militated against this danger while at the same time keeping aristocratic power in check with a representative parliament that was responsive to, but not subject to, the

---

63 Ibid. 64 Dunleavy & Dunleavy, *The O'Conor papers*, pp 219–20, 233–4, 271–2; idem, 'Reconstruction, reform, and Romanism', pp 24–35.

views of the majority. It was this limited form of representative government that the O'Conor Don believed 'had raised England to the highest degree of moral and material prosperity'.[65]

It may come as no surprise then that the O'Conor Don held somewhat controversial and ill-defined views on Irish home rule. At a meeting on the subject in Roscommon on 15 October 1873, he praised the British constitution as one that provided the greatest 'liberty of the subject' and 'protection to life and property' while at the same time responding to the 'wants' and 'feelings' of the people. This, he felt, compared favourably to a system of government subject to the 'tyranny of the multitude', which, although not specifically stated, was almost certainly a reference to the American constitution. But despite his regard for the British constitution, he claimed to support the idea of home rule because Ireland did not have the 'same ... right to self[-]government that England had', resulting in many of England's laws being completely different to Ireland's. This self-governing imbalance was a result of the want of 'regard' among 'British members' for Irish issues; the want of 'responsibility on the part of Irish members' due to their feeling of powerlessness in the situation; 'and [the] want of time on the part of both' due to parliament being overburdened with legislation concerning the constituent parts of the United Kingdom. These, according to the O'Conor Don, were 'the three great evils of the existing system'. However, he thought Butt's federal plan unworkable, for the simple reason that it would not gain the consent of all the nations of the union, particularly England. The only thing he felt that an English-dominated imperial parliament might consent to for Ireland was 'absolute independence', but there would first have to be 'a union amongst Irishmen' and a demonstration 'by their conduct that their object was not the disruption of the Empire'.[66] What 'absolute independence' meant, as a form of home rule, was not made clear, but perhaps he was thinking of a devolved Irish parliament connected to Great Britain and the empire through the crown. In other words, some version of the old, vaguely defined, and failed O'Connellite call for repeal.[67] What seems clear, however, from his call for 'a union among Irishmen' and the security of the British empire, is that he thought Ireland was not yet ready for self-government. This was reflective of liberal thinking at the time, which in short was that, despite British misrule, Ireland was not yet politically or culturally mature enough for self-government.[68]

A further impracticality of Butt's federal home rule plan was the proposal for an Irish house of lords based on the Westminster model. On this point

---

65 Essay on representative government, 1865–6, O'Conor papers, CH, 9.3.HL.308. 66 *Irish Times*, 16 Oct. 1873; *Roscommon Messenger*, 18 Oct. 1873. 67 Foster, *Modern Ireland*, pp 308–9. 68 Reid, 'Isaac Butt, home rule and federalist political thought', pp 354–6.

the O'Conor Don pleaded with those assembled to 'imagine what would be the position of affairs' if there was a hereditary upper house, dominated by landlords, having the power to oppose legislation passed in a representative lower house dominated by men of no property, who sought to pass popular measures on land reform. This, he argued, would result in rancour and division, with the Irish peers 'throw[ing] themselves back on England, the superior power, and the English would say the Irish were not fit to govern themselves'.[69] What this meant in terms of the kind of Irish parliament he thought would work is not clear, but it is clear that he thought men of property should maintain a position of influence in an Irish parliament, just not as hereditary peers. However, given that the O'Conor Don went on to oppose both of Gladstone's home rule bills, one can only speculate as to whether this meant he preferred a unicameral parliament with a cohort of representative peers or a bicameral parliament with a separate chamber of representative peers elected on a limited franchise.

Uncertainty around home rule models aside, the O'Conor Don was also concerned about protecting Ireland's sense of nationality in a parliament potentially dominated by those who criticized the Catholic Church for subordinating Ireland's quest for nationhood to its own quest for power and influence. Although not specifically stated, this was a clear reference to the growing influence of Fenianism in Irish politics, both within and without the home rule movement. As a devout Catholic who believed in the natural law of God, and a liberal who believed in a limited form of representative government and the maintenance of the British connection, the O'Conor Don was fundamentally opposed to the Fenian ideal of a secular Irish republic, obtained by revolution, if necessary, where the Catholic Church would be, in theory, subordinate to the state. For him, the Catholic faith was, due to the persecutions of the past, one of the cornerstones of Ireland's nationality. His concern was that, like the demise of the Irish language under the *de jure* state system of secular national education, the centrality of the Catholic faith to Irish national life could be undermined in a *de facto* secular state.[70] While this may seem, in hindsight, a somewhat fanciful view on the likely demise of religious belief among Catholics in Ireland, it was a view shared by the pope, Cardinal Cullen and many of the bishops and clergy in Ireland, who still felt keenly the vulnerable position of the church in revolutionary France and, more recently, nationalist Italy.[71] The O'Conor Don witnessed first-hand the consternation in Rome as the forces of Victor Emmanuel and Giuseppe Garibaldi descended on the Papal States in 1860, so it is not that surprising that he

---

69 *Roscommon Messenger*, 18 Oct. 1873.   70 Ibid.   71 O.P. Rafferty, '"Eternity is not long enough nor hell hot enough …": the Catholic Church and Fenianism', *History Ireland*, 16:6 (Nov.–Dec. 2008), 30–4.

feared what the influence of republican ideals could mean for the fate of the Catholic Church in a self-governing Ireland influenced by republican ideals.[72] Moreover, from his encounters with Fenianism at home and abroad, he clearly felt that a considerable number of the clergy were, at the very least, complicit in the spread of its ideals by the use of disloyal and anti-English rhetoric. This encouragement of revolutionary sentiment was a cause of concern for Cullen, with vocal clerics such as Father Patrick Lavelle, as well as Archbishops John MacHale and Thomas Croke, reflecting and influencing the growing nationalist sentiment and its often-strong republican undertones in 1870s Ireland.[73]

The O'Conor Don's views on home rule were reasonably accurately summed up by the *Roscommon Messenger* as a statement of his intention to 'continue as an Independent Liberal member' who would not 'vote against every Government' that opposed 'the claim of the people of Ireland to Home Rule'.[74] The *Nation*, however, took issue with his opposition to an Irish house of lords, arguing that objecting to it on the grounds of a comparison with the British house of lords made a folly of his admiration for the British constitution. In any event, it was felt 'that the Irish Peers, in the bracing atmosphere of a national legislature', would not 'display the bigotry and treasonable obstructiveness indicated by the O'Conor Don'.[75] On the other hand, the O'Conor Don had support from the ultramontane, anti-home rule and now distinctly English Catholic magazine the *Tablet*, which was owned by his confidante, Herbert Vaughan, the bishop of Salford. Here he was praised for discussing 'most fully' the ideas of federalism and repeal within the framework of the empire, while coming out 'in favour of a qualified scheme of Repeal, with Irish representation in the Imperial Parliament'.[76] This was a reasonable enough deduction, but the O'Conor Don did not specifically mention repeal, the kind of Irish parliament he envisaged or whether Irish representation should be retained at Westminster or not. Thus, while he did not think a federal union would work, he did not reveal an alternative 'scheme' as Monsell suggested he might do.

Neither did he clarify his position at the national home rule conference in Dublin in November 1873, where, by his own admission, he got himself 'into trouble'.[77] Although he reiterated his scepticism about an Irish house of lords, the O'Conor Don felt that his scepticism had been misconstrued as a declaration 'that the Irish people and their leaders should sit down with folded arms and do nothing until they got unanimity amongst the Irish Peers and … aristocracy in favour of this movement'. This he dismissed as 'nonsense'

---

72 See chapter two, pp 46–7. 73 Rafferty, 'The Catholic Church and Fenianism', pp 30–4. 74 *Roscommon Journal*, 18 Oct. 1873. 75 *Nation*, 1 Nov. 1873. 76 *Tablet*, 25 Oct. 1873. Bishop Herbert Vaughan was co-celebrant at the O'Conor Don's marriage to Ellen More O'Ferrall in 1879. See *Freeman's Journal*, 17 Sept. 1879. 77 Diary of the O'Conor Don, 19 Nov. 1873, O'Conor papers, CH, 9.3.SH.306.

because no one could ever expect unanimity of opinion in any form of 'constitutional representative government'. But in response to calls from the floor to provide an alternative scheme, he declined to do so because he was not 'in opposition to the programme laid down by the Home Rule Association', having only 'pointed to the weak places' in the plan 'as a friend, not as an enemy'. Indeed, he felt that to propose an alternative scheme at this early stage would only serve to undermine the home rule movement, and as such he would be 'acting the part of a traitor'. With this in mind, the O'Conor Don urged the conference not to insist on a strict adherence to its resolutions or to get bogged down in the details of how the federalist plan might work. This, he believed, would only distract from the fundamental principle that Ireland needed some form of self-government, a principle he adhered to 'from the moment I entered into public life'.[78] Generally speaking, this was a reasonably convincing way of saying that consensus had to be established on the end of Irish self-government before any consensus could be reached on the means of achieving it. According to Alan O'Day, this is what Isaac Butt was actually trying to achieve, in the sense that he did not view his federalist plan as the definitive solution, but rather a springboard for debate on how home rule might best work.[79] It is not known if the O'Conor Don ever had this kind of means and ends discussion with Butt, but his vocal opposition to federalism somewhat contradicted his argument that fixating on the means would undermine the end of self-government. In addition, his claim of adherence to the principle of self-government 'from the moment I entered into public life' is not easily verifiable. It was not mentioned in his 1860 election address or in his maiden speech to the House in 1861. Nor did he ever table a motion on the issue in parliament or make a public speech on it before 1873.[80] One can always allow for privately held views, but his thoughts on representative government in the mid-1860s could hardly be interpreted as advocating more democracy in the form of Irish home rule.

One way or another, the O'Conor Don's criticism of Butt's federal plan was not welcomed by A.M. Sullivan, the proprietor of the *Nation* and executive council member of the HGA.[81] Sullivan insisted that the O'Conor Don 'must say yea or nay' to the resolutions, as adherence was necessary to counter the arguments of those opposed to home rule on the grounds that it was nothing more than a ruse for complete separation from the union. In an attempt to cajole and flatter the O'Conor Don, he declared there was 'no man in all the land whom I ... am so heartily ambitious to see at the head of this movement

---

[78] *Proceedings of the home rule conference held at the Rotunda, Dublin, on the 18th, 19th, 20th, and 21st November 1873 ...* (Dublin, 1874), pp 82–3   [79] O'Day, *Irish home rule*, p. 9   [80] *Roscommon Journal*, Mar. 1860; HC Deb., 22 May 1862, vol. 166, cc 2032–40.   [81] P. Maume, 'Sullivan, Alexander Martin (1830–84)', *DIB*.

as the Chief of Roscommon' because the 'Irish people reverence social distinction and historical distinctions', and, as such, they would be 'proud to see their natural leaders … in their natural places'.[82] It seems likely that Sullivan's appeal to the O'Conor Don's sense of patriotic spirit and social standing was at least somewhat exaggerated, but how exaggerated is impossible to determine. Either way, as Jonathan Wright has demonstrated, it was not unusual for men of the O'Conor Don's social rank to be described, or to describe themselves, as 'natural leaders'.[83] He certainly believed in the necessity of a 'natural' ruling class, so it seems likely that he regarded himself as a natural leader.[84] But the chance of taking his 'natural place' in a new home rule order was not enticing enough for the O'Conor Don and he refused to support the resolutions because he was:

> not a man who ever endeavours to conceal his opinions. When it has been unpopular to express them, I have not dreaded that unpopularity. I say, then, that if you propose at the present moment … to establish the federal constitution aimed at in these resolutions, and I were asked if I did believe that, this would tend to the peace, prosperity, and tranquillity of Ireland, I would feel in my conscience obliged to answer, no … I never will court popularity at the expense of my convictions … and … as long as I am in public life I will never attempt to deceive.[85]

As we have seen in relation to his opposition to Butt's land bill in 1876, the O'Conor Don was clear in his mind that an MP should be able to reserve the right to maintain independent judgment, regardless of popular opinion.[86] Therefore, his views here are an earlier exposition of the argument that an MP was a representative not a delegate mandated to express the views of the people who voted him in – an argument that remains current. Unsurprisingly, these very public pronouncements on self-government and political representation led the O'Conor Don to doubt his chances of re-election. Monsell assured him that his position was safe but was otherwise gloomy about the political outlook for 'the country we belong to', adding that 'the day [Gladstone's] university bill was thrown out was an evil day for us'. Given the O'Conor Don's opposition to the bill, one must wonder whether Monsell was gently scolding him for contributing to the situation they now found themselves in.[87]

Nonetheless, despite his concerns, the O'Conor Don and fellow Catholic landlord Charles French were selected as the two 'Home Rule candidates' for

---

[82] *Proceedings of the home rule conference*, p. 88. [83] Wright, *The 'natural leaders'*, pp 49–52. [84] Campbell, *The Irish establishment*, p. 156. [85] *Proceedings of the home rule conference*, pp 91–2. [86] See chapter four, p. 93. [87] William Monsell to the O'Conor Don, 2 Dec. 1873, O'Conor papers, CH, 9.4.HS.230.

County Roscommon in January 1874.[88] In his election address, the O'Conor Don made the somewhat laboured commitment 'to support any scheme which would, consistently with the preservation of all justly recognised rights, confer on my country the inestimable benefits of real Self-Government'.[89] The absence of any mention of home rule or federalism was clearly by design to avoid tying himself to any particular position, but this mattered little as both he and French faced no opposition and were duly returned the following month.[90] The pretence on both sides continued at a meeting of the Roscommon HGA on 16 February 1874, where, although not present, the O'Conor Don was proposed as a member and then promoted as one of the association's vice-presidents. His cousin Thomas Mapother, also not present, was elected president. The nationalist *Roscommon Journal* declared that this was 'practical proof' of the O'Conor Don's support for home rule, but this rather ambitious claim was clearly justification for having no other choice but to select a candidate who in reality had declined to join the association, had publicly opposed Butt's federal home rule scheme and never actually called himself a home ruler.[91]

THE HOME RULE PARTY, 1874–80

On 3 March 1874, a meeting of the fifty-nine Irish MPs returned as home rulers took place at Dublin City Hall. The O'Conor Don did not attend but his brother Denis – who fully endorsed Butt's federal scheme at the November conference and declared himself a home ruler before the election – attended and was elected to the party's executive committee. Most significantly, the meeting resolved that all home rule MPs should act as a party in the commons, independent of all other political parties.[92] After receiving a copy of this resolution, the O'Conor Don decided not to join Butt's embryonic Home Rule Party, which rather contradicts Lawrence McCaffrey's claim that he 'considered himself a member of the Irish party'.[93] Although he agreed with 'the desirability of general unity of action amongst the parliamentary representatives favourable to the cause of Home Rule', and hoped to work 'in Parliament with the majority of Irish representatives', he nonetheless refused to 'concur in any resolutions' that might compromise his independent stance, 'having clearly stated to my constituents previous to the late election that I would

---

88 *Roscommon Messenger*, 7 Jan. 1874. 89 *Freeman's Journal*, 30 Jan. 1874. 90 *Irish Times*, 4 Feb. 1874. 91 *Roscommon Journal*, 21 Feb. 1874. 92 *Sligo Champion*, 7 Feb. 1874; Thornley, *Isaac Butt*, pp 212–13; O'Day, *Irish home rule*, p. 41. 93 L.J. McCaffrey, 'The Home Rule Party and Irish nationalist opinion, 1874–1876', *Catholic Historical Review*, 43:2 (July 1957), 160.

not accept election unless on the understanding that I was free to preserve my ... independence of action'.[94] Upon receiving the censure of the local press for not attending the meeting, the O'Conor Don made it abundantly clear that he could not have assented to the proposed resolutions because they suggested the creation of a 'separate Irish party in the House of Commons', which he did not approve of.[95] This did not, however, stop the O'Conor Don from supporting Butt's motion in July 1874 for the establishment of a select committee to investigate the 'present Parliamentary relations between Great Britain and Ireland'. Again, this demonstrated his preference for deliberate parliamentary process over party or popular politics. Butt's motion subsequently instigated the first lengthy debate on the subject of home rule in the new session, but the views expressed by the O'Conor Don were not welcomed by many of his Irish colleagues. By pointing out 'other difficulties' in the way of home rule, which he felt 'arose from the very great differences of opinion' on the subject in Ireland, he touched on some obvious, but largely unspoken, problems:

> It was quite true that three of the Provinces of Ireland [Connaught, Munster, and Leinster] might be claimed as supporting this proposal; but there were even in these Provinces many influential classes without whose co-operation the scheme could not be worked, and whose support had not yet been secured. On the other hand, in the North of Ireland, almost the whole country was opposed to the proposal. ("No!") There was, at least, a very large, influential, and powerful class against it, and until there was more unanimity and cordiality in the demand he felt that success was unattainable.[96]

Inextricably linked with these problems was what the O'Conor Don identified as Butt's 'vague notion' that home rule would lead to 'the restoration of a great and glorious Irish nationality'.[97] Like Monsell, then, the O'Conor Don's objections were based on a frank acceptance of the likely opposition of the majority of Irish Protestants, particularly in Ulster, to the idea of home rule. This is what transpired when Gladstone introduced his first home rule bill in 1886, with the O'Conor Don's scepticism about the creation of a 'glorious' national identity under a home rule parliament being one of main tenets of Protestant unionist opposition at the time.[98] That said, his scepticism was based on the acceptance of an Irish national identity largely shaped by an

94 The O'Conor Don to Anon., 11 Mar. 1874, O'Conor papers, CH, 9.4.HS.220. 95 *Roscommon Journal*, 14 Nov. 1874. 96 HC Deb., 2 July 1874, vol. 220, cc 918–65. 97 Ibid. 98 O'Day, *Irish home rule*, pp 114–15; P. Buckland, *Irish unionism 1: the Anglo-Irish and the new Ireland, 1885–1922* (Dublin, 1972), p. 10.

adherence to the Catholic faith and the teachings of the Catholic Church, rather than the fear and rejection of it. How he envisaged squaring that particular circle is not clear, but the lack of a coherent sense of Irish national identity was one of the reasons why he thought Ireland was not ready for home rule.

As it turned out, the O'Conor Don's comments had little practical effect on Butt's motion as it was easily defeated by a Conservative government with a comfortable majority. This majority put paid to Butt's land and university education bills in 1876–8, and he and the Home Rule Party struggled to make an impact because of his prolonged absences from London due to professional commitments in Dublin and deteriorating personal finances, which did little to encourage party discipline. The party also struggled due to the obstructionist tactics employed by Parnell and his allies, which consisted of long-winded speeches on obscure points of detail in order to frustrate the order of business in the House.[99] In June 1876, the O'Conor Don's brother, Denis, communicated his frustrations with Butt and the obstructionists to their cousin, Roderick MacDermot, but his complaints met with an unsympathetic reception. In a revealing rejection of the O'Conor Don's politics, Roderick insisted the obstructionists were justified in their actions and prophesized others like them would fill the seats of those like the O'Conor Don who opposed Butt's land bill. Denis disagreed, arguing that his brother had had the courage of his convictions and would not be corralled, like others, into voting for the bill. Indeed, in an alternative assessment of the sort of political opportunism normally levelled at Irish liberals, Denis suggested that many of those who voted for Butt's bill had simply done so in order to save their seats, as they knew it would not pass. Rather gloomily, he declared that he would not stand if 'there were an election tomorrow' because he was 'not at all satisfied with the way things are going on'. Indeed, he felt that 'unless there be a change before the next election I will have done with the whole thing … It is no honour to be in the House of Commons just at present and I certainly never will go to the hustings … as a number of Butts party'.[100]

That a professed home ruler like Denis O'Conor was so disillusioned with Butt did not bode well for his leadership of the party. The O'Conor Don was close to his brother and would have been aware of and sympathized with his frustrations. Butt continued to try and win him over, requesting, in January 1877, that he attend the annual meeting of the Home Rule Party. The O'Conor Don declined to attend, but nonetheless stated that he was

---

99 HC Deb., 2 July 1874, vol. 220, cc 965–9; Hoppen, *The mid-Victorian generation*, p. 630; O'Day, *Irish home rule*, pp 41–53.   100 Denis O'Conor to Roderick MacDermot, 1 June 1876, O'Conor papers, CH, 9.4.HS.133.

happy to support measures that 'may be beneficial to the country' by 'meeting and consulting' with Irish parliamentary colleagues 'without committing myself to a system of party ... of which I cannot approve'.[101] In August of that year, Butt moved to censure the actions of the obstructionists and again sought the O'Conor Don's support, sending him a signed notice from those 'Members of the Irish Parliamentary Party' who 'declare that the course of action which has been recently pursued by a small section of our number has been taken without the sanction or approval of the party and has tended to impair our usefulness and influence'.[102] It is not known if the O'Conor Don responded, but it is clear, from a letter he received from Edmund Dease on the subject, that he thought 'the obstructionists have won' and 'Butt is not able to put them down'. Dease himself believed 'the future' was 'very bleak' because Parnell and the obstructionists sought 'to get at dormant Fenianism in Ireland' through their 'agitation' in parliament.[103] Here we can see that liberals like the O'Conor Don and Dease were convinced that there was a latent sympathy for republican ideals in the Irish body politic and that Parnell and his followers were seeking to tap into those sympathies to popularize the cause of home rule. It was this fear of Fenianism, long-held at this point, that partly drove the O'Conor Don's opposition to the home rule.

SOCIAL REFORM

Although the O'Conor Don refused to join Butt's party, opposed his land bill, and only nominally supported his university bill, he did not sit on his hands in parliament. In 1875–6, he worked as a member of the parliamentary commission on factory legislation, which led to the factory and workshop act of 1878. This act streamlined the legislation of the previous seventy years, regulating the hours of work for children and women and seeking to improve standards in hygiene and educational instruction in factories and workshops in Ireland and Great Britain.[104] In January 1878, he brought forward a Sunday closing bill to regulate the sale of alcohol in Ireland, which followed years of supporting the efforts of other Liberal MPs to get a bill debated at various stages in the 1860s and 1870s. Indeed, this particular issue was one of the few that involved

---

101 The O'Conor Don to Isaac Butt, Jan. 1877, O'Conor papers, CH, 9.4.HS.224. 102 Isaac Butt to the O'Conor Don, 6 Aug. 1877, O'Conor papers, CH, 9.4.HS.133. 103 Edmund Dease to the O'Conor Don, 29 Aug. 1877, O'Conor papers, CH, 9.4.HS.133. 104 *Report of the commissioners appointed to inquire into the working of the factory and workshops acts, with a view to their consolidation and amendment ...*, HC 1876 [C.1443], xxix; D. Greer & J.W. Nicolson, *The factory acts in Ireland, 1802–1914* (Dublin, 2003), pp 1–28, 31–8, 46, 49, 52, 60–85.

cross-confessional cooperation within Irish liberal ranks, with the Catholics Myles O'Reilly and Sir Dominic Corrigan, the Presbyterians Richard Smyth and Thomas McClure, and the Quaker Jonathan Pim all involved at one stage or another throughout the period. However, although the campaign for Sunday closing was unique in nineteenth-century Irish politics in that it garnered support from across the political and religious divides in parliament, it struggled to compete with the issues of land reform, home rule and education. It was also the case that many Irish and English conservative MPs, as well as some home rulers, were reliant on the support of the drinks industry and were therefore hostile to legislation in this area. What transpired with the O'Conor Don's bill in the spring and summer of 1878 was one of the longest legislative debates in parliamentary history, as the bill faced a small but ferocious opposition from those MPs who either had a personal interest in defending the drinks industry or rejected the legislation on the grounds that it was an overbearingly moralistic restriction on the right of the working man to have a drink on his day off.[105] Despite this, the O'Conor Don stuck to his task tenaciously, which was no surprise given that he believed it was the duty of all Sunday closing supporters to 'destroy … this great evil of intemperance', which brought 'calamities … to individuals, to families, and to nations' on a daily basis.[106] Working across the House – including with Parnell and Gladstone, both of whom supported the legislation – he eventually got the bill passed on 10 August 1878, much to the delight of temperance associations in Ireland and Great Britain, and the Irish and English bishops.[107] Finally, as demonstrated in the previous chapter, he worked behind the scenes in the lead-up to the Intermediate Education Act in 1878, which increased funding for intermediate education and put the Irish language on the curriculum. Moreover, he introduced a university bill in 1879 that led to the passing the University Education of Ireland Act and, subsequently, the establishment of the Royal University of Ireland in 1880.[108]

This was all tangible evidence that moderate social reforms were possible if Irish MPs worked across the religious and political divides in the commons. It is also clear evidence of the O'Conor Don's pragmatism, in that he pursued

---

[105] E. Malcolm, *'Ireland sober, Ireland free': drink and temperance in nineteenth-century Ireland* (Dublin, 1986), pp 198–9, 202–3, 217–51; J. Regan-Lefebvre, *Cosmopolitan nationalism in the Victorian empire: Ireland, India and the politics of Alfred Webb* (Basingstoke, 2009), pp 1–3, 21–2, 42. [106] *Freeman's Journal*, 25 Mar. 1879. [107] Malcolm, *'Ireland sober, Ireland free'*, pp 217–51; Recollections part 1, O'Conor papers, CH, 9.4.HS.156, pp 82–3; Letters of congratulations to the O'Conor Don from various temperance associations, Aug. 1878, O'Conor papers, CH, 9.4.HS.175; W.E. Gladstone to the O'Conor Don, 10 Aug. 1878, O'Conor papers, CH, 9.4.HS.228; The O'Conor Don to Gladstone, 13 Aug. 1878, Gladstone papers, BL, add. 4457, f. 205. For Cardinal Manning's praise for the O'Conor Don's efforts, see *Freeman's Journal*, 29 Aug. 1878. [108] See chapter five, pp 129–35.

an agenda of moderate reform when more advanced Irish reforms, like land purchase, were unlikely to be forthcoming from the Conservative government. In pursuing this agenda, he remained a resolutely independent liberal MP detached from all overt party politics.

ELITISM AND EMPIRE

All the while, however, the O'Conor Don maintained his links with Irish and British elites. In 1875, he signed a circular with the duke of Norfolk, the earl of Denbigh, the marquess of Ripon and Lord Petre calling for the establishment of a new Catholic Club to replace the financially failing Stafford Club in London. Officially opened on 27 November that year, it was hoped the new St George's Club would be 'in every respect a first-class Club … for Catholics of the upper classes', as well as a place for 'young men … coming to London from Catholic Colleges and Schools'. While it would seem that St George's was not a resounding success, the O'Conor Don's membership of it gives us a clear indication that he still moved in Irish and English landed Catholic circles.[109]

The O'Conor Don also maintained his links with the top brass in the Liberal Party. In 1876, he joined the Devonshire Club, after encouragement from the joint leader of the party, Lord Hartington.[110] Hartington and the O'Conor Don ended up on the same side when the Liberal Party split on home rule in 1886, and thereafter consulted fairly regularly on Irish issues, particularly land purchase.[111] They were natural allies in the sense that they were landed liberals with whiggish instincts on government and democracy. At the same time, the O'Conor Don was still attached to the former leader of the party, Gladstone, even though he published a pamphlet in 1874 that attacked the declaration of infallibility and questioned the loyalty of Catholics to the British state. Indeed, the O'Conor Don and many of his liberal Catholic colleagues flocked to meet Gladstone when he visited Ireland in October/November 1877.[112]

---

[109] Norfolk House circular, 23 June 1875, O'Conor papers, CH, 9.4.SH.177. *Freeman's Journal*, 29 Nov. 1875. Among the 350 members who joined were the earls of Kenmare and Gainsborough; Viscount Molesworth; lords Emly, O'Hagan, Howard, Clifford, Herries and Norreys; Baron Gerard; W.H.G. Bagshawe, Denis O'Conor, John Pope Hennessey and Joseph MacKenna. [110] Lord Hartington to the O'Conor Don, 23 July 1874 & 16 May 1876, O'Conor papers, CH, 9.4.HS.230; Jenkins, *Gladstone, whiggery and the Liberal Party*, pp 47–51. [111] Jenkins, *Gladstone, whiggery and the Liberal Party*, p. 7. See chapter seven, p. 180. [112] E.R. Norman, *Anti-Catholicism in Victorian England* (Oxford & New York, 2016), p. 216; Recollections part 1, O'Conor papers, CH, 9.4.HL.156, p. 81; Jackson, *Home rule*, pp 29–30.

Perhaps liberal Catholic faith in Gladstone was restored by his commons speech on the eastern question on 7 May 1877, which, in light of the Ottoman atrocities in Bulgaria, called on the Conservative government to review British support for the Ottomans and to consider supporting some form of autonomy for the Bulgarians. Or perhaps they saw in him a better chance for electoral survival if he returned to the leadership of the Liberal Party. In any case, he regarded Gladstone's speech on the eastern question one 'as the most eloquent ... I ever heard'.[113] But while one of the main foreign policy concerns for Catholic MPs was Russia's poor record on the treatment of Catholics in Poland, and the official line of the papacy was to support the Muslim Ottomans on account of what was thought to be their favourable treatment of Catholics within their empire, the O'Conor Don and his brother Denis supported Gladstone's resolutions on the eastern question, whereas the majority of home rulers, apparently in two minds as to what to do, abstained from the vote.[114] It is not clear, however, if the O'Conor Don held particularly strong views on the reported massacres of Christians in Bulgaria, or how the British government should position itself in the face of the perceived Russian threat in the region. He later recalled the 'great reception' lords Beaconsfield (Disraeli) and Salisbury received on their return from the Berlin conference, which maintained Ottoman influence in Bulgaria, which was the policy favoured by Disraeli all along. This would suggest that while the O'Conor Don agreed with Gladstone's more light-touch, moralistic foreign policy, he ultimately supported British imperial interests.[115] After all, the empire was something of a family affair, with the O'Conor Don benefitting directly from its proceeds and his cousin, Sir Nicholas O'Conor, being a high-ranking British diplomat.[116]

Finally, the extent to which the O'Conor Don continued to move in high Irish and British circles was further evidenced by his attendance at a meeting of the British Association in Dublin in August 1878. As a showcase for scientific progress in the mid-Victorian period, the association provided the space for devout Catholics like the O'Conor Don, Lord Emly and Sir John Lentaigne to demonstrate that their Catholicism was not incompatible with an engagement with the latest developments in scientific research. This was not a new endeavour for the O'Conor Don given his involvement with associations for the promotion of educational and scientific endeavour since the

---

113 Recollections part 1, O'Conor papers, CH, 9.4.HS.156, pp 79, 84. 114 J.P. Rossi, 'Catholic opinion on the eastern question, 1876–1878', *Church History*, 51:1 (Mar. 1982), 54–70; Hoppen, *The mid-Victorian generation*, pp 619–27; HC Deb., 14 May 1877, vol. 234, cc 864–97. 115 Recollections part 1, O'Conor papers, CH, 9.4.HL.156, p. 84; Hoppen, *The mid-Victorian generation*, p. 626. 116 The O'Conor Don to Sir Nicholas O'Conor, 21 Jan. 1896 & 21 Sept. 1899, O'Conor papers, CAC, OCON2/4/32.

1860s, but even so, it is another example of the ease with which he moved in elite Irish and British circles, both Catholic and Protestant.[117]

ELECTION DEFEAT AND REACTION

But neither O'Conor Don's social status, nor his successes in educational or social reform, could protect him from the unpopularity of his opposition to fixity of tenure and federal home rule. In the run-up to the general election of 1880, there was a sustained political campaign against him by local nationalists and the nationalist press, with the initial momentum provided by the Irishtown meeting in neighbouring County Mayo, in April 1879, which effectively launched the Land League.[118] A constable from the village of Ballinlough, County Roscommon, informed Dublin Castle officials how Matt Harris had 'denounced the O'Conor Don' and presented John Ferguson of Glasgow as a suitable alternative candidate for the constituency.[119] Indeed, although Harris subsequently congratulated him on his views on land purchase, he had long been a critic of the O'Conor Don as 'the worst class of Irishman', a member of the 'shawneen' party, who could no longer use the influence of the bishops for electoral cover.[120] That same month an editorial in the *Roscommon Journal* recommended that the voters of the county reconsider their support of the O'Conor Don and Charles French in light of their failure to support the Home Rule Party. Although the integrity of both men was admitted and the O'Conor Don's contribution to the university question was not ignored, it was thought that 'when great national interests are at stake … private feelings must be set aside'.[121] At a meeting of the Home Rule League in Dublin on 21 August 1879, W.H. O'Sullivan labelled the O'Conor Don 'a specimen of the Whig class who shelter themselves under the name of Home Rulers'.[122] On 18 November, the O'Conor Don found himself continually interrupted at a meeting in Roscommon while Parnell was greeted with a 'perfect storm of cheers'. On 7 December, Parnell, Michael Davitt and T.D. Sullivan attended a meeting in Castlerea where the O'Conor Don was again deemed a whig who was now surplus to requirements by the local nationalist Patrick Egan.[123]

---

117 *Freeman's Journal*, 15 Aug. 1878; Bew, *The glory of being Britons*, pp 145, 169–70.   118 D.G. Boyce, *Nineteenth-century Ireland: the search for stability* (Dublin, 2005), p. 177.   119 Unnamed police constable to Dublin Castle, 19 Apr. 1879 and clipping from the *Connaught Telegraph*, 21 Apr. 1879, CSORP, NAI, 1885/8039.   120 Matt Harris to J.W. Flanagan, 15 Sept. 1876, O'Conor papers, CH, 9.4.HS.181. 'Shawneen' is thought to be the English-sounding pronunciation of the Irish pet or nickname Seanín, often given to children named Sean. It was used in derogatory terms by some nationalists to describe Irish people who they deemed to be more English than Irish. See O'Neill, *Catholics of consequence*, p. 17.   121 *Roscommon Journal*, 23 Aug. 1879.   122 *Freeman's Journal*, 22 Aug. 1879.   123 *Freeman's Journal*, 8 Dec. 1879.

Although Parnell was reluctant to push the O'Conor Don out of his seat, any personal efforts he may have made to get him on board with the 'New Departure' in Irish politics would have fallen flat given the O'Conor Don's liberal sensibilities.[124] In any event, Parnell very quickly lost any sympathy he might have had for him when he denounced the O'Conor Don as a 'symbol of West Britonism in Ireland' at a meeting in Roscommon the following month.[125]

The O'Conor Don's only response to this barrage of criticism was to slightly vary his position on home rule in his election address. He now asserted that 'Irishmen have a right to claim more real control over legislation affecting only their own country than they at present possess' because the 'Imperial Parliament' was unable to 'efficiently perform' all the 'duties thrown on it'. This was tempered however by his having 'not felt it necessary to renounce my Liberal principles or to abjure connection with that political party, as an independent member of which I have hitherto appeared before you'.[126]

The nominations for the Roscommon election were made on 30 March 1880 at a meeting presided over by Bishop Gillooly. With Charles French standing down, Major John Talbot D'Arcy of Ballinasloe was to run alongside the O'Conor Don, but he resigned in favour of the Parnellite candidate Andrew Commins, a Liverpool-based barrister and president of the Home Rule Confederation of Great Britain. It would seem this arrangement, upon the 'impeachable testimony of the Most Rev Dr Gillooly', was come to prior to the meeting with the proviso that Commins would step down if another Parnellite candidate entered the fray. As it turned out, a second Parnellite candidate, James Joseph O'Kelly, was nominated on the morning of the contest on 6 April.[127] As a radical, anti-clerical member of the Irish Republican Brotherhood, O'Kelly's arrival on the scene from America would have fuelled all the O'Conor Don's suspicions about the real aims of Parnell and the Home Rule Party.[128] Commins offered to withdraw from the contest upon O'Kelly's nomination, but in an extraordinary act of hubris and electoral self-harm the O'Conor Don refused the offer because he 'felt sure of beating' both Commins and O'Kelly 'and thought it would be a cowardly thing to sneak in by a private arrangement without letting the constituency have any voice in the matter'.[129] His refusal occasioned the nomination of a fourth candidate, Thomas Mapother, who was a local landlord and his cousin.[130] Although the

---

124 Bew, *Conflict and conciliation*, p. 51; *Freeman's Journal*, 27 Mar. 1880. 125 See chapter four, pp 94–5. 126 *Roscommon & Leitrim Gazette*, 3 Apr. 1880. 127 *Roscommon Journal*, 3 Apr. 1880; C.J. Woods, 'Commins, Andrew', *DIB*. 128 L. Gibbons, 'Roscommon in literature, 1600–2000' in Farrell et al. (eds), *Roscommon history and society*, pp 729–30. 129 The O'Conor Don to Lord Emly, 10 Apr. 1880, Monsell papers, NAI, MS/1075/19/2. 130 *Roscommon Journal*, 3 Apr. 1880.

O'Conor Don had the support of Bishop Gillooly, he was defeated in the resulting contest, coming third behind Commins and O'Kelly.[131]

While a shock to the political establishment, the O'Conor Don's defeat was not especially unusual as many Irish landlords lost their seats in 1880.[132] Nonetheless, in a letter to Monsell, the O'Conor Don said how his 'defeat was most unexpected … and has caused me much disappointment'. To his credit, he admitted that he 'was probably a little to[o] confident and thought it would be impossible' for both candidates 'to beat me'.[133] This confidence was evident from his diary entry on the 3 April where he stated that 'Things look pretty favourable and I expect to win.'[134] Misplaced though his confidence was, the O'Conor Don still thought 'Everyone was astonished at the result.' In the end, he put his defeat down to Parnell's influence over the people, who 'will do anything he advises', and the consequent waning of clerical influence.[135]

The O'Conor Don's defeat occasioned several condemnations in the press from moderate home rulers and liberals. The Quaker, temperance supporter and secretary of the Home Rule Party Alfred Webb, in a letter to the *Freeman's Journal*, declared it a 'deplorable mistake to refuse the service of a man like The O'Conor Don' given that 'there was no danger of his ever preferring Whig policy or Tory policy to what he believed [were] Irish interests'.[136] In a letter to the *Irish Times*, the Catholic former head inspector of the national schools James Kavanagh condemned the 'ungrateful, unfortunate, and lamentable' decision of the electors of Roscommon to not return 'the trusted champion of Catholic claims throughout these two trying decades of our educational struggles'.[137] A personal friend of the O'Conor Don's, Kavanagh prayed that Ireland would be saved from 'her new dictators', which, of course, was a swipe at Parnell.[138] Monsell, for his part, was 'astounded' at the O'Conor Don's defeat because he 'looked upon' him 'as the coming Irish chief secretary and our misguided people have neglected you – it does fill ones [*sic*] mind with despair'.[139] Although the O'Conor Don thought it would not have been possible to accept the position of Irish chief secretary if he had been elected as an independent liberal MP for County Roscommon, he admitted that he 'would have ambition enough to aspire' to the position, thinking that it would not 'be impossible even now' if 'it were thought for the public good that I should hold

---

131 *Roscommon & Leitrim Gazette*, 10 Apr. 1880.   132 Bew, *Land and the national question*, p. 98; M. Bence Jones, *The twilight of the Ascendancy* (London, 1987), p. 30.   133 The O'Conor Don to Lord Emly, 10 Apr. 1880, Monsell papers, NAI, MS/1075/19/2.   134 Diary of the O'Conor Don, 3 Apr. 1880, O'Conor papers, CH, 9.4.SH.247.   135 The O'Conor Don to Lord Emly, 10 Apr. 1880, Monsell papers, NAI, MS/1075/19/2.   136 *Freeman's Journal*, 15 Apr. 1880.   137 *Roscommon Journal*, 17 Apr. 1880.   138 James Kavanagh to the O'Conor Don, 10 Apr. 1880, O'Conor papers, CH, 9.4.HS.083.   139 Lord Emly to the O'Conor Don, 4 Apr. 1880, O'Conor papers, CH, 9.4.HS.083.

the post'.¹⁴⁰ While it is not known if he was ever seriously considered for the post, the Irish peer, Mervyn Wingfield, Viscount Powerscourt, told Gladstone it was 'a pity the O'Conor Don is not returned' because he would have made 'a capital Chief Secretary', while the English liberal William Rathbone thought 'a good Irishman' like the O'Conor Don should be made a 'permanent under secretary'. As for Gladstone, he felt it necessary to convey his 'extreme concern at not finding' the O'Conor Don 'among us in the hour of liberal triumph', hoping that he would 'not be displeased with the … appointment of Mr. [W.E.] Forster'.¹⁴¹ Gladstone's condolences were made in response to a letter from the O'Conor Don, in which he congratulated the prime minister on his return to power, while also reminding him that he lost his seat 'mainly through a refusal to desert the Liberal Party and to join the nationalists'. Indeed, the O'Conor Don went to great lengths to outline his commitment to the party during his time in parliament; his support for Gladstone's Irish and foreign policies; and how he and his brother spent £8,000 to win the 'conservative stronghold' of County Sligo for the party. All this, he felt, gave him a strong 'claim' to have his 'recommendation' for one of the Irish appointments heard: namely that of his cousin Hugh Hyacinth MacDermot QC, for the position of sergeant at law.¹⁴²

It seems, then, that O'Conor Don had shaken off his earlier worries about being perceived as a whig placeman, being ambitious for a position in a liberal government and indeed feeling that the party owed him something for his commitment to the liberal cause. To realize this ambition, he would need to re-enter parliament; and when A.M. Sullivan resigned his County Louth seat shortly after the election, Archbishop Edward McCabe encouraged him to stand. The O'Conor Don was receptive, telling McCabe that 'having spent 20 years of the best part of my life in public affairs I scarcely like giving them up all at once on my first defeat'. Indeed, he had 'every reason for believing' that a sense of 'regret' regarding his defeat was 'the prevailing feeling in Ireland'.¹⁴³ Subsequently, McCabe was advised against the idea by a local man, who cited the example of Lord Carlingford's defeat in County Louth in 1874, despite having the support of 'most of the clergy of the County'.¹⁴⁴ It is not known if this influenced the O'Conor Don's decision or not, but he chose not to

---

140 The O'Conor Don to Lord Emly, 10 Apr. 1880, Monsell papers, NAI, MS/1075/19/2. 141 Viscount Powerscourt to W.E. Gladstone, 11 Apr. 1880, Gladstone papers, BL, add. 44463, ff 109–12; Wiliam Rathbone to W.E. Gladstone, 17 Apr. 1880, Gladstone papers, BL, 44463, ff 142–6; W.E. Gladstone to the O'Conor Don, 26 Apr. 1880, Gladstone papers, BL, add. 44463, f. 201. 142 The O'Conor Don to W.E. Gladstone, 25 Apr. 1880, Gladstone papers, BL, add. 44463, f. 189; A. Pole, 'MacDermot, Hugh Hyacinth O'Rorke', *DIB*. 143 The O'Conor Don to Archbishop McCabe, 19 Apr. 1880, McCabe papers, DDA, 337/5. 144 J. Levins to Archbishop McCabe, 22 Apr. 1880, McCabe papers, DDA, 346/2.

contest the seat. With no other opportunities on the horizon, he busied himself with his work on Gladstone's land law commission, which as we have seen resulted in him producing a separate report that, much to Gladstone's dismay, called for compulsory land purchase. After the passing of Gladstone's land act in April 1881, the O'Conor Don and his sons set out for northern France, where the latter were to receive some form of tuition.[145]

---

145 Recollections part 2, O'Conor papers, CH, 9.4.HS.156, pp 96–100.

7 / 'I could not speak as an admirer or lover of the Union': the O'Conor Don, liberalism, nationalism and unionism, 1880–1900

Sometime towards the end of his life, the O'Conor Don typed some recollections of his life. Mostly these are brief, matter of fact descriptions of the when, what, where and who of the main political events and meetings that took place in his life from year to year, not a detailed recalling of what he thought about these particular events or meetings. But every now and then, he added a few extra thoughts. One such time was his recollection of the reasons why he did not attend a unionist meeting in Dublin in 1893, organized in opposition to Gladstone's second home rule bill. Although originally down to attend and speak at the meeting, the O'Conor Don pulled out, recalling that while he was:

> opposed to the Home Rule scheme on the ground that it would be disastrous to my country, I could not speak as an admirer or lover of the Union. If I believed that a Home Rule scheme would be secured that would be good for Ireland, I would be its warmest supporter, having no intrinsic love of the Union.[1]

The O'Conor Don's sentiments here point to a kind of nationalist-unionist no-man's-land, occupied by an independent-minded liberal who refused to join one or other camp in the often-heated debates on home rule in the 1880s and 1890s. This is reflective of the fact that a minority of Irish Catholics assumed a unionist position in this period while remaining strongly attached to their sense of Irish national identity and often criticizing aspects of the union and British government policy in Ireland.[2] In that sense, they were, like many Irish Protestants, nationalist-minded, constructive unionists.[3] The O'Conor Don was a devout Catholic possessed of a strong sense of Irish national identity, but his social milieu and natural political home was that of unionists and unionism. For him, there was no contradiction in this at all. Indeed, even though he remained critical of the union and stood aloof

---

1 Recollections part 2, O'Conor papers, CH, 9.4.HL.156, p. 150.   2 Potter, *William Monsell*, pp 1–5; R. Keogh & J. McConnel, 'The Esmonde family of County Wexford', pp 274–91; É. Phoenix, 'Catholic unionism', pp 292–304.   3 Reid, 'Isaac Butt, home rule and federalist political thought', pp 333–4; T. West, 'Plunkett, Horace Curzon', *DIB*; P. Maume, 'Quin, Windham Thomas Wyndham', *DIB*; A. Jackson, *The two unions: Ireland, Scotland, and the survival of the United Kingdom, 1707–2007* (Oxford, 2012), p. 137.

from unionist party organization after his election defeat in 1880, he continued to work towards Irish reforms with liberal and conservative unionists while opposing home rule, remaining loyal to the crown, and supporting the empire.

LIBERALISM AND UNIONISM, 1880–6

The O'Conor Don's reward for his loyalty to the liberal standard before 1880 was his appointment to the privy council in October 1881, something which occasioned even closer contact with prominent Irish and English Catholics such as the marquess of Ripon, the earls of Kenmare and Albemarle, and lords Emly, Montagu and Howard.[4] It also helped forge stronger links with senior figures in the Irish administration, with his diaries regularly mentioning walks in the Phoenix Park with the chief secretary, W.E. Forster, who he commented always carried a revolver with him as a result of police advice.[5] In November 1882, he was also elected to the Kildare Street Club 'with only one black ball'.[6] Although a predominantly Protestant and conservative club, the O'Conor Don was one of a growing number of Catholics to join in the 1880s, including the earls of Westmeath, Granard and Kenmare, Viscount Gormanston, Sir Walter Nugent, Colonel Gerald Dease, Ambrose More O'Ferrall and Edward Martin.[7]

But did this mean that the O'Conor Don the liberal had now suddenly become a unionist, or was he always thus? As Jonathan Parry has pointed out, to be a British liberal was to be a unionist, in the sense that whether a liberal supported home rule or not, they were still a unionist.[8] After all, when Gladstone brought forward his home rule bills in 1886 and 1893, he did so with a view to preserving and strengthening the union, rather than breaking it up. In other words, all British liberals considered themselves unionists, although those liberals who opposed it called themselves liberal unionists.[9] But the politics of home rule was different in Ireland, with those opposed to it identifying as unionists and those who supported it identifying as nationalists. As is clear from his views on home rule in 1873–4, and his comments in the run-up to the 1880 election, the O'Conor Don was an independent liberal who opposed home rule on what can be described as typically unionist grounds.

4 Privy council office to the O'Conor Don, 3 Aug. 1881, O'Conor papers, CH, 9.4.HS.197; Recollections part 2, O'Conor papers, CH, 9.4.HL.156, pp 89–90; *Catholic Directory*, Jan. 1882. 5 Recollections part 2, O'Conor papers, CH, 9.4.HL.156, p. 89. 6 Ibid., p. 104. 7 Bence Jones, *The twilight of the Ascendancy*, pp 55–6; Campbell, *The Irish establishment*, pp 178–9. 8 Parry, *Liberal government in Victorian Britain*, p. 4. 9 Jackson, *Home rule*, p. 82.

This naturally aligned him with Irish and British liberals and conservatives, both Catholic and Protestant, who described themselves as unionists. Taking all this into consideration, his position on the privy council and membership of the Kildare Street Club was as much of a natural progression as it was a shift in political allegiances. It is therefore more than reasonable to describe the O'Conor Don as a unionist at this point. This does not mean that he was any 'less' Catholic, Irish or patriotic, but he could not be described in any meaningful political sense as a nationalist, for he did not move in nationalist circles; was deeply suspicious of the republican forces at work within the Irish nationalist movement; and preferred the status quo of the union as it stood to the prospect of a union with home rule.

Nonetheless, in the early 1880s, the O'Conor Don still described himself as a liberal and remained loosely attached to the Liberal Party. In June 1883, he was urged by the party whip, Richard Grosvenor, to stand in the up-coming by-election for the borough of Wexford. He consented to stand on 10 July, even though he felt there was little chance of success.[10] Bishop Gillooly backed his candidature, but it was not received well in the nationalist press, with the *Freeman's Journal* denouncing it as the work of his 'brother members of the Kildare Street Club' and the cosy 'coalition of Liberals and Conservatives' in the Wexford borough. At a public meeting in Wexford town on 15 July, he was derided by the nationalist Tim Healy as 'a carpet bagger from Connaught' whose cabal of lawyers would 'slake their thirst out of … [his] money bags'. A man with a particular talent for invective, Healy also made the rather outlandish claim that the O'Conor Don had conspired, through his position on the privy council, to have Parnell and J.J. O'Kelly jailed in 1882 as revenge for his election defeat. More rooted in the real world perhaps, given the speculations after his defeat in 1880, was Michael Davitt's claim that the O'Conor Don had put himself forward in Wexford 'to qualify himself for the position of Chief Secretary to Dublin Castle, where he could carry out the infamous policy of the infamous party to which he belonged'.[11] Such claims matter little, however, as the O'Conor Don was soundly defeated by the home rule candidate, William Redmond, younger brother of John Redmond. The O'Conor Don later recalled how there was 'great excitement in the town' on the day of election, but that this excitement turned to violence when he was 'pelted with sods and stones' by an angry crowd, from which he had to be protected from by the police and his political opponents Tim Healy and Thomas Sexton.[12]

10 Recollections part 2, O'Conor papers, CH, 9.4.HL.156, pp 106–7; A.C. Bell & H.C.G. Matthew, 'Grosvenor, Richard de Aquila, first Baron Stalbridge', *ODNB*. 11 *Freeman's Journal*, 16 July 1883; P. Maume, 'Gillooly, Laurence', *DIB*. 12 Recollections part 2, O'Conor papers, CH, 9.4.HL.156, pp 106–7; T. Denman, 'Redmond, William Hoey Kearney ('Willie')', *DIB*.

When news of his defeat reached Roscommon, bonfires were lit in celebration on the outskirts of the town.[13]

On 26 July 1883, shortly after the Wexford by-election, the O'Conor Don's younger brother, Denis, passed away prematurely. This was another big personal blow, as they had always been close, but the O'Conor Don was mentioned as a possible candidate to contest the now vacant County Sligo seat.[14] This did not materialize, however, most likely because Bishop Gillooly directed the Sligo clergy to support the nationalist candidate, Nicholl P. Lynch, a London bank director.[15] Although Gillooly thought the possibility of the O'Conor Don's success would have been better were it not 'for the unfortunate Wexford campaign', he explained how it would be 'fatal not only to religion but to social order' if the clergy sided with candidates who the electorate saw as their opponents. In his opinion, Lynch was 'a moderate man' and the popular candidate among the people.[16] A realistic assessment of the situation, it was symptomatic of a growing distance between the two men and, in a broader sense, of the burgeoning alliance between the Catholic hierarchy and political nationalism in the early 1880s.[17] Gillooly had been a critic of the Land League and Parnell in the early 1880s but had come to accept the new political reality by the middle of the decade. As for the O'Conor Don, he was critical of Gillooly's lack of vocal opposition to clerical involvement in the Plan of Campaign in 1886–8; and by the early 1890s, the two men had fallen out when Gillooly refused to recognize the O'Conor Don's right to 'present' priests for appointment in the parishes of Ballinagare, Ballintober and Castlerea. It is not clear if this was an argument over the appointment of a particular priest, but it seems likely. The O'Conor Don temporarily withdrew his financial support to the local clergy until he had the decision overturned by the pope, after having failed with an appeal to the Irish archbishops.[18] Thus, although he and Gillooly seemed to have patched things up by 1893, the O'Conor Don's relationship with the Catholic hierarchy, particularly after Cardinal Edward McCabe's death in 1885, was fraught with political tension.[19] This, in turn, was further evidence of how his liberal and unionist political views were leading to his marginalization in Irish politics.

Between 1883 and 1886, the O'Conor Don's political activity was sporadic and increasingly hesitant. This kind of incoherence and retreat was

13 *Freeman's Journal*, 19 July 1883. 14 Recollections part 2, O'Conor papers, CH, 9.4.HL.156, p. 108; *Freeman's Journal*, 16 Aug. 1883. 15 *Tablet*, 11 Aug. 1883. 16 Bishop Gillooly to the O'Conor Don, 14 Aug. 1883, O'Conor papers, CH, 9.4.HS.204. 17 Jackson, *Home rule*, pp 46–7. 18 The O'Conor Don to Bishop Gillooly, 20 Oct. 189[?], O'Conor papers, CH, 9.4.ES.238; Supplemental abstract of title, Land commission papers, DAFF, box 237, sch. E, no. 6, record no. 1119; Maume, 'Gillooly, Laurence', *DIB*. 19 Diary of the O'Conor Don, 23 Feb. 1893, O'Conor papers, CH, 9.4.SH.247. Gillooly stayed with the O'Conor Don at Clonalis.

not unusual among Irish liberals, but their inability to work together in this period was brutally exposed by the discipline and organizational capacity of Parnell's Irish Parliamentary Party. Although still attached to the Liberal Party, the O'Conor Don seemed to be somewhat bitter about the fact that it had not done him much good. Indeed, in May 1884 he was protesting with Earl Spencer for not granting the position of sergeant at law to his cousin, Hugh MacDermot, reminding the viceroy that he had supported the Liberal Party throughout his time in parliament, spending 'many thousands in contesting [elections] in the liberal interest', and standing for the party in Wexford against his better judgment.[20] Such feelings of personal slight reveal more than a degree of self-importance, but they were, in any event, unwarranted, as Gladstone appointed MacDermot solicitor general for Ireland in 1885 and attorney general in 1892.[21]

Despite his disgruntlement with the party, the O'Conor Don was present at a meeting of Irish liberals at the viceregal lodge in August 1884, attended by William Findlater, MP for County Monaghan; Thomas Dickson, MP for County Tyrone; Rowland Ponsonby Blennerhassett, MP for County Kerry; John Naish, Irish lord chancellor; and Courtenay Boyle, Earl Spencer's private secretary. The main purpose of the meeting was to consider the implications of Gladstone's proposals for franchise reform in February of that year, with a view to devising a scheme for proportional representation so that the 'loyal minority' could 'gain some seats at the next election'.[22] Although Blennerhassett followed up with letters to the O'Conor Don, urging the need for organization in the 'South and West', nothing seems to have come of the initiative.[23] In January 1885, he was contacted by the newly founded Proportional Representation Society (PRS) because it was felt he 'took a deep interest' in the subject. Once again, there is no evidence of active involvement, even though the radical MP for Bodmin, and founding member of the PRS, Leonard Courtney, visited to Clonalis in September 1890. Nonetheless, the O'Conor Don and other Irish unionists saw the introduction of PR as a way of protecting their political interests, particularly in the three southern provinces.[24]

20 The O'Conor Don to Earl Spencer, 10 May 1884, Althorp papers, BL, add. 76997, art.1. 21 A. Pole, 'MacDermot, Hugh Hyacinth O'Rorke', *DIB*. 22 Recollections part 2, O'Conor papers, CH, 9.3.HS.156, p. 113; A. Findlater, *Findlaters: the story of a Dublin merchant family, 1774–2001* (Dublin, 2001), pp 54–71; Thompson, *The end of liberal Ulster*, pp 277–9; P.M. Geoghegan' 'Naish, John', *DIB*; J.H. Murphy, *Ireland's czar: Gladstonian government and the lord lieutenancies of the red Earl Spencer, 1868–86* (Dublin, 2014), p. 9. 23 R.P. Blennerhassett to the O'Conor Don, 19 Aug. 1884, O'Conor papers, CH, 9.4.HS.217. 24 A. Cromwell White to the O'Conor Don, 29 Jan. 1885, O'Conor papers, CH, 9.4.HS.218; Recollections part 2, O'Conor papers, CH, 9.4.HL.156, p. 140; J. Hart, *Proportional representation: critics of the British electoral system, 1820–1945* (New York, 1992), pp 72, 81–5, 102.

The Liberal government's franchise and constituency-redistribution reforms of 1884 and 1885 saw the Irish electorate expand by some half a million people to 700,000. However, with no proportional element the possibility of Irish liberal successes in future elections were even more unlikely.[25] It is not clear if the O'Conor Don opposed these reforms outright, but he was certainly less than enthusiastic about them. When Lord Carlingford expressed his 'disappointment … about Irish affairs, especially the extension of the suffrage', the O'Conor Don had little sympathy for the former lord privy seal, who did not 'seem to realise that he … [was] one of the cabinet who had to decide on this'.[26] Meanwhile, towards the end of 1884, there was a flurry of communications between Gladstone, Parnell and Joseph Chamberlain on the subject of Irish local government reform. And on 21 January 1885, Parnell made his 'march of a nation' speech in Cork where he demanded, at the very least, the restoration of 'Grattan's Parliament'.[27]

The prospect of a home rule majority in Ireland at the next general election spurred conservative unionists into swifter action than their liberal counterparts. In April 1885, the O'Conor Don received an invitation from Arthur Kavanagh and other prominent landlords to join the Irish Loyal and Patriotic Union (ILPU), so as to meet the 'gravity of the present political crisis'. A mainly southern, Protestant and landed endeavour, the ILPU's objectives were to oppose nationalists wherever possible; to advocate proportional representation as a way to protect the loyal minority; to assess how other organizations such as the 'citizens committee' and the 'labourers union' could be incorporated; and to campaign for the establishment of a royal residence in Ireland.[28] Significantly, the O'Conor Don declined to join, even though Lord De Vesci tried to persuade him to reconsider. Claiming that 'the movement has been warmly taken up and has every prospect of success', De Vesci warned him that 'if no resistance is offered to the Parnellite party … they will have succeeded entirely from a policy of bray'.[29] In response, the O'Conor Don stated that local government and land purchase needed to be prioritized, but while De Vesci agreed with the latter, he thought the former 'will only be as a stepping stone to complete and entire separation'.[30]

The O'Conor Don also had concerns about the largely Protestant and conservative complexion of the ILPU, which he conveyed to Edward O'Brien,

25 E. Biagini, *British democracy and Irish nationalism 1876–1906* (Cambridge, 2007), p. 144; Hoppen, *The mid-Victorian generation*, pp 651–3; Thompson, *The end of liberal Ulster*, pp 290–5. 26 Recollections part 2, O'Conor papers, CH, 9.4.HL.156, p. 114. 27 O'Day, *Irish home rule*, pp 94–7. 28 Arthur Kavanagh to the O'Conor Don, 30 Apr. 1885, O'Conor papers, CH, 9.4.HS.215; Canadine, *British aristocracy*, p. 473. 29 Lord De Vesci to the O'Conor Don, 27 May & 17 June 1885, O'Conor papers, CH, 9.4.HS.215; O'Day, *Irish home rule*, p. 97. 30 Lord De Vesci to the O'Conor Don, 17 June 1885, O'Conor papers, CH, 9.4.HS.215.

a County Limerick landowner and son of the former Young Irelander William Smith O'Brien. In response, O'Brien assured him that the ILPU was 'perfectly impartial as between liberals and conservatives', with 'nothing sectarian in religion or politics', and with a sole purpose of opposing 'the Parnellites on ... the maintenance of the Union' in the upcoming elections. In a not-too-subtle chiding of the O'Conor Don, he cited 'local cowardice and apathy' as the main obstacle to finding local candidates to take up the challenge and he implored him to 'reconsider his decision' because 'surely everyone who is interested in not allowing the Country to pass under the Domination of Mr Parnell ought to exert himself'.[31] The O'Conor Don remained unmoved, even though O'Brien questioned how he could decline to join the ILPU on the grounds of its conservative, Protestant, landed make-up when he had already joined the Irish Landowners' Convention, another largely Protestant and conservative organization. For the O'Conor Don, the distinction was that the Landowners' Convention was 'formed on ex-political lines' with no electoral ambitions, but while the latter point was technically true, it could hardly be argued that the Landowners' Convention was non-political.[32] One can only assume, then, that being a liberal and a Catholic were factors in his decision not to join the ILPU, as well as the ever-present reluctance to get involved in anything party political in Ireland. He was not alone, however, with the ILPU receiving very little support from the many upper- and middle-class Catholics who were loyalists and unionists. Colonel Gerald Dease was the ILPU's vice-president, but he and Sir Rowland Blennerhassett, MP for County Kerry, were two of the relatively few Catholics who joined.[33]

So how were Catholics like the O'Conor Don to display their loyalism and unionism if not through an organization like the ILPU? In April 1885, Edmund Dease wrote a letter to the *Tablet*, which begged the question 'Is loyalty a duty?' His answer was emphatic: 'There was never a time when loyalty to the throne, and respect for the government was so great an obligation as now.'[34] The O'Conor Don would have undoubtedly agreed, but still he declined to assent to a request from his in-law, Ambrose More O'Ferrall, to join him, Dease, William Cogan and other 'respectable' Catholics, 'who consider loyalty a duty', in signing an 'address to the holy father ... setting forth submission to his spiritual authority and also to the temporal authority of the Queen'.[35]

[31] Edward O'Brien to the O'Conor Don, 17 Oct. 1885, O'Conor papers, CH, 9.4.HS.215; De Burgh, *The landowners of Ireland*, p. 343. [32] Recollections part 2, O'Conor papers, CH, 9.4.HL.156, p. 149. [33] Buckland, *Irish unionism 1*, pp 13–15; J. Biggs-Davidson & G. Chowdharay-Best, *The cross of Saint Patrick: the Catholic unionist tradition in Ireland* (Bourne End, 1984), p. 249; J. Quinn, 'Blennerhassett, Sir Rowland', *DIB*. [34] Edmund Dease to Earl Spencer, 25 Apr. 1885, Althorp papers, BL, add. 76998, art. 2. [35] Ambrose More O'Ferrall to the O'Conor Don, 9 & 16 May 1885, O'Conor papers, CH, 9.4.HS.217.

Again, it is not clear why the O'Conor Don declined, but one suspects it was a combination of his stubbornly independent streak and a political judgment that it might make matters even worse for liberal Catholic candidates come election time. One way or another, the general election results of November/December 1885 demonstrated that Irish Catholic loyalties lay predominantly with Parnell and the IPP, which captured eighty per cent of the Irish vote and the balance of power in the house of commons. The ILPU, on the other hand, failed to win any seats, despite fielding fifty-two candidates.[36] Notably, in a rather unusual intervention in the run-up to the election, the English Catholic convert and philanthropist Lady Elizabeth Herbert tried to persuade the O'Conor Don to stand for the ILPU in the newly created constituency of North County Dublin. She did so through their mutual acquaintance Walter Hussey Walsh, a Catholic landowner in County Roscommon, to whom she confidently predicted that if the O'Conor Don stood as an 'anti-separatist candidate ... he would be returned by a very large majority' because 'all the moderate men in Ireland ... liberal and conservative would support him warmly'.[37] Monsell also encouraged him to stand, relaying how Lord De Vesci thought his 'election would be certain'.[38] Again, the O'Conor Don was unmoved, telling Hussey Walsh that 'Lady Herbert must be sadly deceived' if 'she thinks that ... any anti-Parnellite candidate could win' or 'even make a respectable fight' of it in an 'overwhelming Nationalist' constituency like North County Dublin.[39] This was a correct assessment, with the nationalist John Joseph Clancy winning the seat by a large margin. Even so, this episode once again demonstrates the O'Conor Don's squeamishness about sticking his head above the electoral parapet for the sake of making his unionism explicit.[40]

THE FIRST HOME RULE BILL AND LIBERAL UNIONISM, 1886–92

Although the O'Conor Don was becoming an ever more marginal figure in Irish and British politics, spending more time on his estates and compiling his history of the O'Conors of Connaught, he remained engaged with the main political issues of the day. On the face of it, a minority Conservative government taking up the reins of power in June 1885 was a positive development

---

36 Hoppen, *The mid-Victorian generation*, pp 679–80; O'Day, *Irish home rule*, p. 106; Cannadine, *British aristocracy*, p. 473. 37 Lady Elizabeth Herbert to Walter Hussey Walsh, 8 Nov. 1885, O'Conor papers, CH, 9.4.HS.217; Diaries of the O'Conor Don, 3 Feb. 1864 & 11 Apr. 1893, O'Conor papers, CH, 9.4.SH.247; Bence Jones, *Catholic families*, pp 204, 207, 237. 38 Lord Emly to the O'Conor Don, 10 Nov. 1885, O'Conor papers, CH, 9.4.HS.217. 39 The O'Conor Don to Walter Hussey Walsh, 11 Nov. 1885, O'Conor papers, CH, 9.4.HS.217. 40 C.J. Woods, 'Clancy, John Joseph', *DIB*.

for Irish unionists, but many were alarmed when secret discussions between the Irish viceroy, Lord Carnarvon, and Parnell on the issue of self-government were made public in August 1885. It was also known that Parnell had been communicating with Gladstone on the subject through his partner, Katherine O'Shea. Shortly after the election in December 1885, Gladstone's son, Herbert, made public his father's conversion to home rule. Thus, when Gladstone returned to power in February 1886, home rule was now on the legislative cards.[41]

The O'Conor Don's thoughts on home rule at this point seemed to be those of a man resigned to the reality of politics in Ireland, but still resistant to it. When Lord Monteagle wrote to optimistically ponder whether Parnell's support for home rule was simply 'a question of pocket', and whether he might 'allow the HR question to be hung up' if he was not 'afraid of losing the farmers support or of his Fenian tail wagging him, or both', the O'Conor Don's response was to state bluntly that 'Beyond any shadow of doubt amongst the greater part of the Catholics of Ireland there is a strong National feeling in favour of Home Rule'. He did not dispute that there was 'self[-]interest' and a desire for 'power amongst mod[ern] men', but nonetheless felt that Parnell and the IPP were moving 'in the same direction' as 'this National feeling'.[42] However, despite conceding the popularity of home rule, the O'Conor Don opposed Gladstone's home rule bill, criticizing the 'great chief' for thinking that accompanying the bill with a land-purchase scheme would make the prospect of home rule any more palatable to Irish landlords.[43] Edmund Dease was likewise conflicted. On the one hand, he rather fancifully told Earl Spencer that he was 'perhaps in advance' of Gladstone on the question of home rule and regretted that he had not dealt with it sooner. On the other, he opposed Gladstone's bill because there was 'a great danger, to the liberty of the R[oman] C[atholic] Church under a domestic legislature' dominated by Parnell and the IPP. This, he believed, was the view of many prominent Catholics 'within the church', who were 'afraid to speak publicly' on the matter 'for the sake of appearing to be of one mind on this national question'. Indeed, Dease recounted a conversation he had with Cardinal Cullen, who, based on the experience of the Catholic Church in revolutionary France and Italy, feared for its position in Ireland under a 'native Parliament'. Therefore, although he supported the idea of home rule, he did not trust the 'fabulous results' promised by the 'agitators' in Parnell's party, who had 'absolute separation' in mind, which he felt 'would have the most

41 O'Day, *Irish home rule*, pp 97–108.   42 Lord Monteagle to the O'Conor Don, 4 Feb. 1886, O'Conor papers, CH, 9.4.HS.219; The O'Conor Don to Lord Monteagle, 7 Feb. 1886, O'Conor papers, CH, 9.4.HS.219.   43 See chapter four, p. 101.

disastrous results [for] Ireland'.⁴⁴ Dease reiterated these arguments in a letter to the *Tablet* in March 1886, where he declared himself to be 'A Catholic first, [and] an Irishman Afterwards'.⁴⁵

This was, more or less, the O'Conor Don's position on home rule; he supported the idea of it but thought most Irish nationalists were in fact republicans bent on an independent, secular Irish republic by any means necessary. But, once again, he declined to support a public declaration of Catholic loyalty, this time from the earl of Granard, who in turn had been contacted by the leading English Catholic, the duke of Norfolk, about the possibility of organizing it.⁴⁶ Indeed, although the duke and Lord Randolph Churchill were convinced that there were many loyal Irish Catholics whose voices had not been heard, there was no coordinated declaration of loyalty from the O'Conor Don, Monsell, Dease, Granard, More O'Ferrall and the many other Catholic loyalists who moved in their circles.⁴⁷

The defeat of Gladstone's home rule bill on 8 June 1886 led to a general election in July, which saw the conservatives returned to office with the support of seventy-four liberal unionists, who seceded from the Liberal Party over the question of home rule.⁴⁸ Significantly, the O'Conor Don met with Lord Hartington, the leader of the liberal unionists, on 3 June at Devonshire House, where they had 'a long talk ... on public affairs and the home rule bill'.⁴⁹ This indicates a degree of cooperation between Irish and English liberal unionists, but any semblance of unionist organization in Ireland was mainly confined to Ulster.⁵⁰ Indeed, it was not until Hartington and George Goschen visited Dublin in November 1887, for the launch of the Liberal Union of Ireland (LUI), that things got somewhat underway in southern Ireland. On 7 November, the O'Conor Don received word from the secretary of the LUI, Rowland Ponsonby Blennerhassett, requesting that his 'name ... be placed on the reception committee to receive' Hartington and Goschen in Dublin. Although Blennerhassett assured him that LUI had support of 'many of the leading Catholic Merchant and professional men' in the country, the O'Conor Don once again declined to get involved.⁵¹ While he had 'the highest admiration for Lord H[artington] and respect [for] his companion', he told Blennerhassett that he had come 'to the conclusion some years ago that whilst

---

44 Edmund Dease to Earl Spencer, 24 Apr. 1886, Althorp papers, BL, add. 76998, art. 2. **45** *Tablet*, 27 Mar. 1886. **46** Lord Granard to the O'Conor Don, 22 & 25 Feb. 1886, O'Conor papers, CH, 9.4.HS.217. **47** *Irish Times*, 23 Feb. 1886; *Belfast Weekly News*, 27 Feb. 1886. **48** C. Shannon, 'The Ulster liberal unionists and local government reform, 1885–98', *Irish Historical Studies*, 18:71 (Mar. 1973), p. 409. **49** Recollections part 2, O'Conor papers, CH, 9.4.HL.156, p. 121. **50** Shannon, 'Ulster liberal unionists', p. 412. **51** R.P. Blennerhassett to the O'Conor Don, 7 Nov. 1887, O'Conor papers, CH, 9.4.HS.271; *Irish Times*, 7 Nov. 1887.

out of public life I would not go out of my way to take part in any political demonstration'.⁵² Thus, although happy to meet with Hartington in a private capacity, as he had done on a number of occasions in 1887, the O'Conor Don was clearly reluctant to be openly associated with anything resembling a unionist political party. He was clearly not alone in this, with the lack of public Catholic support for the liberal unionist cause evident at their conference at Westminster on 8 December 1887, where Sir Rowland Blennerhassett and William Kenny QC appear to have been the only liberal Catholics in attendance.⁵³

In October 1890, the O'Conor Don was present at an informal meeting of liberal unionists held at the Shelbourne Hotel in Dublin, which discussed the need to promote 'any measure of Local Government for Ireland' that included a provision for the 'representation of minorities' and scheduled a further meeting to draw up a memorandum along these lines. Other Catholics in attendance were William Kenny, a founding member of the LUI who helped organize Hartington's Dublin visit in 1887, and Sir George Errington, mentioned in chapter three as Gladstone's unofficial envoy to Rome in 1886.⁵⁴ Also present were the Protestants Rowland Ponsonby Blennerhassett and William Findlater, as well as the Quaker Frederic W. Pim. Findlater and Pim were Dublin businessmen closely associated with leading Ulster liberal unionists such as John Givan, Andrew Porter, Sir Thomas Lea, Sir Thomas McClure, Thomas Dickson MP and James Richardson.⁵⁵ Despite the O'Conor Don's reticence, then, he was part of a loose network of liberal unionists across Ireland who were willing to work together to promote electoral, local government and land reform.⁵⁶

Typically, though, the O'Conor Don also worked with leading conservative unionists to achieve Irish reforms. Between 1888 and 1892, he met with the Irish chief secretary, Arthur Balfour, on several occasions to discuss local government, land purchase, funds for the River Suck drainage scheme, and the construction of a railway line between Castlerea and Ballaghaderreen.⁵⁷ In 1891, Salisbury's conservative government passed a land purchase act, which, although it would not have gone far enough for the O'Conor Don, provided more substantial funds for the transfer of land from landlord to tenant than any previous acts.⁵⁸ Moreover, in 1892, the conservatives introduced an Irish

---

52 The O'Conor Don to R.P. Blennerhassett, 11 Nov. 1887, O'Conor papers, CH, 9.4.HS.271. 53 *The liberal unionist conference and banquet* (London, 1888). 54 Local government memorandum, 18 Oct. 1890, O'Conor papers, CH, 9.4.HS.188; Burnand, *Catholic who's who*, p. 222. See chapter three, pp 79–80. 55 Findlater, *Findlaters*, pp 54–71. 56 J. McNabb, 'Frederic William Pim', *DIB*; B. Hourican & J. Quinn, 'Jonathan T. Pim', *DIB*. 57 Recollections part 2, O'Conor papers, CH, 9.4.HL.156, pp 122–45; The O'Conor Don to Arthur Balfour, 16 Nov. 1890, CSORP, NAI, 17955. 58 See chapter four, p. 100.

local government bill formulated on the model of recent local government reforms in England and Scotland. The bill proposed the establishment of county and district councils elected on the parliamentary franchise, but the absence of PR voting drove the majority of unionists to oppose it, while nationalists opposed the provisions of a cumulative vote for landlords and grand juries being granted the power to censor council resolutions.[59] According to Andrew Gailey, the conservatives' proposals for local government were a 'classic unionist alternative' to home rule, rather than being any attempt 'to undercut Home Rule and reconcile the politically concerned in Ireland to the Union'.[60] However, this is not how the O'Conor Don would have seen it. He was clearly resigned to home rule becoming a reality at some point but felt that a range of economic and political reforms were needed before it could be considered. As such, he saw land purchase, local government reform and proportional representation as ways to provide protection for the position of landowners and unionists in the event of a home rule settlement, rather than an actual alternative to home rule. This was in contrast to many conservative unionists in the ILPU, who, like the conservative government, thought land purchase would 'kill Home Rule with Kindness' and allow landlords, on much reduced estates, to maintain some kind of political influence in Irish society.[61]

Generally speaking, then, O'Conor Don was in broad agreement with liberal and conservative unionists about the policies that were required in Ireland, even though he would have disagreed that these policies would 'kill' home rule altogether. Once the initial panic over home rule and associated issues over party or organizational allegiance subsided in 1886–7, he busied himself lobbying for land purchase, arterial drainage, state ownership of railways, local government reform and proportional representation. All of these policies were advocated by liberal and conservative unionists across Ireland.[62] But although the O'Conor Don was clearly moving in unionist circles and on the unionist side of the argument against home rule, he was very reluctant to pin his colours publicly and consistently to the unionist mast. On the other hand, although he opposed home rule, he accepted that there was a majority Catholic national feeling in favour of it. It could be that the O'Conor Don was torn between a shared national feeling with his fellow Catholics and a shared political conviction with his fellow unionists, but there is little doubt that the latter consistently trumped the former.

59 Shannon, 'Ulster liberal unionists', pp 415–18; Gailey, *The death of kindness*, pp 27, 43. 60 Jackson, *The Ulster Party*, pp 170–2; Gailey, *The death of kindness*, p. 41. 61 Gailey, *The death of kindness*, pp 27, 43; Canadine, *British aristocracy*, p. 475. 62 Shannon, 'Ulster liberal unionists', pp 410–15; O'Day, *Irish home rule*, p. 146.

THE SECOND HOME RULE BILL AND CATHOLIC UNIONISM, 1892–3

In December 1890, the IPP split over Parnell's affair with Katherine O'Shea. Less than one year later, in October 1891, Parnell had passed away. His death was a significant blow to the coherence of the nationalist movement in Ireland, but the return of Gladstone to power in August 1892 temporarily overshadowed the bitter feud in the IPP and rallied the Parnellite and anti-Parnellite camps behind the home rule standard. Irish unionists, on the other hand, held large anti-home rule demonstrations in Belfast and Dublin in June 1892 in anticipation of Gladstone's return to power.[63] The O'Conor Don did not attend these demonstrations, but after Gladstone introduced his second home rule bill in February 1893 he agreed to attend and speak at a unionist demonstration at Leinster Hall on 15 March 1893. As already noted, however, he pulled out at the last minute because, although 'opposed to the Home Rule scheme on the ground that it would be disastrous to my country', he 'could not speak as an admirer or lover of the Union'.[64]

What we can see from this recollection of events is that, like in 1873–4, the O'Conor Don was sticking to the argument that he supported the idea of home rule while opposing the practical application of it. But his continued resistance to any form of home rule clearly demonstrates that he preferred the status quo of the union as it stood over a union with a devolved Irish parliament. After all, it was not either the union or home rule; it was a union with home rule. The O'Conor Don was, therefore, less a lover of home rule than the union. In any event, his recollection of his reason for not attending the meeting in Dublin is rather contradicted by a letter he wrote to the *Freeman's Journal* at the time, in which he said his absence was 'involuntary' and not because of any lack of 'sympathy with the opposition to the Home Rule Bill'. Indeed, he 'would have been glad' of the 'opportunity' to speak against it and hoped that he would be able to do so on a 'future occasion'. Such an occasion presented itself at a unionist demonstration at the Albert Hall in London on 25 April 1893, but while the O'Conor Don attended he did not speak.[65]

The O'Conor Don's unionism was, however, confirmed by his retrospective signing of a Catholic unionist petition to parliament in opposition to Gladstone's home rule bill, which was published in the *Freeman's Journal* on the same day of the Leinster Hall meeting on 15 March 1893. Signed by Monsell,

---

63 O'Day, *Irish home rule*, pp 142–55, 152–9; *Irish Times*, 3, 6, 7, 8, 11, 15, 16 Mar. 1893.   64 Recollections part 2, O'Conor papers, CH. 9.4.HL.156, p. 150; *Irish Times*, 15 Mar. 1893. Other prominent Catholics such as Sir Richard Martin, Sir Percy Grace, Sir John Lentaigne and Walter Hussey Walsh had no qualms about attending the demonstration.   65 Recollections part 2, O'Conor papers, CH. 9.4.HS.156, p. 151; *Freeman's Journal*, 16 Mar. 1893.

Dease, Cogan, More O'Ferrall, Kenny and others, it stated their 'unshaken' loyalty to the British crown and constitution, as well as their belief that the maintenance of the union between 'England and Ireland' was vital to protect the 'full civil and religious liberty' Catholics enjoyed under the crown and constitution. Moreover, in an accompanying letter, it was argued that, notwithstanding 'certain anti-Catholic utterances', a 'false impression' existed, which portrayed a straight 'contest between a Roman Catholic majority' in favour of the bill 'and a Protestant minority' against. Their opposition to the bill was based on 'purely secular considerations, heartily in accord with our fellow Unionists ... that Home Rule, if imposed on Ireland, would ... foster a revolutionary spirit disastrous to the true interests of our religion'.[66] It was, of course, accurate to say that a binary Catholic nationalist-Protestant unionist divide was not representative of the full spectrum of opinion on home rule in Ireland, but the failure of Catholic unionists to organize among themselves or alongside their Protestant counterparts gave the rather strong impression that such a clear binary represented the totality of Irish political opinion. Clearly, a majority of Catholics supported home rule and a majority of Protestants opposed it, but there were many Catholic unionists like the O'Conor Don who opposed it and many Protestant nationalists like Parnell who supported it. Conversely, many landed Catholics supported home rule (John Redmond being the obvious example), while most landed Protestants (of which Parnell was one) opposed it.[67]

That the O'Conor Don still claimed to be a supporter of home rule, while at the same time signing a Catholic unionist petition opposing it, proved irksome for the *Freeman's Journal*. In an editorial on 'Recreant Home Rulers', it dismissed his position as 'utterly indefensible', 'scarcely honest' and inconsistent with the views he expressed at the home rule conference in 1873. True to form, the O'Conor Don rejected the charges of 'inconsistency and recreancy', arguing that his present position was consistent with that of 1873 because he still believed an Irish parliament could only be 'demanded ... upon ... two grounds': those of nationality and utility. On nationality, he argued that, under Gladstone's bill, 'Ireland can no longer be a nation' given that the imperial parliament would 'continue to legislate upon every one of the subjects committed to the Irish Legislature just as it did before'. It was therefore a 'deceit' to claim that an Irish parliament would lead to greater sense of Irish

---

66 *Freeman's Journal*, 15 & 16 Mar. 1893. Other signatories included the earls of Fingall, Kenmare and Westmeath, Lord De Freyne, James Talbot Power, John Smithwick, Nicholas Synnott, John Ross, Christopher and Henry Grattan Bellew, Daniel and Maurice O'Connell, Colonel Gerald Dease, Percy Grace and John Whyte.   67 Campbell, *The Irish establishment*, pp 156–7. J.A. Blake, Charles Meldon, W.H.K. Redmond and Francis O'Beirne were other landed Catholic home rulers.

nationhood. Moreover, pointing to what was perhaps an uncomfortable truth, he argued that if the supremacy of the imperial parliament were admitted, 'not even a packed convention in Dublin would dare to accept the bill'. Conversely, if imperial supremacy were not admitted, and the bill passed, he felt it would 'lead to future trouble' when supremacy became apparent; in other words, calls for complete separation from Great Britain.[68] On the grounds of utility, the O'Conor Don felt that he could not see the political advantage of home rule given that the 'proposed legislature' would be 'inferior in its powers not merely to those enjoyed by a British Colony but to those enjoyed by one of the States of the American Union'. Nor could he see the economic advantage because the proposed parliament would be 'Starting with a bankrupt exchequer' and 'forced to live by taxation of capital', with 'all industry, enterprise and energy' driven out of the country. In such circumstances, he rather sarcastically remarked that 'nothing would remain to be taxed but the unfortunate holders or occupiers of land, of whose rights you so kindly make me the champion'.[69]

The *Freeman's* response was to denounce the O'Conor Don as a 'traitorous' and 'whey-blooded Catholic ... who thinks it no curtailment of Catholic liberty that a Catholic is debarred by statute from representing his Sovereign in the Government of Ireland'.[70] By this it referred to the constitutional bar on a Catholic holding the office of Irish lord lieutenant, which it was thought made a mockery of the Catholic unionist claim that Catholics enjoyed 'full civil and religious liberty' under the British constitution. The O'Conor Don's response was to rather sarcastically call on the *Freeman's* to campaign for the removal of the Catholic bar, but even more sarcastic was his line that not 'every Catholic peasant would rise from his bed' thinking himself 'freer and more independent' if one of his fellow Catholics, 'who would probably be dubbed ... a "Cawtholic"', could become lord lieutenant and 'embrace the ladies at the next Drawingroom in Dublin Castle'.[71] This rather ungratifying recourse to name-calling and sarcasm masked the fact that the O'Conor Don's concerns about the limited powers of the proposed Irish parliament were similarly voiced by nationalists in the commons debates on the bill. Nonetheless, although the leader of the Parnellite faction, John Redmond, publicly expressed his dissatisfaction, he adopted a position of accepting the bill as a first instalment of Irish autonomy.[72] On the other hand, the majority of unionists, like the O'Conor Don, focused on the impracticality of having an Irish parliament subordinate to the imperial parliament, and on the economic ruin of Ireland. These arguments were also made at the time of first home rule bill in 1886,

68 *Freeman's Journal*, 17 Mar. 1893.   69 Ibid.   70 *Freeman's Journal*, 18 Mar. 1893.   71 *Irish Independent*, 18 Mar. 1893   72 O'Day, *Irish home rule*, pp 16–5.

with Irish liberal unionist and historian W.H. Lecky, and the English liberal unionist and constitutional theorist Albert Venn Dicey two of their foremost proponents.[73] The O'Conor Don may have been influenced by Lecky and Dicey, but his opposition to home rule had most likely hardened anyway given the land agitations of the previous thirteen years; worsening political relations with the hierarchy and clergy; and the failure of successive Conservative governments to introduce a comprehensive scheme of land purchase.

After passing through the commons on 2 September 1893 with a majority of thirty-three votes, Gladstone's second home rule bill was predictably thrown out by the house of lords.[74] The newspaper and journal campaign against home rule continued for a time afterwards and the O'Conor Don joined the chorus of opposition in December with an article in the unionist *National Review* entitled 'The Unsolved Irish Problem'. Here he dismissed Gladstone's bill as 'impracticable' and 'unworkable', suggesting that it 'probably passed the House of Commons because it was well known it would be thrown out by the House of Lords'.[75] The dominant theme of the article, however, was the O'Conor Don's contempt for nationalist leaders who he accused of drifting from a position of 'extravagant talk and incitement to disturbance' to the pretence of being 'coadjutors in preserving the public peace' with the Irish chief secretary, John Morley.[76] He singled out his old foe John Dillon for presenting a false position on the home rule bill because it 'did not give them [nationalists] all, or anything like all, that they wanted'. While acknowledging that nationalist opposition to the bill 'would have been madness', the O'Conor Don insisted their support was based on the hope 'that they could use it as a lever to obtain more'. In other words, nationalists saw home rule as a step towards complete independence from Great Britain, the crown and the empire, which was not what he, Butt or Gladstone wanted.[77] Questioning the probity of the nationalist leadership was a feature of the unionist critique of home rule, with Lecky particularly scathing of their associations with the combinations of the Plan of Campaign. To his mind this was a sure sign that once nationalists gained control of Irish affairs confiscation of landed property would ensue.[78] The O'Conor Don held the same view, arguing that the land

---

73 D. McCartney, 'Lecky, William Edward Hartpole', *DIB*; R.A. Cosgrove, 'Dicey, Albert Venn', *ODNB*; H. Mulvey, 'The historian Lecky: opponent of Irish home rule', *Victorian Studies*, 1:4 (June 1958), 337–51; W.E.H. Lecky, 'Some aspects of home rule', *Contemporary Review*, 63 (May 1893), 626–38; A.V. Dicey, 'The defence of the union', *Contemporary Review*, 61 (Mar. 1892), 314–31; Buckland, *Irish unionism 1*, pp 12–15; O'Day, *Irish home rule*, p. 168. 74 O'Day, *Irish home rule*, pp 165–8. 75 C.O. O'Conor, 'The unsolved Irish problem', *National Review*, 22 (Dec. 1893), p. 531. 76 O'Conor, 'The unsolved Irish problem', pp 532–3. 77 O'Conor, 'The unsolved Irish problem', pp 533–5; *Freeman's Journal*, 18 Mar. 1893. 78 Buckland, *Irish unionism 1*, pp 8–10; Lecky, 'Some aspects of home rule', pp 626–30.

question would have to be resolved 'before any form of Home Rule or any very extensive system of local government can be safely granted to Ireland'.[79]

Despite his opposition to home rule, however, the O'Conor Don was, like Lecky, willing to recognize the veracity of Irish national sentiment.[80] In a significant development from his arguments on nationality in 1874, he referred to the difficulties of reconciling 'two distinct and separate nationalities ... divided by the most marked lines of different religions, different likings and antipathies, and, looking back on past history, with the most antagonistic prejudices'. Those who prided themselves on their 'British extraction', he argued, were bound to oppose Gladstone's bill.[81] On the other hand, the O'Conor Don recognized that the demand for home rule would continue regardless of this opposition, and that not even 'the most extreme Unionist' could 'shut his eyes' to the fact that the bill was 'passed by the Democratic branch of the Legislature of the United Kingdom'. Although he felt Ireland was more or less 'self-governed' because 'the minority in Ireland often belongs to the Party composing the majority of the whole Kingdom', the O'Conor Don nonetheless conceded that this did not 'satisfy the cravings of Irish national sentiment' among the Catholic majority. The problem therefore was to secure 'to the minority [in Ireland] the least possible interference with [their] individual rights, in which alone consists true liberty'. An alternative to Gladstone's proposals was therefore required because 'Ireland must be governed in the same degree as England is by the Imperial Parliament ... or she must get real independence'.[82] What he meant by 'real independence' is not made explicit, but it echoes his contention in 1873 that an English-dominated imperial parliament would be more likely to grant 'absolute independence' than anything else. Whether or not this 'real' or 'absolute' independence meant the old O'Connellite idea of repealing the Act of Union while maintaining the constitutional connection with Great Britain through the crown is again not clear, but what we do know is that the O'Conor Don certainly did not support complete Irish separation from Great Britain and the empire. He was not of 'British extraction', and he would not have seen himself as an 'extreme' unionist, but he was certainly attached to the British connection and supported the unionist opposition to home rule.

The O'Conor Don's alternative to home rule was that a session of 'the Parliament of the United Kingdom', comprised of all members, but dealing mainly with Irish issues, should be held in Dublin 'every year, or every alternate year, for a few months'. This, he argued, would not be too far removed

79 O'Conor, 'The unsolved Irish problem', pp 537–8, 541. 80 Mulvey, 'The historian Lecky', pp 337–51. 81 O'Conor, 'The unsolved Irish problem', pp 532–3. 82 Ibid., pp 535–8.

from the current situation where Irish issues were to a large degree treated separately at Westminster, but in moving a session of the imperial parliament to Dublin, Irish MPs would gain more 'practical control over their own legislation'. Running alongside this, the O'Conor Don proposed the establishment of a permanent royal residence in Dublin, which 'would not fail to revive and strengthen that personal loyalty to the Throne which ... has always been shown by the Irish'. Together, these initiatives would 'raise' Dublin 'to the status of one of the capital cities of a great Empire', and would gratify 'that sentiment of nationality' in Ireland 'in a far more conclusive way than by the relegation of certain topics to a petty subordinate Legislature invested with much power but with little honour or dignity ... [and] without real responsibility'.[83] The argument here, it would seem, was that home rule gave too much power to nationalists, many of whom had too narrow a conception of Irish national identity and rejected the British connection in all its forms. Better to foster an Irish national identity that recognized that although Irish Catholics had 'lived through centuries of misrule and persecution', the Protestant 'settlers in Ireland' were now 'more Irish than the Irish themselves'. The O'Conor Don therefore argued that it was the 'task before us to guide and gratify' this national sentiment 'into channels where Irishmen of all races and creeds could unite in upholding it'.[84]

'A more ridiculous policy it would be hard to frame' was the damning verdict of the *Freeman's Journal*.[85] Although these were harsh words that overlooked the O'Conor Don's admirably nuanced understanding of Irish national sentiment based on the country's fractious, religiously divisive history, his proposal for a rotating imperial parliament and a permanent royal residence was more like wishful thinking than a serious, viable alternative to Gladstone's home rule proposals. Gladstone's proposals were fraught with their own difficulties, with the 1886 bill proposing a unicameral parliament and no Irish representation at Westminster, while the 1893 bill proposed a bicameral parliament with the retention of Irish representation at Westminster. In 1886, Parnell was undecided on the retention of Irish representation at Westminster and dissatisfied with the fiscal aspects of Gladstone's proposals. This was broadly representative of the confusion among nationalist MPs over what exactly home rule meant and how it might work in practice.[86] Even so, one would have to conclude that the O'Conor Don's proposals were not an alternative form of home rule, but rather a rehashing of the partially colonial system of governance already in place in Ireland and in other parts of the empire.[87]

83 O'Conor, 'The unsolved Irish problem', pp 538–40. 84 Ibid., p. 541. 85 *Freeman's Journal*, 6 Dec. 1893. 86 Lyons, *Parnell*, pp 351–8, 461–4; O'Day, *Irish home rule*, pp 109, 161–2. 87 A. Jackson, 'Ireland,

The O'Conor Don's support for the empire, and Ireland's place of prominence within it, was one of the principal motivations for his desire to see a royal residence in Dublin. Similar arguments had been made by Daniel O'Connell in the 1820s and Sir Colman O'Loghlen in the 1860s, while Earl Spencer and Gladstone considered the idea during the 1868–74 administration. Spencer raised the prospect again when the prince of Wales visited Ireland in 1885, but the queen's opposition made it an unlikely eventuality at any point during her reign. In any event, as James H. Murphy and James McConnel have both demonstrated, expressions of loyalty to the crown and support for the empire were common enough among moderate Catholic nationalists.[88] Indeed, McConnel has argued that although John Redmond sometimes called for the overthrow of landlordism and employed the rhetoric of Irish independence from Great Britain, he was a man of his class: a landlord with a gentlemanly, socially conservative temperament that considered attachment to the crown and the empire 'compatible with his Catholic faith and Irish patriotism'.[89] According to James Loughlin, a key factor in maintaining this attachment across the political and religious divides was the ceremony of monarchy, performed through royal visits and the court of the viceroy.[90] But royal visits were often a source of great tension among nationalists, with John Dillon repulsed by Redmond's welcome for the queen's visit to Ireland in 1900. While Redmond himself was conflicted, having declared that Irish nationalists would not congratulate the queen on her jubilee in 1897 or take any part in the King Edward's coronation in 1902.[91] The O'Conor Don was not conflicted in this way, being a regular attendee at royal and viceregal levees throughout his life, dining with the queen at the viceregal lodge in 1900, and being the standard bearer for Ireland at King Edward's coronation in 1902.[92] Moreover, unlike Redmond, the O'Conor Don opposed home rule on the grounds that it would lead to a complete break with Great Britain, the crown and the empire.

But what does the O'Conor Don's loyalism, imperialism and unionism tell us about his sense of national identity? Or, in other words, did he see himself as Irish or Irish and British? He certainly saw himself as a liberal and, as noted in the introduction, recent scholarship has argued that Irish liberals tended to be patriots, loyalists and unionists; and, as such, were

---

the union, and the empire, 1800–1960' in K. Kenny (ed.), *Ireland and the British empire* (Oxford, 2004), p. 124. **88** J.H. Murphy, *Abject loyalty*, pp 83, 102, 187–91, 240, 245, 259, 290; McConnel, 'John Redmond and Irish Catholic loyalism', 83–111. **89** McConnel, 'John Redmond and Irish Catholic loyalism', p. 110. **90** Murphy, *Abject loyalty*, pp xi–xxxiv; J. Loughlin, *The British monarchy in Ireland: 1800 to the present* (Cambridge, 2007), pp 57–101, 148–68, 241–69. **91** Quoted in McConnel, 'John Redmond and Irish Catholic loyalism', p. 108. **92** Diary of the O'Conor Don, 5 Apr. 1900, O'Conor papers, CH, 0.1.SH.041.

possessed of a dual Irish-British identity.[93] The O'Conor Don spoke about the existence of 'separate' Irish and British national identities in Ireland, divided along Catholic and Protestant lines, but he clearly thought it was possible to be both Irish and British because the descendants of Protestant British settlers had become 'more Irish than the Irish themselves'. At the same time, while he was critical of 'extreme' unionist denials of a Catholic nationalist majority in favour of home rule, he took a strong unionist line against home rule. This involved signing a Catholic unionist petition against Gladstone's bill in 1893, which confirmed his unionism, loyalism and imperialism, all of which strongly suggests an attachment to a form of British identity.[94]

Still, the O'Conor Don was a devout Catholic and a proud Irishman who often chafed at 'English' misrule in Ireland, whether that was in the historical sense of the confiscations and the penal laws, which were deeply personal for him, or in the course of his political life, whether on the issue of disestablishment or the provision of Catholic education. But was the O'Conor Don, in any meaningful sense of the word, a nationalist? Alvin Jackson and Colin Reid have recently argued that a 'unionist nationalism' or a 'national unionism' was discernible in the thinking of Daniel O'Connell and Isaac Butt.[95] This argument has a good deal of merit given that both sought to achieve some form of federal or devolved home rule that would preserve the connection with Great Britain, but the O'Conor Don's rejection of both these options places him firmly in the anti-nationalist, unionist camp in the political sense at least. He was, however, an Irish patriot possessed of a strong Irish national sentiment, as evidenced through his support for Catholic education and the inclusion of the Irish language at all levels of the education system. That said, he did not get involved with the Gaelic Union's successor, the Gaelic League, when it formed in 1893, which would suggest that he was wary of the associations between the promotion of the Irish language, the wider Gaelic revival and mainstream nationalist politics. Indeed, it was not unusual for unionists to support the preservation of the Irish language while rejecting the 'Irish Ireland', anti-British rhetoric of popular Catholic nationalist politics.[96] The O'Conor Don was a friend of Douglas Hyde, the Protestant president of the League, who dedicated his life to the revival of the Irish language but kept

---

93 Potter, *William Monsell*, pp 49–53; Ridden, 'Making good citizens', pp 7–21; J. Ridden, 'Britishness as an imperial and diasporic identity' in P. Gray, *Victoria's Ireland?: Irishness and Britishness, 1837–1901* (Dublin, 2003), pp 89–91.   94 *Freeman's Journal*, 15, 16 & 18 Mar. 1893.   95 Jackson, *The two unions*, p. 137; Reid, 'Isaac Butt, home rule and federalist political thought', pp 333–4.   96 *Freeman's Journal*, 13 Nov. 1882, 31 Dec. 1883, 24 & 29 Mar. 1886; Ó Conchubhair, 'The Gaelic League and Irish Ireland', pp 196–219; Foster, 'The Irish literary revival', pp 169–82; Garvin, *Nationalist revolutionaries*, pp 78–99.

his distance from nationalist party politics and was eventually ousted as the League's leader in 1915 for being too politically moderate.[97] Thus, while both men cleaved to moderation in politics and believed that the Irish language needed to be preserved, the O'Conor Don was a unionist who did not, like Hyde, want to 'de-Anglicize' Ireland. Rather he wanted to maintain Ireland's constitutional connection to Great Britain and foster an Irish national identity that incorporated British identity. All things considered, then, it can be argued that his political unionism incorporated a moderate form of cultural nationalism.

HOME RULE AND THE FINANCIAL QUESTION, 1895–8

Although still engaged with the issues of home rule and land purchase, the O'Conor Don was now a marginal figure in Irish politics. His desire to remain completely detached from party politics suggests that this was a state of affairs he would have been content with. Indeed, his interest in the Irish language, his writing of the O'Conors of Connaught and his involvement with the Royal Society of Antiquaries of Ireland are indicative of man with wider cultural interests.[98] Nonetheless, between 1895 and 1898, the O'Conor Don was drawn back in from the margins of Irish politics to some extent through his role in the royal commission on the financial relations between Great Britain and Ireland.

Before standing down as prime minster in 1894, Gladstone appointed a commission to examine the financial relations between Great Britain and Ireland, with a view to considering the merits of separate taxation for the latter.[99] But given that the liberals, under Lord Rosebery, lost the 1895 general election, it was Lord Salisbury and the conservatives who had to deal with the commission's findings, which inevitably became a proxy war for the case for and against home rule. The former liberal chancellor of the exchequer and home rule supporter Hugh Childers had been made chairman, but his death in January 1896 saw the O'Conor Don put in his place. Given that he did not think Ireland was ready for home rule, the O'Conor Don certainly did not take up his position in the commission to make the case for it. The majority of the commissioners did, however, support home rule, including the nationalists John Redmond, Thomas Sexton and Edward Blake, and the liberals lords

---

97 P. Maume, 'Hyde, Douglas (de hÍde, Dubhghlas)', *DIB*.   98 For his involvement in the Royal Society of Antiquaries of Ireland, see pp 22 & 39.   99 Lyons, *Parnell*, pp 350–3; Gailey, *The death of kindness*, pp 100–1.

Farrer and Welby, Sir Robert Hamilton and B.W. Currie. The other unionists on the commission were Sir David Barbour, Sir Thomas Sutherland, G.W. Wolff and Charles E. Martin.[100]

The commission's report, leaked to the press in June 1896, made the controversial claim that Ireland was being over-taxed by £2.75 million per annum through a disproportionately high contribution to the imperial exchequer. This contribution was calculated to be one-eleventh of the whole and the commissioners agreed that one-twentieth would better reflect what Ireland could afford given the disparities of wealth between her and Great Britain. It was thought that the over-taxation of Ireland was largely a result of the imposition of indirect taxes on popularly consumed goods such as tea, tobacco and spirits, but the report also provided an historical dimension to Ireland's fiscal maltreatment, arguing that, between 1793 and 1801, the country's national debt was unfairly and exponentially increased due to government expenditure on internal security and, to a greater extent, on war with France. Moreover, even though it was envisaged under article seven of the Act of Union that Ireland would be taxed separately in proportion to her capacity, the proportion of her contribution to the imperial exchequer – set at one-seventh – was judged to have been too severe. Indeed, it was claimed that 'In the sixteen years which followed the Union, the debts of Ireland were quadrupled, her taxation was increased fourfold, and at the end of the period she was ... nearly bankrupt'.[101] This, it was argued, led to a situation in 1817 where the Irish and British exchequers were consolidated under the false premise that Ireland's debt would be shared, and that she would contribute to the imperial exchequer 'in proportion to her resources'.[102] The experience of the Famine was thought to have revealed the falseness of this premise, with Gladstone's introduction of income tax to Ireland in 1853 being condemned as an unwarranted extra tax burden on a country still recovering from the social and economic devastation caused by the catastrophe.[103]

From a unionist perspective, the crux of the financial question lay in whether it was consistent with the fundamentals of unionism to consider

---

[100] *Final report by Her Majesty's commissioners appointed to inquire into the financial relations between Great Britain and Ireland*, HC 1896 [C.8008] [C.8262], xxxiii, 59, 291, p. iv. Hereafter referred to as *Financial relations commission*; W. Carr & H.C.G. Matthew, 'Childers, Hugh Culling Eardley', *ODNB*; M. Laffan, 'Redmond, John Edward', *DIB*; S. Boylan, 'Martin, Charles Edward', *DIB*; J. Davis, 'Farrer, Thomas Henry, first Baron Farrer', *ODNB*; M. Wright, 'Welby, Reginald Earle, Baron Welby', *ODNB*; A.F. Pollard & D. Huddleston, 'Hamilton, Sir Robert George Crookshank', *ODNB*; R. Davenport-Hines, 'Currie, Bertram Wodehouse', *ODNB*; F. Harcourt, 'Sutherland, Sir Thomas', *ODNB*; M.S. Moss, 'Wolff, Gustav Wilhelm', *ODNB*. [101] *Financial relations commission*, pp 4–6, 21; Gailey, *The death of kindness*, p. 101. [102] *Financial relations commission*, pp 7, 25. [103] Ibid., pp 9–11, 25.

Ireland as a separate taxable entity.[104] The prime minister, Lord Salisbury, the chancellor of the exchequer, Sir Michael Hicks Beach, and the first lord of the treasury, Arthur Balfour, all rejected the claim of over-taxation. They did so firstly on the basis that imperial and local expenditure were two different things; in other words, money taken from the imperial exchequer for the maintenance of civil government in Ireland was deemed local expenditure, and that this expenditure offset Ireland's supposedly high tax contribution to the exchequer. Second, it was argued that uniformity of taxation was an intrinsic component of the union and the commissioners' recommendation of separate taxation was unduly influenced by their bias towards home rule. Separate taxation for Ireland, it was argued, could involve having to reduce indirect taxes on commodities such as tobacco and alcohol, or introduce new ones on commodities like meat, timber and grain, or on property transactions and licences for businesses. Indeed, these were the recommendations of Sir Robert Giffen, a board of trade official and one of the chief witnesses to the commission, who incidentally denied that he was a home ruler. While Hicks Beach was apparently open to suggestions for the diversification of indirect taxes, the 'huge implications' of Giffen's proposals caused him to think again. In the confusion, he turned to his treasury secretary, Sir Edward Hamilton, the other main witness for the commission, to assist him in combating the commission's report. In a memorandum submitted to the cabinet, Hamilton turned the report on its head by arguing that if Ireland was treated as a separate taxable entity, then her contribution to the imperial exchequer would have to be increased rather than decreased. Nonetheless, his alternative of establishing a separate Irish exchequer had equally controversial implications for the fundamentals of unionism, ensuring that the government ignored his findings along with those of the commission.[105]

Much to the chagrin of Salisbury and the embarrassment of the Irish administration, however, many Irish unionists supported the commission's claim. The O'Conor Don, lords Dunraven and Castletown, the earl of Mayo, the junior minister T.W. Russell and the MP for South Dublin, Horace Plunkett, were all prominent in the organization of a national campaign that saw unionists sharing platforms with nationalists up and down the country towards the end of 1896 and throughout 1897. Indeed, on Plunkett's suggestion, an All-Ireland Committee was established in February 1897 to help coordinate the campaign.[106] As a member of the recess committee in 1896, the O'Conor Don had worked with Plunkett in his efforts to promote agricultural industry,

---

104 Gailey, *The death of kindness*, pp 99–114.   105 A. Jackson, 'Irish unionism and the Russellite threat', *Irish Historical Studies*, 15:100 (Nov. 1987), 376–404; Gailey, *The death of kindness*, pp 101–9.   106 *Freeman's Journal*, 14 Dec. 1896; *Irish Times*, 10 Feb. 1897

and both men put similar emphasis on the need for encouraging non-partisan politics in Ireland.[107] In June 1897, the Irish Financial Reform League was established as a 'non-party' national organization to lobby parliament for the redress of Ireland's financial grievance.[108] League meetings were held in Dublin, Cork, Sligo and Roscommon, with the O'Conor Don now praised by the *Freeman's Journal* for his willingness to foster an atmosphere of unity between nationalists and unionists. Nonetheless, it was thought his emphasis on a moderate approach could be misconstrued as 'compromising with the wrong'.[109] The central problem for unionists, according to *Freeman's*, was the difficulty they faced in squaring their support for the union with their support for financial reform. Indeed, it was argued that unionists would have to face up to the reality that 'either the taxation of Ireland under the Act of Union can be proportioned to her needs and capacity, or the system of government established by the Union is inconsistent with Irish progress'.[110] This was a commonly held view among nationalists, who optimistically envisioned that 'unionism would disappear' if the commission's report 'were explained to the rank and file'.[111] A mass awakening among 'rank and file' unionists was of course highly unlikely, while 'the uneasy alliance' of unionist and nationalist MPs 'was easily contained' by a Conservative government with a comfortable majority in the commons.[112] There was also significant opposition to the findings of the commission in the English press, with the *Times* and the *Daily Telegraph* questioning the financial expertise of the commissioners and calling for 'uniformity of taxation'.[113]

In February 1897, the O'Conor Don took it upon himself to publish an article on 'The over-taxation of Ireland' in the unionist *National Review*, which rebuked both government and press criticisms. On the supposed home rule bias of the commission, he argued that its terms of reference were not solely 'contemplated in connection with the Home Rule Bill of 1893'. Instead, their 'true origin' could be found in the Conservative government's appointment of a select committee to investigate the 'financial relations between England, Scotland, and Ireland' in 1890. Indeed, he named the 'true author of the phrase "separate financial entities"' as the liberal unionist George Goschen, a member of the select committee who, at that time, was chancellor of the exchequer in Salisbury's Conservative government. As for the credibility of the commission's findings, the O'Conor Don pointed to the financial expertise of its members, many of whom had worked for the treasury or in the world of

---

107 C. King, 'The recess committee, 1895–6', *Studia Hibernica*, 30 (1998/9), 21–46; West, 'Plunkett, Horace Curzon', *DIB*. 108 *Irish Times*, 5 June 1897. 109 *Freeman's Journal*, 4, 9, 14, 23, 29 Dec. 1896, 4 Jan. 1897. 110 Ibid., 13 Sept. 1896. 111 P. Maume, *The long gestation: Irish nationalist life, 1891–1918* (Dublin, 1999), p. 21 112 Gailey, *The death of kindness*, pp 114–20. 113 Ibid., p. 111.

banking and trade, and all of whom agreed that Ireland should be treated as a separate taxable entity.[114] Moreover, in a further reveal of his adherence to the new political economy, he drew on the arguments of Mill when he claimed that it was impossible to impose a uniform tax – direct or indirect – without considering people's ability to pay it. As such, he rejected the notion that indirect taxation was 'optional' in the sense that it was usually 'levied ... upon luxuries' that people did not necessarily have to consume. And in any event, he felt this 'identity of taxation' had little or nothing to do with the principle set out in the Act of Union, whereby Ireland was to contribute to the imperial exchequer in proportion to her capacity.[115]

In dealing with the wider political implications, the O'Conor Don explicitly stated his intention to deal with the question from 'a Unionist point of view', which was, along with the Catholic unionist petition in 1893, the closest he had come to publicly conceding that he was, in fact, a unionist. Politics aside, he rejected the treasury's argument that expenditure on civil government in Ireland could be categorized as local expenditure and therefore act as an offset for Ireland's high tax contribution to the imperial exchequer. Indeed, he argued that 'this division of Imperial expenditure into classes' was by its very nature a separatist argument because if 'the civil government of any part of the United Kingdom' was deemed to be 'local, instead of ... Imperial ... it follows ... that the control of that civil government, the expenditure on it and everything connected with it, should also be local'.[116] Having neatly revealed this contradiction in the government's position, the O'Conor Don went on to argue that while 'the countries are united under one Parliament, Imperial expenditure, regulated and controlled by that Parliament, cannot be regarded as local, and cannot be cut up and divided without destroying that central authority'.[117] Indeed, he thought it 'strange' for those who opposed the findings of the commission 'to taunt Unionists, who join in making the claim, with separatist ideas, when their claim and their demand are founded upon the provisions of the Act of Union itself'.[118] The O'Conor Don had already made this argument at a public meeting in Dublin at the end of 1896 where he noted that recognizing the constitutional provision for separate taxation under the Act of Union was no different to accepting the constitutional fact that Great Britain and Ireland had very different laws. None of this, he felt, undermined 'Ireland's union ... with Great Britain' because it was 'too close, too intimate, to be regarded as a matter of purely local concern'. For him, the union was not 'maintained ... merely for the benefit of Irishmen but because it is supposed,

114 C.O. O'Conor, 'The over-taxation of Ireland', *National Review*, 28 (Feb. 1897), pp 739–41; T.J. Spinner, 'Goschen, George Joachim, first Viscount Goschen', *ODNB*. 115 O'Conor, 'The over-taxation of Ireland', pp 745–6. 116 Ibid., pp 749–50. 117 Ibid., p. 750. 118 Ibid., p. 751.

and I believe rightly supposed, that Great Britain is deeply interested in it. Not only is it Imperial in its essence, but is managed exclusively as Imperial and by an Imperial Parliament.'[119] In other words, although they were two separate and, in many ways, different countries, Great Britain and Ireland were bound together, in a mutually beneficial way, by a political union that oversaw the governance of a vast empire.

But despite the O'Conor Don's making of the unionist case for separate taxation, the unionist campaign for financial reform came undone over the growing distance between southern and Ulster unionists. The ILPU – which in 1891 became the Irish Unionist Alliance – had always been a predominantly southern enterprise, while Ulster unionists had, since 1893, been organizing more specifically along Ulster lines with the establishment of the Ulster Convention League and the Unionist Clubs Council. Thus, although relations between southern and northern unionists remained good in this period, the 'Ulstermen', as Buckland has argued, 'preferred to fight it [home rule] in their own way'.[120] The financial controversy aggravated these divisions, as evidenced by the O'Conor Don's attendance at a meeting on the financial question in the Ulster Hall, Belfast, in May 1897. Things started off well as he remarked how significant it was that he, 'a pronounced Roman Catholic', was sharing a platform with the 'Grandmaster of the Orangemen of Belfast', Dr Robert Kane. Declaring that they were 'all Irishmen first', he went on to lavish praise on the province of Ulster, and the city of Belfast in particular, for showing 'what the Irish could do by perseverance, energy, and industry'. This, in turn, showed 'that under Legislative Union Irishmen could be prosperous ... [and] compete in manufacturing industry with the great centres of industry on the other side of the channel'. Having dispensed with the niceties, the O'Conor Don addressed the elephant in the room: home rule. On this he sought to reassure the audience of his desire to approach the financial question 'from a Unionist point of view', and that the commission was not formed with home rule in mind. Indeed, although he admitted that some of the commissioners were home rulers, he argued that the commission's work was based 'on the supposition that the Union was to last'. This of course made perfect sense, because home rule, as understood by its liberal proponents at least, was a union-saving rather than a union-wrecking enterprise. But the *Belfast Newsletter* was not convinced, describing the meeting a 'conspicuous failure' and declaring that the 'Imperial Province' of Ulster would 'take no part or lot in a movement that may be designed or tend to help Home Rule'. Rejecting the O'Conor Don's arguments as separatist, it was felt Ireland had nothing to

---

119 *Freeman's Journal*, 29 Dec. 1896.   120 Buckland, *Irish unionism 1*, pp 16–17; P. Buckland, *Irish unionism 2: Ulster unionism and the origins of Northern Ireland, 1886–1922* (Dublin, 1973), pp 16–17.

'grumble about' given that the alleged over-taxation was largely confined to indirect taxes on commodities that were voluntarily purchased and consumed. Ulster unionists were therefore advised to look for increased government support for Irish industry, rather than pursue a 'ridiculous' grievance premised on the 'separation' of Ireland from the union.[121]

Despite this setback, the O'Conor Don continued to defend the findings of the commission and address the wider issue of home rule. At a meeting in Cork, where the audience would have been sympathetic to home rule, he admitted that the majority wanted a 'unified', self-governing Ireland. However, he warned, without explicitly saying so, that this desire was mostly felt by Catholics. At the same time, he stated that his conception of Irish 'unity' was 'of a more ... truly national character embracing all classes, all creeds, and all races'; a conception which drew its inspiration from the 'noble words' of the United Irishmen 'one hundred years ago'. Given his ancestors involvement in the United Irishmen, and his mixed social and political milieu throughout his life, this admirably tolerant and liberal articulation of Irish unity is not that surprising. The bishop of Cloyne, Robert Browne, was not convinced, however. While he praised the O'Conor Don's articulation of a unified Ireland, he rather disappointedly concluded that he did so as a unionist. This was an accurate assessment given the O'Conor Don's track record on home rule up to that point, but quite apart from all that he was obviously drawing on the generosity of spirit in the United Irish message and, once again, not so subtly making the point that Ireland was not ready for home rule because Protestants and Catholics were not agreed on the case for it or on what it meant to be Irish. Thus, although he refrained from explicitly stating that he approached his Cork speech from 'a unionist point of view', the O'Conor Don asked the assembled crowd whether it was not possible to be 'united Irishmen in the truest, broadest, and at the same time the most constitutional sense' within the United Kingdom.[122]

In his attempts to placate unionist and nationalist audiences in this way, the O'Conor Don was once again demonstrating that he was a patriot possessed of national sympathies, who, at the same time, maintained allegiance to the union, the crown and the empire. His allegiance to the union was not, however, unconditional, and this was made clear again in his response to English criticisms of the case for separate Irish taxation within the union.[123] Arthur Balfour infamously reduced the commission's claim to the Irishman's appetite for whiskey, and the O'Conor Don was not the only Irish politician

---

121 *Belfast Newsletter*, 12 May 1897; *Freeman's Journal*, 12 May 1897. 122 *Freeman's Journal*, 3 Nov. 1897. 123 C.O. O'Conor, *The over-taxation of Ireland: speech of the right hon. O'Conor Don, in answer to the English case, 8 December, 1897* (Dublin, 1897); idem, *The speech of the right hon. O'Conor Don in reply to the right hon. A.J. Balfour, MP delivered at the Mansion House, Dublin, on January 4th, 1899* (Dublin, 1899).

to scold him for this.[124] The position taken by Sir John Lubbock, who published an article on the subject in November 1897, was no less distasteful to him. A Liberal MP for the borough constituency of London University and an opponent of home rule, Lubbock rejected the theory of separate taxable entities within the United Kingdom for two main reasons. First, if Ireland was entitled to separate treatment, then other regions of Great Britain would make the case for it. Second, attributing the over-taxation of Ireland to indirect taxation on tea, tobacco, beer and spirits was a fallacy because such commodities were just as heavily consumed in Great Britain. On the latter point, Lubbock thought taxes on these unnecessary luxuries were a good thing for the fabric of society and suggested that supporters of temperance in Ireland – no doubt alluding to the O'Conor Don – would hardly endorse a reduction on the levy on alcohol given the Irishman's apparent propensity for over-consumption.[125]

The O'Conor Don's reply, at a meeting of the Irish Financial Reform League on 8 December 1897, was to denounce Lubbock as 'the typical Englishman' who, having placed himself 'on a pinnacle of high morality', 'looks down upon the inhabitants … of Ireland, as beings of an inferior caste'.[126] On a personal level, he thought there was nothing more 'offensive' than the 'patronising air' of 'ostentatious patronage and generosity' by supposedly 'well-intentioned Englishmen'; for the Irish people more generally, he felt sure there was nothing 'more irritating' or 'more humiliating than this mode of treatment'.[127] Having vented his anger at the perceived English arrogance, the O'Conor Don went on to deconstruct Lubbock's opposing arguments. He rejected the idea that separate taxation for Ireland would mean the same for smaller regions in Great Britain because, unlike Ireland, no treaty existed which recognized their existence as a separate taxable entity within the United Kingdom.[128] As for Lubbock's suggestion that high duties on tea, tobacco and spirits acted as a useful deterrent for over-consumption, the O'Conor Don argued that indirect taxation was 'not imposed for the purpose of punishing the consumers', but rather 'for the purpose of [raising] revenue'. In other words, people would not stop consuming these goods as a result of prohibitively high prices.[129] In the end, the O'Conor Don warned that the passing of a local government measure, with its predicted funding of £700,000, could not 'be taken as an acquittal of the debt due to us'.[130]

The Conservative government had introduced a local government bill towards the end of 1897, which, according to Gailey, was 'a hurried decision'

124 Gailey, *The death of kindness*, p. 106; O'Conor, *Speech … in reply to … A.J. Balfour*, pp 4–11.   125 J. Lubbock, 'On the financial relations of Great Britain and Ireland', *Nineteenth Century*, 42:249 (Nov. 1897), pp 791–8; T.L. Alborn, 'Lubbock, Sir John William, third baronet', *ODNB*.   126 *Irish Times*, 9 Dec. 1897.   127 O'Conor, *Speech … in answer to the English case*, p. 4   128 Ibid., pp 7–8   129 Ibid., pp 10–12   130 Ibid., p. 15.

made in reaction to the furore caused by the financial question and subsequent calls by many nationalist MPs for a £750,000 government grant to subsidize the payment of Irish local rates.[131] The government's immediate reaction to the finance question had been to introduce an Irish agriculture and industries bill in the spring of 1897, but it ran aground amid nationalist and unionist dissatisfaction with the allocation of a mere £150,000 for the establishment of an Irish board of agriculture. After this embarrassment, the government renewed its commitment to local government reform on the basis that grants in aid of local rates could not be made without first reforming local authorities. The local government bill eventually introduced in February 1898 by the Irish chief secretary, Gerald Balfour, was of a far more democratic nature than the one devised by his brother in 1892. Grand juries and the £50 county franchise were to be abolished and replaced by district and county councils elected with a vote for all owner-occupiers. That it passed through both houses without much opposition in August 1898 was due to nationalist willingness to accept a measure they believed was a stepping-stone towards home rule and unionist reluctance to oppose a policy that was accompanied by a reasonably generous financial package.[132]

LOCAL GOVERNMENT, 1898–9

The campaign for the county and district council elections was the occasion for the O'Conor Don's last foray into electoral politics. His local profile had been raised again in February 1896 on his appointment to the lord lieutenancy of County Roscommon, while his role in the finance question had brought him back into the national spotlight.[133] Added to this was John Redmond's plea, made at a Parnellite meeting in October 1898, for nationalists to show 'toleration' for politicians of moderate views in the selection of candidates for the council elections. A fellow landed Catholic, Redmond felt that the O'Conor Don, as 'a representative of the old chieftains' and a man of 'great ability', could perhaps be brought into the 'National ranks' if toleration were shown for his views. Redmond's broader political reasoning was that a policy of toleration, as opposed to the exclusion advocated by his nationalist rival William O'Brien, would demonstrate to the British government that unionists and nationalists could find a middle ground, and that Ireland was therefore

131 Gailey, *The death of kindness*, pp 43–4. 132 Shannon, 'Ulster liberal unionists', pp 420–1; Gailey, *The death of kindness*, p. 44. 133 Christopher Palles to Baron Ashbourne, 18 Jan. 1896, Cadogan papers, NLI, 826; Baron Ashbourne to the earl of Cadogan, 20 Jan. 1896, Cadogan papers, NLI, 828; The O'Conor Don to the earl of Cadogan, 27 Feb. 1896, Cadogan papers, NLI, 843.

capable of self-government.¹³⁴ Paul Bew has argued that 'Redmond must have known ... that he was asking a particular favour from Roscommon Parnellites' in accepting the O'Conor Don because 'they were being asked to expend their own political capital to ensure the continued local influence of a man who ... had a rather "weak" stance on the key questions of the day'.¹³⁵ While Redmond's request for toleration was indeed expecting a lot from Roscommon nationalists, Bew's assessment overlooks the O'Conor Don's advanced position on the land question – something nationalists continually ignored or dismissed. That said, there is no doubt that the O'Conor Don's opposition to home rule, while still claiming to support the principle of it, was tenuous to say the least.

In contrast to Redmond's calls for toleration, O'Brien 'pulverized' the O'Conor Don's candidature in the columns of the *Freeman's Journal* by imploring the people of Roscommon to ignore the 'rubbish talked about these old Catholic families', who, it was said, deserved respect for holding onto their estates. Instead, he suggested that 'the Queen's O'Conors' had held on to their estates 'by proving false to faith and fatherland' and were now 'shivering in their mansions saving their bacon' as members of the hated landed class.¹³⁶ O'Brien's sentiments were somewhat echoed at a meeting of the Castlerea branch of the United Irish League, where it was pronounced that although the O'Conor Don was 'a very able man ... and a great Catholic', he would ultimately strive 'to save his own bacon' as a landlord.¹³⁷ Because of this, the branch advocated the election of candidates who supported home rule, the restoration of evicted tenants, the release of political prisoners, the redress of the financial grievance and an equal distribution of grasslands.¹³⁸ Redmond's plea for toleration was also rejected by the agrarian radical Jasper Tully through the pages of his newspaper, the *Roscommon Herald*.¹³⁹ An election leaflet further demonstrated the strength of local feeling against the candidature of the O'Conor Don, and that of his cousin, Thomas Mapother. Here the 'working classes' of Roscommon were implored to take 'no act nor part in placing the O'Conor Don or Mapother in [the] position of chairman of the County or District Council' because 'As anti-nationalists ... these gentlemen' would not support their demand for home rule.¹⁴⁰

One would have thought that in the face of such vocal opposition the O'Conor Don might have had second thoughts about contesting the election. This was not the case, however, and it can only be assumed that he believed he had enough support in the county to secure a council seat. The unionist

---

134 *Freeman's Journal*, 11 Oct. 1898; Laffan, 'Redmond, John Edward', *DIB*.   135 Bew, *Conflict and conciliation*, pp 50–1   136 *Roscommon Herald*, 25 Mar. 1899.   137 Ibid., 14 Jan. 1899.   138 Ibid., 21 Jan. 1899.   139 Bew, *Conflict and conciliation*, p. 33; *Roscommon Herald*, 15 Oct. 1898.   140 Roscommon county council election leaflet, n.d. but most likely Oct.–Dec. 1898, O'Conor papers, CH, 9.4.HS.250).

Irish Times certainly believed this to be the case, predicting that the people of Roscommon would ignore O'Brien's appeals and place the O'Conor Don at the top of the poll. In fact, the paper felt that it had been a 'mistake' for the county 'to have ever slighted … so superior a logician, and earnest a patriot, as The O'Conor Don', and that it would be 'a day of woe for Ireland when the natural leaders amongst us are wholly extinguished'.[141] On 5 February 1899, at a meeting for the selection of candidates for the Castlerea district, the O'Conor Don put himself forward and urged those present to choose on the basis of the candidate's ability to do the job rather than concentrating on their political views. While he conceded that people were most likely to support candidates who they felt adequately represented their political aspirations, he urged them not to shut out those, like him, with opposing views who might fulfil a useful role.[142] The subsequent election of the O'Conor Don to the Castlerea District Council demonstrated that he still had support in the county and that some moderate nationalists were prepared to take Redmond's line. Indeed, his election was one of those rare instances where a landlord had been 'tolerated' by voters in the three southern provinces. Already outnumbered by nationalists on the poor law boards, the council elections virtually wiped out landlord influence in southern Irish local politics. Out of a total of 676 council seats in Ireland, nationalists won 551, the majority of which were in the three southern provinces. Unionists, on the other hand, won 125 seats, 86 of which were in Ulster.[143]

On 15 April 1899, the O'Conor Don was appointed chairman of the Castlerea District Council, with John Fitzgibbon, one of the most prominent nationalists in Castlerea, selected as vice-chairman. There was no position of seniority for him on Roscommon County Council, with Farrell MacDonnell, another local nationalist, appointed chairman and Fitzgibbon once again occupying the position of vice-chairman.[144] The O'Conor Don was, in any event, just as well pleased, as he felt that the meetings of the county council were a talking shop for 'all sorts of absurd political resolutions'.[145] But it was not long before his position as chairman of the district council was taken up with the politics of the day. At a meeting on 4 November 1899, a resolution of sympathy with the Boers, in their war with 'the tyrannous British Government', was passed. The O'Conor Don was absent from this meeting, but at the next gathering of the council on 13 November he stated his opposition to the resolution, arguing that it would have been more appropriate if the resolution had expressed a 'regret that war had broken out', or 'contained

---

141 *Irish Times*, 22 Mar. 1899.   142 *Roscommon Herald*, 11 Feb. 1899.   143 Campbell, *Irish establishment*, p. 31.   144 *Roscommon Herald*, 15, 22, 29 Apr. 1899.   145 The O'Conor Don to Sir Nicholas O'Conor, 21 Sept. 1899, O'Conor papers, CAC, OCON2/4/32.

a severe censure on the government for having acted in such a way as to bring ... [about a] war', rather than openly taking sides with the Boers. Indeed, the O'Conor Don thought the resolution deserved 'the epithet of disloyalty' and that those who passed it did so with the full knowledge that 'they can neither help the Boers nor injure England'. This, to his mind, was hardly 'a dignified position ... to occupy', and he challenged the 'manliness' of those who pass 'vain paper resolutions which manifest nothing but impotent disloyalty'. A lack of manhood and loyalty aside, the O'Conor Don rather more awkwardly questioned the logic of home rulers criticizing the very government they wished to procure home rule from, wondering how they could expect to 'secure the votes of the English people' with such treacherous resolutions.[146] But with the loyalist gauntlet thrown down, the O'Conor Don's position on the district council was now a precarious one and he was not re-elected for the chairmanship the following year. Unsurprisingly, his position went to the local nationalist organizer John Fitzgibbon.[147]

Although still chairman of the Castlerea board of guardians, the O'Conor Don's departure from the district council marked his ultimate and final rejection in Irish politics. This must have been a personal blow for a man who had served the local community with diligence for the entirety of his political career, but his final exit from electoral politics did not mean that he rested on his laurels. The O'Conor Don continued to wield influence on the debate on land reform as a member of the executive committee of the Landowners' Convention, although he ultimately recoiled from taking a prominent role by declining to attend the 1902 land conference. He also continued to fulfil his duties as a landlord, avoiding being engulfed by the agitation on surrounding estates while he negotiated, not without dispute, purchase terms with tenants. His love for shooting game with the local gentry also continued unabated, as did his willingness to roll up his sleeves and oversee the less 'gentlemanly' tasks of getting in the hay, sorting potatoes and sheep dipping. Elsewhere in politics, he continued to take an interest in the education question, serving as a member of a royal commission on Irish university education in 1901–3, where he again made the case for denominational education. Finally, his attachment to all things viceregal and royal continued, as both a frequent attendee at Dublin Castle levees and the standard bearer for Ireland at King Edward VII's coronation in 1902. Nonetheless, there is little doubt that by the turn of the century the O'Conor Don felt like a man out of place and out of time. Indeed, on the occasion of his sixty-second birthday in May

---

146 Meeting of the Castlerea District Council, 13 Nov. 1899, O'Conor papers, CH, O.1.ES.109; *Freeman's Journal*, 7, 13 Nov. 1899. 147 *Freeman's Journal*, 8 June 1900.

1900, he rather wistfully remarked how many of his 'old friends' were 'drifting off', and how he was feeling 'very old' and did not 'expect to see many more' birthdays.[148]

---

[148] The O'Conor Don's diary, 7 May 1900, O'Conor papers, CH, o.1.SH.041.

Conclusion

On 30 June 1906, the O'Conor Don passed away at Clonalis House after a bout of pneumonia. On 3 July, his body was removed from the house and taken to the Catholic Church in Castlerea, with the coffin carried on the shoulders of tenants from the estate. The following day, he was buried at the new cemetery, Clonalis, Castlerea, on land which he had donated to the Catholic Church. He was survived by his wife, Ellen, and three sons, Denis, Owen and Charles. The funeral Mass was attended by other family members and friends; local archbishops, bishops and clergy; a representative of the lord lieutenant; many of the local gentry; and a large crowd of people from the local community.[1] It was a fitting send-off for a man who had been a staunch Catholic and had indeed shown great commitment to his roles as a landlord and a politician.

But what, in the end, are we to make of the O'Conor Don's life and political career? And what, in turn, does this add to our understanding of religion, politics and identity in nineteenth-century Ireland? In the first instance, it is clear that the O'Conor Don's family history played a significant part in shaping his understanding of Irish history, his political outlook and his life trajectory. Given his emphasis on the loyalist and constitutionalist nature of his ancestors' politics in his writing of his family history, the O'Conor Don's understanding of Irish history was almost certainly that rebellion and sectarian division had heaped devastation on his country and should therefore be avoided at all costs. He clearly had a high regard for his great-great grandfather, Charles O'Conor of Ballinagare, who made the nascent liberal Catholic case for reform of the penal laws through constitutional political means, which included declaring Catholic loyalty to the British crown. And he clearly wished to follow in the liberal political footsteps of his grandfather, Owen, and father, Denis, both of whom supported the charismatic leadership of Daniel O'Connell during the campaign for Catholic emancipation in the 1820s and became Liberal MPs for County Roscommon in the 1830s and 1840s.

The rising economic fortunes of the O'Conor Don's immediate ancestors went hand in hand with their position of political prominence. In spite of the penal laws of the eighteenth century, his family slowly regained their position through legal battles to retain land, lucky inheritance, astute marriages, the consolidation of family branches and the purchase of more

---

1 *Irish Times*, 5 July 1906; *Newry Reporter*, 19 June 1906.

land once the penal laws were relaxed. This enabled his father to integrate into the wider Irish and British landed elite in the early nineteenth century through education in England and Ireland, European travel, high society in Dublin and London, and Westminster politics. The O'Conor Don's family background, plus his own inheritance, English education and Continental travels set him up for a life in politics. He duly pursued that path when the opportunity presented itself, albeit at the second time of asking in 1860. His family's politics were liberal, and he saw himself as the torch bearer of that political tradition, although he was clearly determined to avoid his father's fate of being perceived as a whig placeman, resolving to remain independent of government office. In terms of his social status, the O'Conor Don's position as a wealthy landed Catholic enabled him to move in a world of local, national and transnational connections that was cross-confessional and politically hybrid. Thus, although the Catholic gentry, aristocracy and hierarchy of Ireland and England dominated his social circles, and he married an English Catholic, he also moved relatively freely among the Protestant gentry and aristocracy, as well as Protestant political circles in Dublin and London.

But the O'Conor Don was not some aloof aristocrat who toured the country houses, race meets, levees and balls at the expense of being engaged with the running of his estates. Quite the opposite in fact. From his coming of age in 1859 to his death in 1906, the O'Conor Don's life as a landlord was a remarkable rollercoaster ride of contrasting fortunes. The highly favourable financial circumstances of the Moore inheritance enabled him to expand his estates by over 5,000 acres between 1859 and 1876, but this was completely turned on its head between 1879 and 1906, with over 8,000 acres sold, albeit the majority of that just after his death. The MacDermots undoubtedly played an important role in the sound management of his estates, but it ultimately came down to the O'Conor Don's pro-active and even-handed approach to the business of being a landlord. He treated his tenants well and there was, as a consequence, little of what could be defined as organized or violent agitation on his estates. His status as the O'Conor Don – the descendant of the last high king of Ireland and therefore the rightful owner of his estates – probably helped shield him from the worst effects of the Land League and Plan of Campaign agitations, but the respect and kudos that went with his title would have counted for nought if he had, like Lord De Freyne, been an indebted, authoritarian landlord determined to get the better of his tenants, or had like the earls of Kenmare and Granard been an incompetent landlord who spent lavishly beyond his means. He may well have treated his Catholic tenants well out of a sense of religious solidarity, but it seems far more likely that he did so because he was a fair and reasonable man with a paternalistic sense of duty towards his tenants and the local community. Indeed, it is telling that one of the O'Conor Don's greatest causes of frustration and anger during the 1880s was the involvement of the Catholic clergy in the Plan of Campaign. Catholic landlords like him were finding themselves in the rather awkward position of having to condemn their own clergy for either ignoring or openly encouraging the agitation. Once their allies, the majority of the priests and bishops had gradually come down on the side of the tenants and the rising tide of Irish nationalism. In the face of such opposition to their very existence, the O'Conor Don and his fellow Catholic landlords sought to use whatever little remaining power and influence they had with the British state and the papacy to have the land agitation, and the clergy's involvement, condemned. This dual appeal to Protestant British and Roman Catholic power raised all sorts of uncomfortable questions about where their loyalties lay vis-à-vis Ireland and its majority, home rule-supporting Catholic population, which was a recurring theme that caused them great difficulty in the world of politics.

The worlds of landlordism and politics were inextricably linked and inevitably influenced the O'Conor Don's views on land reform. Although he was not the first to proclaim advanced views on the subject, his proposal for compulsory state-aided land purchase in the late 1870s was a radical one in the context of an Irish and British political establishment that was largely dismissive of the idea at that time. In the 1860s and early 1870s, most Irish landlords were at the very least pragmatic enough to realize that supporting tenant right and fixity of tenure had a certain amount of political capital when their seats were coming increasingly under threat by nationalists, and Gladstone was determined to legislate in that direction anyway. And even though land purchase became the official policy of the Home Rule Party after Parnell became leader in 1880, fixity of tenure was still the favoured policy of many nationalists. When the O'Conor Don again voiced his support for compulsory land purchase as a member of the land law commission in 1881, this was a minority view, with the majority of landlords on the commission, and Gladstone's Liberal government, favouring the 3fs. However, as the issue of home rule became more prominent, opinion on land purchase shifted in Westminster and Lord Salisbury's first Conservative government passed the first meaningful land purchase act in 1885. Gladstone reluctantly embraced the idea in 1886, in the hope that it would bring Irish landlords over to the cause of home rule. The O'Conor Don opposed this policy and sided with the liberal unionists, who split from the Liberal Party on the issue of home rule. The conservatives dominated government for the remainder of the century and presided over a policy of piecemeal voluntary land purchase in the hope of killing home rule with kindness. The O'Conor Don did not think this policy would work either, as he felt home rule would have to happen at some point in the future. For him, the point was to prepare Ireland for it and one of the ways to do that was to bring about a radical but orderly overhaul of landownership through compulsory state-aided land purchase. By the land conference of 1902, land purchase had been accepted by most Irish landlords as a *fait accompli*. The O'Conor Don's status as one who had long advocated the principle meant his support was sought after by those in the Landowners' Convention who supported and opposed the idea of a conference with the leaders of the Irish Parliamentary Party and the United Irish League. His refusal to attend the conference seems to have been part distaste for the idea of landlords negotiating with the leaders of the United Irish League; part insistence that negotiations on any terms other than compulsory purchase would prove to be worthless; and part squeamishness about getting involved in the politics of it all. But while the O'Conor Don failed to make any practical contribution to the conference, his overall contribution to the debate on land reform between the late 1870s and early 1900s was still considerable. That he had a vested interest in land purchase is self-evident, but his opinions were also shaped by his experiences as a landlord; his support for a new political economy and a more interventionist state; his opposition to a home rule parliament under nationalist control; and his hope that a complete overhaul of the pattern of landownership would pacify Ireland.

Similarly, the O'Conor Don's position on the university question was driven by a combination of factors. As a devout Catholic, he believed in the principle of denominational education, but as a liberal he believed in freedom of religion. For him, this freedom was the hallmark of a tolerant, liberal state, which in the sphere of university education ought to mean all denominations being enabled to provide the type of education they wanted with support from the state. His support for denominationalism aligned him with the views of the hierarchy, but they differed on the degree of clerical control in education and on the practical politics of what was an acceptable compromise between a Catholic university and a system of secular university education. His denominationalism also aligned him with many nationalists, but, although he was sure the majority of Catholics wanted a Catholic university, he was not keen on majoritarian political causes if they did not align with his views. Crucially, though, in terms of the state of liberalism in Ireland, the O'Conor Don's denominationalism set him odds with liberal Catholics and Protestants who embraced the idea that secular education would help heal the old sectarian divisions in Ireland. For them, the demand for a Catholic university was nothing other than the demand of an ultramontane hierarchy seeking to dominate the provision of education in Ireland and the political and cultural life of Irish Catholics more generally. The leadership of the Liberal Party was convinced of these arguments, but liberal Catholics like the O'Conor Don still hoped that Gladstone would rule Ireland by Irish ideas, or in this case Irish Catholic ideas. His bill of 1873, proposing a national university with affiliated colleges of all denominations and none, was the O'Conor Don's preferred solution, but he rejected it on account of the absence of endowment for the Catholic college. That he later regretted this decision speaks to the failure of liberalism in Ireland and his role in it at the time. Despite this failure, his role in spurring the Conservative government into action with his own university bill in 1879 was no mean achievement, demonstrating his ability to work with the clergy, the bishops, nationalist MPs and the Conservative government to achieve the compromise solution of a central examining university that provided state funding for Catholics through the back door. Indeed, somewhat ironically, the independent-mindedness that prevented the O'Conor Don from working more closely with his liberal colleagues in parliament between 1860 and 1874 was the very thing that enabled him to negotiate this tricky terrain and make a tangible contribution to the reform of Ireland's system of university education.

This independent-mindedness was something that pretty much defined the O'Conor Don's political career. Throughout his time as an MP, he pursued an agenda of mostly moderate reforms, while maintaining a stubbornly independent stance in parliament, free from the constraints of Irish or British party politics, and from being overly reliant on clerical influence. In the mid-1860s, he steered clear of the National Association and a place in Lord Russell's Liberal government, while supporting Gladstone's policy of ruling Ireland with Irish ideas, in the hope that it would steer popular Irish opinion away from the allure of Fenianism and home rule. The O'Conor Don's indifference to any kind of national or popular political movement was not that unusual, however. Indeed, his conduct in this regard was reflective of a general indifference among Irish liberals to co-ordinated party action along Irish lines, even though they often expressed anti-English sentiments in their criticisms of British government policy in Ireland, and even though party discipline was still in its infancy. Thus, although Irish Liberals did see themselves as a distinct group or party, they failed to act as one, mostly due to a combination of gentlemanly independent-mindedness and indifference; religious divisions over education and the influence the Catholic Church in Irish society; and a preference for working within the broader umbrella of the Liberal Party. Their support for the Liberal Party was vindicated by the convincing electoral victory of 1868, but the shaky British-Irish liberal alliance was soon undermined by dissatisfaction with Gladstone's land act, coercion, a Fenian amnesty and the failure of Gladstone's university bill. All this provided a fillip for Isaac Butt's home rule movement, which from Butt's point of view was an attempt to avert the spread of Fenianism by finding a way to satisfy the demand for Irish self-determination while preserving the union. Once Butt's federal home rule proposals became a serious issue for political debate in 1873–4, the O'Conor Don's whiggishly liberal views on public representation and representative government, as well as his fear of the Fenian influences within Irish nationalism, drove his opposition to it. Thus, even though he raised pragmatic considerations such as the unviability of an Irish house of lords, Ulster Protestant opposition and the likely opposition of an English-dominated imperial parliament, his claim to support the idea of home rule while opposing Butt's federal proposals rang hollow, especially when he failed to propose an alternative. Thereafter, between 1874 and 1880, he continued to pursue a moderate reform agenda, contributing to tangible changes in factory laws, the sale of alcohol, intermediate and university education and Irish language provision. But his ability to work across the House with nationalists, liberals and conservatives in helping to achieve these reforms was completely overshadowed by his opposition to federal home rule, refusal to join Butt's Home Rule Party and opposition to fixity of tenure for tenant farmers. Parnell's rise within Butt's party, and alliance with radical nationalist forces in 1879, ensured that this was the case for the O'Conor Don in the 1880 general election campaign. Even Bishop Gillooly's support could not ensure his safe return, but it was his over-confidence in defeating all comers that ultimately proved to be his undoing. Nonetheless, the O'Conor Don remained optimistic that it would not be the end of his political career, apparently shaking off prior concerns about being perceived as a whig placeman and entertaining the idea of joining Gladstone's second liberal administration if he could manage to get himself re-elected elsewhere. The position of Irish chief secretary was most likely beyond what might have been offered to him, but even if it was not, his independent-mindedness would probably have ensured that he either would have turned it down or would not have lasted long in that or any other government role.

The O'Conor Don's independent liberal streak continued to define the increasingly marginal part he played in Irish and British politics after 1880. Having failed to get himself re-elected in the Wexford by-election in 1883, he seems to have been somewhat bitter about the lack of recognition for his service to the Liberal Party and resigned himself to quitting any kind of party politics altogether. Thus, while the O'Conor Don worked with liberal and conservative unionists to achieve land, local government and electoral reform between 1883 and 1903, he declined to join the Irish Loyal and Patriotic Union in 1885 and the Liberal Union of Ireland in 1887. He also absented himself from Irish unionist demonstrations in 1892 and 1893. This reluctance to fully engage with a predominantly Protestant Irish unionism was contrasted by his signing of a Catholic unionist petition, attendance at a unionist demonstration in London and public opposition to Gladstone's second home rule bill in 1893. His stated preference for a continuation of a form of colonial administration in Ireland at this point confirmed his loyalism, unionism and imperialism. His unionism was underpinned by deep-seated fears about the maintenance of law and order, the fair transfer of land, the protection of minorities and the advance of a secular and separatist republicanism under a nationalist-dominated Irish parliament. However, the lack of advanced Irish reforms under the Conservative governments of the 1890s, particularly in land and local government, left the O'Conor Don disillusioned. His involvement in the financial relations commission in 1895–6 emphasized what he already believed was Ireland's mistreatment as an inferior partner in the union, but the O'Conor Don's patriotism, lack of enthusiasm for the union and nationalist-sounding criticisms of English arrogance did not lead him to advocate for devolved home rule as a solution to Ireland's problems. This was evidenced during the brief campaign for financial reform in 1896–7 when he was once again thrown into the melting pot of Irish politics. All this achieved, however, was a renewed sense of frustration for the O'Conor Don, as he found himself unable to articulate what he believed was the misapplication of the rules governing Ireland's tax contribution to the imperial exchequer without being dragged into a debate on whether the union was being undermined by highlighting the wrong, and the case for home rule therefore strengthened. For the O'Conor Don, it was a matter of reforming the financial arrangements of the union so that Ireland might benefit fully and fairly from them. Being disillusioned with or openly critical of this aspect of the union arrangement did not entail a rejection of the union. His attempt to make the case for separate Irish taxation from a unionist point of view failed to convince Ulster unionists and southern nationalists. Yet still, the nationalist leader John Redmond wanted his supporters in County Roscommon to 'tolerate' the O'Conor Don in the run-up to the local government elections in 1899, in the hope that he could be won over to the nationalist side. Although duly tolerated and elected, the O'Conor Don was far from won over, with his stint as chair of Castlerea District Council a brief one due to a clash with nationalists over their disloyal support for the Boers. His participation in the 1902 royal coronation made clear that his support for the crown and the empire trumped any doubts or misgivings he had about the union.

To summarize, then, the O'Conor Don was a liberal Catholic and a unionist whose sense of Irish national identity incorporated a form of British identity. But these are not hard and fast, easily definable political views and cultural identities. The O'Conor Don's liberalism was shaped by a conservative Catholicism that opposed the advance of secularism, which in turn undermined his desire for a more tolerant, pluralist sense of Irish national identity that incorporated the aspects of British culture and identity that he was attached to. His unionism was of the national kind in the sense that he critiqued the union from a mostly Irish Catholic perspective and conceded that some form of Irish home rule would eventually have to be granted by the British state because the majority of Irish Catholics supported it. However, even though the O'Conor Don acknowledged that home rule was required and had majority support, he could not see his way to actually supporting it. There were a number of reasons for this. First, like many Irish and British liberals, he believed in the necessity of a natural ruling class within a limited form of representative democracy where those who governed made decisions based on popular opinion and what they thought was in the best interest of the country. This whiggishly liberal view of government and democracy was shaped by a number of factors: his education and understanding of history and philosophy; his European and American travels; his hereditary status as one of Ireland's so-called natural leaders; and his generally paternalistic outlook on society, influenced by his role as a landlord. Second, like all liberal and conservative unionists, the O'Conor Don believed that the nationalist politics which sought to bring about home rule were in fact strongly republican and had in mind Ireland's complete independence from Great Britain, the crown and the empire. Third, like many Catholic unionists, he felt that the republican forces within Irish nationalism sought to create a secular Irish republic in which the Catholic Church would be subordinate to the state.

In the final analysis, however, the hybrid nature of O'Conor Don's liberal Catholic and unionist outlook gradually became impossible as politics became increasingly polarized along Catholic nationalist and Protestant unionist lines in late nineteenth- and early twentieth-century Ireland. In those circumstances, the possibility for a pluralist Irish national identity, which incorporated British identity, also became gradually impossible. However, this is not to write the O'Conor Don off as some obscure figure who is not worthy of our attention. There is no doubting that he did become an increasingly marginal figure in Irish politics after 1880 because of his views on politics, identity and society more generally. But perhaps looking at the politics and identity of someone like the O'Conor Don, with all its diversity and apparent contradictions, might help us to better understand the complex patchwork of Irish, Northern Irish and British identities that exist in today's Ireland.

Appendix 1: The O'Conor Don's family tree

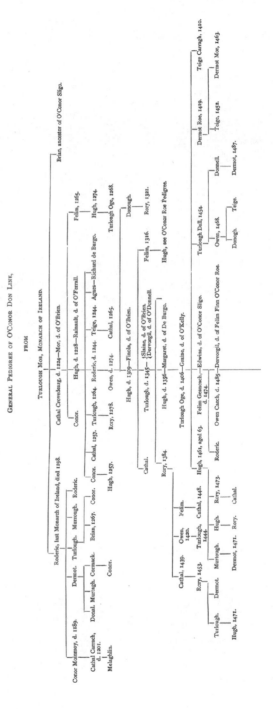

Appendix 1: The O'Conor Don's family tree

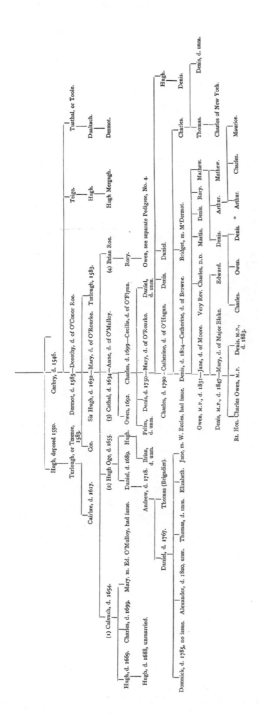

Source: C.O. O'Conor, *The O'Conors of Connaught: an historical memoir* (Dublin, 1891). Courtesy of the Board of Trinity College Dublin.

Appendix 2.1: Map of Ireland, with counties Roscommon and Sligo highlighted

Appendix 2.2: Maps of counties Sligo and Roscommon with the civil parishes in which the O'Conor Don owned land

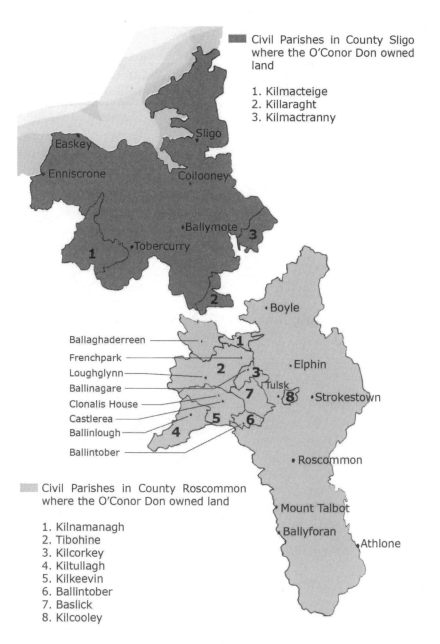

Civil Parishes in County Sligo where the O'Conor Don owned land

1. Kilmacteige
2. Killaraght
3. Kilmactranny

Civil Parishes in County Roscommon where the O'Conor Don owned land

1. Kilnamanagh
2. Tibohine
3. Kilcorkey
4. Kiltullagh
5. Kilkeevin
6. Ballintober
7. Baslick
8. Kilcooley

Appendix 3: Landownership tables

Tables 1 and 2 contain details of the O'Conor Don's land by county, parish and townland, complete with acreage and whether he inherited, purchased, or sold the land. It is not, however, a definitive list of all the land he owned between 1860 and 1906.

Table 1: County Roscommon

Parish	Townland	Acreage (*a., r., p.*)			Notes
Ballintober	Ballintober	44	1	3	Purchased in 1892 for £5,100 from Pakenham-Mahon estate.
	Rosmeen	163	0	28	
Baslick	Pollranny	137	1	23	Purchased in 1876 for £7,850 from Dominick Trant estate. Purchase includes Carrowreagh in Kilcorkey parish below.
	Rathmoyle	89	0	34	
	Toberelva	125	2	38	
Kilcooley	Clooneigh	215	0	33	Purchased after 1859. Sold in 1906 under 1903 land purchase act.
	Lissaphuca	111	1	5	Purchased after 1859. Sold in 1906 under 1903 land purchase act.
Kilcorkey	Annaghmaghera	477	3	22	Inherited. Sold 169*a.* 3*r.* 10*p.* in 1906 under 1903 land purchase act.
	Ballaghcullia	361	0	11	Inherited. Sold and re-purchased in 1906 under 1903 land purchase act.

Appendix 3: Landownership tables

Parish	Townland	Acreage (a., r., p.)			Notes
	Ballinagare	314	1	30	Inherited. Sold 314a. 1r. 30p. and re-purchased 204a. 0r. 23p. in 1906 under 1903 land purchase act.
	Ballincool	118	3	31	Inherited. Sold in 1906 under 1903 land purchase act.
	Ballynahowna	286	1	0	Inherited
	Carrowreagh	672	1	2	See Trant purchase above in Baslick parish. Sold 58a. 1r. 39p. c.1896–1902 under 1891 land purchase act. Sold 2a. 0r. 6p. in 1906 under 1903 land purchase act.
	Cashel	86	0	8	Inherited. Sold 69a. 2r. 1p. in 1906 under 1903 land purchase act but re-purchased 2r. 10p.
	Cornamucklagh and Falmore	478	1	20	Inherited. Sold 232a. 1r. 20p. in 1906 under 1903 land purchase act.
	Derreen	250	2	15	Inherited. Sold 188a. 2r. 15p. in 1906 under 1903 land purchase act.
	Drummin	265	2	34	Inherited. Sold and re-purchased in 1906 under 1903 land purchase act.
	Gortnagoyne	250	0	30	Inherited. Sold 124a. 0r. 39p. in 1906 under 1903 land purchase act.

Parish	Townland	Acreage (a., r., p.)			Notes
	Knockroe	274	3	28	Inherited. Sold 211a. 0r. 29p. in 1906 under 1903 land purchase act.
	Tullaghan	237	1	24	Inherited 2a. 3r. 19p. Purchased remainder sometime after 1859. Sold in 1906 under 1903 land purchase act.
Kilcooley	Clooneigh	215	0	33	Purchased after 1859. Sold in 1906 under 1903 land purchase act.
	Lissaphuca	111	1	5	Purchased after 1859. Sold in 1906 under 1903 land purchase act.
Kilkeevin	Arm (seems to have included parts of Meelickaduff)	426	1	24	Purchased in 1860 for £11,385 from William Lloyd estate. Sold 27a. 2r. 17p. in 1899 under the 1891 land purchase act. Sold 82a. 3r. 21p. in 1906 under the 1903 land purchase act.
	Breanabeg	150	0	10	Purchased in 1878 for £503 from John McCreery estate. Sold in 1906 under 1903 land purchase act.
	Cloonaff	345	2	7	Inherited. Sold 85a. 1r. 20p. in 1906 under 1903 land purchase act.
	Cloonalis	315	2	27	Inherited. Sold and re-purchased in 1906 under 1903 land purchase act.

Appendix 3: Landownership tables

Parish	Townland	Acreage (a., r., p.)			Notes
	Cloonboniff	234	0	17	Inherited. Sold 189a. 3r. 28p. in 1906 under 1903 land purchase act.
	Cloonconra	0	2	20	Purchased after 1859. Sold in 1906 under 1903 land purchase act.
	Clooncoose North	771	0	14	Inherited. Sold 423a. 0r. 23p. in 1906 under 1903 land purchase act.
	Clooncoose South	118	3	22	Inherited.
	Clooncraffield	291	0	8	Inherited. Sold 254a. 1r. 16p. in 1906 under 1903 act.
	Cloonree	2	3	0	Purchased after 1859. Sold in 1906 under 1903 land purchase act.
	Cloonsuck	347	1	10	Inherited. Sold in 1906 under 1903 land purchase act.
	Cloontrask	211	2	0	Purchased in 1860 for £3,195 from William Lloyd estate. Sold 210a in 1906 under 1903 land purchase act.
	Creglahan	447	3	6	Inherited. Sold 327a. 0r. 23p. in 1906 under 1903 land purchase act.
	Derreen	129	1	9	Inherited. Sold 96a. 1r. 0p. in 1906 under 1903 land purchase act.

Parish	Townland	Acreage (a., r., p.)			Notes
	Drumalough	169	0	9	Purchased in 1876 from Dominick Trant estate. Sold in 1906 under 1903 land purchase act.
	Meelickaduff	16	1	23	Not clear if he owned all of this townland (99a. 3r. 0p. in total) but part of it seems to have been included in Arm purchase above. Sold 16a. 1r. 23p. in 1906 under 1903 act.
Kilnamanagh	Ardmoyle	115	2	33	Purchased in 1859 for £3,000 from Marcus McCausland estate
Kiltullagh	Carrick	457	2	23	Purchased in 1858 for £2,490 from Colonel Fulkes Greville estate. Sold 340a. 3r. 19p. in 1899–1901 under the 1891 land purchase act. Sold 44a. 3r. 20p. in 1906 under the 1903 land purchase act.
	Clooncrim	34	0	24	See Grange, below.
	Coolatinny	213	0	37	Purchased in 1858 for £2,200 from Colonel Fulkes Greville estate. Sold 134a. 1r. 38p. in 1899–1901 under the 1891 land purchase act.

Appendix 3: Landownership tables

Parish	Townland	Acreage (*a., r., p.*)			Notes
	Corrasluastia	519	0	34	Purchased in 1858 for £4,275 from Colonel Fulkes Greville estate. Sold 401*a*. 1*r*. 23*p*. in 1899–1901 under the 1891 land purchase act. Sold 4*a*. 3*r*. 8*p*. in 1906 under the 1903 land purchase act.
	Grange	389	2	5	Purchased in 1858 for £3,320 from Colonel Fulkes Greville estate (amount includes purchase of Clooncrim, above). Sold 246*a*. 6*r*. 24*p*. in 1899–1900, under 1891 land purchase act. Sold 15*a*. 2*r*. 21*p*. in 1906 under 1903 land purchase act.
Roscommon	Ardnanagh	8	3	23	Purchase in 1859 for £1,500 from Marcus McCausland.
Tibohine	Carrrowgarve	536	0	25	Purchased in 1860 for £10,000 from Patrick Balfe estate. Purchase includes Cartronmore below. Sold to the Congested Districts Board in 1909.
	Cartronmore	392	3	14	See above.

Parish	Townland	Acreage (*a.*, *r.*, *p.*)			Notes
	Leggatinty	156	2	28	Purchased 61*a.* 2*r.* 28*p.* after 1859. Purchased 95 acres in 1878 for £1,380 from Michael Fox estate. Sold 156*a.* 2*r.* 28*p.* in 1906 under 1903 land purchase act.

Note: The O'Conor Don sold 55*a.* 2*r.* 25*p.* in County Roscommon in 1890 under the 1885 land purchase act but it is not clear which townland/s

Table 2. County Sligo

Parish	Townland	Acreage			Notes
Killaraght	Ardsoreen	419	1	1	Inherited. Sold *c.*1877–89 under the landed estates court.
	Ardmoyle	260	1	11	Purchased after 1859.
Kilmacteige	Drimina	635	1	17	Inherited. Sold *c.*1877–9 under the landed estates court.
Kilmactranny	Carricknagrip	131	3	1	Inherited.
	Carrigeenboy	296	0	29	Inherited.

Note: The O'Conor Don sold 359*a.* 0*r.* 30*p.* in County Sligo in 1890 under the 1885 act but it is not clear which townland/s.

Bibliography

ARCHIVAL SOURCES

British Library, London
Althorp papers; Gladstone papers; Iddelseigh papers; Ripon papers

Churchill Archives Centre, Cambridge
Nicholas O'Conor papers

Clonalis House, Castlerea, County Roscommon
O'Conor papers

Department of Agriculture, Food & Forestry, Portlaoise
Land commission papers

Dublin Diocesan Archives, Dublin
Cullen papers; Hamilton papers; McCabe papers; Woodlock papers

Elphin Diocesan Archives, Sligo
Gillooly papers

Hull History Centre, Hull
Chichester papers

Irish College, Rome (online)
Kirby papers

Jesuit Archives, Dublin
Delany papers

National Archives of Ireland, Dublin
Chief Secretary's Office Registered Papers; Land League papers; Landed estates court rentals; Monsell papers

National Library of Ireland, Dublin
Copy of the will of Denis O'Conor; Cadogan papers; Castletown papers; Clonbrock papers; Diary of Denis Maurice O'Conor (microfilm); Landed estates court rentals; Monsell papers

Public Record Office of Northern Ireland, Belfast
Bladensburg papers; McCausland papers; O'Conor family documents; O'Hagan papers

PARLIAMENTARY RECORDS

Hansard Parliamentary Debates, 3rd series (1830–91)
Royal commission of inquiry into state of law and practice in respect to occupation of land in Ireland, minutes of evidence, part II, 1845 (616), xx.1.
Correspondence from July, 1846, to January, 1847, relating to the measures adopted for the relief of the distress in Ireland: commissariat series, HC 1847 (761), li.
Copy of a letter on the subject of national education in Ireland, addressed to the chief secretary in the month of July last by certain members of parliament, HC 1861 (212), xlviii.
Select committee to inquire how education of destitute and neglected children may be assisted by public funds: report, proceedings, minutes of evidence, appendix, index 1861, HC 1861 (460) (460-I), vii.
Royal commission to inquire into operation of acts relating to transportation and penal servitude: report, appendix, minutes of evidence, HC 1863 (3190) (3190-I), xxi.1.
Report from the select committee on scientific institutions (Dublin); together with the proceedings of the committee, minutes of evidence, appendix and index, HC 1864 (495), xiii.
Select committee on art union laws: report, proceedings, minutes of evidence, appendix, index, HC 1866 (332) (332-I) vii.1.
Select committee on home and foreign trade in animals by sea and railroad: report, proceedings, minutes of evidence, appendix, index, HC 1866 (427) (427-I) xvi.
Report from the select committee on tramways (Ireland) acts amendment bill; together with the proceedings of the committee, minutes of evidence, and appendix, HC 1866 (418) xi.
A bill to extend the Industrial Schools Act to Ireland, HC 1867–8 (6), ii.
Copy of further correspondence relative to the proposed charter to a Roman Catholic University in Ireland, HC 1867–8 (288) (380), liii.
Copy of declaration of the Catholic laity of Ireland, on the subject of university education in that select committee on laws under which monies are raised by grand jury presentments in Ireland: report, proceedings, index, HC 1867–8 (392) (392-I) x.
Copy of declaration of the Catholic laity of Ireland, on the subject of university education in that country, lately laid before the prime minister, HC 1870 (140), liv.
Report from the select committee on Callan schools; together with the proceedings of the committee, minutes of evidence, and appendix, HC 1873 (255), ix.
Return of names of proprietors and area and valuation of properties in counties in Ireland, held in fee or perpetuity, or long leases at chief rents, HC 1876 (412), lxxx.

Bibliography

Report of the commissioners appointed to inquire into the working of the factory and workshops acts, with a view to their consolidation and amendment; together with the minutes of evidence, appendix, and index, vol. I, HC 1876 [C.1443], xxix.

Royal commission to inquire into working of penal servitude acts: report, minutes of evidence, appendix, index, HC 1878–9 (C.2368) (C.2368-I) (C.2368-II), xxxvii.1, 67, xxxviii.1.

A bill intituled an act to promote the advancement of learning, and to extend the benefits connected with university education in Ireland, HL 1878–9 (250), vii.

A bill [as amended in committee] intituled An act to promote the advancement of learning, and to extend the benefits connected with university education in Ireland, HL 1878–9 (283), vii.

Report of the Intermediate Education Board for Ireland for the year 1879, HC (1880), xxiii.

Copy of the charter of the Royal University of Ireland, HC 1881 (203), lxxiii.

Copy of list of the names of the members of the senate of the Royal University of Ireland, HC 1881 (204), lxxiii.

Report of Her Majesty's commissioners of inquiry into the working of the Landlord and Tenant (Ireland) Act, 1870, and the acts amending the same, HC 1881 (73), xviii & (825), xxix.

Relief of Distress (Ireland) Acts (Loans), HC 1881 (99), lvii.

Return according to provinces and counties of judicial rents fixed by sub-commissions and civil bill courts, as notified to the Irish land commission during the month of December 1882, HC 1883 (121), lvi.

Return according to provinces and counties of judicial rents fixed by sub-commissions and civil bill courts, as notified to the Irish land commission during the month of January 1883, HC 1883 (237), lvi.

Return according to provinces and counties of judicial rents fixed by sub-commissions and civil bill courts, as notified to the Irish land commission during the month of October 1883, HC 1884 (233), lxv.

Return of payments made to landlords by the Irish land commission, pursuant to the 1st and 16th sections of the act; and also a return of rent-charges cancelled pursuant to the 15th section of the Arrears of Rent (Ireland) Act 1882, HC 1884 (97), lxiv.

Royal commission on reformatories and industrial schools: report, minutes of evidence, appendices, index, HC 1884 [C.3876] [C.3876-I], xlv.

Return according to provinces and counties of judicial rents fixed by sub-commissions and civil bill courts, as notified to the Irish land commission during the month of April 1884, HC 1884 (413), lxvi.

Return according to provinces and counties of judicial rents fixed by sub-commissions and civil bill courts, as notified to the Irish land commission during the month of November 1884, HC 1884–5 (193), lxv.

First report of the royal commission on Irish public works, HC 1887 (471) (509), xxv.

The agricultural districts of Ireland, for the year 1887, HC 1888 (106), cvi.

Return according to provinces and counties of judicial rents fixed by sub-commissions and civil bill courts, as notified to the Irish land commission during the months of January and February 1888, HC 1888 (229), lxxxiv.

Return according to provinces and counties of judicial rents fixed by sub-commissions and civil bill courts, as notified to the Irish land commission during the months of May and June 1888, HC 1888 (621), lxxxiv.

Return showing the gross and net revenues of Trinity College, Dublin for the year 1888, the total amount of the incomes of the provost and of the senior fellows, and the total amount of the incomes of the junior fellows, the salary attached to each professional chair, and whether the chair is held by a fellow or not; the number of undergraduates on the college books on 31 December 1888, and how many belong to each religious denomination classified as (a.) Protestant Episcopalians; (b.) Presbyterians; (c.) Roman Catholics; and (d.) all other denominations, HC 1889 (334), lix.

Return according to provinces and counties of judicial rents fixed by sub-commissions and civil bill courts, as notified to the Irish land commission during the months of January and February 1889, HC 1889, lxiii.

Return according to provinces and counties of judicial rents fixed by sub-commissions and civil bill courts, as notified to the Irish land commission during the month of May 1890, HC 1890 (477), lxi.

Return according to provinces and counties of judicial rents fixed by sub-commissions and civil bill courts, as notified to the Irish land commission during the month of June 1890, HC 1890 (653) (811), lxi.

Return according to provinces and counties of judicial rents fixed by sub-commissions and civil bill courts, as notified to the Irish land commission during the month of August 1890, HC 1890–1 (219), lxv.

Return giving the names of the landowners the purchase of whose properties under 'the Land Purchase (Ireland) Act, 1885', has been sanctioned by the Irish land commission since 1st January 1889, HC 1890 (115), lx.

Return according to provinces and counties of judicial rents fixed by sub-commissions and civil bill courts, as notified to the Irish land commission during the months of September, October, and November 1891, HC 1892 (177), lxvi.

Return according to provinces and counties of judicial rents fixed by sub-commissions and civil bill courts, as notified to the Irish land commission during the months of March and April 1893, HC 1893–4 (553), lxxv.

Return according to provinces and counties of judicial rents fixed by sub-commissions and civil bill courts, as notified to the Irish land commission during the months of September and October 1893, HC 1893–4 (871), lxxv.

Royal commission on labour. The agricultural labourer, vol. iv: Ireland, part iv: Reports by Mr Arthur Wilson Fox (assistant commissioner), upon certain selected districts in the counties of Cork, Mayo, Roscommon and Westmeath; with summary report prefixed, HC 1893–4 (341), xxxvii.

Return according to provinces and counties of judicial rents fixed by sub-commissions and civil bill courts, as notified to the Irish land commission during the months of May and June 1895, HC 1895 (583), lxxxii.

Return according to provinces and counties of judicial rents fixed by sub-commissions and civil bill courts, as notified to the Irish land commission during the months of September, October, November, and December 1895, HC 1896 (85), lxx.

Final report by Her Majesty's commissioners appointed to inquire into the financial relations between Great Britain and Ireland, HC 1896 [C.8008] [C.8262], xxxiii.

Royal commission of inquiry into the procedure and practice and the methods of valuation followed by the land commission, the land judge's court, and the civil bill courts in Ireland under the land acts and the land purchase acts, vol. II: minutes of evidence, HC 1898 (41), xxxv.

Return according to provinces and counties of judicial rents fixed by sub-commissions and civil bill courts, as notified to the Irish land commission during the month of November 1897, HC 1898 (375), lxxv.

Return of advances under the Purchase of Land (Ireland) Act, 1891, 1899–1900, HC 1900 (302), lxix.

Return of advances under the Purchase of Land (Ireland) Act, 1891, 1900–1901, HC 1901 (308), lxi.

Return of advances under the Purchase of Land (Ireland) Act, 1891, 1901–1902, HC 1902 (334), lxxxiv.

Return of advances under the Purchase of Land (Ireland) Act, 1891, 1902–1903, HC 1903 (335), lvii.
Return of untenanted lands in rural districts, distinguishing demesnes on which there is a mansion, showing: rural district and electoral division; townland; area in statute acres; valuation (poor law); names of occupiers as in valuation lists (land-landlord and tenant (Ireland): untenanted lands), HC 1906 (250), c.

NEWSPAPERS

Belfast Newsletter
Belfast Weekly News
Catholic Directory
Catholic Telegraph
Dublin Evening Post
Freeman's Journal
Irish Independent
Irish News
Irish Times
Nation

Newry Reporter
Roscommon Herald
Roscommon Journal
Roscommon & Leitrim Gazette
Roscommon Messenger
Sligo Champion
Sligo Independent
Tablet
Times

CONTEMPORARY BOOKS, ARTICLES AND PAMPHLETS

Association of Graduates, *The Queen's University and the O'Conor Don's university bill: report of proceedings at a meeting held in Belfast, 2 June 1879* (Belfast, 1879).
Blackwood, F. Temple, *Irish emigration and the tenure of land in Ireland* (London, 1867).
——, *The land question, Ireland, vi: Lord Dufferin on the three fs* (Dublin, 1881).
Blennerhassett, Rowland, *Peasant proprietors in Ireland* (London, 1884).
Butt, Isaac, *The problem of Irish education: an attempt at its solution* (London, 1875).
Cairnes, John E., *The character and logical method of political economy* (London, 1857).
——, 'University education in Ireland', *Theological Review*, 3 (Jan. 1866), 116–49.
——, *Political essays* (London, 1873).
——, *Some leading principles of political economy newly expounded* (London, 1874).
Croskery, Thomas, 'Irish university education', *Edinburgh Review*, 125 (Jan.–Apr. 1872), 166–96.
Declaration of Irish Catholic laity in favor of religious equality (Dublin, 1860), pp 1–27.
Dicey, Albert V., 'The defence of the union', *Contemporary Review*, 61 (Mar. 1892), 314–31.
Dun, Finlay, *Landlords and tenants in Ireland* (London, 1881).
Gibbon, Skeffington, *The recollections of S.G. from 1796 to the present year, 1829; being an epitome of the lives and characters of the nobility and gentry of Roscommon the genealogy of those who are descended from the kings of Connaught; and a memoir of Madame O'Conor Don* (Dublin, 1829).
Lecky, William E.H., 'Some aspects of home rule', *Contemporary Review*, 63 (May 1893), 626–38.

Lubbock, John, 'On the financial relations of Great Britain and Ireland', *Nineteenth Century*, 42:249 (Nov. 1897), pp 791–8.
Maguire, Thomas, *Letter to Henry Fawcett on the Irish university question* (Galway, 1872).
Monsell, William, 'University education in Ireland', *Home and Foreign Review*, 2 (Jan. 1863), 32–58.
Norbert Birth, D.H., *Downside: the history of St Gregory's school from its commencement at Douay to the present time* (London, 1902).
O'Conor, Charles Owen, *A few remarks on the evidence received by the Irish taxation committee: together with a brief review of the subject* (Dublin, 1865).
——, *What is meant by freedom of education, or, the Catholic objections to pure secularism considered* (Dublin, 1872).
——, 'Ballintubber Castle, County Roscommon', *Journal of the Royal Historical and Archaeological Association of Ireland*, 9:78 (Jan.–Mar. 1889), 24–30.
——, *The O'Conors of Connaught: an historical memoir* (Dublin, 1891).
——, 'The unsolved Irish problem', *National Review*, 22 (Dec. 1893), 531–41.
——, 'The over-taxation of Ireland', *National Review*, 28 (Feb. 1897), 739–51.
——, *The over-taxation of Ireland: speech of the right hon. O'Conor Don, in answer to the English case, 8 December, 1897* (Dublin, 1897).
——, *The speech of the right hon. O'Conor Don in reply to the right hon. A.J. Balfour, MP delivered at the Mansion House, Dublin, on January 4th, 1899* (Dublin, 1899).
——, *The Irish land bill, 1903: speech of the right hon. the O'Conor Don at the Irish Landowners' Convention, Dublin, 24 April, 1903* (Dublin, 1903).
O'Conor, Matthew, *The history of the Irish Catholics from the settlement in 1691, with a view of the state of Ireland from the invasion by Henry II to the revolution* (Dublin, 1813).
O'Donnell, F.H., *Public education: its necessity, and the ideas involved in it: an essay on the principles of national instruction: with some of their applications to Irish university systems* (Dublin, 1867).
O'Hagan, John, 'The constitutional history of the University of Dublin, with some account of its present condition and suggestions for improvement', *Dublin Review*, 22 (Sept. 1847), 228–51.
O'Reilly, Myles, 'The connection of the state with education in England and Ireland', *Dublin Review*, 52 (Nov. 1862), 106–54.
——, 'University education', *Dublin Review*, 52 (Apr. 1863), 423–67.
Proceedings, *Journal of the Royal Society of Antiquaries of Ireland*, 5:3 (Sept. 1895), 235–316
Proceedings of the home rule conference held at the Rotunda, Dublin, on the 18th, 19th, 20th, and 21st November 1873: with list of conference ticket holders, index to speakers, index to subjects treated of in the debates, constitution and laws of the Irish Home Rule League, and final report of the Home Government Association (Dublin, 1874).
Sullivan, W.K., *University education in Ireland; letter to Sir John Dalberg Acton* (Dublin, 1866).
The liberal unionist conference and banquet (London, 1888).
Thornton, William T., *A plea for peasant proprietors; with the outlines of a plan for their establishment in Ireland* (London, 1848).
Whittle, James L., *Freedom of education: what it means* (Dublin, 1866).
——, 'How to save Ireland from an ultramontane university', *Fraser's Magazine for Town and Country*, 77 (Apr. 1868), 433–51.

BOOKS, ESSAYS AND JOURNAL ARTICLES

Adelman, Juliana, *Communities of science in nineteenth-century Ireland* (London, 2009).

Akenson, Donald H., *The Irish education experiment: the national system of education in the nineteenth century* (London & Toronto, 1970).

Altholz, J.L., *The liberal Catholic movement in England: the rambler and its contributors, 1848–1864* (London, 1962).

Auchmuty, J.J., *Irish education: a historical survey* (London, 1937).

Barnes, Jane, *Irish industrial schools, 1868–1906: origins and development* (Dublin, 1989).

Barr, Colin, *Paul Cullen, John Henry Newman, and the Catholic university of Ireland, 1845–1865* (Herefordshire, 2003).

——, *The European culture wars in Ireland: the Callan schools affair, 1868–1881* (Dublin, 2010).

Bartlett, Thomas, *The fall and rise of the Irish nation: the Catholic question, 1690–1830* (Dublin, 1992).

—— (ed.), *The Cambridge history of Ireland* (Cambridge, 2018), vol. 4.

Beckett, J.C. & T.W. Moody, *Queen's Belfast, 1845–1949: the history of a university* (London, 1959), vol. 1.

Bence Jones, Mark, *The twilight of the Ascendancy* (London, 1987).

——, *The Catholic families* (London, 1992).

Bernstein, G.L., 'British liberal politics and Irish liberalism after O'Connell' in Brown, S.J. & D.W. Miller (eds), *Piety and power in Ireland, 1760–1960: essays in honour of Emmet Larkin* (Belfast, 2000), pp 43–65.

Bew, John, *The glory of being Britons: civic unionism in nineteenth-century Belfast* (Dublin, 2009).

Bew, Paul, *Land and the national question in Ireland, 1858–82* (Dublin, 1978).

——, *Charles Stewart Parnell* (Dublin, 1980).

—— & Frank Wright, 'The agrarian opposition in Ulster politics, 1848–87' in Clark, Samuel & J.S. Donnelly Jnr, *Irish peasants: violence and political unrest, 1780–1914* (Madison, WI, 1983), pp 192–229.

——, *Conflict and conciliation in Ireland, 1890–1910 – Parnellites and radical agrarians* (New York, 1987).

Biagini, Eugenio, *British democracy and Irish nationalism 1876–1906* (Cambridge, 2007).

Biggs-Davidson, John & George Chowdharay-Best, *The cross of Saint Patrick: the Catholic unionist tradition in Ireland* (Bourne End, 1984).

Bligh, John, 'John Fitzgibbon of Castlerea: "A most mischievous and dangerous agitator"' in Brian Casey (ed.), *Defying the law of the land* (2013), pp 201–19.

Bouchilloux, Hélène, 'Pascal and the social world' in Hammond, Nicholas (ed.), *The Cambridge companion to Pascal* (Cambridge, 2003), pp 201–15.

Boyce, D.G., *Nineteenth-century Ireland: the search for stability* (Dublin, 2005).

—— & Alan O'Day (eds), *Defenders of the union: a survey of British and Irish unionism since 1801* (London & New York, 2001).

Boyne, Patricia, *John O'Donovan (1806–1861): a biography* (Kilkenny, 1987).

Breathnach, Ciara, *The Congested Districts Board, 1891–1923: poverty and development in the west of Ireland* (Dublin, 2005).

Buckland, Patrick, *Irish unionism 1: the Anglo-Irish and the new Ireland, 1885–1922* (Dublin, 1972).

——, *Irish unionism 2: Ulster unionism and the origins of Northern Ireland, 1886–1922* (Dublin, 1973).
Bull, Philip, *Land, politics and nationalism: a study of the Irish land question* (Dublin, 1996).
Campbell, Fergus, *Land and revolution: nationalist politics in the west of Ireland, 1891–1921* (New York, 2005).
——, *The Irish establishment: 1879–1914* (New York, 2009).
Cannadine, David, *The decline and fall of the British aristocracy* (London, 1996).
Carty, P.J., 'Roscommon: landownership, land occupation and settlement' in Farrell et al. (eds), *Roscommon history and society* (2018), pp 411–40.
Casey, Brian (ed.), *Defying the law of the land: agrarian radicals in Irish history* (Dublin, 2013).
Clarke, Joseph, *Christopher Dillon Bellew and his Galway estates, 1763–1862* (Dublin, 2003).
Coleman, Anne, *Riotous Roscommon: social unrest in the 1840s* (Dublin, 1999).
Colley, Linda, *Britons: forging the nation, 1707–1837* (New Haven & London, 2012).
Comerford, R.V., *The fenians in context, Irish politics and society, 1848–82* (Dublin, 1998).
——, 'Churchmen, tenants, and independent opposition' in Vaughan (ed.), *A new history of Ireland*, (1989), v, pp 396–414.
Connolly, Paul, *The landed estates of County Roscommon* (Galway, 2018).
Corcoran, Donal, *The Irish brigade in the pope's army, 1860: faith, fatherland and fighting* (Dublin, 2018).
Corish, P.J. (ed.), *A history of Irish Catholicism* (Dublin, 1971), vol. 6.
Crossman, Virginia, *Politics, law and order in nineteenth-century Ireland* (Dublin, 1996).
Curtis, L.P., 'Incumbered wealth: landed indebtedness in post-Famine Ireland', *American Historical Review*, 85:2 (Apr. 1980), 332–67.
D'Alton, Ian, 'A "first voice": Henry Villers Stuart (1827–95) and the cause of the Irish agricultural labourers' in Casey (ed.), *Defying the law of the land* (2013), pp 164–75.
Donnelly Jnr, J.S., *The land and people of nineteenth-century Cork: the rural economy and the land question* (London, 1975).
——, 'The Kenmare estates during the nineteenth century', *Journal of the Kerry Archaeological and Historical Society*, 1:21 (1988), 29–41.
——, 'The Kenmare estates during the nineteenth century', *Journal of the Kerry Archaeological and Historical Society*, 3:23 (1990), 20–33.
Dooley, Terence, *The decline of the Big House in Ireland: a study of Irish landed families, 1860–1960* (Dublin, 2001).
——, 'Landlords and mortgagees in late nineteenth-century Ireland: the case of Lord Granard and the trustees of Maynooth College, 1871–89', *Journal of the County Kildare Archaeological Society*, 18 (1998), 612–25.
Dowling, P.J., *A history of Irish education: a study in conflicting loyalties* (Cork, 1971).
Duddy, Tom, *A history of Irish thought* (London & New York, 2002).
Dunleavy, Gareth W. & Janet E., 'Reconstruction, reform, and Romanism, 1865–85: America as seen by Charles O'Conor and Charles Owen O'Conor Don, MP', *Éire Ireland*, 15:3 (Fall, 1980), 15–35.
Dunne, Tom & Gerard O'Brien (eds), *Catholic Ireland in the eighteenth century: collected essays of Maureen Wall* (Dublin, 1989).

Enright, Aidan, 'Catholic elites and the Irish university question: European solutions for an Irish dilemma, 1860–1880' in B. Heffernan (ed.), *Life on the fringe? Ireland and Europe, 1800–1922* (Dublin & Portland, OR, 2012), pp 177–95.

Fagan, Patrick, *Catholics in a Protestant country: the papist constituency in eighteenth-century Dublin* (Dublin, 1998).

Farrell, Richie, et al. (eds), *Roscommon history and society: interdisciplinary essays on the history of an Irish county* (Dublin, 2018).

Feingold, William, 'The tenants' movement to capture the Irish Poor Law Boards, 1877–1886' in O'Day, Alan (ed.), *Reactions to Irish nationalism 1865–1914* (London, 1987), pp 79–94.

Findlater, Alex, *Findlaters: the story of a Dublin merchant family, 1774–2001* (Dublin, 2001).

Foster, R.F., *Modern Ireland, 1600–1972* (London, 1988).

——, 'The Irish literary revival' in Bartlett (ed.), *Cambridge history of Ireland* (2018), iv, pp 168–95.

Gailey, Andrew, *Ireland and the death of kindness: the experience of constructive unionism, 1890–1905* (Cork, 1987).

Garvin, Tom, *Nationalist revolutionaries in Ireland, 1858–1928* (Oxford, 2005).

Geary, Laurence M., *The Plan of Campaign 1886–1891* (Cork, 1986).

Gibbons, Luke & Kieran O'Conor (eds), *Charles O'Conor of Ballinagare: life and works* (Dublin, 2015).

Gibbons, Luke, 'Roscommon in literature, 1600–2000' in Farrell et al. (eds), *Roscommon history and society* (2018), pp 721–52.

Goodlad, G.D., 'The Liberal Party and Gladstone's land purchase bill of 1886', *Historical Journal*, 32:3 (Sept. 1989), 627–41.

Grant, Alexander & Keith J. Stringer (eds), *Uniting the kingdom? The making of British history* (London & New York, 2014).

Gray, John (ed.), *John Stuart Mill: 'On liberty' and other essays* (New York, 1998).

Gray, Peter, *Famine, land and politics: British government and Irish society 1843–50* (Dublin, 1999).

——, *The making of the Irish poor law, 1815–43* (Manchester, 2009).

Greer, Desmond & James W. Nicolson, *The factory acts in Ireland, 1802–1914* (Dublin, 2003).

Hall, Gerald R., *Ulster liberalism, 1778–1876: the middle path* (Dublin, 2010).

Hart, Jennifer, *Proportional representation: critics of the British electoral system, 1820–1945* (New York, 1992).

Harvey, Karen J., *The Bellews of Mount Bellew: a Catholic gentry family in eighteenth-century Ireland* (Dublin, 1998).

Hawkins, Angus, *British party politics, 1852–1886* (Basingstoke, 1998).

Hoppen, K.T., 'Tories, Catholics, and the general election of 1859', *Historical Journal*, 13:1 (1970), 48–67.

——, *Elections, politics and society in Ireland, 1832–1885* (Oxford, 1984).

——, *The mid-Victorian generation, 1846–1886* (Oxford, 1998).

——, *Governing Hibernia: British politicians and Ireland, 1800–1921* (Oxford, 2016).

Jackson, Alvin, 'Irish unionism and the Russellite threat', *Irish Historical Studies*, 15:100 (Nov. 1987), 376–404.

——, *Colonel Edward Saunderson: land and loyalty in Victorian Ireland* (New York, 1995).

—, *Home rule: an Irish history* (London, 2003).

—, 'Ireland, the union, and the empire, 1800–1960' in Kenny, Kevin (ed.), *Ireland and the British empire* (Oxford, 2004), pp 123–53.

—, *The two unions: Ireland, Scotland, and the survival of the United Kingdom, 1707–2007* (Oxford, 2012).

Jenkins, T.A., *Gladstone, whiggery and the Liberal Party, 1874–1886* (New York, 1988).

Kendle, John, *Ireland and the federal solution: the debate over the United Kingdom constitution, 1870–1921* (Kingston, Ontario, 1989).

Kenny, Colum, 'Paradox or pragmatist? "Honest" Tristram Kennedy (1805–85): lawyer, educationalist, land agent and member of parliament', *Proceedings of the Royal Irish Academy*, 92:1 (1992), pp 1–35.

Keogh, Richard, '"Nothing is so bad for the Irish as Ireland alone": William Keogh and Catholic loyalty', *Irish Historical Studies*, 38:150 (2012), 230–48.

Keogh, Richard & James McConnel, 'The Esmonde family of County Wexford and Catholic loyalty' in Rafferty (ed.), *Irish Catholic identities* (2013), pp 274–91.

Ker, Ian, *John Henry Newman: a biography* (Oxford, 1988).

Kerr, Donal, *'A nation of beggars'? Priests, people and politics in Famine Ireland, 1846–1852* (Oxford, 1994).

Kinealy, Christine, *This great calamity: the Irish Famine, 1845–52* (Dublin, 2006).

King, Carla, 'The recess committee, 1895–6', *Studia Hibernica*, 30 (1998/1999), 21–46.

Kinzer, Bruce, 'John Stuart Mill and the Irish university question', *Victorian Studies*, 31 (Autumn, 1987), 59–77.

—, *England's disgrace?: J.S. Mill and the Irish question* (Toronto, 2001).

Knowlton, Stephen, 'The voting behaviour of the Independent Irish Party, 1850–59', *Éire-Ireland* (Spring, 1991), 57–62.

Lane, P.G., 'The encumbered estates court, Ireland, 1848–1849', *Economic and Social Review*, 19 (1972), 413–53.

Larkin, Emmet, 'The devotional revolution in Ireland, 1850–75', *American Historical Review*, 77:3 (June 1972), 625–52.

—, *The Roman Catholic Church and the Plan of Campaign in Ireland, 1886–88* (Cork, 1978).

—, *The Roman Catholic Church and the emergence of the modern political system, 1874–1878* (Dublin, 1996).

Lock, Alexander, *Catholicism, identity and politics in the age of Enlightenment: the life and career of Sir Thomas Gascoigne, 1745–1810* (Woodbridge, 2016).

Loughlin, James, *The British monarchy in Ireland: 1800 to the present* (Cambridge, 2007).

Lyne, G.J., 'John Townsend Trench's reports on the Lansdowne estates in Kerry', *Journal of the Kerry Archaeological and Historical Society*, 19 (1986), 5–64.

Lyons, F.S.L., *John Dillon: a biography* (London, 1968).

—, *Charles Stewart Parnell* (Dublin, 2005).

Macaulay, Ambrose, *The Holy See, British policy and the Plan of Campaign in Ireland, 1885–93* (Dublin, 2002).

MacDermot, Dermot, *MacDermot of Moylurg: the story of a Connacht family* (Nure, Co. Leitrim, 1996).

MacDonagh, Oliver, *The emancipist: Daniel O'Connell, 1830–47* (London, 1989).
MacDowell, R.B., et al. (eds), *The writings of Theobald Wolfe Tone, 1763–98* (Oxford, 1998), vol. 1.
Macintyre, Angus, *The Liberator: Daniel O'Connell and the Irish Party, 1830–1847* (London, 1965).
Mackail, J.W. & Guy Wyndham, *Life and letters of George Wyndham* (London, 1925), vol. 2.
MacSuibhne, Peadar, *Paul Cullen and his contemporaries: with their letters from 1820–1902* (Naas, 1961), vol. 3.
Malcolm, Elizabeth, *'Ireland sober, Ireland free': drink and temperance in nineteenth-century Ireland* (Dublin, 1986).
Matthew, H.C.G. (eds), *The Gladstone diaries with cabinet minutes and prime-ministerial correspondence, ix: January 1875–December 1880* (Oxford, 1986).
Maume, Patrick, *The long gestation: Irish nationalist life, 1891–1918* (Dublin, 1999).
McBride, Ian, *Eighteenth-century Ireland: the isle of slaves* (Dublin, 2009).
McCaffrey, Lawrence J., 'The Home Rule Party and Irish nationalist opinion, 1874–1876', *Catholic Historical Review*, 43:2 (July 1957), 160–77.
——, 'Isaac Butt and the home rule movement: a study in conservative nationalism', *Review of Politics*, 22:1 (Jan. 1960), 77–82.
McCartney, Donal, 'Lecky and the Irish university question', *Irish Ecclesiastical Record*, 5 (1967), 102–12.
McClelland, V. Alan, 'Church and state: the Manning-Gladstone correspondence, 1833–1891', *British Catholic History*, 32:3 (2015), 383–412.
McConnel, James, 'John Redmond and Irish Catholic loyalism', *English Historical Review*, 125:512 (Feb. 2010), 83–111.
McGrath, Fergal, *Newman's university: idea and reality* (London, 1951).
——, 'The Irish university question' in Corish (ed.), *A history of Irish Catholicism* (1971), vi, pp 84–142.
Moody, T.W., 'The Irish university question of the nineteenth century', *History*, 43 (1958), 90–109.
Morrissey T.J., SJ, *Towards a national university, William Delany, SJ (1835–1924): an era of initiative in Irish education* (Dublin, 1983).
Mulvey, Helen, 'The historian Lecky: opponent of Irish home rule', *Victorian Studies*, 1:4 (June 1958), 337–51.
Murphy, James H., *Abject loyalty: nationalism and monarchy in Ireland during the reign of Queen Victoria* (Cork, 2001).
——, *Ireland's czar: Gladstonian government and lord lieutenancies of the Red Earl Spencer, 1868–86* (Dublin, 2014).
Murphy, Joseph, *The Redingtons of Clarinbridge: leading Catholic landlords in the nineteenth century* (Dublin, 1999).
Murphy, Sean J., *Twilight of the chiefs: the MacCarthy Mór hoax* (Dublin, 2004).
Melvin, Patrick, 'Roscommon estates and landowners: diversity and durability' in Farrell et al. (eds), *Roscommon history and society* (2018), pp 327–48.
Moran, Gerard, 'James Daly and the rise and fall of the Land League in the West of Ireland, 1879–82', *Irish Historical Studies*, 29:114 (Nov. 1994), pp 189–207.

Moran, Mary, 'Father Michael O'Flanagan' in Farrell et al. (eds), *Roscommon history and society* (2018), pp 561–87

Norman, E.R., *The Catholic Church in the age of rebellion, 1859–1873* (New York, 1965).

——, *Anti-Catholicism in Victorian England* (Oxford & New York, 2016).

O'Brien, Eoin, *Conscience and conflict: a biography of Sir Dominic Corrigan, 1802–1880* (Dublin, 1983).

O'Brien, Paul, *The Glynns of Kilrush, County Clare, 1811–1940: family, business and politics* (Dublin, 2019).

O'Cathaoir, Brendan, *John Blake Dillon: Young Irelander* (Dublin, 1990).

Ó Conchubhair, Brian, 'The culture war: the Gaelic League and Irish Ireland' in Bartlett (ed.), *Cambridge history of Ireland* (2018), iv, pp 196–220.

O'Day, Alan, *Irish home rule, 1867–1921* (Manchester, 1998).

O'Ferrall, Fergus, *Catholic emancipation: Daniel O'Connell and the birth of Irish democracy* (Dublin, 1985).

O'Gara-O'Riordan, Maura, 'Count Charles O'Gara 1699–1777', *Corran Herald*, 46 (2013/14), 66–9.

O'Neill, Ciaran, *Catholics of consequence: transnational education, social mobility, and the Irish Catholic elite, 1850–1900* (Oxford, 2014).

Ó Siochrú, Micheál, *Confederate Ireland, 1642–1649: a constitutional and political analysis* (Dublin, 1999).

Ó Súilleabháin, S.V., 'Secondary education' in Corish (ed.), *A history of Irish Catholicism* (1971), vi, pp 55–83.

Ó Tuathaigh, Gearóid, 'Ireland under the union: historiographical reflections', *Australian Journal of Irish Studies*, 2 (2002), 1–22.

——, 'Political history' in Geary, Lawrence M. & Margaret Kelleher (eds), *Nineteenth-century Irish history: a guide to recent research* (Dublin, 2005), pp 1–26.

Parkes, Susan, 'Higher education in Ireland, 1793–1908' in W.E. Vaughan (ed.), *A new history of Ireland, vi: Ireland under the union, II, 1870–1921* (Oxford, 1996), pp 539–70.

Parry, Jonathan P., *Democracy and religion: Gladstone and the Liberal Party* (Cambridge, 1989).

——, *The rise and fall of liberal government in Victorian Great Britain* (New Haven, 1993).

Pašeta, Senia, 'The Catholic hierarchy and the Irish university question, 1880–1908', *History*, 85 (2000), 268–84.

——, 'Trinity College, Dublin, and the education of Irish Catholics, 1873–1908', *Studia Hibernica*, 30 (1998/9), 7–20.

Phoenix, Éamon, 'Catholic unionism: a case study: Sir Denis Stanislaus Henry (1864–1925)' in Rafferty (ed.), *Irish Catholic identities* (2013), pp 292–304.

Pocock, J.G.A., 'British history: a plea for a new subject', *Journal of Modern History*, 47 (1975) 601–21.

Pomfret, J.E., *The struggle for land in Ireland, 1800–1923* (Princeton, NJ, 1930).

Potter, Matthew, *William Monsell of Tervoe, 1812–1894: Catholic unionist, Anglo-Irishman* (Dublin, 2009).

——, 'Local government in Co. Roscommon' in Farrell et al. (eds), *Roscommon history and society* (2018), pp 279–99.

Power, T.P. & Kevin Whelan (eds), *Endurance and emergence: Catholics in Ireland in the eighteenth century* (Dublin, 1990).
Purcell, Mary, 'Dublin Diocesan Archives: Hamilton papers (3)', *Archivium Hibernicum*, 46 (1991/2), pp 22–134.
Purdue, Olwen, *The Big House in the north of Ireland: land, power and social elites, 1878–1960* (Dublin, 2009).
Rafferty, Oliver P. (ed.), *Irish Catholic identities* (Manchester & New York, 2013).
—, '"Eternity is not long enough nor hell hot enough …": the Catholic Church and Fenianism', *History Ireland*, 16:6 (Nov.–Dec. 2008), 30–4.
Regan-Lefebvre, Jennifer, *Cosmopolitan nationalism in the Victorian empire: Ireland, India and the politics of Alfred Webb* (Basingstoke, 2009).
Reid, Colin, '"An experiment in constructive unionism": Isaac Butt, home rule and federalist political thought during the 1870s', *English Historical Review*, 129:537 (2014), 333–7.
Ridden, Jennifer, 'Britishness as an imperial and diasporic identity' in Gray, Peter, *Victoria's Ireland?: Irishness and Britishness, 1837–1901* (Dublin, 2003), pp 88–105.
Rossi, J.P., 'Catholic opinion on the eastern question, 1876–1878', *Church History*, 51:1 (Mar. 1982), 54–70.
Shannon, Catherine, 'The Ulster liberal unionists and local government reform, 1885–98', *Irish Historical Studies*, 18:71 (Mar. 1973), 407–23.
Share, Bernard & Cornelius F. Smith (eds), *Whigs on the green: the Stephen's Green Club, 1840–1900* (Dublin, 1990).
Shields, Andrew, *The Irish Conservative Party: land, politics and religion, 1852–1868* (Dublin, 2007).
Socolofsky, H.E., 'William Scully: Ireland and America, 1840–1900', *Agricultural History*, 48:1 (Jan. 1974), 155–75.
Solow, Barbara L., *The land question and the Irish economy* (Cambridge, 1971).
Steele, E.D., *Irish land and British politics: tenant-right and nationality, 1865–1870* (London, 1974).
Supple, Jennifer F., 'Ultramontanism in Yorkshire, 1850–1900', *British Catholic History*, 17:2 (Oct. 1985), 274–86.
Thompson, F.M.L. (ed.), *The University of London and the world of learning, 1836–1986* (London, 1990).
Thompson, Frank, *The end of liberal Ulster: land agitation and land reform, 1868–1886* (Belfast, 2001).
Thornley, David, *Isaac Butt and home rule* (London, 1964).
Vaughan, W.E. (ed.), *A new history of Ireland, v: Ireland under the union, I, 1801–70* (Oxford, 1989).
—, 'Landlord and tenant relations in Ireland between the Famine and the Land War, 1850–1878' in Cullen, L.M. & T.C. Smout (eds), *Comparative aspects of Scottish and Irish economic history, 1600–1900* (Edinburgh, 1977), pp 216–26.
—, 'Ireland, c.1870' in Vaughan (ed.), *A new history of Ireland* (1989), v, pp 726–800.
—, *Landlords and tenants in mid-Victorian Ireland* (New York, 1994).
Wall, Maureen, 'Catholics in economic Life' in Dunne & O'Brien (eds), *Catholic Ireland* (1989), pp 73–92.
—, 'The quest for Catholic equality, 1745–1778' in Dunne & O'Brien (eds), *Catholic Ireland* (1989), pp 115–33.

——, 'The making of Gardiners' relief act, 1781–2' in Dunne & O'Brien (eds), *Catholic Ireland* (1989), pp 135–48.
——, 'The Catholics and the establishment, 1782–93' in Dunne & O'Brien (eds), *Catholic Ireland* (1989), pp 149–62.
Ward C.C. & R.C. Ward, 'The Catholic pamphlets of Charles O'Conor (1710–1791)', *Studies: An Irish Quarterly Review*, 68:272 (Winter 1979), 259–64.
Ward, C.C. & R.E. Ward (eds), *Letters of Charles O'Conor* (Ann Arbor, MI, 1980), 2 vols.
Whelan, Kevin, *The tree of liberty: radicalism, Catholicism and the construction of Irish Identity, 1760–1830* (Cork, 1996).
Whyte, J.H., *The Independent Irish Party, 1850–9* (London, 1958).
Wright, Jonathan Jeffrey, *The 'natural leaders' and their world: politics, culture and society in Belfast, c.1801–1832* (Liverpool, 2012).
Yates, Nigel, *The religious condition of Ireland, 1770–1850* (New York, 2006).

THESES

Casey, Brian J., 'Land, politics and religion on the Clancarty estate, east Galway, 1851–1914' (PhD, NUIM, 2011).
Dyer Wolf, Daphne, 'Two windows: the tenants of the De Freyne rent strike 1901–1903' (PhD, DU, May 2019).
Horgan, David T., 'The Irish Catholic whigs in parliament, 1847–74' (PhD, UM, 1975).
McKenna, Kevin, 'Power, resistance, and ritual: paternalism on the Clonbrock estates,1826–1908' (PhD, NUIM, 2011).
Melvin, Patrick, 'The landed gentry of Galway, 1820–1880' (PhD, TCD, 1991).
Phillips, Jonathan, 'The Irish university question, 1873–1908' (PhD, UC, 1978).
Pole, Adan, 'Landlord responses to the Irish Land War, 1879–82' (PhD, TCD, 2006).
Ridden, Jennifer, '"Making good citizens": national identity, religion and liberalism among the Irish elite c.1800–1850' (PhD, UL, 1998).

REFERENCE WORKS

Burnand, F.C. (ed.), *The Catholic who's who and yearbook, 1908* (London, 1908)
Connacht & Munster landed estates database, www.landedestates.ie, accessed 25 Jan. 2021.
Dictionary of Irish biography www.dib.ie/, accessed 02 November 2021
Dunleavy, Gareth W. & Dunleavy, Janet E., *The O'Conor papers: a descriptive catalog and surname register of the materials at Clonalis House* (Madison, WI, 1977).
Griffith's valuation www.askaboutireland.ie/griffith-valuation/, accessed 2 Nov. 2021.
History of parliament online www.historyofparliamentonline.org/, accessed 2 Nov. 2021.
Hussey De Burgh, U.H., *The landowners of Ireland: an alphabetical list of the owners of estates of 500 acres or £500 valuation and upwards in Ireland, with the acreage and valuation in each county* (Dublin, 1878).

Oxford dictionary of national biography www.oxforddnb.com/, accessed 2 Nov. 2021.

Royal Irish Academy list of members 2001, giving the names of the council and officers, members, honorary members and Cunningham medallists, with an appendix listing the officers of the Academy since its foundation (Dublin, 2001).

Stenton, Michael (ed.), *A who's who of British members of parliament: a biographical dictionary of the house of commons based on annual volumes of 'Dod's parliamentary companion' and other sources*, i: 1832–1885 (Sussex, 1976).

Index

Abercorn, duke of, 98, 104, 106, 133
Act of Union (1801), 33–5, 186, 191, 193–4
Acton, Lord, 116, 119–20
Amnesty Association, 146; see also Fenian amnesty
anti-Catholicism, 16, 20, 28, 53, 112, 123, 183
anti-Englishness, 47, 143, 149, 155, 207; see also anti-British, 19, 46, 189
Antrim, earl of, 98
Ashbourne act, 82, 99; see also land reform

Balfe, Patrick, 61, 69, 91
Balfour, Arthur, 101, 180, 192, 196
Balfour, Gerald, 198
Ball, John Thomas, 128
Ballaghaderreen (town), 61–2, 76, 78, 180
Ballinagare (village), 27–35, 62, 65–7, 79, 84
Ballinlough (village), 61–2, 79, 82, 165
Ballintober (village), 27–8, 33–4, 37, 63, 173
Baillargeon, Charles-Francois (bishop of Quebec), 151
Barbour, Sir David, 191
Bellews of Moutbellew, 28–9, 59, 183n66
Belmore, earl of, 98, 128
Berkley, George, 31
Bessborough, earl of, 95
Bessborough commission, 95–6, 98
Betham, Sir William, 35
Bitham Hall, Warwickshire, 52–3, 64
Blake, Edward, 190
Blake, Helen, 63
Blake, Major Maurice, 37
Blake, Valentine (b. 1843), 67
Blakes of Towerhill, 37, 52, 59, 66–8
Blennerhassett, Rowland Ponsonby, 90, 174, 179–80
Blennerhassett, Sir Rowland, 51n47, 79, 98–9, 116, 121, 141, 176, 180
Bourke, Walter, 58–9
Brady, John, 114
British empire (support for), 16–18, 22–3, 38, 42, 44, 109, 153, 155, 163–5, 171, 187–8, 195–6, 210

British identity, 19–20, 22, 45, 188–90, 210–11; see also Irish identity
British liberalism, 20–1, 115, 135–65, 171–81
Browne, Catherine, 32
Burke, Sir John Bernard, 26
Burke, Thomas Henry, 51n47, 137n3
Butt, Isaac, 20, 127–31, 185, 189, 208; and Fenian amnesty, 146; land bill, 90–3; university bill, 125–7; home rule, 147–8, 153–6, 158–61

Cairnes, John Elliott, 93, 120
Callan schools affair, 123–4
Castlerea (town), 23, 28, 40, 56, 62, 65, 75, 77, 79, 91, 94, 116, 165, 173, 180, 199, 203
Castlerea board of guardians, 50, 202
Castlerea district council, 25, 50, 200, 209
Castletown, Lord, 53, 129, 192
Catholic Church, 19, 26, 45, 112, 160, 203, 207; and ultramontanism, 21–2, 109–10, 115, 119–20, 124, 207; university education, 108–9, 113–15, 122, 130–3; Irish nationalism, 46–8, 76–81, 154–5, 178; Italian nationalism, 46–8, 112, 116, 137 178;
Catholic landlords, 15–16, 46, 51, 58–60, 76–81, 205
Catholic loyalty (to the crown), 18, 27–8, 31–2, 35, 38, 44, 142–3, 163, 176, 179, 183, 187–8, 201, 203,
Catholic loyalty (to the pope), 46, 49, 80
Catholic unionism, 15, 18, 176, 182–90, 194, 209–10
Catholic University, 36, 46, 108–11, 113–14, 118, 120, 126, 134, 136, 140, 206–7
Chichester, Charles Raleigh, 91
Chichester Fortescue (Lord Carlingford), 145, 168, 175
Childers, Hugh, 190
Clancarty, earl of, 69–70, 76, 78
Clarke, Lieutenant William Thomas, 151
Clonalis House (new), 12, 30, 62, 64, 82–3, 203; and old, 64

238

Index

Clonbrock, Lord, 54, 66–7, 69–70, 73–4, 76, 78, 84, 104, 106
Cogan, William Henry, 51n47, 113, 137n4, 146, 176, 183
confiscations (Cromwellian), 27–9, 57, 189
conservative Catholicism, 21–2, 46, 124, 135–6, 210; *see also* ultramontanism
Conservative government, 79, 85, 99–100, 103, 108, 114, 125–9, 131, 133, 142, 145, 160, 163–4, 177–81, 185, 190, 193, 198, 205–9
Corrigan, Sir Dominic, 51n47, 114, 121, 162
Corry, James, 128
Courtney, Leonard, 131, 174
Crofton, Lord (and estate), 53, 83–4
Croke, Thomas (archbishop), 130, 132, 155
Croskery, Thomas, 120–1
Cullen, Paul (cardinal), 51, 73, 110, 114–15, 118, 122–4, 139–40, 154–5, 178
Currie, B.W., 191
Curry, Dr John (1702?–86), 31

Davitt, Michael, 94–5, 165, 172
De Vesci, Lord, 65, 98, 175
Dease, Edmund, 51, 80, 122, 129, 133, 161, 176, 178–9, 183,
Dease, Colonel Gerald, 171, 176
Dease, John A., 139n11, 140
Delany, Father William, 51, 129–31
Denbigh, earl of, 79, 163
Derby, earl of, 114, 142
Dicey, A.V., 185
Dickson, Thomas, 174, 180
Dillon, John, 67, 76–8, 81, 126, 185, 188
Dillon, Lord, 65, 81, 84
Dillon, Mary, 32
Dillon, William, 126
disestablishment (of the Church of Ireland), 21, 48, 51, 116, 120–1, 135, 139–41, 145, 148, 189
Disraeli, Benjamin, 114, 123, 125, 127, 129, 142, 164
Döllinger, J.J. Ignaz Von, 119–20
Dowd, Father Patrick, 151
Downside College, 43–5, 68, 86, 111
Doyle, James (bishop), 38
Dufferin, Lord, 54, 58, 93, 96–7

Duggan, James (bishop of Chicago), 151
Dunraven, earl of, 105–6, 192

education (of Irish Catholics), 18–19, 22, 27, 30, 33, 36–7, 39, 42–5
education question, 18, 21, 46, 48, 50–2, 88, 108–34, 136, 139, 142, 145, 189, 201, 206; *see also* university question
encumbered estates court, 59, 66
English Catholics (landed), 16, 30, 39, 44, 51–3, 91, 116, 171, 179, 204
Errington, George (archbishop), 52
Errington, Sir George, 51n47, 79, 180
evictions, 58, 66, 73–9, 89–90, 95, 102

factory reform, 21, 161, 208
Famine (the Irish Famine), 39–41, 49, 59, 66, 71–2, 74, 85–6, 191
Farrer, Lord, 191
Fawcett, Henry, 115, 117, 123, 125
federalism, 92, 94, 147–58, 165, 189, 208; *see also* home rule
Fenian amnesty, 89, 145–7, 208
Fenianism, 24, 47, 131, 136–49, 154–5, 161, 178, 207–8
Ferrall, Daniel Henry, 59
financial relations question, 190–8, 209; *see also* taxation
Findlater, William, 174, 180
Fingall, earl of, 51n47, 183n66
Fitzgibbon, John, 77, 200–1
Forbes, Priscilla, 35
Forster, W.E., 55n61, 96–7, 168, 171
French, Arthur (Lord De Freyne), 58–9, 65–8, 72–3, 77–8, 81, 84, 183n66, 204
French, Charles, 145, 157–8, 165–6
French, Fitzstephen (1801–73), 47, 49
Frenches of Frenchpark, 28–9
Frenchpark (town), 28, 59, 62, 65–6, 75

Gaelic League, 189
Gaelic Union, 127–8, 189
Gaffrey, James, 68–9
Galway (county), 29, 42, 52, 59, 66–7, 69–70, 73, 76, 78, 97,
Gavin, George, 122

Gillooly, Lawrence (bishop), 48–9, 51–2, 80, 88, 124, 130, 139–42, 166–7, 172–3, 208
Givan, John, 180
Gladstone, W.E., 55, 70–1, 73, 79, 85, 88–91, 95, 97–100, 112, 114–26, 133–4, 138, 141–2, 145–8, 154, 157, 159, 162–4, 168–71, 174–5, 178–91, 205, 207–9
Goff, Captain Thomas, 48–9
Gormanston, Viscount, 51n47, 171
Goschen, George, 179, 193
Grace, Oliver (1791–1871), 37, 47–8, 142
Granard, earl of, 51n47, 59, 78–9, 133, 171, 179, 204
Granite Hall, Kingstown (Dún Laoghire), 53, 65, 83
Grant, General Ulysses S., 151
Grehan, Patrick, 33, 48, 59

Hamilton, John (archdeacon), 41–2
Hamilton, Sir Edward, 192
Hamilton, Sir Robert, 191
Harris, Matt, 98, 165
Hartington, Lord, 163, 179–80
Healy, Tim, 172
Henry, Mitchell, 131
Herbert, Lady Elizabeth, 177
Hicks Beach, Sir Michael, 128, 192
Home Government Association, 147–8, 156, 158
home rule, 15, 18–19, 22–3, 25, 38, 50, 55, 75, 85, 92, 94–5, 99–100, 116, 123, 125, 135–6, 147–67, 170–201, 205–10
home rule bills, (first) 100, 154, 171, 177–82, 184; (second) 100, 154, 170–1, 182–90
Home Rule Party, 24, 72, 90, 98–9, 102–3, 125–7, 131, 136, 158–61, 166–7, 205, 208
Hyde, Douglas, 55n61, 56, 68, 189–90

Johnson, Andrew (US president), 152

industrial schools, 21, 112, 144
intermediate education, 50, 102, 127–8, 134, 162
Irish identity, 15–22, 44–5, 159–60, 170, 187–90, 210–11; *see also* British identity
Irish Landowners' Convention, 24, 50, 54, 56, 84, 101, 103–6, 176, 201, 206
Irish language, 21, 30, 50, 55, 127, 154, 162, 189–90, 208
Irish liberalism, 15–24, 31, 34–5, 38–9, 46, 50–1, 108–21, 135–55, 160–4, 166–9, 171–81, 188, 196, 203–10; *see also* British liberalism
Irish Loyal and Patriotic Union, 175–7, 181, 195
Irish nationalism (general) 19, 22, 44, 94, 135–47, 170–90, 205, 208, 210; moderate nationalism, 15, 17, 22–3, 44, 94–5, 131, 167, 188, 200; cultural nationalism, 127, 190; republicanism 19, 22, 44, 47, 94, 135–6, 155, 161, 166, 172, 179, 209–10; *see also* Fenianism
Irish Parliamentary Party, 44, 103, 105–6, 161, 174, 177–8, 182, 206
Italian nationalism, 46, 48, 112, 116, 137

Kane, Robert, 119,
Kavanagh, Arthur, 54, 78, 90, 97, 131, 175
Kavanagh, James, 51n47, 167
Keenan, Sir Patrick, 51n47, 124, 127, 137n3
Kelly, J.J., 67, 75, 79, 82
Kenmare, earl of, 51n47, 78, 133, 163n109, 171, 183n66, 204
Kenny, William, 180, 183
Keogh, William, 49, 51n47, 87
King-Harman, Edward, 99; and King-Harman estates, 53, 65, 72, 84
King-Tenison, Edward, 48, 54, 149; and King-Tenison estates, 53, 65, 72, 84

Lalor Sheil, Richard (1791–1851), 36, 38, 137n3
Land League, 74–6, 94–8, 165, 173, 204
land reform (general), 18, 21, 24–5, 54–5, 85–107, 136, 145, 154, 162, 180, 201, 205–6; tenant right & 1870 land act, 86–90; 3fs & 1881 land act, 90–8; land purchase & 1885–1903 land acts, 98–107
landed estates court, 23, 59–60, 82, 87, 89–91
landlordism, 57–84
Leahy, John, 42–3
Lecky, W.H., 185–6
Lee, General Robert E., 151
Leitrim (county), 48, 54, 59

Index

Lentaigne, Sir John, 164, 182n64
liberal Catholicism, 15–20, 35, 51, 109–21, 134, 136–47, 163–4, 171–82, 206–7, 210
Liberal government, 15, 39, 48–9, 88, 95, 100, 111, 114, 124, 133–4, 136–7, 141–2, 145, 175, 205, 207
Liberal Party, 18, 21, 24, 47, 100, 109–11, 115–17, 136–7, 139–41, 145, 163, 168, 172–4, 179, 205, 207–8
liberal Protestants, 17–18, 20–2, 108–9, 116, 120–1
Liberal Union of Ireland, 24, 179–80, 209
local government reform, 21, 144, 175, 180–1, 186, 197–202, 209
Longford (county), 59, 78–9
Longford, Lord, 65
Loughglynn (village), 60, 65–6, 81
Lowther, James, 128–9, 131
Lubbock, Sir John, 197
Lucas, Frederick, 87
Lynch, Edward Whitby, 67, 76
Lynch, Nicholl P., 173
Lynch, Patrick (bishop of Charleston), 151

MacDermot, Charles (1794–1873), 66
MacDermot, Fanny, 66
MacDermot, Hugh Hyacinth, 51n47, 168, 174
MacDermot, Roderick (1812–99), 45, 52, 60, 66, 86, 160, 204
MacDermot, Thomas (1810–79), 47–8, 52, 60–1, 66–8, 74–5, 86, 204
MacDermots of Coolavin, 28, 66, 68
MacDonnell, Sir Anthony, 51n47, 69, 137n3
MacDonnell, Farrell, 200
Maguire, Thomas, 119–21
Manning, Henry (cardinal), 52, 162n107
Marlborough, duke of, 128–30
Martin, Charles E., 191
Martin, Edward, 171
Martin, Sir Richard, 182
Mayo (county), 37, 42, 47, 52, 58–9, 64, 67, 97, 165
Mayo, earl of, 105–6, 114, 192
McCabe, Edward (cardinal), 51, 130–3, 168, 173

McCallum, Colonel Daniel, 151
McCloskey, John (archbishop), 151
McClure, Sir Thomas, 162, 180
McCracken, Ernest, 151
McDonnell, Martin, 94
McLaren, Duncan, 131
Meagher, Thomas Francis, 39, 44
Mill, John Stuart, 92–3, 100, 194
Monsell, William (Lord Emly), 17–18, 21n13, 51, 59, 80, 98–9, 112–16, 119, 121, 127, 133, 137, 140, 144, 148–50, 155, 157–9, 167, 177, 179, 182
Monteagle, Lord, 55n61, 100, 178,
Montesquieu, Charles-Louis, 31
Montgomery, Hugh de Fellenberg, 105–6
Moore, Charles, 114
Moore, Edward (d. 1787), 33
Moore, Edward (d. 1851), 41–2, 50, 60, 63, 204
Moore, George Henry, 47–8, 87, 139n11
Moran, D.P., 44
More O'Ferrall, Ambrose, 171, 176, 179, 183
More O'Ferrall, John Lewis, 53, 65
More O'Ferrall, Richard, 51n47, 112, 137n4

National Association, 24, 136, 139–40, 207
Newman, John Henry (cardinal), 46, 52, 110–11, 118, 120,
Norfolk, duke of, 79, 163, 179
Nugent, Sir Walter, 171

O'Beirne, Connell, 59, 61
O'Beirne, Hugh, 59, 61
O'Brien, Edward, 99, 175–6
O'Brien, William, 78, 81, 102, 104–5, 199–200
O'Carolan, Turlough, 30
O'Connell, Daniel, 34, 37–9, 49, 87, 147, 153, 186, 188–9, 203
O'Connor, Valentine (1744–1814), 33–4, 37, 42
O'Conor, Alexander (1735–1820), 33–4
O'Conor, Charles (1584–1655), 28
O'Conor, Charles (1710–91), 30–3, 65, 203
O'Conor, Charles (1736–1808), 32–4
O'Conor, Revd Charles (1764–1828), 34–6

O'Conor, Charles (1804–84), 141, 151–2
O'Conor, Charles (1872–1939), 52, 83, 203
O'Conor, Charles Owen, the O'Conor Don (1838–1906): Gaelic ancestry, 15, 26–7, 58; family background, 26–40; *The O'Conors of Connaught: an historical memoir*, 27, 177, 190; clubs, 53–5, 163, 171–2; inheritance, 15, 42, 50, 60, 62–4, 204; education, 42–5; travel, 46–7, 132–4; marriage, 52–4, 57; positions & memberships, 50; management of his estates, 57–84; liberalism, 15–23, 46, 48–51, 88, 94, 108–21, 135–69, 170–81, 188, 203–10; whiggism, 21, 50, 135, 163, 208, 210; unionism, 15, 22–3, 54, 170–202; conservative Catholicism, 21–2, 46, 124, 135–6, 210; Irish & British identity 15–22, 44–5, 159–60, 170, 187–90, 210–11; views on & relationship with Catholic Church & hierarchy, 22, 48–9, 51–2, 80, 88, 109, 112, 124, 130, 135–6, 139–41, 154–5, 159–60, 166–7, 172–3, 179, 203 ; views on education (*see also* university question), 108–34, 136–9, 142, 161–2, 164, 189, 201, 206–7; nationalism/ Fenianism/republicanism, 22–3, 47, 89, 94, 127, 135–61, 165–9, 170–202; land reform, 85–107, 136, 154; home rule, 22–3, 75, 92–5, 100, 116, 123, 135–202, 205–10; British empire, 16–18, 22–3, 44, 109, 153–5, 163–5, 185–8, 195–6, 210; government and democracy, 15, 21, 50, 135–6, 147–58, 163, 210; local government, 21, 70, 144, 175, 180–1, 186, 197–202; taxation (imperial), 21, 25, 190–8, 209; social reform, 21, 24, 137, 144, 161–3; Irish language, 21, 50, 55, 127–8, 154, 162, 189–90.
O'Conor, Daniel (1612–89), 28
O'Conor, Denis (1674–1750), 28, 30
O'Conor, Denis (1732–1804), 32–3, 35
O'Conor, Denis MP (1794–1847), 36–42, 137n3, 203
O'Conor, Denis Charles (1869–1917), 52, 65, 68, 80–1, 83–4 , 203
O'Conor, Denis Maurice MP (1840–83), 41–6, 50, 53, 62–3, 66, 145, 147, 149, 158, 160, 164, 173

O'Conor, Dionysia, 41
O'Conor, Dominick, 33
O'Conor, Edward (1796–1838), 37, 66
O'Conor, Ellen (née More O'Ferrall) (1857–1932), 53, 65, 83, 203
O'Conor, Eugenia, 41
O'Conor, Georgina (née Perry) (1847–72), 52–4, 57, 64, 148–9
O'Conor, Honoria (d. 1857), 41–2, 60
O'Conor, Honoria (née Blake), 37, 66
O'Conor, Jane, 41
O'Conor, Josephine, 41
O'Conor, Kate, 41
O'Conor, Mary (née Blake), 37, 41
O'Conor, Sir Nicholas (1843–1908), 51n47, 81, 137n3, 164
O'Conor, Major Owen (1632–92), 28
O'Conor, Owen MP (1763–1831), 33–7, 203
O'Conor, Owen Phelim (1870–1943), 52, 83, 203
O'Conor, Roderic (d. 1198), 26
O'Conor, Roderick (1872–8), 52–3
O'Conor-Blake, Valentine (1808–79), 41–2, 60, 67
O'Donnell, Frank Hugh, 118
O'Donoghue, Daniel ('the O'Donoghue'), 46–7, 51, 90, 113, 137n4, 139n11, 140, 141n18
O'Gara, Count Charles (1699–1777), 32
O'Hagan, John, 118
O'Hagan, Thomas (Lord), 51n47, 114–15, 121, 128, 133, 137n3, 140, 146–9, 163n109
O'Kelly, J.J., 166–7, 172
O'Loghlen, Sir Colman, 51n47, 113, 137n4, 188
O'Reilly, Myles (1825–80), 46–7, 51, 90, 113–14, 119, 122, 137n4, 139–40, 141n18, 162
O'Rourke, Thaddues (bishop of Killala), 30
O'Rourke, Mary, 30
O'Rourke, Colonel Tiernan, 30
O'Sullivan, W.H., 165

Pakenham-Mahons, 63, 65–6, 69, 72, 77, 84
Palles, Christopher, 44, 128

Palmerston, Lord, 87, 112, 137, 141
papal infallibility, 21–2, 36, 116, 119, 163
papal states, 46–7, 137, 154
Parnell, Charles Stuart, 9, 72, 94–5, 98–100, 102, 127, 130–1, 136, 160–2, 165–7, 172–8, 182–4, 187, 198, 205, 208
Perry, Thomas, 52–3
Petre, Lord, 52n50, 163
Pim, Frederic, 180
Pim, Jonathan, 55n61, 162
Plan of Campaign, 76–81, 185, 204
Plunkett, Horace, 55n61, 192
Pope Leo XIII, 79
Pope Pius IX, 21, 46, 110
Porter, Andrew, 180

Queen's colleges, 43, 110–11, 114, 119, 121, 127–8, 132–4
Queen's University, 110, 114, 120–1, 130–2, 134
Quill, Albert William, 120–1

Redington, Christopher, 98
Redington, Sir Thomas, 137n3
Redingtons of Clarinbridge, 52n48, 59
Redmond, John, 18, 23, 44, 103, 172, 183, 188, 190, 198–200, 209
repeal (of the Act of Union), 35, 37, 39, 147, 153, 155, 186
Richardson, James, 180
Ripon, marquess of, 125, 163, 171
River Suck drainage scheme, 69, 180
Roscommon (county), 15, 23, 26–7, 30, 32, 34, 37, 47–8, 50, 52–4, 59, 61–3, 66–7, 69, 71–2, 74, 76–7, 81–4, 89, 91, 99, 103, 142, 158, 165, 167, 177, 193, 203, 209
Roscommon (town), 37, 39, 49, 61, 67, 89, 91, 93–4, 105, 143, 153, 165–6
Ross, John of Bladensburg, 79–80, 183n66
Royal Dublin Society, 50, 113
Royal Irish Academy, 32, 50, 113
Royal Society of Antiquaries of Ireland, 33, 50
Royal University of Ireland, 50, 128, 132–4, 162
Royal Zoological Society, 113

Russell, Lord John, 39, 49, 114, 124, 136, 141–2, 207
Russell, Thomas Wallace, 55n61, 102, 105, 192

Sadlier, John, 49, 87
Salisbury, Lord, 79, 99, 102, 164, 180, 190, 192–3, 205
Salmon, Revd George, 128
Scott, William Henry, 46
Scully, William, 58
Shaw, William, 131
Shawe Taylor, Captain John, 103–4
Sheil, Richard Lalor, 36, 38, 137n3
Sligo (county), 15, 28, 34–5, 37, 50, 61–3, 66–7, 73–4, 78, 82, 145, 168, 173, 193
Society for the Preservation of the Irish Language, 50, 127–8
Spencer, earl of, 76, 100, 146, 149, 174, 178, 188
Strickland, Charles, 60, 66
Strokestown (town), 62–3, 65–6, 79
Sullivan, A.M., 156–7, 168
Sullivan, T.D., 165
Sullivan, William, 120
Sunday closing, 161–2; *see also* temperance
Sutherland, Sir Thomas, 191

Talbot Crosbie, Lindsay, 103–6
taxation (imperial), 21, 25, 190–8, 209
temperance, 55, 162, 167, 197; *see also* Sunday closing
Thompson, William Thorton, 92
Trinity College, Dublin, 32, 36–7, 43, 110–11, 115–25, 130–4
Tully, Jasper, 98, 199

ultramontanism, 21–2, 110, 115, 119–20, 124, 132, 155, 207
unionism & unionists (general), 15–25, 39, 44, 54, 85, 128, 159, 170–202; Catholic unionism, 182–90; constructive or national unionism, 146, 170–1, 189–90; conservative unionism, 175–7, 180–1; liberal unionism, 171–5, 177–81; Ulster unionism, 102, 180, 195–6

university question (general), 108–33; the supplemental charter, 114–15, 120; Gladstone's university bill, 121–3; Butt's university bill, 125–6; the O'Conor Don's university bill, 129–32; the Royal University of Ireland, 50, 132–4, 162; National University of Ireland & Queen's University Belfast, 134

Vaughan, Herbert (cardinal), 52, 155

Walsh, Walter Hussey, 177, 182n64
Walsh, William (archbishop), 80
West Britonism, 19, 44, 50, 94, 166
Westmeath, earl of, 171, 183n66
Wexford (by-election), 172–4, 208
Whigs & Whig-Liberal (British & Irish), 15, 17, 21, 21n13, 31, 39, 49–50, 130, 135–7, 163, 165, 167–8, 204, 208, 210
Whittle, James Lowry, 119–22
Wills-Sandford, 53, 65, 77, 81
Wiseman, Nicholas (cardinal), 46
Woodlock, Bartholonew (monsignor), 51, 111–14, 122, 125–6, 128–30, 133
Woufle, Stephen (1787–1840), 36
Wyndham, George, 55n61, 56, 81; and the Wyndham land act, 83–4, 102–7; *see also* land reform
Wyse, Thomas (1701?–70), 31
Wyse, Sir Thomas (1791–1862), 36, 38, 44, 137n3